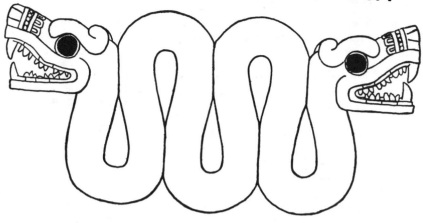

Enduring Praise for
The Discovery and Conquest of Mexico

"The most complete and trustworthy of the chronicles of the Conquest. The translation has adroitly preserved all the charm and the simplicity of the original . . . The design and illustrations carry out well the spirit of the incomparable old soldier and his times, whose memory of the tragic drama he helped to enact was so vivid fifty years later that he decided to leave to his descendants 'this true story' that they might 'find out what a wonderful story it is'."
—Carlos Castaneda, *New York Times*

"Bernal Díaz's pages quiver with life, raw, painful, appalling."
—*The Boston Transcript*

"[The author] speaks to us from the past. But it is a clear, simple voice full of incredible tales that put fiction in the shade."
—*Christian Science Monitor*

"[*The Discovery and Conquest of Mexico* is] one of the primary documents in the history of the Americas, and its artless depiction of the atrocities committed in the 'long shadow of the white man' is for North Americans the opening episode of a drama that ends 371 years later in a frozen gulch at Wounded Knee, South Dakota."
—Frederick W. Turner III, editor of *The Viking Portable North American Indian Reader*

"This detailed, exciting, unpolished narrative of one of the most thrilling adventure stories of all time is a joy to read in this translation." —*Library Journal*

"[Bernal Díaz's memoir is] the most reliable narrative that exists and conveys across the centuries the spirit and motivations of the actors in that golden age." —*Chicago Sunday Tribune*

"What perhaps is most delightful in all of Bernal Díaz's vivid story of misery, pathos, and blood is his drawing of himself— 'simple, enduring, splendidly courageous, and unaffectedly vain,' as Professor Maudslay writes." —*Spectator*

"Bernal Díaz's own abiding sense of wonder at what he and his comrades saw and did illumines his pages and makes this a thoroughly interesting adventure story." —*Commonweal*

"Bernal Díaz wrote something rather more than an historical document of the first importance. His narrative is also captivatingly readable, so that one's interest and admiration are equally divided between the stupendous events he records and the charming revelations that he makes of his own character and general outlook." —*Saturday Review*

"[Bernal Díaz's history] is as interesting to the casual reader as it is valuable to the historian. What warms the heart of the reader are the strong human interest and gossipy detail . . . The prowess of an old friend in battle and how he died, the color of a horse and his good points, are some of the details set down with a faithfulness to actuality that will make the book a fireside companion for generations to come for those who love the Homeric in man's story." —*New York Herald Tribune*

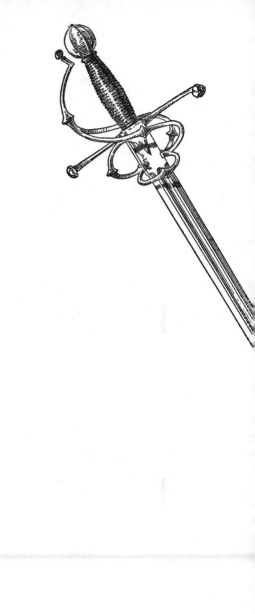

HERNANDO CORTÉS

THE

DISCOVERY

AND

CONQUEST

OF

MEXICO 1517–1521

by Bernal Díaz del Castillo

Edited from the only exact copy of the original MS
(and published in Mexico) by Genaro García. Translated
with an Introduction and Notes by A. P. Maudslay,
and a new Introduction by Hugh Thomas

DA CAPO PRESS • NEW YORK

Library of Congress Cataloging in Publication Data

Díaz del Castillo, Bernal, 1496–1584.
[Historia verdadera de la conquista de la Nueva España. English]
The discovery and conquest of Mexico, 1517–1521 / by Bernal Díaz
del Castillo; edited from the only exact copy of the original MS (and
published in Mexico) by Genaro García; translated with an introduction and notes by A.P. Maudslay; new introduction by Hugh Thomas.
   p.   cm.
Originally published: New York: Farrar, Straus, and Cudahy, 1956.
ISBN 0-306-80697-5 (alk. paper)
   1. Mexico—History—Conquest, 1519–1540. 2. Cortés, Hernán,
1485–1547. I. Title.
F1230.D56513 1996   95-45871
972'.02—dc20   CIP

First Da Capo Press edition 1996

This Da Capo Press edition of *The Discovery and Conquest of Mexico*
is an unabridged republication of the edition published in New York
in 1956, here supplemented by a new introduction by Hugh Thomas.

A.P. Maudslay edited this edition from his own 1908 translation of
The True Story of the Conquest of New Spain, Bernal Díaz's account
of his campaigns in Mexico and other countries, published in five
volumes by the Hakluyt Society.

Published by Da Capo Press, Inc.
A Subsidiary of Plenum Publishing Corporation
233 Spring Street, New York, N.Y. 10013

CONTENTS

Introduction

Bernal Díaz's memoir of his time as a soldier in the service of Hernán Cortés is one of the great books of the sixteenth century. It is indeed one of the very few books of the sixteenth century which are still readable in the twentieth, because it is written very naturally, with none of the flourishes and affectations with which most writers of the Renaissance felt it necessary to embellish their style. It is written with energy, and the story it tells is absolutely compelling.

The book is one of the main sources for the history of the Conquest. It was begun, it is true, about 35 years after the Conquest was over, at a time when the author, then nearly sixty, was living in Santiago de Guatemala. On occasion Bernal Díaz's memory is at fault and where his account clashes with documentary evidence or memories nearer the time, the conscientious historian will probably prefer the alternative account. But where Bernal Díaz remembers individuals, the passing of the years does not matter. Thus, when he describes Pánfilo de Narváez as having a voice so deep that it sounded as if it came from a vault, or when he remembers Cortés's seductive style of eloquence, he makes major points of permanent value.

Some of the set pieces in Bernal Díaz's book rank with the best historical reporting. No one, for instance, will forget his account of the conquistadors coming down the mountains which divide, then as now, the valley of Mexico from the temperate zone and seeing, for the first time, the great capital of the Mexica, Tenochtitlan, in what is now the center of Mexico City. Bernal Díaz also allows into his recollection of the sight a touch of melancholy: how beautiful it was, how ruined it all now is!

Bernal Díaz was born in the Castilian city of Medina del Campo about 1495. He was accordingly between 24 and 27 when he participated in the extraordinary events which are the subject of his book. Nothing is known of his youth, though he himself said that his father, Francisco Díaz del Castillo, "el Galán," "the Gallant" as he seems to have been known, was a *regidor*, or councillor of the city. His mother was María Díez Rejón. He was related to two other conquistadors who formed part of Cortés's little army, Francisco de Lugo and Juan Velázquez de León. The former was also born in Medina del Campo. The latter relation caused him to be connected with the large clan of the Velázquez who came from Cuéllar, not far away from Medina, and whose imperial representative was Diego Velázquez, the conqueror and first Spanish governor of Cuba. Later in life, Bernal Díaz explained that he was related to Gutierre Velázquez, then *oidor* of the Council of the Indies.

Medina del Campo in Bernal Díaz's youth was one of the most interesting cities of Castile, being the site of one of the great markets of Europe. The main square where the market was held, though rebuilt in the sixteenth century at least once, still survives to remind the modern traveller of the size of this fascinating place of enterprise and exchange. Bernal Díaz compared the market in Tlatelolco, on the north side of Tenochtitlan, to that in his home city. The two seemed to be arranged in much the same way, he thought.

The city was almost as famous for its lawyers as for its market. Queen Isabel the Catholic, who died in the place in 1504 (Bernal Díaz must have remembered the occasion), said once that, if she had been given a choice by God, she would have had three sons, of whom the first of course would have been her heir as monarch; the second would have been archbishop of Toledo; and the third would have been a notary (*escribano*) of Medina del Campo.

Bernal Díaz's father Francisco had one interesting colleague on the town council of Medina. That was Garci Ro-

dríguez de Montalvo, who rewrote for publication in 1508
the famous romance known as *Amadís de Gaula*, by far the
most successful book of the sixteenth century in Spain. *Amadís*
was a romance probably written in the fourteenth century.
Montalvo only edited and revised it, though he added a
fourth book to it, as well as writing a sequel, *Las Sergas de
Esplandián*, published in 1510. This fellow citizen of Bernal
Díaz's turned the work into a bestseller, especially admired by
conquistadors who wanted something to read on long voyages, as eloquently explained by Irving Leonard in his famous
work, *Books of the Brave*. Perhaps the influence was even
greater than that. For Chapter 90 of *Las Sergas de Esplandián*
describes how the hero removes a lion standing guard at the
gate of a tomb containing an enchanted treasure:

> And in this fashion it befell him in the tomb, of which
> he raised the outermost glass door; the inner one, col-
> ored skyblue, was guarded by a lock of pure emerald
> in which was inserted a key of diamond . . . The
> hinges were of precious rubies. And when he opened
> the tomb he saw within an idol of pure gold, all inlaid
> with precious stones and a huge mother of pearl.

The paragraph can be easily compared with Bernal Díaz's reporting of how Cortés saw the inside of the great temple of
Huitzilopochtli on top of the pyramid in Tenochtitlan.

Bernal Díaz also compared Tenochtitlan itself to a city in
Amadís, a famous comparison which strikes anyone who has
read that novel as farfetched, since the cities described in it
are modest affairs, certainly much smaller than Tenochtitlan.

The author of *The Discovery and Conquest of Mexico*
went to the Indies (the Spaniards' term for the Americas in
those days) in 1514, as part of an expedition led by the aged
and experienced warrior, Pedrarias Avila. (The reference in the
Archivo de Indias, also for 1514, to the journey of a "Bernal
Díaz" of Medina del Campo, and reported by the archivist
Bermúdez Plata, must refer to another person of that name,
perhaps a cousin, for that individual was the son of a Lope
and Teresa Díaz.) Pedrarias's aim was to establish the first

Spanish colony on mainland America at Darien, in what is now Panama.

There is a famous description of how Pedrarias left Seville with a brave company of well-dressed knights, all expecting to find gold very easily in the rivers and to return as millionaires without much trouble. For that reason they called the place *Castillo de Oro*, Castle of Gold. Alas, the enterprise was doomed: many died; the rest found it hard to survive; there was very little gold; they killed native Indians without consideration; and they quarreled among themselves. Unfortunately, Bernal Díaz does not go into much detail about that part of his experience, but hurries on to describe how he and some other friends went to Cuba, where they thought that they would be well looked after by cousin Diego Velázquez. But that governor had his own difficulties. The Indian population was declining with alarming speed; there were no more indigenous people to distribute in *encomiendas* (grants of indigenous people with the land on which they lived) to needy adventurers such as Bernal Díaz. So the latter was quite ready to embark on the next expedition of exploration which Velázquez was keen to send out in 1517 towards the west. At that time the Caribbean, the north coast of South America, and much of the coastline of Florida as far as the Mississippi had been discovered by Ponce de León. But the zone in between, from Honduras (where Columbus had briefly touched in 1502) to the Mississippi, was unknown. It was generally believed that there must be a channel there, or perhaps just a strait, which would lead easily and quickly to China, which was still thought to be no distance away.

Velázquez was probably influenced by a story told to him in 1514: how on occasion "certain Indians had come from other islands beyond Cuba, towards the north, navigating five or six days by canoe and that these gave news of other islands which lie beyond those from which they came." These people could not have come from Florida. Perhaps, as Carl Sauer suggested in *The Early Spanish Main*, they came from Yucatan.

The first expedition in that direction despatched by Velázquez, that of Francisco Hernández de Córdova, was a failure. They found no strait to China and the leader was mortally wounded in a fight with Maya Indians. But he did find some gold. The second expedition was led by a nephew of Velázquez's, Juan de Grijalva. That conquistador went to Yucatan and sailed along the Mexican coast as far as modern Veracruz. He found evidence of a large settled monarchy, that of the Mexica. (No one at the time called them Aztecs, a nineteenth-century usage which should be forgotten.) He also received clear evidence that these people produced jewelry of considerable subtlety as well as many other remarkable artifacts, including feather and turquoise mosaics, carved wood, and sculpture-reliefs, both monumental and portable. The conquistadors (the word was in use at the time) realized too that they had encountered a civilization superior to anything which the Spaniards had discovered in the Caribbean. Some of the jewels obtained were sent home.

Velázquez then mounted his third expedition, led by Hernán (at the time known usually as Hernando) Cortés, an ex-secretary of his own, a man who had been trained as a lawyer and came from a family of hidalgos in Extremadura, though his branch was poor.

Bernal Díaz described himself as having been on all these expeditions. In the 1940s Henry Wagner, in *The Rise of Hernando Cortés*, argued that he could not have been on Grijalva's expedition since there was nothing in his account which could not have been found in the history of his ex-comrade in Darien, Oviedo. Wagner pointed out that in a statement of Bernal Díaz's services and merits in 1539 he did not say that he had been with Grijalva, which he would have done had there not been at that time many people alive who would have remembered the truth. That is quite unproven, though it is true that Bernal Díaz's account of Grijalva's expedition is unrevealing. Still, there are other passages where Bernal Díaz is inadequate: for example, he does not tell us anything of the campaign in and around the city of Tepeaca in 1520, nor does he describe the terms on which the Tlaxcalteca agreed to support Cortés and the Spaniards. The reason for that omission may have been that he was still recovering from his wounds suffered during the *noche triste*. Even the toughest warrior cannot be everywhere in a campaign lasting two years. (The terms of the alliance with Tlaxcala were noted by various witnesses in a forgotten "Información de Tlaxcala" of 1565, published in Mexico in 1876 as volume XX in a useful collection known as the Biblioteca Ibérica.)

Of course, there are other omissions in Bernal Díaz's book. There are also some errors, or so I see them. For example, the author says that in 1522 the arrival of Catalina Suárez Marcayda, Cortés's first wife, was a surprise to that conquistador. That view cannot be sustained since a statement of the 1560s, inspired by Catalina's family, shows that Cortés sent for her to come. (The transcript of this document of the Archivo de Indias is in the Conway papers in the University Library in Aberdeen, Scotland.) There are other such mistakes, perfectly natural in a long book. They must be taken into account by the historian, but such things do not alter the magnificent sweep, and the value, of the book as a whole.

After the conquest Bernal Díaz established himself first with an *encomienda* in the region of Coatzacoalcos and then journeyed with Cortés on the long and exhausting voyage to Honduras. On his return to Mexico-Tenochtitlan, which was beginning to be known simply as Mexico, he settled down with an Indian girl who had been presented to him by Montezuma and whom he called Doña Francisca. By her he had two daughters. He presented a sworn testimony of his services to the Crown, as did so many other conquistadors, an *Información de Servicios y Méritos* in 1539, of which the record is also to be found in the Archivo de Indias in Seville, and which may be described as the first draft—the first germ, in the words of Miguel León-Portilla—of *The Discovery and Conquest of Mexico*.

Bernal Díaz went home to Spain in 1540 and again in 1549 to try and establish his claim to favor at the court. In between, he settled in Guatemala, where he lived with another Indian girl, Angelina, by whom he had a son, Diego Luis del Castillo. Then he married Teresa Becerra, a Castilian widow, who had been married to Juan Durán and was the daughter of a conquistador of Guatemala, Bertolomé Becerra. By her he had nine sons, of whom one, Francisco, would concern himself with his father's book after his death. In Guatemala, Bernal Díaz became a *regidor*, councillor, just as his father had been so long before in Medina del Campo. His son Diego obtained a grant of arms from Philip II in 1558.

Bernal Díaz seems to have begun to write his book about 1555, again hoping thereby to gain favor from the Crown. He is said to have turned the book into a memoir when he read the elegant but classically written life of Cortés by Francisco López de Gómara, a decided humanist, with whom Bernal Díaz was always comparing himself adversely, as a rough-and-ready writer with no frills in his style, but an honest one. López de Gómara's book appeared in 1552 and was republished several times in the next few years. Bernal Díaz was anxious to point that it was not just the leader, nor the leaders, who should be seen as the victors of the battles against the Mexica: the soldiers also counted. Further, he was at pains to point out that Cortés consulted the soldiers at every step, a judgment which may concede more than he expected to the figure of the leader. Like every good general, Cortés made a show of consultation when he really made up his own mind on what to do, and then persuaded his men to follow him by means of intelligent speeches.

Bernal Díaz wrote a draft of the book, then corrected it over thirty years. He presumably used information from other surviving conquistadors who lived in Guatemala as he did from Leonor, daughter of Pedro de Alvarado by "Doña Luisa," daughter herself of Xicoténcatl, one of the rulers of Tlaxcala in 1519.

Bernal Díaz died in 1584, probably on February 3, and was probably buried in the Cathedral of Santiago de Guatemala. He of course died without knowing that his book would be read by millions and that after Cortés and perhaps even more than Alvarado, he is the conquistador who is today most known to the general public. One version of the manuscript was sent to Madrid in 1575 and was there touched up by a mercedarian friar, Alonso Remón. Bernal Díaz's son Francisco also added things to a deteriorated copy of the text which was kept in Guatemala.

The book was published in 1632 in Madrid but it included Remón's additions. Various editions followed thereafter. Translations appeared. All these used the flawed version of 1632 as their basis. Next in 1904 a Mexican scholar, Génaro García, went to Guatemala and published a version which excluded not only the friar's additions but those of Bernal Díaz's son. Then in 1932 a third manuscript, which seemed to be an early revision by Bernal Díaz himself, now known as the Alegría MSS., was found in Murcia.

The best edition in Spanish is a critical one edited in 1982 by Fr. Carmelo Sáenz de Santa María; an excellent popular version of that text, though without the notes, was published by *Historia 16* in Madrid in 1984, with a fine introduction by Miguel León-Portilla, prince of Mexican Mexicanists.

The present translation is the work of Alfred Maudslay, an admirable British scholar, one more writer among the many distinguished men who devoted their lives to Mexico and the Mexicans and who are scarcely remembered in their own country (a biography by the Harvard archaeologist, Ian Graham, is under way which will surely do justice to this forgotten giant). Maudslay's translation of Bernal Díaz is based on Génaro García's edition of 1904. It is a vast work, executed with an energy and panache fully worthy of the original, written in an English of a generation educated in the classics, and without modern jargon. When writing my own *Conquest*, I occasionally thought that I had tripped Maudslay up in some version of the Spanish but, in the end, I almost always had to concede that I had deceived myself. This new edition of a long out-of-print work will be a service to scholars as well as the general reader interested in studying the most important event in the history of the Americas.

HUGH THOMAS
London
August 1995

Hugh Thomas is the highly acclaimed author of Conquest: Montezuma, Cortés, and the Fall of Old Mexico *and* The Spanish Civil War, *among others.*

Extracts from the Introduction by
Señor Don Genaro García[1]

The True History of the Conquest of New Spain, written by
Bernal Díaz del Castillo, one of the Conquerors, was known to,
and appreciated by historians and bibliographers before it was
published. Antonio de Herrera[2] quotes it frequently, Friar Juan
de Torquemada[3] also refers to it on several occasions, and the
Licentiate Antonio de Leon Pinelo[4] devotes some lines to it in
his brief bibliography.

Although the original manuscript has always been kept in
Guatemala, first by the Author and afterwards by his descendants, and still later by the Municipality of the Capital, in whose
archives it is preserved to-day, a copy of it was made in the sixteenth century and sent to Spain to King Philip II[5] and was
there consulted by the Royal chroniclers. After its publication

---

[1] The following extracts are translated direct from Señor Don Genaro García's Introduction. Any differences entertained with regard to the names of persons or places or
the routes followed, will be explained in note attached to the translation of the text
of Bernal Díaz's narrative.

[2] *Historia general de los hechos de los castellanos en las Islas i Tierra Firme del Mar
Oceano.* Madrid, 1726–30, Decada 2ª passim. The first edition was published in 1601.

[3] *Los Veinte i un libros rituales y Monarchia Indiana.* Madrid, 1723, Tomo I passim.
The first edition was published in 1615.

[4] *Epitome de la Biblioteca Oriental i Occidental, Nautica y Geografica* (Madrid, 1629),
p. 75.

[5] So it was stated by Juan Rodriguez Cabrillo de Medrano in 1579. In the *Historia
de Guatemala ó Recordacion Florida,* by D. Francisco Antonio de Fuentes y Guzmán
(Madrid, 1882–3), Vol. i, p. 398.—G. G.

in Madrid by Friar Alonzo Remón of the Order of Mercy in the year 1632 the *True History* was universally accepted from that time onwards as the most complete and trustworthy of the chronicles of the Conquest of New Spain. A second edition followed almost immediately, in the same city, some four years later, a third, a fourth, and a fifth. It was translated into English by Maurice Keatinge in 1800 and John Ingram Lockhart in 1844; into German by Ph. J. von Rehfues in 1838 and Karl Ritter in 1848; into French by D. Jourdanet in 1876 and José María de Heredia in 1877,[1] and into Hungarian by Károly Brózik in 1878 and Moses Gaal in 1899.

Several of these translations obtained the honours of a second edition, as that of Keatinge in 1803, that of Rehfues in 1843, and that of Jourdanet in 1877.

†

It must be pointed out that no secret has ever been made of Remón's extensive corruption of the original text. Don Antonio de Leon Pinelo, in his account of the *True History* in 1629, says, no doubt without malice, that Friar Alonzo Remón kept in readiness a "corrected" copy for publication. It was no sooner printed than the author of the *Isagoge Histórico Apologét co*[2] found in it "many things added which were not found in the original". More explicitly and with a better judgment Don Francisco Antonio de Fuentes y Guzmán, the great-great-grandson of the author, and at that time the possessor of the manuscript, wrote at the end of the same century that the book, published by the reverend father Friar Alonzo Remón, differs considerably from the original, "for in some places there is more and in others less than what my great-grandfather the author wrote, for I find corruptions in chapters 164 and 171, and in the same way in other parts in the course of the history, in which not only is the credibility and fidelity of my Castillo clouded over, but many real heroes are defrauded of their just merit."

Fuentes y Guzmán states that this corruption (of the text)

[1] The French translations were—although an interval of one year lay between their publication—written simultaneously by the distinguished author of the *Influence de la pression de l'air sur la vie de l'homme*, and the excellent poet to whom France is indebted for the inimitable *Les Trophées*. This synchronism strongly indicates the extraordinary importance attributed to the *Historia Verdadera*.—G. G.

[2] Published in Madrid, 1892.

was not the least important of the motives that induced him to write his own work.[1] At the beginning of the following century Friar Francisco Vásquez proved that Friar Bartolomé de Olmedo was not in Guatemala at the time of its conquest, as is stated in the edition of Remón, and therefore he was not the first to spread the Christian faith through that province, unless, as he says, one should concede another miracle such as that of Saint Anthony of Padua, who managed to be in two different places at the same time.

Some years afterwards Don Andrés González Barcia, referring to the charge that Fuentes y Guzmán had launched against Remón, arbitrarily surmised that the differences that existed between the edition published by the latter and the original manuscript were matters of no importance, and simply inferred that it was "easy to believe that in copying the author should make some alterations, as ordinarily happens". This defence was not convincing, and on this account our great bibliographer in Mexico, Don Juan José de Eguiara y Eguren, delicately objected that P. Vásquez had declared even the first edition to be falsified, while in Spain the indefatigable chronicler Don Juan Bautista Muñoz endeavoured to procure a copy of the original manuscript with the object of ascertaining the alterations due to Padre Remón.

Finally, if there could be any doubt remaining about the bad faith of Remón, it was completely dispelled by the Guatemalan historians Padre Domingo Juarros Don José Milla, the Bishop Don Francisco de Paula García Paláez, and Don Ramón A. Salazar, who from personal inspection fully corroborated what had been asserted by their predecessors the author of the *Isagoge,* Fuentes y Guzmán, and Vásquez.

As a matter of fact we can see at a glance in the following notes (par. iv, and Appendix No. 2)[2] that Fray Alonzo Remón in printing the *True History* suppressed whole pages of the manuscript, interpolated others, garbled the facts, changed the names of persons and places, increased or lessened the numbers,

---

[1] *Historia de Guatemala ó Recordación Florida,* p. 8.

[2] This paragraph and appendix has not been translated. As we have now before us an accurate copy of the original text, the reader would not be much interested in a discussion of the corruptions of the text by Padre Remón. In most instances these corruptions of the text were introduced for the purpose of magnifying the importance of Padre Olmedo and the Friars of the Order of Mercy, of which Order Padre Remón was himself a member. In the edition of Don Genaro García these matters are fully investigated, and a complete bibliography is given.

modified the style, and modernized the orthography moved thereto either by religious fervour and false patriotism, or by personal sympathy and vile literary taste. As all the later editions, and all the translations without exception were copied from the first edition published by Remón, it results that in reality we do not know the *True History*.

†

On the 20th October, 1895, Don Emilio León, the Envoy Extraordinary and Minister Plenipotentiary from the Republic of Guatemala accredited to Mexico, presented in the name of his Government to ours, "as a proof of friendship and especial regard", a photographic reproduction of the original manuscript. It was then, with some reason, believed that, at last, we should see the *True History* published; but this could not be carried out, for accompanying the gift of the reproduction was a prohibition against its being copied and printed.

Five years later, when I wrote my book entitled *Caracter de la Conquista Española en America y en México,* I was convinced that to perfect our Ancient history an exact edition of the *True History* was indispensable, and I desired to carry this work through.

Soon afterwards, in August, 1901, I wrote to the then President of Guatemala, Don Manuel Estrada Cabrera, telling him of my wish to print the precious manuscript.

This distinguished official had the kindness to reply on the first of the following month that on that very day he had decreed that "an exact and complete copy of the manuscript" should be made and sent to me for the purpose that I had stated. Señor Don Juan I. Argueta, Secretary of the Interior and Justice in that Republic, at once began punctually to send me instalments of the copy as soon as they were made, which copy I corrected here, and perfected with all care and accuracy by comparing it with the photographic reproduction already referred to, which is preserved in our National Library.

†

The author says that, after making a fair copy of his narrative, two licentiates of Guatemala begged him to lend it to them, and that he did so most willingly; but he warned them not to correct it in any way, neither by addition nor deletion, for all he had written was true.

Assuredly with regard to truth the author would find no fault with us, for we have taken care to religiously respect the original text, without introducing the slightest variation, not even of the artless orthography or punctuation.

Any change would have been dangerous, and we might have fallen into the same error that we attribute to Remón; everybody knows that by a single comma one might reverse the meaning of a statement.

We reproduce in notes placed at the foot of the page all the erasures that can have any interest for inquiring readers, and in like manner we have transcribed all the various words blotted out, which, besides exhibiting important variations, give an idea of the method of composition employed by the author.

Occasionally, when a full understanding of the text necessitates it, or for the purpose of finishing off a clearly implied word or phrase, or of correcting some manifest numerical error, we have ventured to insert some word or number between brackets, so that it can be known at once that it is not the author who is speaking, and the readers are left at liberty to admit or reject the slight interpolation; finally, we have allowed ourselves to indicate by dotted lines the gaps that are found in the original manuscript, which, happily, are very few in number, except on the first and last pages, which, in the course of time, have naturally suffered more than the others.

May our modest effort meet with the approbation of the intelligent and learned, for we long for it as much as we fear their censure.

BERNAL DÍAZ DEL CASTILLO

Bernal Díaz del Castillo was born in the very noble, famous, and celebrated town[1] of Medina del Campo in the year 1492 at the very time when Christopher Columbus was joining the two worlds.

Bernal tells us that at the time that he made up his mind to

---

[1] "Muy noble é insigne y muy nombrada Villa". In old Spain towns and cities were formally granted such titles of honour.

come to New Spain, about the year 1517, he was a youth "of about twenty-four years", a statement which corroborates the date of his birth.

His parents were Don Francisco Díaz del Castillo and Doña María Diez Rejón.

†

Bernal was not the only son, he tells us of his brother, probably older than himself, whom he wished to imitate.

†

Bernal himself writes that he was a gentleman,[1] and that his grandparents, his father, and his brother were always servants of the Crown and of their Catholic Majesties Don Fernando and Doña Isabel, which Carlos V. confirms by calling them "our retainers and servants".

If the family of Bernal had not enjoyed esteem and respect in Medina del Campo, the inhabitants would not have chosen Don Francisco as their *Regidor*.[2] On the other hand, his financial position must have been a very modest one, for the author most certainly came here to seek his fortune, and often complains of his poverty.

After all, the fact that in the *True History* he discloses a very scrupulous moral sense, a fair amount of learning, accurate philosophy, and a piety out of the common, permits us to infer that his family educated him with great care: it would be exceptional for a man illiterate and untaught during his youth to acquire such qualities in his old age; it is proven, on the other hand, that the author knew how to write when he reached New Spain. Nevertheless, we know nothing for certain about the childhood and youth of Bernal, our information begins in the year 1514.

The author was then twenty-two years old.

From some of his remarks one may judge that he was tall or of middle height, active, quick, well made, and graceful; his comrades called him "the elegant" (el galan).

†

Following the example of so many other Spanish youths, Bernal left his country in the year 1514 to emigrate to America in

[1] Hijodalgo.
[2] *Regidor* = magistrate, prefect.

search of adventures and riches, resolved to be worthy of his ancestry. He accompanied Pedro Arias de Avila, the Governor of Tierra Firme, as one of his soldiers.

When he reached Nombre de Dios he remained there three or four months, until an epidemic that broke out and certain disputes that arose between the Governor and his son-in-law, Vasco Nuñez de Balboa, obliged him to flee to Cuba, to his relation, Diego Velásquez, who was Governor of the Island.

During three years Bernal "did nothing worthy of record", and on that account he determined to set out on the discovery of unknown land with the Captain Francisco Hernández de Córdova and one hundred and ten companions.

They sailed in three ships from the port of Ajaruco on the 8th February, 1517, and after enduring a passage occupying twenty-one days and one fierce gale, they arrived at Cape Catoche, where the natives gave them a hostile reception.

After touching at Lázaro they stopped at Champotón, where the natives killed forty-eight Spaniards, captured two of them, and wounded the rest, including the captain, who received ten arrow wounds, and the author, who received "three, and one of them in the left side which pierced my ribs, and was very dangerous".

The survivors returned by way of Florida to Cuba, disillusioned and in ill-health, suffering from burning thirst and barely escaping shipwreck, for the ships were leaking badly. When recounting these calamities the author exclaims: "Oh! what a troublesome thing it is to go and discover new lands and the risks we took it is hardly possible to exaggerate".

Nevertheless Bernal was not discouraged by experience; his poverty, which, of necessity, increased daily, impelled him to seek his fortune even at the risk of losing his life, and his youth made him naturally impatient; he did not care to wait for the Indians which Diego Velásquez had promised to give him as soon as there were some unemployed, and he at once enlisted in a second expedition, composed of four ships and two hundred soldiers, under the command of Juan de Grijalva, which weighed anchor in the port of Matanzas on the 8th April, 1518.

The author says that he went "as ensign", but it is doubtful.

The expedition went by way of Cozumel and Champotón, whose intrepid inhabitants wounded Grijalva and broke two of his teeth, and killed seven soldiers, by the Boca de Términos, the Rio de Tabasco which they called the Rio de Grijalva, La Rambla, the Rios de Tonalá or de Santo Antón, de Coatza-coalcos, de Papaloapan or de Alvarado, and the Rio de Ban-deras, where they obtained by barter "more than sixteen thou-sand pesos in jewels and low grade gold". They sighted the Isla Blanca and the Isla Verde and landed on the Isla de Sacrificios and the sand dunes of Ulúa; thence Alvarado, accom-panied by certain soldiers, returned to Cuba in search of rein-forcements, while Grijalva, with the rest of his followers, in-cluding the author, pushed ahead by Tuxtla,[1] Tuxpan and the Rio de Canoas, where the Spaniards were attacked by the na-tives of Cape Rojo; then Grijalva, yielding to the entreaties of his soldiers, agreed to return to Cuba.

Velásquez, fascinated beyond measure by the gold which Grijalva had obtained by barter, organized a third expedition consisting of "eleven ships great and small", and appointed Hernan Cortés to command it. Bernal again enlisted, as at this time he found himself much in debt. Cortés set out from the Port of Trinidad on the 18th February, 1519. The author had started eight days earlier in the company of Pedro de Alvarado. All met together again at the Island of Cozumel, where a review was held, which showed a muster of five hun-dred and eight soldiers, "not including ship-masters, pilots, and seamen, who numbered one hundred and sixteen horses and mares". Keeping on their course, they passed close by Cham-potón without venturing to land; they stopped at Tabasco, where they fought with the natives, who gave the author "an arrow wound in the thigh but it was not a severe wound", and finally they arrived at Ulúa.

They went inland and marched to Cempoala and Quiahuizt-lan, and in the neighbourhood of the latter they founded the Villa Rica de la Vera Cruz, and they determined to push on to México, whose Prince, Motecuhzoma,[2] had been exciting their cupidity by rich presents of gold and other objects of value.

Before undertaking this march, the friends of Cortés (one of whom was Bernal) advised him to destroy the ships, lest any of the soldiers should mutiny and wish to return to Cuba, and so that he could make use of the ship-masters, pilots and

[1] This is an error. Tuxtla was passed before reaching the Isla de Sacrificios.
[2] Montezuma.

seamen "who numbered nearly one hundred persons" as we have already stated. When this had been done, "without concealment and not as the chronicler Gómara describes it", they started for Mexico in the middle of August, probably on the sixteenth, and passed without incident through Jalapa Xicochimalco, Ixhuacan, Texutla, Xocotla, and Xalacingo, but on reaching the frontiers of Tlaxcala they were stopped by the natives, who fought against them for several days. There the author received "two wounds, one on the head from a stone, and the other an arrow wound in the thigh", from which he was seriously ill in the Capital of Tlaxcala, after Cortés had made peace and an alliance with the inhabitants.

"On the 12th October" they continued their march by Cholula, where they committed a shocking massacre, Itzcalpan, Tlamanalco, and Itztapalatengo. Here Cacamatzin the Lord of Tetzcoco met them in royal state to welcome them in the name of Motecuhzoma, and they accompanied him along the causeway of Itztapalapa, which crossed the lake in a straight line to Mexico, and from it could be seen on both sides innumerable "cities and towns", some in the water and others on dry land, all of them beautified by stately temples and palaces. This wonderful panorama, as picturesque as it was novel, made the deepest impression on Bernal and his companions, and he says, "we were amazed and said that it was like the enchantments they tell us of in the story of Amadis, on account of the great towers and *cues*[1] and buildings rising from the water, and all built of masonry. And some of our soldiers even asked whether the things that we saw were not all a dream".

When they reached the junction of the causeways of Itztapalapa and Coyohuacan they met many Caciques and Chieftains of importance coming in advance of Motecuhzoma, who received the Spaniards a little further on, almost at the gates of Mexico, with sumptuous pomp and extreme ceremony. Many times the Mexican sovereign had contemplated attacking the Spaniards, but weighted down by superstition and rendered powerless by a timid and vacillating character, he now conducted them into the great Tenochtitlan, only to deliver it up to them at once. The autocrat felt himself fatally conquered before beginning the struggle.

[1] *Cue* = temple. This is not a Nahua or Maya word but one picked up by the Spaniards in the Antilles.

Thence step by step within a few days he suffered seven
Spaniards, among whom was Bernal, to make him a prisoner
in his own palace; he allowed his jailors to burn [to death]
Quauhpopoca and other native chieftains, whose crime consisted in having, by his own orders, given battle to Juan de
Escalante and other Spanish soldiers; he handed over to Cortés
Cacamatzin, Totoquihuatzin, Cuitláhuac and Cuauhtémoc,
lords respectively of Tetzcoco, Tlacopan, Itztapalapan and
Tlatelolco, who wished to set their sovereign at liberty, and
finally, weeping like a tender unhappy woman, he swore fealty
to the King of Spain.

With ease and in a short time Cortés was able to collect an
immense treasure which amounted to "seven hundred thousand
gold dollars", which he found it necessary to divide among his
soldiers; nevertheless, he made the division with such trickery
and cunning that there fell to the soldiers "a very small share,
only one hundred dollars each, and it was so very little that
many of the soldiers did not want to take it, and Cortés was left
with it all". If the author did not complain of this as much
as some of his companions, for example, as Cárdenas, who even
"fell ill from brooding and grief", it was owing to his having
already received from Motecuhzoma some presents of "gold
and cloths", as well as of "a beautiful Indian girl . . . the
daughter of a chieftain", whom he ventured to beg of the
sovereign through the good offices of the page Orteguilla, a
gift which he certainly thought that he had gained by his
respectful courtesy "for whenever I was on guard over him,
or passed before him, I doffed my helmet to him with the
greatest respect".

The Spaniards began to enjoy the gold divided among them,
abandoning themselves to a life of licentious pleasure, when
in March, 1520, Pánfilo de Narvaez arrived at Ulúa with sixteen ships,[1] fourteen hundred soldiers, ninety crossbowmen,
seventy musketeers, and eighty horses.

Diego Velásquez had sent him to punish Cortés and his
followers as traitors, because they had rebelled against him
without reason. However, as Cortés was immensely rich, and
there is no power greater than riches, he soon won over almost

---

[1] The author says that there were nineteen, but the Oidor Lucas Vásquez de Ayllon,
who accompanied Narvaez, writes that there were sixteen (Hernan Cortés, *Cartas y
Relaciones*, Paris, 1866: (p. 42).—G. G.

all the soldiers of Narvaez with ingots and jewels of gold, in such a way that when the fight took place at Cempoala, Narvaez was the only man who fought in earnest, until he was wounded and lost an eye. The author figures among his captors: "the first to lay hands on him was Pedro Sanchez Farfan, a good soldier, and I handed him (Narvaez) over to Sandoval".

After his victory, Cortés returned with all speed to Mexico, where the inhabitants had risen in arms with the purpose of avenging the inhuman massacre carried out by Pedro de Alvarado in the precincts of the great Teocalli, which Alonzo de Avila pronounced to be disgraceful, saying that it would for ever remain "an ill memory in New Spain". Cortés now brought with him over thirteen hundred soldiers, eighty crossbowmen and as many musketeers, and ninety mounted men, without counting his numerous native allies.

Although they all reached the great Tenochtitlan "on the day of San Juan de Junio (St John's Day) in the year 1520", they could not make a stand against the Mexicans, who, under the command of Cuitláhuac and Cuahtémoc, killed the greater number of the invaders and forced the rest, wounded and ruined, for they were unable to save the riches they had collected, to flee to Tlaxcala. The Tlaxcalans received them, lodged them and attended to them with affection. When they were somewhat recovered, the Spaniards began Vandal-like forays through Tepeyácac, Cachula, Guacachula, Tecamachalco, the town of the Guayabos, Ozúcar, Xalacingo, Zacatami, and other places in the neighbourhood, enslaving and branding with a hot iron all the youths and women they met with; "they did not trouble about the old men": the inhuman mark was placed "on the face", and not even the most beautiful young women escaped it.

The author did not assist in all these forays because "he was very ill from fever and was spitting blood".

Cortés then founded a second city, which he named Segura de la Frontera.

After the Spaniards had been reinforced by various expeditions that had come from Cuba, they resolved to return to Mexico to recover their lost treasure, and they forthwith took the road to Tetzcoco.

They took with them many thousands of native allies.

When the headquarters had been established at Tetzcoco,

Cortés opened hostilities by an assault on Itztapalapa, where he and his followers nearly lost their lives by drowning, for the Mexicans "burst open the canals of fresh and salt water and tore down a causeway": the author was "very badly wounded by a lance thrust which they gave me in the throat near the windpipe, and I was in danger of dying from it, and retain the scar from it to this day".

Cortés did not think of a direct attack on Mexico, he understood that it could lead to no satisfactory result; he proposed merely to invest the city and reduce it by starvation; so as to accomplish this he had entrusted to the Tlaxcalans the construction of thirteen launches, which he anxiously awaited.

Meanwhile, he attacked the neighbouring towns with fire and sword. The author did not join in these earlier combats as he was still ill from his dangerous wound, but as soon as it healed, he again took up arms, and accompanied Cortés, who went to assist the natives of Chalco, and distinguished himself among the most intrepid soldiers.

On his side, Cuauhtémoc, who was now Lord of Mexico, took measures for the defence of his country with unequalled courage; he had obtained from his subjects a promise "that they would never make peace, but would either all die fighting or take our lives".

The strife was remarkably prolonged and bloody, and no quarter was given.

The siege began on the 21st May, 1521, and lasted eighty-five days. Not for one moment did the Mexicans show signs of discouragement, notwithstanding the scarcity of fresh water and provisions, the superiority of the arms of the Spaniards, and the immense number of their native allies;[1] each day as it came was for them as the first day of the strife, so great was the determination and the strength with which they appeared on the field of battle, and, moreover, they never ceased fighting "from dawn to dusk".

When the greater number of them had already perished, the few who still remained stoically resisted thirst, hunger, weariness, and pestilence in the defence of their country, and even then refused, with indomitable fortitude, the proposals of peace

[1] The author makes immoderate efforts to lessen the number of the allies, but Cortés informs us that there were "numberless people", "an infinite number", "which could not be counted", that those that accompanied him alone numbered "more than one hundred and fifty thousand men".—G. G.

which Cortés repeatedly made to them. In this manner only did they die.

The army which was to attack the Mexicans by land was divided from the beginning into three sections. It fell to the lot of the author to serve in that of Tlacopan, commanded by Pedro de Alvarado. Many times Bernal was in danger of losing his life, first of all when the siege had just been commenced; a few days later when the Mexicans succeeded in seizing him, "many Indians had already laid hold of me, but I managed to get my arm free and our Lord Jesus Christ gave me strength so that by some good sword thrusts that I gave them, I saved myself, but I was badly wounded in one arm"; on another occasion they succeeded in taking him prisoner, but "it pleased God that I should escape from their power"; and, finally, at the end of June on the day that Cortés suffered his terrible defeat, the author received "an arrow wound and a sword thrust".

The siege ended on the 13th of August, 1521, with the capture of the north-east corner of the city where the few surviving Mexicans still offered a heroic resistance.

Prefatory Note

In 1908 the Hakluyt Society published my translation of *The True Story of the Conquest of New Spain* by Bernal Diaz del Castillo with maps and notes in five volumes, and I wish to express my thanks to the Council of that Society for permitting me to use that translation for the present volume, which tells the story so far as it relates to the discovery and conquest of Mexico in Bernal Diaz's own words, omitting all unnecessary passages, and ends with the fall of Mexico City.

Some extracts from the letters of Hernando Cortés are added to make clear the topography of the siege of the City.

The latter part of Bernal Diaz's history deals with the march to Honduras, which is another story.

A. P. M.

Preface by the Author

I have observed that the most celebrated chroniclers, before they begin to write their histories, first set forth a Prologue and Preface with the argument expressed in lofty rhetoric in order to give lustre and repute to their statements, so that the studious readers who peruse them may partake of their melody and flavour. But I, being no Latin scholar, dare not venture on such a preamble or prologue, for in order properly to extol the adventures which we met with and the heroic deeds we accomplished during the Conquest of New Spain and its provinces in the company of that valiant and doughty Captain, Don Hernando Cortés (who later on, on account of his heroic deeds, was made Marqués del Valle) there would be needed an eloquence and rhetoric far beyond my powers. That which I have myself seen and the fighting I have gone through, with the help of God, I will describe quite simply, as a fair eye witness without twisting events one way or another. I am now an old man, over eighty-four years of age, and I have lost my sight and hearing, and, as luck would have it, I have gained nothing of value to leave to my children and descendants but this my true story, and they will presently find out what a wonderful story it is.

BOOK ONE

THE
DISCOVERY

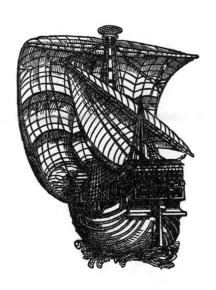

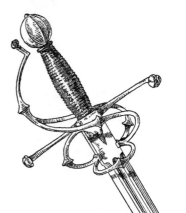

I

The Expedition Under Cordova

I, Bernal Díaz del Castillo, citizen and Regidor of the most loyal city of Santiago de Guatemala, one of the first discoverers and conquerors of New Spain and its provinces, and the Cape of Honduras and all that lies within that land, a Native of the very noble and distinguished town of Medina del Campo, and the son of its former *Regidor,* Francisco Díaz del Castillo, who was also called "The graceful" (may his soul rest in glory), speak about that which concerns myself and all the true conquerors my companions who served His Majesty by discovering, conquering, pacifying, and settling most of the provinces of New Spain, and that it is one of the best countries yet discovered in the New World, we found out by our own efforts without His Majesty knowing anything about it.

In the year 1514, there went out as Governor of Tierra-firme,[1] a gentleman named Pedrárias Dávila. I agreed to go with him to his Government and the country conquered by him, and we arrived at Nombre de Dios, for so it was named.

Some three or four months after the settlement was formed, there came a pestilence from which many soldiers died, and in addition to this, all the rest of us fell ill and suffered from bad ulcers on the legs. Then disputes arose between the Governor and a nobleman named Vasco Nuñez de Balboa, the captain, who had conquered that province, to whom Pedrárias Dávila had given his daughter in marriage. But it seems that after

[1] *Tierra-firme* = the Spanish Main.

marriage, he grew suspicious of his son-in-law, believing that
he would rise in rebellion and lead a body of soldiers towards
the South Sea, so he gave orders that Balboa should have his
throat cut and certain of the soldiers should be punished.

As we were witnesses of what I have related, and of other
revolts among the captains, and as the news reached us that the
Island of Cuba had lately been conquered and settled, and that
a gentleman named Diego Velásquez, who was my kinsman,
had been made Governor of the Island, some of us gentlemen
and persons of quality, who had come out with Pedrárias
Dávila, made up our minds to ask him to give us permission to
go to Cuba, and he willingly did so.

As soon as leave was granted we embarked in a good ship
and with fair weather reached the Island of Cuba. On landing
we went at once to pay our respects to the Governor, who was
pleased at our coming, and promised to give us Indians as soon
as there were any to spare. I was then twenty-four years old.

When three years had gone by, counting both the time we
were in Tierra-firme and that which we had passed in the Island of Cuba, and it became evident that we were merely wasting our time, one hundred and ten of us got together, most of
us comrades who had come from Tierra-firme, and the other
Spaniards of Cuba who had had no Indians assigned to them,
and we made an agreement with a gentleman named Francisco
Hernández de Córdova, that he should be our leader, for he
was well fitted for the post, and that we should try our fortune
in seeking and exploring new lands where we might find employment.

With this object in view, we purchased three ships, two of
them of good capacity, and the third, a bark, bought on credit
from the Governor, Diego Velásquez, on the condition that all
of us soldiers should go in the three vessels to some islands lying between Cuba and Honduras, which are now called the
Islands of the Guanajes,[1] and make war on the natives and load
the vessels with Indians, as slaves, with which to pay him for
his bark. However, as we soldiers knew that what Diego Velásquez asked of us was not just, we answered that it was neither
in accordance with the law of God nor of the king, that we
should make free men slaves. When he saw that we had made
up our minds, he said that our plan to go and discover new

[1] Roatan, Bonacca, etc. Islands near the coast of Honduras.

countries was better than his, and he helped us in providing food for our voyage.

To return to my story, we now found ourselves with three ships stored with Cassava bread, which is made from a root, and we bought some pigs which cost three dollars apiece, for in those days there were neither sheep nor cattle in the Island of Cuba, for it was only beginning to be settled, and we added a supply of oil, and bought beads and other things of small value to be used for barter. We then sought out three pilots, of whom the chief, who took charge of the fleet, was called Anton de Alaminos, a native of Palos. We also engaged the necessary number of sailors and procured the best supply that we could afford of ropes, cordage, cables, and anchors, and casks for water and other things needed for the voyage, and this all to our own cost.

When all the soldiers were mustered, we set out for a port on the North coast. In order that our voyage should proceed on right principles we wished to take with us a priest named Alonso González, and he agreed to come with us. We also chose for the office of *Veedor*[1] (in His Majesty's name) a soldier named Bernaldino Yñiguez, so that if God willed that we should come on rich lands, or people who possessed gold or silver or pearls or any other kind of treasure, there should be a responsible person to guard the Royal Fifth.

After all was arranged we set out on our voyage in the way I will now relate.

† II

On the eighth day of the month of February in the year fifteen hundred and seventeen, we left the port on the North coast, and in twelve days we doubled Cape San Antonio. When we had passed this Cape we were in the open sea, and trusting to luck we steered towards the setting sun, knowing nothing of the depth of water, nor of the currents, nor of the winds which usually prevail in that latitude, so we ran great risk of our lives, when a storm struck us which lasted two days and two nights, and raged with such strength that we were nearly lost. When the weather moderated, we kept on our course, and twenty-one

[1] *Veedor*=overseer.

days after leaving port, we sighted land, at which we rejoiced greatly and gave thanks to God. This land had never been discovered before, and no report of it had reached us. From the ships we could see a large town standing back about two leagues from the coast, and as we had never seen such a large town in the Island of Cuba nor in Hispaniola, we named it the Great Cairo.

We arranged that the two vessels which drew the least water should go in as near as possible to the Coast, to examine the land and see if there was any anchorage near the shore. On the morning of the 4th March, we saw ten large canoes, called *piraguas,* full of Indians from the town, approaching us with oars and sails. The canoes were large ones made like hollow troughs cleverly cut out from huge single logs, and many of them would hold forty Indians.

They came close to our ships, and we made signs of peace to them, beckoning with our hands and waving our cloaks to induce them to come and speak to us, although at the time we had no interpreters who could speak the languages of Yucatan and Mexico. They approached quite fearlessly and more than thirty of them came on board the flagship, and we gave them each a present of a string of green beads, and they passed some time examining the ships. The chief man among them, who was a *Cacique,* made signs to us that they wished to embark in their canoes and return to their town, and that they would come back again another day with more canoes in which we could go ashore.

These Indians were clothed in cotton shirts made like jackets, and covered their persons with a narrow cloth, and they seemed to us a people superior to the Cubans, for the Cuban Indians go about naked, only the women wearing a cloth reaching to the thighs.

The next morning the same *Cacique* returned to the ships and brought twelve large canoes, with Indian rowers, and with a cheerful face and every appearance of friendliness, made signs that we should go to his town.

He kept on saying in his language, *"cones catoche," "cones catoche,"* which means "come to my houses," and for that reason we called the land Cape Catoche, and it is still so named on the charts.

When our captain and the soldiers saw the friendly overtures

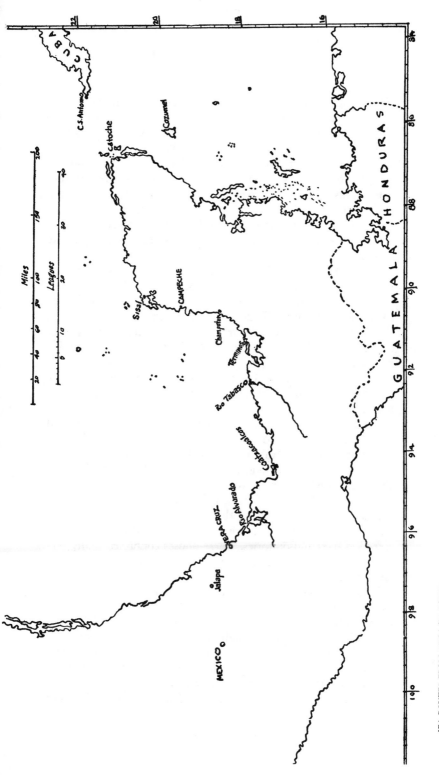

SEA ROUTES FROM CUBA TO MEXICO

the chief was making to us, we agreed to lower the boats from our ships, and in the vessel of least draught, and in the twelve canoes, to go ashore all together, and because we saw that the shore was crowded with Indians from the town, we arranged to land all of us at the same moment. When the Cacique saw us all on shore, but showing no intention of going to his town, he again made signs to our captain that we should go with him to his houses, and he showed such evidence of peace and good-will, that we decided to go on, and we took with us fifteen crossbows and ten muskets, so with the Cacique as our guide, we began our march along the road, accompanied by many Indians.

We moved on in this way until we approached some brush-covered hillocks, when the Cacique began to shout and call out to some squadrons of warriors who were lying in ambush ready to fall upon us and kill us. On hearing the Cacique's shouts, the warriors attacked us in great haste and fury, and began to shoot with such skill that the first flight of arrows wounded fifteen soldiers.

These warriors wore armour made of cotton reaching to the knees and carried lances and shields, bows and arrows, slings and many stones.

After the flight of arrows, the warriors, with their feathered crests waving, attacked us hand to hand, and hurling their lances with all their might, they did us much damage. However, thank God, we soon put them to flight when they felt the sharp edge of our swords, and the effect of our guns and crossbows, and fifteen of them fell dead.

A short distance ahead of the place where they attacked us, was a small *plaza* with three houses built of masonry, which served as *cues* and oratories. These houses contained many pottery Idols, some with the faces of demons and others with women's faces.

Within the houses were some small wooden chests, and in them were some other Idols, and some little discs made partly of gold but more than half of copper, and some necklaces and three diadems, and other small objects in the form of fish and others like the ducks of the country, all made of inferior gold.

When we had seen the gold and the houses of masonry, we felt well content at having discovered such a country.

In these skirmishes we took two Indians prisoners, and later on, when they were baptized, one was named Julian and the other Melchior, both of them were cross-eyed. When the fight was over we returned to our ships, and as soon as the wounded were cared for, we set sail.

† III

We travelled with the greatest caution, sailing along the coast by day only, and anchoring by night. After voyaging in this manner for fifteen days, we descried from the ship, what appeared to be a large town, and we thought that there might be a river or stream there, where we could provide ourselves with water of which we had great need, because the casks and other vessels which we had brought with us, were not watertight.

We agreed to approach the shore in the smallest of the vessels, and in the three boats, with all our arms ready, so as not to be caught as we had been at Cape Catoche.

In these roadsteads and bays the water shallows vary considerably at low tide, so that we had to leave our ships anchored more than a league from the shore.

We went ashore near the town which is called Campeche, where there was a pool of good water, for as far as we had seen there were no rivers in this country. We landed the casks, intending to fill them with water, and return to our ships. When the casks were full, and we were ready to embark, a company of about fifty Indians, clad in good cotton mantles, came out in a peaceful manner from the town, and asked us by signs what it was we were looking for, and we gave them to understand that we had come for water, and wished to return at once to our ships. They then made signs with their hands to find out whether we came from the direction of the sunrise, repeating the word "Castilan" "Castilan" and we did not understand what they meant by Castilan. They then asked us by signs to go with them to their town, and we decided to go with them, keeping well on the alert and in good formation.

They led us to some large houses very well built of masonry, which were the Temples of their Idols, and on the walls were figured the bodies of many great serpents and other pictures of evil-looking Idols. These walls surrounded a sort of Altar covered with clotted blood. On the other side of the Idols were symbols like crosses, and all were coloured. At all this we stood wondering, as they were things never seen or heard of before.

It seemed as though certain Indians had just offered sacrifices to their Idols so as to ensure victory over us. However, many Indian women moved about us, laughing, and with every appearance of good will, but the Indians gathered in such numbers that we began to fear that there might be some trap set for us, as at Catoche. While this was happening, many other Indians approached us, wearing very ragged mantles and carrying dry reeds, which they deposited on the plain, and behind them came two squadrons of Indian archers in cotton armour, carrying lances and shields, slings and stones, and each captain drew up his squadron at a short distance from where we stood. At that moment, there sallied from another house, which was an oratory of their Idols, ten Indians clad in long white cotton cloaks, reaching to their feet, and with their long hair reeking with blood, and so matted together, that it could never be parted or even combed out again, unless it were cut. These were the priests of the Idols, and they brought us incense of a sort of resin which they call *copal,* and with pottery braziers full of live coals, they began to fumigate us, and by signs they made us understand that we should quit their land before the firewood which they had piled up there should burn out, otherwise they would attack us and kill us. After ordering fire to be put to the reeds, the priests withdrew without further speech. Then the warriors who were drawn up in battle array began to whistle and sound their trumpets and drums. When we perceived their menacing appearance and saw great squadrons of Indians bearing down on us we remembered that we had not yet recovered from the wounds received at Cape Catoche, and had been obliged to throw overboard the bodies of two soldiers who had died, and fear fell on us, so we determined to retreat to the coast in good order, and began to march along the shore towards a large rock which rose out of the sea, while the boats and the small bark laden with the water casks coasted along close in shore. We had not dared to embark near the town where we had landed, on account of the great press of Indians, for we felt sure they would attack us as we tried to get in the boats. As soon as we had embarked and got the casks on board the ships, we sailed on for six days and nights in good weather, then we were struck by a *norther* which is a foul wind on that coast and it lasted four days and nights, and so strong was the storm that it nearly drove us ashore, so that we had to drop anchor, but we broke two cables, and one ship began to drag her anchor. Ah! the danger was terrible, for if our last cable had given way we should have been driven ashore to destruction, but thank God we were able to ease the strain on the cable by lashing it with pieces of rope and hawsers, and at last the weather moderated. Then we kept on our course along the coast, going ashore whenever we were able to do so to get water, for, as I have already said, the casks we carried were leaky, and we hoped that by keeping near the coast we should be able to find water, whenever we landed, either in pools or by digging for it.

As we were sailing along on our course, we came in sight of a town, and about a league on the near side of it, there was a bay which looked as though it had a river running into it; so we determined to anchor. On this coast the tide runs out so far that there is a danger of ships being stranded, so for fear of this we dropped anchor at the distance of a league from the shore, and we landed from the vessel of least draught and from the boats, well armed and carrying all our casks along with us. This landing place was about a league from the town, near to some pools of water, and maize plantations, and a few small houses built of masonry. The town is called Champoton.

† IV

As we were filling our casks with water there came along the coast towards us many squadrons of Indians clad in cotton armour reaching to the knees, and armed with bows and arrows, lances and shields, and swords like two handed broad swords, and slings and stones and carrying the feathered crests, which they are accustomed to wear. Their faces were painted black and white, and ruddled and they came in silence straight towards us, as though they came in peace, and by signs they asked whether we came from where the sun rose, and we replied that we did come from the direction of the sunrise. We were at our wits end considering the matter, and wondering what the words were which the Indians called out to us for they were the same as those used by the people of Campeche, but we never made out what it was that they said.

All this happened about the time of the Ave Maria, and the Indians then went off to some villages in the neighbourhood, and we posted watchmen and sentinels for security.

While we were keeping watch during the night we heard a great squadron of Indian warriors approaching from the town and from the farms, and we knew well, that their assembly boded us no good, and we took counsel together as to what should be done. However, some said one thing and some said another. While we were still taking counsel and the dawn broke, and we could see that there were about two hundred Indians to every one of us, and we said one to the other "let us strengthen our hearts for the fight, and after commending ourselves to God let us do our best to save our lives."

As soon as it was daylight we could see, coming along the coast, many more Indian warriors with their banners raised. When their squadrons were formed up they surrounded us on all sides and poured in such showers of arrows and darts, and stones thrown from their slings that over eighty of us soldiers were wounded, and they attacked us hand to hand, some with lances and the others shooting arrows, and others with two-handed knife edged swords,[1] and they brought us to a bad pass. At last feeling the effects of our sword play they drew back a little, but it was not far, and only enabled them to shoot their stones and darts at us with greater safety to themselves.

While the battle was raging the Indians called to one another in their language *"al Calachuni, Calachuni"* which means "let us attack the Captain and kill him," and ten times they wounded him with their arrows; and me they struck thrice, one arrow wounding me dangerously in the left side, piercing through the ribs. All the other soldiers were wounded by spear thrusts and two of them were carried off alive.

Our captain then saw that our good fighting availed us nothing; other squadrons of warriors were approaching us fresh from the town, bringing food and drink with them and a large supply of arrows. All our soldiers were wounded with two or three arrow wounds, three of them had their throats pierced by lance thrusts, our captain was bleeding from many wounds and already fifty of the soldiers were lying dead.

[1] *Macana* (or *Macuahuitl*), a wooden sword edged with sharp flint or obsidian.

Feeling that our strength was exhausted we determined with stout hearts to break through the battalions surrounding us and seek shelter in the boats which awaited us near the shore; so we formed in close array and broke through the enemy.

Ah! then to hear the yells, hisses and cries, as the enemy showered arrows on us and hurled lances with all their might, wounding us sorely.

Then another danger befell us; as we all sought shelter in the boats at the same time they began to sink, so in the best way we could manage hanging on to the waterlogged boats and half swimming, we reached the vessel of lightest draught which came in haste to our assistance.

Many of us were wounded while we embarked, especially those who were sitting in the stern of the boats, for the Indians shot at them as targets, and even waded into the sea with their lances and attacked us with all their strength. Thank God! by a great effort we escaped with our lives from the clutches of those people.

Within a few days we had to cast into the sea five others who died of their wounds and of the great thirst which we suffered. The whole of the fighting occupied only one hour.

† v

After we had attended to the wounded (and there was not a man among us who had not two, three or four wounds, and the Captain was wounded in ten places and only one soldier escaped without hurt) we decided to return to Cuba.

As almost all the sailors also were wounded we were shorthanded for tending the sails, so we abandoned the smallest vessel and set fire to her after removing the sails, cables and anchors, and we divided the sailors who were unwounded between the two larger vessels. However, our greatest trouble arose from the want of fresh water, for owing to the attack made on us and the haste with which we had to take to the boats, all the casks and barrels which we had filled with water were left behind.

So great was our thirst that our mouths and tongues were cracked with the dryness, and there was nothing to give us relief. Oh! what hardships one endures, when discovering new lands, in the way we set out to do it; no one can appreciate the excessive hardships who has not passed through them as we did.

We kept our course close to the land in hope of finding some stream or bay where we could get fresh water, and at the end of three days we found a bay where there appeared to be a creek which we thought might hold fresh water. Fifteen of the sailors who had remained on board and were unwounded and three soldiers who were out of danger from their wounds went ashore, and they took hoes with them, and some barrels; but the water of the creek was salt, so they dug holes on the beach, but there also the water was as salt and bitter as that in the creek. However, bad as the water was, they filled the casks with it and brought it on board, but no one could drink such water and it did harm to the mouths and bodies of the few soldiers who attempted to drink it.

There were so many large alligators in that creek that it has always been known as the *éstero de los Lagartos*.

While the boats went ashore for water there arose such a violent gale from the North East that the ships began to drag their anchors and drift towards the shore. The sailors who had gone on shore returned with the boats in hot haste and arrived in time to put out other anchors and cables, so that the ships rode in safety for two days and nights. Then we got up anchor and set sail continuing our voyage back to the island of Cuba.

The pilot Alaminos then took counsel with the other two pilots, and it was settled that from the place we then were we should cross over to Florida, for he judged that it was about seventy leagues distant, and that it would be a shorter course to reach Havana than the course by which we had come.

We did as the pilot advised, for it seems that he had accompanied Juan Ponce de Leon on his voyage of discovery to Florida fourteen or fifteen years earlier. After four days' sail we came in sight of the land of Florida.

† vi

When we reached land, it was arranged that twenty of the soldiers, those whose wounds were best healed, should go ashore. I went with them, and also the Pilot, Anton de Alaminos, and we carried with us such vessels as we still possessed, and hoes, and our crossbows and guns. As the Captain was very badly wounded, and much weakened by the great thirst he had endured, he prayed us on no account to fail in bringing back fresh water, as he was parching and dying of thirst, for the water we had on board was salt and not fit to drink.

We landed near a creek, the Pilot Alaminos carefully examined the coast and said that it was at this very spot when he came with Juan Ponce de Leon that the Indians of the country had attacked them and had killed many soldiers, and that it behoved us to keep a very sharp look out. We at once posted two soldiers as sentinels while we dug holes on a broad beach where we thought we should find fresh water, for at that hour the tide had ebbed. It pleased God that we come on very good water, and so overjoyed were we that what with satiating our thirst, and washing out cloths with which to bind up wounds, we must have stayed there an hour. When, at last, very well satisfied, we wished to go on board with the water, we saw one of the soldiers whom we had placed on guard coming towards us crying out, "to arms, to arms! many Indian warriors are coming on foot and others down the creek in canoes." The soldier who came shouting, and the Indians reached us nearly at the same time.

These Indians carried very long bows and good arrows and lances, and some weapons like swords, and they were clad in deerskins and were very big men. They came straight on and let fly their arrows and at once wounded six of us, and to me they dealt a slight arrow wound. However, we fell on them with such rapidity of cut and thrust of sword and so plied the crossbows and guns that they left us to ourselves and set off to the sea and the creek to help their companions who had come in the canoes and were fighting hand to hand with the sailors, whose boat was already captured and was being towed by the canoes up the creek, four of the sailors being wounded, and the Pilot Alaminos badly hurt in the throat. Then we fell upon them, with the water above our waists, and at the point of the sword, we made them abandon the boat. Twenty of the Indians lay dead on the shore or in the water, and three who were slightly wounded we took prisoners, but they died on board ship.

As soon as the skirmish was over we asked the soldier who

had been placed on guard what had become of his companion. He replied that he had seen him go off with an axe in his
hand to cut down a small palm tree, and that he then heard
cries in Spanish, and on that account he had hurried towards us
to give us warning, and it was then that his companion must
have been killed.

The soldier who had disappeared was the only man who had
escaped unwounded from the fight at Champoton, and we at
once set to work to search for him. We found a palm tree partly
cut through, and near by the ground was much trampled by
footsteps, and as there was no trace of blood we took it for certain that they had carried him off alive. We searched and
shouted for more than an hour, but finding no trace of him we
got into the boats and carried the fresh water to the ship, at
which the soldiers were as overjoyed as though we had given
them their lives. One soldier jumped from the ship into the
boat, so great was his thirst, and clasping a jar of water to his
chest drank so much water that he swelled up and died within
two days.

As soon as we had got the water on board and had hauled
up the boats, we set sail for Havana, and during the next day
and night the weather was fair and we were near some Islands
called *Los Martires,* when the flagship struck the ground and
made water fast, and with all of us soldiers working at the
pumps we were not able to check it, and we were in fear of
foundering.

Ill and wounded as we were, we managed to trim the sails
and work the pump until our Lord carried us into the port,
where now stands the city of Havana, and we gave thanks to
God.

We wrote in great haste to the Governor of the Island, Diego
Velásquez, telling him that we had discovered thickly-peopled
countries, with masonry houses, and people who covered their
persons and went about clothed in cotton garments, and who
possessed gold and who cultivated maize fields, and other matters which I have forgotten.

From Havana our Captain Francisco Hernández went by
land to the town of Santispíritus; but he was so badly wounded
that he died within ten days.

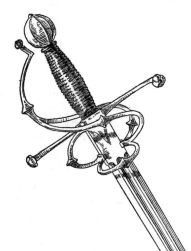

II

The Expedition Under Grijalva

In the year 1518 the Governor of Cuba, hearing the good account of the land which we had discovered, which is called Yucatan, decided to send out another fleet, and made search for four vessels to compose it. Two of these vessels were two of the three which had accompanied Francisco Hernández, the other two were vessels which Diego Velásquez bought with his own money.

At the time the fleet was being fitted out, there were present in Santiago de Cuba, where Velásquez resided Juan de Grijalva, Alonzo de Ávila, Francisco de Montejo, and Pedro de Alvarado, who had come to see the Governor on business, for all of them held *encomiendas* of Indians in the Island. As they were men of distinction, it was agreed that Juan de Grijalva who was a kinsman of Diego Velásquez, should go as Captain General, that Alonzo de Ávila, Pedro de Alvarado, and Francisco de Montejo should each have command of a ship. Each of these Captains contributed the provisions and stores of Cassava bread and salt pork, and Diego Velásquez provided the four ships, crossbows and guns, some beads and other articles of small value for barter, and a small supply of beans. Then Diego Velásquez ordered that I should go with these Captains as ensign.

As the report had spread that the lands were very rich, the soldiers and settlers who possessed no Indians in Cuba were greedily eager to go to the new land, so that 240 companions were soon got together.

Then every one of us, out of his own funds, added what he could of stores and arms and other suitable things; and I set out again on this voyage as ensign, as I have already stated.

As soon as all of us soldiers had got together and the pilots had received their instructions and the lantern signals had been arranged, after hearing mass, we set out on the 8th April, 1518.

In ten days we doubled the point of San Anton and after eight days sailing we sighted the Island of Cozumel, which was then first discovered, for with the current that was running we made much more lee-way than when we came with Francisco Hernández de Córdova, and we went along the south side of the Island and sighted a town with a few houses, near which was a good anchorage free from reefs.

We went on shore with the Captain and a large company of soldiers, and the natives of the town had taken to flight as soon as they saw the ships coming under sail, for they had never seen such a thing before.

We soldiers who landed found two old men, who could not walk far, hidden in the maize fields and we brought them to the Captain. With the help of the two Indians Julianillo and Melchorejo whom Francisco Hernández brought away, who thoroughly understood that language the captain spoke kindly to these old men and gave them some beads and sent them off to summon the cacique of the town, and they went off and never came back again.

While we were waiting, a good-looking Indian woman appeared and began to speak in the language of the Island of Jamaica, and she told us that all the men and women of the town had fled to the woods for fear of us. As I and many of our soldiers knew the language she spoke very well, for it is the same as that spoken in Cuba, we were very much astonished, and asked the woman how she happened to be there; she replied that two years earlier she had started from Jamaica with ten Indians in a large canoe intending to go and fish near some small islands, and that the currents had carried them over to this land where they had been driven ashore, and that her husband and all the Jamaica Indians had been killed and sacrificed to the Idols. When the Captain heard this it seemed to him that this woman would serve very well as a messenger, so he sent her to summon the people and caciques of the town, and he gave her two days in which to go and return. We were afraid that the Indians Melchorejo and Julianillo if once they got away from us would go off to their own country which was near by, and on that account we could not trust them as messengers.

To return to the Indian woman from Jamaica, the answer she brought was that notwithstanding her efforts she could not persuade a single Indian to approach us.

As the Captain Juan de Grijalva saw that it would be merely losing time to wait there any longer, he ordered us to go on board ship, and the Indian woman went with us, and we continued our voyage, and in eight days we reached the neighbourhood of the town of Champoton which was the place where the Indians of that province had defeated us, as I have already related. As the tide runs out very far in the bay, we anchored our ships a league from the shore and then making use of all the boats we disembarked half the soldiers close to the houses of the town.

The Indians of the town and others from the neighbourhood at once assembled, as they had done on the other occasion when they killed over fifty-six of our soldiers and wounded all the rest, and for that reason they were now very proud and haughty, and many of them had their faces painted black and others red and white. They were drawn up in array and awaited us on the shore, ready to fall on us as we landed. As we had already gained experience from our former expedition, we had brought with us in the boat some falconets and were well supplied with crossbows and guns.

As we approached the shore they began to shoot arrows and hurl lances at us with all their might, and although we did them much damage with our falconets, such a hail storm of arrows fell on us before we could land that half of us were wounded. As soon as all the soldiers got on shore we checked their ardour with our good sword play and with our crossbows, and although they still shot at us we were protected by our cotton armour. However, they kept up the fight against us for a good while until we drove them back into some swamps near to the town. In this fight seven soldiers were killed, and our

Captain Juan de Grijalva received three arrow wounds, and had two of his teeth broken, and more than sixty of us were wounded.

When we saw that all the enemy had taken to flight we entered the town and attended to the wounded and buried the dead. We could not find a single person in the town, nor could we find those who had retreated into the swamp for they had all disappeared. In that skirmish we captured three Indians one of whom was a chief, and the Captain sent them off to summon the cacique of the town, giving them clearly to understand through the interpreters Julianillo and Melchorejo that they were pardoned for what they had done, and he gave them some green beads to hand to the cacique as a sign of peace, and they went off and never returned again. So we believed that the Indians, Julianillo and Melchorejo had not repeated to the prisoners what they had been told to say to them but had said something quite different.

At that town we stayed for three days.

I remember that this fight took place in some fields where there were many locusts, and while we were fighting they jumped up and came flying in our faces, and as the Indian archers were pouring a hail storm of arrows on us we sometimes mistook the arrows for locusts and did not shield ourselves from them and so got wounded; at other times we thought that they were arrows coming towards us, when they were only flying locusts and it greatly hampered our fighting. Then we embarked and kept on our course and reached what seemed to be the mouth of a very rapid river, very broad and open, but it was not a river as we at first thought it to be, but it was a very good harbour, and we called it the Boca de Terminos.

The Captain Juan de Grijalva went ashore with all the other Captains and we spent three days taking soundings at the mouth of the strait and exploring up and down the bay. On shore we found some houses built of masonry, used as oratories of their Idols, but we found out that the place was altogether uninhabited, and that the oratories were merely those belonging to traders and hunters who put into the port when passing in their canoes and made sacrifices there. We had much deer and rabbit hunting and with the help of a lurcher we killed ten deer and many rabbits. At last when we had finished our soundings and explorations we made ready to go on board ship, but the lurcher got left behind.

As soon as we were all on board again we kept our course close along the shore until we arrived at a river which they call the Rio de Tabasco, which we named Rio de Grijalva.

† VIII

As we came nearer in we saw the water breaking over the bar at the mouth of the river, so we got out boats, and by sounding we found out that the two larger vessels could not enter the river, so it was agreed that they should anchor outside in the sea, and that all the soldiers should go up the river in the other two vessels which drew less water and in the boats.

When we arrived within half a league of the town we could hear the sound of chopping wood for the Indians were making barriers and stockades and getting ready to give us battle. When we were aware of this, so as to make certain, we disembarked half a league from the town on a point of land where some palm trees were growing. When the Indians saw us there a fleet of fifty canoes approached us full of warriors. Many other canoes full of warriors were lying in the creeks, and they kept a little way off as though they did not dare approach as did the first fleet. When we perceived their intentions we were on the point of firing at them, but it pleased God that we agreed to call out to them, and through Julianillo and Melchorejo, who spoke their language very well, we told them that they need have no fear, that we wished to talk to them, for we had things to tell them which when they understood them they would be glad that we had come to their country and their homes. Moreover, we wished to give them some of the things we had brought with us. As they understood what was said to them, four of the canoes came near with about thirty Indians in them, and we showed them strings of green beads and small mirrors and blue cut glass beads, and as soon as they saw them they assumed a more friendly manner, for they thought that they were *chalchihuites*[1] which they value greatly.

Then through Julianillo and Melchorejo as interpreters, the Captain told them that we came from a distant country and

[1] Chalchihuite is Jadeite, which was treasured as a precious stone by the Indians.

were the vassals of a great Emperor named Don Carlos, who had many great lords and chiefs as his vassals, and that they ought to acknowledge him as their lord, and it would be to their advantage to do so, and that in return for the beads they might bring us some food and poultry.

Two of the Indians answered us, and said that they would bring the food which we asked for, and would barter their things for ours; but as for the rest, they already had a chief, that we were only just now arrived, and knew nothing about them, and yet we wanted to give them a chief. Let us beware not to make war on them as we had done at Champoton, for they had more than three *jiquipiles* of warriors from all the provinces around in readiness (every *jiquipil* numbers eight thousand men) and they said that they were well aware that only a few days earlier we had killed and wounded more than two hundred men at Champoton but that they were not weaklings such as those, and for this reason they had come to talk to us and find out what we wanted, and that whatever we should tell them they would go and report to the chiefs of many towns who had assembled to decide on peace or war.

Then our Captain embraced the Indians as a sign of peace, and gave them some strings of beads and told them to go and bring back an answer as soon as possible, but he said that although we did not wish to anger them, that if they did not return we should have to force our way into their town.

The following day more than thirty Indians with their chief came to the promontory under the palm trees where we were camped and brought roasted fish and fowls, and zapote fruit and maize bread, and braziers with live coals and incense, and they fumigated us all. Then they spread on the ground some mats, which here they call *petates,* and over them a cloth, and they presented some golden jewels, some were diadems, and others were in the shape of ducks, like those in Castile, and other jewels like lizards and three necklaces of hollow beads, and other articles of gold but not of much value, for they were not worth more than two hundred dollars. They also brought some cloaks and skirts, such as they wear, and said that we must accept these things in good part as they had no more gold to give us, but that further on, in the direction of the sunset, there was plenty of gold, and they said "Colua, Colua, Méjico, Méjico," but we did not know what this Colua or Méjico could be. Although the present that they brought us was not worth much, we were satisfied, because we thus knew for certain that they possessed gold. Captain Juan de Grijalva thanked them for their gift and gave them a present of beads. It was decided that we should go on board at once, for the two ships were in much danger should a northerly gale blow, for it would put them on a lee shore, and moreover we wanted to get nearer to where we were told there was gold.

We returned on board and set our course along the coast and in two days came in sight of a town called Ayagualulco, and many of the Indians from that town marched along the shore with shields made of the shells of turtle, which sparkled as the sun shone on them, and some of our soldiers contended that they were made of low grade gold.

The Indians who carried them as they marched along the sandy beach, knowing that they were at a safe distance, cut capers, as though mocking at the ships. We gave the town the name of La Rambla, and it is thus marked on the charts.

Coasting along we came in sight of a bay into which flows the river Tonalá.

As we sailed along we noted the position of the great river Coatzacoalcos. Soon we came in sight of the great snow mountains, which have snow on them all the year round, and we saw other mountains, nearer to the sea.

As we followed along the coast, the Captain Pedro de Alvarado, went ahead with his ship and entered a river which the Indians call Papaloapan, and which we then called the Rio de Alvarado because Alvarado was the first to enter it. There, some Indian fishermen, natives of a town called Tlacotalpa gave him some fish. We waited at the mouth of the river with the other three ships until Alvarado came out, and the General was very angry with him for going up the river without his permission, and ordered him never to go ahead of the other ships again, lest an accident should happen when we could not give him help.

We kept on our course, all four ships together until we arrived at the mouth of another river, which we called the Rio de Banderas,[1] because we there came on a great number of Indians with long lances, and on every lance a great cloth banner which they waved as they beckoned to us.

[1] Rio de Banderas is the Rio Jamapa of the modern maps.

† IX

Some studious readers in Spain may have heard that Mexico
was a very great city built in the water like Venice, and that
it was governed by a great prince called Montezuma. Now it
appears that Montezuma had received news of our arrival when
we came first, with Francisco Hernández de Córdova, and of
what had happened at the battle of Catoche and at Champoton,
and also what had happened at the battle of this same Champoton during this voyage, and he knew that we soldiers being
few in number had defeated the warriors of that town and
their very numerous allies, and he knew as well that we had
entered the Rio Tabasco and what had taken place between
us and the caciques of that town, moreover he understood that
our object was to seek for gold, in exchange for the things we
had brought with us. All this news had been brought to him
painted on a cloth made of *henequen*[1] which is like linen, and
as he knew that we were coasting along towards his provinces
he sent orders to his governors that if we should arrive in their
neighbourhood with our ships that they should barter gold for
our beads, especially the green beads, which are something like
their *chalchihuites,* which they value as highly as emeralds;
he also ordered them to find out more about our persons and
our plans.

It is a fact, as we now know, that their Indian ancestors had
foretold that men with beards would come from the direction
of the sunrise and would rule over them. Whatever the reason
may have been many Indians sent by the Great Montezuma
were watching for us at the river I have mentioned with long
poles, and on every pole a banner of white cotton cloth, which
they waved and called to us, as though making signals of peace,
to come to them.

When from the ships we saw such an unusual sight we were
fairly astonished and the General and most of the Captains
were agreed that to find out what it meant we should lower
two of the boats, and that all those who carried guns or crossbows and twenty of the most daring and active soldiers should
go in them, and that Francisco de Montejo should accompany

[1] *Henequen,* or Sisal hemp, is a species of Aloe (*Agave Ixtli*) now largely used for
cordage.

us, and that if we should discover that the men who were waving the banners were warriors that we should at once bring news of it and of anything else that we could find out.

Thank God at that time we had fine weather which is rare enough on this coast. When we got on shore we found three Caciques, one of them the governor appointed by Montezuma, who had many of the Indians of his household with him. They brought many of the fowls of the country and maize bread such as they always eat, and fruits such as pineapples and zapotes, which in other parts are called mameies, and they were seated under the shade of the trees, and had spread mats on the ground, and they invited us to be seated, all by signs, for Julianillo the man from Cape Catoche, did not understand their language which is Mexican. Then they brought pottery braziers with live coals, and fumigated us with a sort of resin.

As soon as the Captain Montejo had reported all that had taken place the General determined to anchor his ships and go ashore with all his captains and soldiers. When the Caciques and governors saw him on land and knew that he was the Captain General of us all, according to their custom, they paid him the greatest respect. In return he treated them in a most caressing manner and ordered them to be given blue and green glass beads and by signs he made them understand that they should bring gold to barter with us. Then the Governor sent orders to all the neighbouring towns to bring jewels to exchange with us, and during the six days that we remained there they brought more than sixteen thousand dollars worth of jewelry of low grade gold, worked into various forms.

When the General saw that the Indians were not bringing any more gold to barter, and as we had already been there six days and the ships ran risk of danger from the North and North East wind, he thought it was time to embark.

So we took [formal] possession of the land in the name of His Majesty, and as soon as this had been done the General spoke to the Indians and told them that we wished to return to our ships and he gave them presents of some shirts from Spain. We took one of the Indians from this place on board ship with us, and after he had learnt our language he became a Christian and was named Francisco, and later on I met him living with his Indian wife.

As we sailed on along the coast we sighted some Islands of

white sand which the sea washed over, and going on further
we saw an Island somewhat larger than the others about a
league and a half off the shore, and in front of it there was a
good roadstead where the General gave orders for the ships to
come to anchor.

As soon as the boats were launched the Captain Juan de
Grijalva and many of us soldiers went off to visit the Island
for we saw smoke rising from it, and we found two masonry
houses very well built, each house with steps leading up to
some altars, and on these altars were idols with evil looking
bodies, and that very night five Indians had been sacrificed
before them; their chests had been cut open, and the arms and
thighs had been cut off and the walls were covered with blood.

At all this we stood greatly amazed, and gave the Island
the name of the Isla de Sacrificios and it is so marked on the
charts.

We all of us went ashore opposite that Island, and many Indians had come down to the coast bringing gold made into
small articles which they wished to barter as they had done at
the Rio de Banderas, and, as we afterwards found out the great
Montezuma had ordered them to do so. These Indians who
brought the gold were very timid and the gold was small in
quantity, for this reason the Captain Juan de Grijalva ordered
the anchors to be raised and sail set, and we went on to anchor
opposite another Island, about half a league from land, and it
is at this Island that the port of Vera Cruz is now established.

We landed on a sandy beach, and so as to escape the swarms
of mosquitos we built huts on the tops of the highest sand
dunes, which are very extensive in these parts.

We stayed there for seven days, but we could not endure the
mosquitos, and seeing that we were wasting time, and that
our cassava bread was very mouldy and dirty with weevils and
was going sour, and that the soldiers of our company were not
numerous enough to form a settlement, all the more so as thirteen soldiers had died of their wounds, it was agreed that we
should send to inform the Governor Diego Velásquez of our
condition, so that he could send us help.

It was therefore decided that the Captain Pedro de Alvarado
should go in a very good ship called the *San Sebastian* to carry
the message.

† x

After the Captain Pedro de Alvarado had left us it was decided to keep in close to the shore and discover all that we were able on the coast. Keeping on our course we came in sight of the Sierra de Tuzpa. As we coasted along, we saw many towns apparently two or three leagues inland. Continuing our course, we came to a great and rapid river which we called the Rio de Canoas and dropped anchor at the mouth of it.

When all three ships were anchored and we were a little off our guard, twenty large canoes filled with Indian warriors came down the river and made straight for the smallest ship. The Indians shot a flight of arrows which wounded five soldiers, and they made fast to the ship with ropes intending to carry her off, and even cut one of her cables with their copper axes. However, the captain and soldiers fought well, and upset three of the canoes, and we hastened to their assistance in our boats. Then we got up anchor and set sail and followed along the coast until we came to a great Cape which was most difficult to double, for the currents were so strong we could make no headway.

Then the pilot, Alaminos, said to the General, that it was no use trying to go further in that direction, and gave many reasons for his opinion. Counsel was taken as to what had best be done, and it was settled that we should return to Cuba.

So we turned round and set all sail before the wind, and aided by the currents, in a few days we reached the mouth of the great Rio de Coatzacoalcos, but we could not enter it on account of unfavourable weather, and going close in shore we entered the Rio de Tonalá. There we careened one of the ships which was making water fast, for on entering the river she had struck on the bar where the water is very shallow.

While we were repairing the ship many Indians came in a most friendly manner from the town of Tonalá, which is about a league distant, and brought maize bread, and fish and fruit, and gave them to us with great good will. The captain showed them much attention and ordered them to be given white and green beads, and made signs to them that they should bring gold for barter and we would give them our goods in exchange;

so they brought jewels of low grade gold, and we gave them beads in return. People came also from Coatzacoalcos and the other towns in the neighbourhood, and brought jewelry, but this did not amount to anything.

Besides these things for barter, the Indians of that province usually brought with them highly polished copper axes with painted wooden handles, as though for show or as a matter of elegance, and we thought that they were made of inferior gold, and began to barter for them, and in three days we had obtained more than six hundred, and we were very well contented thinking that they were made of debased gold, and the Indians were even more contented with their beads, but it was no good to either party, for the axes were made of copper and the beads were valueless.

Going on board ship again, we went on our way and in forty-five days we arrived at Santiago de Cuba where Diego Velásquez was residing, and he gave us a very good reception.

When the Governor saw the gold that we brought, which was worth four thousand dollars, and with that which had already been brought by Pedro de Alvarado, amounted in all to twenty thousand dollars, he was well contented. Then the officers of the King took the Royal Fifth, but when the six hundred axes which we thought were low grade gold were brought out, they were all rusty like copper which they proved to be, and there was a good laugh at us, and they made great fun of our trading.

BOOK TWO

THE
CONQUEST

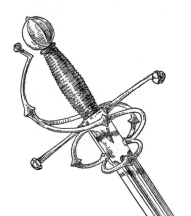

I

The Expedition Under Cortés

After the return of the Captain Juan de Grijalva to Cuba, when the Governor Diego Velásquez understood how rich were these newly discovered lands, he ordered another fleet, much larger than the former one to be sent off, and he had already collected in the Port of Santiago, where he resided, ten ships, four of them were those in which he had returned with Juan de Grijalva, which had at once been careened, and the other six had been got together from other ports in the Island. He had them furnished with provisions, consisting of Cassava bread and salt pork. These provisions were only to last until we arrived at Havana, for it was at that port that we were to take in our stores, as was afterwards done.

I must cease talking of this and tell about the disputes which arose over the choice of a captain for the expedition. There were many debates and much opposition.

Most of us soldiers who were there said that we should prefer to go again under Juan de Grijalva, for he was a good captain, and there was no fault to be found either with his person or his capacity for command.

While things were going on in the way I have related, two great favourites of Diego Velásquez named Andrés de Duero, the Governor's Secretary, and Amador de Lares, His Majesty's accountant, secretly formed a partnership with a gentleman named Hernando Cortés, a native of Medellin, who held a grant of Indians in the Island. A short while before, Cortés had

married a lady named Catalina Juarez la Marcayda. As far as
I know, and from what others say, it was a love match.

I will go on to tell about this partnership, it came about in
this manner:—These two great favourites of Velásquez agreed
that they would get him to appoint Cortés Captain General of
the whole fleet, and that they would divide between the three
of them, the spoil of gold, silver and jewels which might fall
to Cortés' share. For secretly Diego Velásquez was sending to
trade and not to form a settlement, as was apparent afterwards
from the instructions given about it, although it was announced
and published that the expedition was for the purpose of founding a settlement.

Andrés de Duero drew up the documents in very good ink,
as the proverb says, in the way Cortés wished with very ample
powers.

† XII

As soon as Hernando Cortés had been appointed General he
began to search for all sorts of arms, guns, powder and crossbows, and every kind of warlike stores which he could get together, and all sorts of articles to be used for barter, and other
things necessary for the expedition.

Moreover he began to adorn himself and be more careful of
his appearance than before, and he wore a plume of feathers
with a medal, and a gold chain, and a velvet cloak trimmed
with knots of gold, in fact he looked like a gallant and courageous Captain. However, he had no money to defray the expenses I have spoken about, for at that time he was very poor
and much in debt, although he had a good *encomienda* of
Indians who were getting him a return from his gold mines,
but he spent all of it on his person and on finery for his wife,
whom he had recently married, and on entertaining some
guests who had come to visit him. For he was affable in his
manner and a good talker, and he had twice been chosen
Alcalde[1] of the town of Santiago Baracoa where he had settled,
and in that country it is esteemed a great honour to be chosen
as *Alcalde*.

When some merchant friends of his saw that he had ob-

---
[1] *Alcalde* = Mayor.

tained this command as Captain General, they lent him four thousand gold dollars in coin and gave him merchandise worth another four thousand dollars secured on his Indians and estates. Then he ordered two standards and banners to be made, worked in gold with the royal arms and a cross on each side with a legend which said, "Comrades, let us follow the sign of the holy Cross with true faith, and through it we shall conquer." And he ordered a proclamation to be made with the sound of drums and trumpets in the name of His Majesty and by Diego Velásquez in the King's name, and in his own as Captain General, to the effect that whatsoever person might wish to go in his company to the newly discovered lands to conquer them and to settle there, should receive his share of the gold, silver and riches which might be gained, and an *encomienda* of Indians after the country had been pacified, and that to do these things Diego Velásquez held authority from His Majesty.

We assembled at Santiago de Cuba, whence we set out with the fleet more than three hundred and fifty soldiers in number. From the house of Velásquez there came Diego de Ordás, the chief Mayordomo, whom Velásquez himself sent with orders to keep his eyes open and see that no plots were hatched in the fleet, for he was always distrustful of Cortés, although he concealed his fears. There came also Francisco de Morla and an Escobar, whom we called The Page, and a Heredia, and Juan Ruano and Pedro Escudero, and Martin Ramos de Lares, and many others who were friends and followers of Diego Velásquez; and I place myself last on the list for I also came from the house of Diego Velásquez, for he was my kinsman.

Cortés worked hard to get his fleet under way and hastened on his preparations, for already envy and malice had taken possession of the relations of Diego Velásquez who were affronted because their kinsman neither trusted them nor took any notice of them, and because he had given charge and command to Cortés, knowing that he had looked upon him as a great enemy only a short time before, on account of his marriage, so they went about grumbling at their kinsman Diego Velásquez and at Cortés, and by every means in their power they worked on Diego Velásquez to induce him to revoke the commission.

Now Cortés was advised of all this, and for that reason

never left the Governor's side, and always showed himself to be
his zealous servant, and kept on telling him that, God willing,
he was going to make him a very illustrious and wealthy
gentleman in a very short time. Moreover Andrés de Duero
was always advising Cortés to hasten the embarkation of himself and his soldiers, for Diego Velásquez was already changing
his mind owing to the importunity of his family.

When Cortés knew this he sent orders to his wife that all
provisions of food which he wished to take and any other gifts
(such as women usually give to their husbands when starting
on such an expedition) should be sent at once and placed on
board ship.

He had already had a proclamation made that on that day
by nightfall all ships, Captains, pilots and soldiers should be
on board and no one should remain on shore. When Cortés had
seen all his company embarked he went to take leave of Diego
Velásquez, accompanied by his great friends and many other
gentlemen, and all the most distinguished citizens of that town.

After many demonstrations and embraces of Cortés by the
Governor, and of the Governor by Cortés, he took his leave.
The next day very early after having heard Mass we went to
our ships, and Diego Velásquez himself accompanied us, and
again they embraced with many fair speeches one to the other
until we set sail.

A few days later, in fine weather, we reached the Port of
Trinidad, where we brought up in the harbour and went
ashore, and nearly all the citizens of that town came out to meet
us; and entertained us well.

From that town there came to join us five brothers, namely
Pedro de Alvarado and Jorge de Alvarado, and Gonzalo and
Gómez, and Juan de Alvarado, the elder, who was a bastard.
There also joined us from this town Alonzo de Ávila, who went
as a Captain in Grijalva's expedition, and Juan de Escalante
and Pedro Sanchez Farfan, and Gonzalo Mejía who later on
became treasurer in Mexico, and a certain Baena and Juanes of
Fuenterrabia, and Lares, the good horseman, and Cristóbal de
Olid, the Valiant, and Ortis the Musician, and Gaspar Sanchez,
nephew of the treasurer of Cuba, and Diego de Pineda, and
Alonzo Rodríguez, and Bartolomé García and other gentlemen
whose names I do not remember, all persons of quality.

From Trinidad Cortés wrote to the town of Santispíritus

which was eighteen leagues distant, informing all the inhabitants that he was setting out on this expedition in His Majesty's service, adding fair words and inducements to attract many persons of quality who had settled in that town, among them Alonzo Hernándes Puertocarrero cousin of the Count of Medellin, and Gonzalo de Sandoval and Juan Velásquez de Leon came, a kinsman of Diego Velásquez, and Rodrigo Reogel, and Gonzalo Lópes de Jimena, and his brother, and Juan Sedeño also came. All these distinguished persons whom I have named came from the town of Santispíritus to Trinidad, and Cortés went out to meet them with all the soldiers of his company and received them with great cordiality and they treated him with the highest respect.

We continued to enlist soldiers and to buy horses, which at that time were both scarce and costly, and as Alonzo Hernándes Puertocarrero neither possessed a horse nor the wherewithal to buy one, Hernando Cortés bought him a gray mare, and paid for it with some of the golden knots off the velvet cloak which as I have said he had had made at Santiago de Cuba.

At that very time a ship arrived in port from Havana, which a certain Juan Sedeño, a settler at Havana, was taking, freighted with Cassava bread and salt pork to sell at some gold mines near Santiago de Cuba.

Juan Sedeño landed and went to pay his respects to Cortés, and after a long conversation Cortés bought the ship and the pork and bread on credit, and it all came with us. So we already had eleven ships and thank God all was going well with us.

† XIII

I must go back a little from our story to say that after we had set out from Santiago de Cuba with all the ships, so many things were said to Diego Velásquez against Cortés that he was forced to change his mind, for they told him that Cortés was already in rebellion, and that he left the port by stealth, and that he had been heard to say that although Diego Velásquez and his relations might regret it, he intended to be Captain and that was the reason why he had embarked all his soldiers by night, so that if any attempt were made to detain him by force he might set sail. Those who took the leading part in persuading Diego Velásquez to revoke the authority he had given to Cortés were some members of the Velásquez family and an old man named Juan Millan whom some called the astrologer, but others said he had a touch of madness because he acted without reflection, and this old man kept repeating to Diego Velásquez: "Take care, Sir, for Cortés will take vengeance on you for putting him in prison,[1] and as he is sly and determined he will ruin you if you do not prevent it at once."

And Velásquez listened to these speeches and was always haunted by suspicions, so without delay he sent two messengers whom he trusted, with orders and instructions to Francisco Verdugo, the Chief Alcalde of Trinidad, who was his brother-in-law, to the effect that on no account should the fleet be allowed to sail, and he said in his orders that Cortés should be detained or taken prisoner as he was no longer its captain, for he had revoked his commission and given it to Vasco Porcallo. The messengers also carried letters to Diego de Ordás and Francisco de Morla and other dependents of his begging them not to allow the fleet to sail.

When Cortés heard of this, he spoke to Ordás and Francisco Verdugo, and to all the soldiers and settlers at Trinidad, whom he thought would be against him and in favour of the instructions, and he made such speeches and promises to them that he brought them over to his side. Diego Ordás himself spoke at once to Francisco Verdugo, the Alcalde Mayor advising him to have nothing to do with the affair but to hush it up, and bade him note that up to that time they had seen no change in Cortés, on the contrary that he showed himself to be a faithful servant of the Governor, and that if Velásquez wished to impute any evil to him in order to deprive him of the command of the fleet, it was as well to remember that Cortés had many men of quality among his friends, who were unfriendly to Velásquez, because he had not given them good grants of Indians. In addition to this, that Cortés had a large body of soldiers with him and was very powerful and might sow strife in the town, and perhaps the soldiers might sack the town and plunder it, and do even worse damage.

So the matter was quietly dropped and one of the messengers

[1] This refers to an earlier incident in the relations between Cortés and Diego Velásquez.

who brought the letters and instructions, joined our company, and by the other messenger, Cortés sent a letter to Diego Velásquez written in a very friendly manner, saying that he was amazed at His Honour having come to such a decision, that his desire was to serve God and His Majesty, and to obey him as His Majesty's representative, and that he prayed him not to pay any more attention to what was said by the gentlemen of his family, nor to change his mind on account of the speeches of such an old lunatic as Juan Millan. He also wrote to all his friends and especially to his partners Duero and the Treasurer.

When these letters had been written, Cortés ordered all the soldiers to polish up their arms, and he ordered the blacksmiths in the town to make head pieces, and the crossbowmen to overhaul their stores and make arrows, and he also sent for the two blacksmiths and persuaded them to accompany us, which they did. We were ten days in that town.

† XIV

When Cortés saw that there was nothing more to be done at the town of Trinidad he sent Pedro de Alvarado by land to Havana[1] to pick up some soldiers who lived on farms along the road, and I went in his company, and he sent all the horses by land. Cortés then went on board the flagship to set sail with all the fleet for Havana.

It appears that the ships of the Convoy lost sight of the flagship in the night time, and we all arrived at the town of Havana, but Cortés did not appear, and no one knew where he was delayed. Five days passed without news of his ship, and we began to wonder whether he had been lost. We all agreed that three of the smaller vessels should go in search of Cortés, and in preparing the vessels and in debates whether this or the other man—Pedro or Sancho—should go, two more days went by and Cortés did not appear. Then parties began to be formed, and we all played the game of "Who shall be Captain until Cortés comes?"

Let us leave this subject and return to Cortés. In the neigh-

[1] This is the old Havana on the south coast, not the present port.

bourhood of the Isle of Pines, or near the *Jardines,* where there are many shallows, his ship ran aground and remained there hard and fast and could not be floated.

Cortés ordered all the cargo which could be removed to be taken ashore in the boat, for there was land near by where it could be stored, and when it was seen that the ship was floating and could be moved, she was taken into deeper water and was laden again with the cargo, sail was then set and the voyage continued to the port of Havana.

When Cortés arrived nearly all of us gentlemen and soldiers who were awaiting him were delighted at his coming, all except some who had hoped to be Captains, for the game of choosing captains came to an end.

It was here in Havana that Cortés began to organize a household and to be treated as a Lord. The first Marshal of the household whom he appointed was a certain Guzman who soon afterwards died or was killed by the Indians, and he had as *camarero*[1] Rodrigo Ranguel, and for Mayordomo, Juan de Cáceres.

When all this was settled we got ready to embark and the horses were divided among all the ships, and mangers were made for them and a store of maize and hay put on board. I will now call to mind all the mares and horses that were shipped:

The Captain Cortés: a vicious dark chestnut horse, which died as soon as we arrived at San Juan de Ulúa.

Pedro de Alvarado and Hernando López de Ávila: a very good sorrel mare, good both for sport and as a charger. When we arrived at New Spain Pedro de Alvarado bought the other half share in the mare or took it by force.

Alonzo Hernández Puertocarrero: a gray mare, a very good charger which Cortés bought for him with his gold buttons.

Juan Velásquez de Leon: a very powerful gray mare which we called "La Rabona,"[1] very handy and a good charger.

Cristóval de Olid: a dark chestnut horse, fairly good.

Francisco de Montejo and Alonzo de Ávila: a parched sorrel horse, no use for warfare.

Francisco de Morla: a dark chestnut horse, very fast and very easily handled.

[1] *Camarero* = chamberlain.
[1] *La Rabona* = the bob-tailed.

Juan de Escalante: a light chestnut horse with three white stockings, not much good.

Diego de Ordás: a gray mare, barren, tolerably good, but not fast.

Gonzalo Domínguez: a wonderfully good horseman; a very good dark chestnut horse, a grand galloper.

Pedro González de Trujillo: a good chestnut horse, all chestnut, a very good goer.

Moron, a settler at Bayamo: a dappled horse with stockings on the forefeet, very handy.

Baena, a settler at Trinidad: a dappled horse almost black, no good for anything.

Lares, a very good horseman: an excellent horse of rather light chestnut colour, a very good goer.

Ortiz the musician and Bartolomé García, who once owned gold mines: a very good dark horse called "El Arriero",[2] this was one of the best horses carried in the fleet.

Juan Sedeño, a settler at Havana: a chestnut mare which foaled on board ship.

This Juan Sedeño passed for the richest soldier in the fleet, for he came in his own ship with the mare, and a negro and a store of cassava bread and salt pork, and at that time horses and negroes were worth their weight in gold, and that is the reason why more horses were not taken, for there were none to be bought.

† xv

To make my story clear, I must go back and relate that when Diego Velásquez knew for certain that Francisco Verdugo not only refused to compel Cortés to leave the fleet, but, together with Diego de Ordás, had helped him to get away, they say that he was so angry that he roared with rage, and said that Cortés was mutinous. He made up his mind to send orders to Pedro Barba, his lieutenant at Havana, and to Diego de Ordás and to Juan Velásquez de Leon who were his kinsmen praying them neither for good nor ill to let the fleet get away, and to seize Cortés at once and send him under a strong guard to Santiago de Cuba.

[2] *El Arriero* = the muleteer, carrier.

On the arrival of the messenger, it was known at once what he had brought with him, for by the same messenger Cortés was advised of what Velásquez was doing. It appears that a friar of the Order of Mercy wrote a letter to another friar of his order named Bartolomé del Olmedo, who was with us, and in that letter Cortés was informed of all that had happened.

Not one of those to whom Diego Velásquez had written favoured his proposal, indeed one and all declared for Cortés, and lieutenant Pedro Barba above all, and all of us would have given our lives for Cortés. So that if in the Town of Trinidad the orders of Velásquez were slighted, in the town of Havana they were absolutely ignored.

Cortés wrote to Velásquez in the agreeable and complimentary terms which he knew so well how to use, and told him that he should set sail next day and that he remained his humble servant.

† XVI

There was to be no parade of the forces until we arrived at Cozumel. Cortés ordered the horses to be taken on board ship, and he directed Pedro de Alvarado to go along the North coast in a good ship named the *San Sebastian,* and he told the pilot who was in charge to wait for him at Cape San Antonio as all the ships would meet there and go in company to Cozumel. He also sent a messenger to Diego de Ordás, who had gone along the North Coast to collect supplies of food with orders to do the same and await his coming.

On the 10th February, 1519, after hearing Mass, they set sail along the south coast with nine ships and the company of gentlemen and soldiers whom I have mentioned, so that with the two ships absent from the north coast there were eleven ships in all, including that which carried Pedro de Alvarado with seventy soldiers and I travelled in his company.

The Pilot named Camacho who was in charge of our ship paid no attention to the orders of Cortés and went his own way and we arrived at Cozumel two days before Cortés and anchored in the port which I have often mentioned when telling about Grijalva's expedition.

Cortés had not yet arrived, being delayed by the ship commanded by Francisco de Morla having lost her rudder in bad weather, however she was supplied with another rudder by one of the ships of the fleet, and all then came on in company.

To go back to Pedro de Alvarado. As soon as we arrived in port we went on shore with all the soldiers to the town of Cozumel, but we found no Indians there as they had all fled. So we were ordered to go on to another town about a league distant, and there also the natives had fled and taken to the bush, but they could not carry off their property and left behind their poultry and other things and Pedro de Alvarado ordered forty of the fowls to be taken. In an Idol house there were some altar ornaments made of old cloths and some little chests containing diadems, Idols, beads and pendants of gold of poor quality, and here we captured two Indians and an Indian woman, and we returned to the town where we had disembarked.

While we were there Cortés arrived with all the fleet, and after taking up his lodging the first thing he did was to order the pilot Camacho to be put in irons for not having waited for him at sea as he had been ordered to do. When he saw the town without any people in it, and heard that Pedro de Alvarado had gone to the other town and had taken fowls and cloths and other things of small value from the Idols, and some gold which was half copper, he showed that he was very angry both at that and at the pilot not having waited for him, and he reprimanded Pedro de Alvarado severely, and told him that we should never pacify the country in that way by robbing the natives of their property, and he sent for the two Indians and the woman whom we had captured, and through Melchorejo (Julianillo his companion was dead), the man we had brought from Cape Catoche who understood the language well, he spoke to them telling them to go and summon the Caciques and Indians of their town, and he told them not to be afraid, and he ordered the gold and the cloths and all the rest to be given back to them, and for the fowls (which had already been eaten) he ordered them to be given beads and little bells, and in addition he gave to each Indian a Spanish shirt. So they went off to summon the lord of the town, and the next day the Cacique and all his people arrived, women and children and all the inhabitants of the town, and they went about among us as though they had been used to us all their lives, and

Cortés ordered us not to annoy them in any way. Here in this Island Cortés began to rule energetically, and Our Lord so favoured him that whatever he put his hand to it turned out well for him, especially in pacifying the people and towns of these lands, as we shall see further on.

When we had been in Cozumel three days, Cortés ordered a muster of his forces so as to see how many of us there were, and he found that we numbered five hundred and eight, not counting the shipmasters, pilots, and sailors, who numbered about one hundred. There were sixteen horses and mares all fit to be used for sport or as chargers.

There were eleven ships both great and small, and one a sort of launch which a certain Gines Nortes brought laden with supplies.

There were thirty-two crossbowmen and thirteen musketeers, and some brass guns, and four falconets, and much powder and ball.

After the review Cortés ordered Mesa surnamed "the gunner" and Bartolomé de Usagre and Arbenga and a certain Catalan who were all artillerymen, to keep their guns clean and in good order, and the ammunition ready for use. He appointed Francisco de Orozco, who had been a soldier in Italy to be captain of the Artillery. He likewise ordered two crossbowmen named Juan Benítez and Pedro del Guzman who were masters of the art of repairing crossbows, to see that every crossbow had two or three [spare] nuts and cords and fore cords and to be careful to keep them stored and to have smoothing tools and to see that the men should practise at a target. He also ordered all the horses to be kept in good condition.

† XVII

Cortés sent for me and a Biscayan named Martin Ramos, and asked us what we thought about those words which the Indians of Campeche had used when we went there with Francisco Hernández de Córdova, when they cried out "Castilan, Castilan." We again related to Cortés all that we had seen and heard about the matter, and he said that he also had often thought about it, and that perhaps there might be some Spaniards living in the country, and added "It seems to me that it would be well to ask these Caciques of Cozumel if they know anything about them." So through Melchorejo, who already understood a little Spanish and knew the language of Cozumel very well, all the chiefs were questioned, and every one of them said that they had known of certain Spaniards and gave descriptions of them, and said that some Caciques, who lived about two days' journey inland, kept them as slaves. We were all delighted at this news, and Cortés told the Caciques that they must go at once and summon the Spaniards, taking with them letters. The Cacique advised Cortés to send a ransom to the owners who held these men as slaves, so that they should be allowed to come, and Cortés did so, and gave to the messengers all manner of beads. Then he ordered the two smallest vessels to be got ready, under the command of Diego de Ordás, and he sent them off to the coast near Cape Catoche where the larger vessel was to wait for eight days while the smaller vessel should go backwards and forwards and bring news of what was being done, for the land of Cape Catoche was only four leagues distant.

In two days the letters were delivered to a Spaniard named Jerónimo de Aguilar, for that we found to be his name. When he had read the letter and received the ransom of beads which we had sent to him he was delighted, and carried the ransom to the Cacique his master, and begged leave to depart, and the Cacique at once gave him leave to go wherever he pleased. Aguilar set out for the place, five leagues distant, where his companion Gonzalo Guerrero was living, but when he read the letter to him he answered: "Brother Aguilar, I am married and have three children and the Indians look on me as a Cacique and captain in wartime— You go, and God be with you, but I have my face tattooed and my ears pierced, what would the Spaniards say should they see me in this guise? and look how handsome these boys of mine are, for God's sake give me those green beads you have brought, and I will give the beads to them and say that my brothers have sent them from my own country." And the Indian wife of Gonzalo spoke to Aguilar in her own tongue very angrily and said to him: "What is this slave coming here for talking to my husband— go off with you, and don't trouble us with any more words."

When Jerónimo de Aguilar saw that Gonzalo would not accompany him he went at once, with the two Indian mes-

sengers, to the place where the ship had been awaiting his
coming, but when he arrived he saw no ship for she had already departed. The eight days during which Ordás had been
ordered to await and one day more had already expired, and
seeing that Aguilar had not arrived Ordás returned to Cozumel
without bringing any news about that for which he had come.

When Aguilar saw that there was no ship there he became
very sad, and returned to his master and to the town where he
usually lived.

When Cortés saw Ordás return without success or any news
of the Spaniards or Indian messengers he was very angry, and
said haughtily to Ordás that he thought that he would have
done better than to return without the Spaniards or any news
of them, for it was quite clear that they were prisoners in that
country.

† XVIII

We embarked again, and set sail on a day in the month of
March, 1519, and went on our way in fair weather. At ten
o'clock that same morning loud shouts were given from one of
the ships, which tried to lay to, and fired a shot so that all
the vessels of the fleet might hear it, and when Cortés heard
this he at once checked the flagship and seeing the ship commanded by Juan de Escalante bearing away and returning towards Cozumel, he cried out to the other ships which were
near him: "What is the matter? What is the matter?" And a
soldier named Luis de Zaragoza answered that Juan de
Escalante's ship with all the Cassava bread on board was sinking, and Cortés cried, "Pray God that we suffer no such disaster," and he ordered the Pilot Alaminos to make signal to all
the other ships to return to Cozumel.

When the Spaniard who was a prisoner among the Indians,
knew for certain that we had returned to Cozumel with the
ships, he was very joyful and gave thanks to God, and he
came in all haste with the two Indians who had carried the
letters and ransom, and as he was able to pay well with the
green beads we had sent him, he soon hired a canoe and six
Indian rowers.

When they arrived on the coast of Cozumel and were disembarking, some soldiers who had gone out hunting (for there were wild pigs on the island) told Cortés that a large canoe, which had come from the direction of Cape Catoche, had arrived near the town. Cortés sent Andrés de Tápia and two other soldiers to go and see, for it was a new thing for Indians to come fearlessly in large canoes into our neighbourhood. When Andrés de Tápia saw that they were only Indians, he at once sent word to Cortés by a Spaniard that they were Cozumel Indians who had come in the canoe. As soon as the men had landed, one of them in words badly articulated and worse pronounced, cried *Dios y Santa Maria de Sevilla,* and Tápia went at once to embrace him.

Tápia soon brought the Spaniard to Cortés but before he arrived where Cortés was standing, several Spaniards asked Tápia where the Spaniard was? although he was walking by his side, for they could not distinguish him from an Indian as he was naturally brown and he had his hair shorn like an Indian slave, and carried a paddle on his shoulder, he was shod with one old sandal and the other was tied to his belt, he had on a ragged old cloak, and a worse loin cloth, with which he covered his nakedness, and he had tied up, in a bundle in his cloak, a Book of Hours, old and worn. When Cortés saw him in this state, he too was deceived like the other soldiers, and asked Tápia: "Where is the Spaniard?" On hearing this, the Spaniard squatted down on his haunches as the Indians do and said "I am he." Cortés at once ordered him to be given a shirt and doublet and drawers and a cape and sandals, for he had no other clothes, and asked him about himself and what his name was and when he came to this country. The man replied, pronouncing with difficulty, that he was called Jerónimo de Aguilar, a native of Ecija, and that he had taken holy orders, that eight years had passed since he and fifteen other men and two women left Darien for the Island of Santo Domingo, and that the ship in which they sailed, struck on the *Alacranes* so that she could not be floated, and that he and his companions and the two women got into the ship's boat, thinking to reach the Island of Cuba or Jamaica, but that the currents were very strong and carried them to this land, and that the Calachiones of that district had divided them among themselves, and that many of him companions had been sacrificed to the Idols, and that others had died of disease, and the women had died of overwork only a short time before, for they had been made to grind corn; that the Indians had intended him for a sacrifice, but that one night he escaped and fled to the Cacique with whom since then he had been living, and that none were left of all his party except himself and a certain Gonzalo Guerrero, whom he had gone to summon, but he would not come.

Cortés questioned Aguilar about the country and the towns, but Aguilar replied that having been a slave, he knew only about hewing wood and drawing water and digging in the fields, that he had only once travelled as far as four leagues from home when he was sent with a load, but, as it was heavier than he could carry, he fell ill, but that he understood that there were very many towns. When questioned about Gonzalo Guerrero, he said that he was married and had three sons, and that his face was tattooed and his ears and lower lip were pierced, that he was a seaman and a native of Palos, and that the Indians considered him to be very valiant; that when a little more than a year ago a captain and three vessels arrived at Cape Catoche, it was at the suggestion of Guerrero that the Indians attacked them, and that he was there himself in the company of the Cacique of the large town. When Cortés heard this he exclaimed "I wish I had him in my hands for it will never do to leave him here."

On the advice of Aguilar the Caciques asked Cortés to give them a letter of recommendation, so that if any other Spaniards came to that port they would treat the Indians well and do them no harm, and this letter was given to them.

† xix

On the 4th March, 1519, with the good fortune to carry such a useful and faithful interpreter along with us, Cortés gave orders for us to embark in the same order as before, and with the same lantern signals by night.

We sailed along in good weather, until at nightfall a head wind struck us so fiercely that the ships were dispersed and there was great danger of being driven ashore. Thank God, by midnight the weather moderated, and the ships got together again, excepting the vessel under the command of Juan

Velásquez de Leon. However, when she still failed to appear, it was agreed that the whole fleet should go back and search for the missing ship, and we found her at anchor in a bay which was a great relief to us all. We stayed in that bay for a day and we lowered two boats and went on shore and found farms and maize plantations, and there were four *Cues* which are the houses of their Idols, and there were many Idols in them, nearly all of them figures of tall women so that we called that place the *Punta de las Mugeres*.[1]

On the 12th March, 1519, we arrived with all the fleet at the Rio de Grijalva, which is also called Tabasco, and as we already knew from our experience with Grijalva that vessels of large size could not enter into the river, the larger vessels were anchored out at sea, and from the smaller vessels and boats all the soldiers were landed at the Cape of the Palms (as they were in Grijalva's time) which was about half a league distant from the town of Tabasco. The river, the river banks and the mangrove thickets were swarming with Indians, at which those of us who had not been here in Grijalva's time were much astonished.

In addition to this there were assembled in the town more than twelve thousand warriors all prepared to make war on us, for at this time the town was of considerable importance and other large towns were subject to it and they had all made preparation for war and were well supplied with arms.

The reason for this was that the people of Champoton and Lázaro and the other towns in that neighbourhood had looked upon the people of Tabasco as cowards, and had told them so to their faces, because they had given Grijalva the gold jewels and they said that they were too faint hearted to attack us although they had more towns and more warriors than the people of Champoton and Lázaro. This they said to annoy them and added that they in their towns had attacked us and killed fifty-six of us. So on account of these taunts, which had been uttered, the people of Tabasco had determined to take up arms.

When Cortés saw them drawn up ready for war he told Aguilar the interpreter to ask the Indians who passed near us, in a large canoe and who looked like chiefs, what they were so much disturbed about, and to tell them that we had not come

---

[1] *Punta de las Mugeres* = the Cape of the Women.

to do them any harm, but were willing to give them some of the things we had brought with us and to treat them like brothers, and we prayed them not to begin a war as they would regret it, and much else was said to them about keeping the peace. However, the more Aguilar talked to them the more violent they became, and they said that they would kill us all if we entered their town, and that it was fortified all round with fences and barricades of large trunks of trees.

Aguilar spoke to them again and asked them to keep the peace, and allow us to take water and barter our goods with them for food, and permit us to tell the Calachones[1] things which would be to their advantage and to the service of God our Lord, but they still persisted in saying that if we advanced beyond the palm trees they would kill us.

When Cortés saw the state of affairs he ordered the boats and small vessels to be got ready and ordered three cannon to be placed in each boat and divided the crossbowmen and musketeers among the boats. We remembered that when we were here with Grijalva we had found a narrow path which ran across some streams from the palm grove to the town, and Cortés ordered three soldiers to find out in the night if that path ran right up to the houses, and not to delay in bringing the news, and these men found out that it did lead there. After making a thorough examination of our surroundings the rest of the day was spent in arranging how and in what order we were to go in the boats.

The next morning we had our arms in readiness and after hearing mass Cortés ordered the Captain Alonzo de Ávila and a hundred soldiers among whom were ten crossbowmen, to go by the little path which led to the town, and, as soon as he heard the guns fired, to attack the town on one side while he attacked it on the other. Cortés himself and all the other Captains and soldiers went in the boats and light draft vessels up the river. When the Indian warriors who were on the banks and among the mangroves saw that we were really on the move, they came after us with a great many canoes with intent to prevent our going ashore at the landing place, and the whole river bank appeared to be covered with Indian warriors carrying all the different arms which they use, and blowing trumpets and shells and sounding drums. When Cortés saw how matters

[1] Calachiones (?)

stood he ordered us to wait a little and not to fire any shots from guns or crossbows or cannon, for as he wished to be justified in all that he might do he made another appeal to the Indians through the Interpreter Aguilar, in the presence of the King's Notary, Diego de Godoy, asking the Indians to allow us to land and take water and speak to them about God and about His Majesty, and adding that should they make war on us, that if in defending ourselves some should be killed and others hurt, theirs would be the fault and the burden and it would not lie with us, but they went on threatening that if we landed they would kill us.

Then they boldly began to let fly arrows at us, and made signals with their drums, and like valiant men they surrounded us with their canoes, and they all attacked us with such a shower of arrows that they kept us in the water in some parts up to our waists. As there was much mud and swamp at that place we could not easily get clear of it, and so many Indians fell on us, that what with some hurling their lances with all their might and others shooting arrows at us, we could not reach the land as soon as we wished.

While Cortés was fighting he lost a shoe in the mud and could not find it again, and he got on shore with one foot bare. Presently someone picked the shoe out of the mud and he put it on again.

While this was happening to Cortés, all of us Captains as well as soldiers, with the cry of "Santiago!" fell upon the Indians and forced them to retreat, but they did not fall back far, as they sheltered themselves behind great barriers and stockades formed of thick logs until we pulled them apart and got to one of the small gateways of the town. There we attacked them again, and we pushed them along through a street to where other defences had been erected, and there they turned on us and met us face to face and fought most valiantly, making the greatest efforts, shouting and whistling and crying out "al calacheoni," "al calacheoni," which in their language meant an order to kill or capture our Captain. While we were thus surrounded by them Alonzo de Ávila and his soldiers came up.

As I have already said they came from the Palm grove by land and could not arrive sooner on account of the swamps and creeks. Their delay was really unavoidable, just as we also had been delayed over the summons of the Indians to surrender,

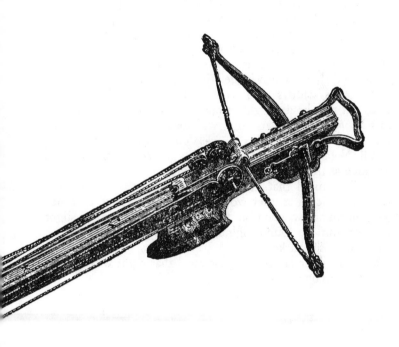

and in breaking openings in the barricades, so as to enable us to attack them. Now we all joined together to drive the enemy out of their strongholds, and we compelled them to retreat, but like brave warriors they kept on shooting showers of arrows and fire-hardened darts, and never turned their backs on us until [we gained] a great court with chambers and large halls, and three Idol houses, where they had already carried all the goods they possessed. Cortés then ordered us to halt, and not to follow on and overtake the enemy in their flight.

There and then Cortés took possession of that land for His Majesty, performing the act in His Majesty's name. It was done in this way; he drew his sword and as a sign of possession he made three cuts in a huge tree called a *Ceiba,* which stood in the court of that great square, and cried that if any person should raise objection, that he would defend the right with the sword and shield which he held in his hands.

All of us soldiers who were present when this happened cried out that he did right in taking possession of the land in His Majesty's name, and that we would aid him should any person say otherwise. This act was done in the presence of the Royal Notary. The partizans of Diego Velásquez chose to grumble at this act of taking possession.

I call to mind that in that hard fought attack which the Indians made on us, they wounded fourteen soldiers, and they gave me an arrow wound in the thigh, but it was only a slight wound; and we found eighteen Indians dead in the water where we disembarked.

We slept there [in the great square] that night with guards and sentinels on the alert.

† xx

The next morning Cortés ordered Pedro de Alvarado to set out in command of a hundred soldiers, fifteen of them with guns and crossbows, to examine the country inland for a distance of two leagues, and to take Melchorejo the interpreter in his company. When Melchorejo was looked for he could not be found as he had run off with the people of Tabasco, and it appears that the day before he had left the Spanish clothes that had been given to him hung up in the palm grove, and

had fled by night in a canoe. Cortés was much annoyed at his flight, fearing that he would tell things to his fellow countrymen to our disadvantage—well, let him go as a bit of bad luck, and let us get back to our story. Cortés also sent the Captain Francisco de Lugo, in another direction, with a hundred soldiers, twelve of them musketeers and crossbowmen, with instructions not to go beyond two leagues and to return to the camp to sleep.

When Francisco de Lugo and his company had marched about a league from camp he came on a great host of Indian archers carrying lances and shields, drums and standards and they made straight for our company of soldiers and surrounded them on all sides. They were so numerous and shot their arrows so deftly that it was impossible to withstand them, and they hurled their fire-hardened darts and cast stones from their slings in such numbers that they fell like hail, and they attacked our men with their two-handed knife-like swords.[1] Stoutly as Francisco de Lugo and his soldiers fought, they could not ward off the enemy, and when this was clear to them, while still keeping a good formation, they began to retreat towards the camp. A certain Indian, a swift and daring runner, had been sent off to the camp to beg Cortés to come to their assistance, meanwhile Francisco de Lugo by careful management of his musketeers and crossbowmen, some loading while others fired, and by occasional charges was able to hold his own against all the squadrons attacking him.

Let us leave him in the dangerous situation I have described and return to Captain Pedro de Alvarado, who after marching about a league came on a creek which was very difficult to cross, and it pleased God our Lord so to lead him that he should return by another road in the direction where Francisco de Lugo was fighting. When he heard the reports of the muskets and the great din of drums and trumpets and the shouts and whistles of the Indians, he knew that there must be a battle going on, so with the greatest haste but in good order he ran towards the cries and shots and found Captain Francisco de Lugo and his men fighting with their faces to the enemy, and five of the enemy lying dead. As soon as he joined forces with Francisco de Lugo they turned on the Indians and drove them

[1] *Macanas,* or *Maquahuitls:* edged with flint or obsidian.

back, but they were not able to put them to flight, and the Indians followed our men right up to the camp.

In like manner other companies of warriors had attacked us where Cortés was guarding the wounded, but we soon drove them off with our guns, which laid many of them low, and with our good sword play.

When Cortés heard of Francisco de Lugo's peril from the Cuban Indian who came to beg for help, we promptly went to his assistance, and we met the two captains with their companies about half a league from the camp. Two soldiers of Francisco de Lugo's company were killed and eight wounded, and three of Pedro de Alvarado's company were wounded. When we arrived in camp we buried the dead and tended the wounded, and stationed sentinels and kept a strict watch.

In those skirmishes we killed fifteen Indians and captured three, one of whom seemed to be a chief, and through Aguilar, our interpreter, we asked them why they were so mad as to attack us, and that they could see that we should kill them if they attacked us again. Then one of these Indians was sent with some beads to give to the Caciques to bring them to peace, and that messenger told us that the Indian Melchorejo whom we had brought from Cape Catoche, went to the chiefs the night before and counselled them to fight us day and night, and said that they would conquer us as we were few in number; so it turned out that we had brought an enemy with us instead of a help.

This Indian whom we despatched with the message went off and never returned. From the other two Indian prisoners Aguilar the interpreter learnt for certain that by the next day the Caciques from all the neighbouring towns of the province would have assembled with all their forces ready to make war on us, and that they would come and surround our camp, for that was Melchorejo's advice to them.

As soon as Cortés knew this for certain, he ordered all the horses to be landed from the ships without delay, and the crossbowmen and musketeers and all of us soldiers, even those who were wounded, to have our arms ready for use.

When the horses were brought on shore they were very stiff and afraid to move, for they had been many days on board ship, but the next day they moved quite freely.

At that time it happened that six or seven soldiers, young men and otherwise in good health, suffered from pains in their loins, so that they could not stand on their feet and had to be carried on men's backs. We did not know what this sickness came from, some say that they fell ill on account of the [quilted] cotton armour which they never took off, but wore day and night, and because in Cuba they had lived daintily and were not used to hard work, so in the heat they fell ill. Cortés ordered them not to remain on land but to be taken at once on board ship.

The best horses and riders were chosen to form the cavalry, and the horses had little bells attached to their breastplates. The men were ordered not to stop to spear those who were down, but to aim their lances at the faces of the enemy.

Thirteen gentlemen were chosen to go on horseback with Cortés in command of them, and I here record their names: —Cortés, Cristóval de Olíd, Pedro de Alvarado, Alonzo Hernández Puertocarrero, Juan de Escalante, Francisco de Montejo, and Alonzo de Ávila to whom was given the horse belonging to Ortiz the musican and Bartolomé García, for neither of these men were good horsemen, Juan Velásquez de Leon, Francisco de Morla, and Lares the good horseman, Gonzalo Domínguez, an excellent horseman, Moron of Bayamo, and Pedro González of Trujillo. Cortés selected all these gentlemen and went himself as their captain.

Cortés ordered Mesa the artilleryman to have his guns ready, and he placed Diego de Ordás in command of us foot soldiers and he also had command of the musketeers and bowmen, for he was no horseman.

Very early the next day which was the day of Nuestra Señora de Marzo [Lady-day, 25th March] after hearing mass, which was said by Fray Bartolomé de Olmedo, we formed in order under our standard bearer, and marched to some large savannas where Francisco de Lugo and Pedro de Alvarado had been attacked, about a league distant from the camp we had left; and that savanna and township was called Cintla, and was subject to Tabasco.

Cortés [and the horsemen] were separated a short distance from us on account of some swamps which could not be crossed by the horses, and as we were marching along we came on the whole force of Indian warriors who were on the way to attack us in our camp. It was near the town of Cintla that we met them on an open plain.

As they approached us their squadrons were so numerous that they covered the whole plain, and they rushed on us like mad dogs completely surrounding us, and they let fly such a cloud of arrows, javelins and stones that on the first assault they wounded over seventy of us, and fighting hand to hand they did us great damage with their lances, and one soldier fell dead at once from an arrow wound in the ear, and they kept on shooting and wounding us. With our muskets and crossbows and with good sword play we did not fail as stout fighters, and when they came to feel the edge of our swords little by little they fell back, but it was only so as to shoot at us in greater safety. Mesa, our artilleryman, killed many of them with his cannon, for they were formed in great squadrons and they did not open out so that he could fire at them as he pleased, but with all the hurts and wounds which we gave them, we could not drive them off. I said to Diego de Ordás: "It seems to me that we ought to close up and charge them," for in truth they suffered greatly from the strokes and thrusts of our swords, and that was why they fell away from us, both from fear of these swords, and the better to shoot their arrows and hurl their javelins and the hail of stones. Ordás replied that it was not good advice, for there were three hundred Indians to every one of us, and that we could not hold out against such a multitude —so there we stood enduring their attack. However, we did agree to get as near as we could to them, as I had advised Ordás, so as to give them a bad time with our swordsmanship, and they suffered so much from it that they retreated towards a swamp.

During all this time Cortés and his horsemen failed to appear, although we greatly longed for him, and we feared that by chance some disaster had befallen him.

I remember that when we fired shots the Indians gave great shouts and whistles and threw dust and rubbish into the air so that we should not see the damage done to them, and they sounded their trumpets and drums and shouted and whistled and cried "Alala! Alala!"

Just at this time we caught sight of our horsemen, and as

the great Indian host was crazed with its attack on us, it did not at once perceive them coming up behind their backs, and as the plain was level ground and the horsemen were good riders, and many of the horses were very handy and fine gallopers, they came quickly on the enemy and speared them as they chose. As soon as we saw the horsemen we fell on the Indians with such energy that with us attacking on one side and the horsemen on the other, they soon turned tail. The Indians thought that the horse and its rider was all one animal, for they had never seen horses up to this time.

The savannas and fields were crowded with Indians running to take refuge in the thick woods near by.

After we had defeated the enemy, Cortés told us that he had not been able to come to us sooner as there was a swamp in the way, and he had to fight his way through another force of warriors before he could reach us, and three horsemen and five horses had been wounded.

As it was Lady-day we gave to the town which was afterwards founded here the name of Santa Maria de la Victoria, on account of this great victory being won on Our Lady's day. This was the first battle that we fought under Cortés in New Spain.

After this we bound up the hurts of the wounded with cloths, for we had nothing else, and we doctored the horses by searing their wounds with the fat from the body of a dead Indian which we cut up to get out the fat, and we went to look at the dead lying on the plain and there were more than eight hundred of them, the greater number killed by thrusts, the others by the cannon, muskets and crossbows, and many were stretched on the ground half dead. Where the horsemen had passed, numbers of them lay dead or groaning from their wounds. The battle lasted over an hour, and the Indians fought all the time like brave warriors, until the horsemen came up.

We took five prisoners, two of them Captains. As it was late and we had had enough of fighting, and we had not eaten anything, we returned to our camp. Then we buried the two soldiers who had been killed, one by a wound in the ear, and the other by a wound in the throat, and we seared the wounds of the others and of the horses with the fat of the Indian, and after posting sentinels and guards, we had supper and rested.

When Aguilar spoke to the prisoners he found out from what they said that they were fit persons to be sent as messengers, and he advised Cortés to free them, so that they might go and talk to the Caciques of the town. These two messengers were given green and blue beads, and Aguilar spoke many pleasant and flattering words to them, telling them that they had nothing to fear as we wished to treat them like brothers, that it was their own fault that they had made war on us, and that now they had better collect together all the Caciques of the different towns as we wished to talk to them, and he gave them much other advice in a gentle way so as to gain their good will. The messengers went off willingly and spoke to the Caciques and chief men, and told them all we wished them to know about our desire for peace.

When our envoys had been listened to, it was settled among them that fifteen Indian slaves, all with stained faces and ragged cloaks and loin cloths, should at once be sent to us with fowls and baked fish and maize cakes. When these men came before Cortés he received them graciously, but Aguilar the interpreter asked them rather angrily why they had come with their faces in that state, that it looked more as though they came to fight than to treat for peace; and he told them to go back to the Caciques and inform them, that if they wished for peace in the way we offered it, chieftains should come and treat for it, as was always the custom, and that they should not send slaves. But even these painted faced slaves were treated with consideration by us and blue beads were sent by them in sign of peace, and to soothe their feelings.

The next day thirty Indian Chieftains, clad in good cloaks, came to visit us, and brought fowls, fish, fruit and maize cakes, and asked leave from Cortés to burn and bury the bodies of the dead who had fallen in the recent battles, so that they should not smell badly or be eaten by lions and tigers. Permission was at once given them and they hastened to bring many people to bury and burn the bodies according to their customs.

Cortés learnt from the Caciques that over eight hundred men were missing, not counting those who had been carried off wounded.

They said that they could not tarry with us either to discuss the matter or make peace, for on the morrow the chieftains and leaders of all the towns would have assembled, and that then they would agree about a peace.

As Cortés was very sagacious about everything, he said, laughing, to us soldiers who happened to be in his company, "Do you know, gentlemen, that it seems to me that the Indians are terrified at the horses and may think that they and the cannon alone make war on them. I have thought of something which will confirm this belief, and that is to bring the mare belonging to Juan Sedeño, which foaled the other day on board ship, and tie her up where I am now standing and also to bring the stallion of Ortiz the musician, which is very excitable, near enough to scent the mare, and when he has scented her to lead each of them off separately so that the Caciques who are coming shall not hear the horse neighing as they approach, not until they are standing before me and are talking to me." We did just as Cortés ordered and brought the horse and mare, and the horse soon detected the scent of her in Cortés' quarters. In addition to this Cortés ordered the largest cannon that we possessed to be loaded with a large ball and a good charge of powder.

About mid-day forty Indians arrived, all of them Caciques of good bearing, wearing rich mantles. They saluted Cortés and all of us, and brought incense and fumigated all of us who were present, and they asked pardon for their past behaviour, and said that henceforth they would be friendly.

Cortés, through Aguilar the Interpreter, answered them in a rather grave manner, as though he were angry, that they well knew how many times he had asked them to maintain peace, that the fault was theirs, and that now they deserved to be put to death, they and all the people of their towns, but that as we were the vassals of a great King and Lord named the Emperor Don Carlos, who had sent us to these countries, and ordered us to help and favour those who would enter his royal service, that if they were now as well disposed as they said they were, that we would take this course, but that if they were not, some of those *Tepustles* would jump out and kill them (they call iron *Tepustle* in their language) for some of the *Tepustles* were still angry because they had made war on us. At this moment the order was secretly given to put a match to the cannon which had been loaded, and it went off with such a thunderclap as was wanted, and the ball went buzzing over the hills, and as it was mid-day and very still it made a great noise, and the Caciques were terrified on hearing it. As they had never seen anything like it they believed what Cortés had told them was true. Then Cortés told them, through Aguilar, not to be afraid for he had given orders that no harm should be done to them.

Just then the horse that had scented the mare was brought and tied up not far distant from where Cortés was talking to the Caciques, and the horse began to paw the ground and neigh and become wild with excitement, looking all the time towards the Indians and the place whence the scent of the mare had reached him, and the Caciques thought that he was roaring at them and they were terrified. When Cortés observed their state of mind, he rose from his seat and went to the horse and told two orderlies to lead it far away, and said to the Indians that he had told the horse not to be angry as they were friendly and wished to make peace.

While this was going on there arrived more than thirty Indian carriers, who brought a meal of fowls and fish and fruits and other food.

Cortés had a long conversation with these chieftains and Caciques and they told him that they would all come on the next day and would bring a present and would discuss other matters, and then they went away quite contented.

† XXII

Early the next morning many Caciques and chiefs of Tabasco and the neighbouring towns arrived and paid great respect to us all, and they brought a present of gold, consisting of four diadems and some gold lizards, and two [ornaments] like little dogs, and earrings and five ducks, and two masks with Indian faces and two gold soles for sandals, and some other things of little value. I do not remember how much the things were worth; and they brought cloth, such as they make and wear, which was quilted stuff.

This present, however, was worth nothing in comparison with the twenty women that were given us, among them one very excellent woman called Doña Marina, for so she was named when she became a Christian. Cortés received this present with pleasure and went aside with all the Caciques, and with Aguilar, the interpreter, to hold converse, and he told them that he gave them thanks for what they had brought with them, but there was one thing that he must ask of them, namely, that they should re-occupy the town with all their people, women and children, and he wished to see it repeopled within two days, for he would recognize that as a sign of true peace. The Caciques sent at once to summon all the inhabitants with their women and children and within two days they were again settled in the town.

One other thing Cortés asked of the chiefs and that was to give up their idols and sacrifices, and this they said they would do, and, through Aguilar, Cortés told them as well as he was able about matters concerning our holy faith, how we were Christians and worshipped one true and only God, and he showed them an image of Our Lady with her precious Son in her arms and explained to them that we paid the greatest reverence to it as it was the image of the Mother of our Lord God who was in heaven. The Caciques replied that they liked the look of the great Teleciguata (for in their language great ladies are called Teleciguatas) and [begged] that she might be given them to keep in their town, and Cortés said that the image should be given to them, and ordered them to make a well-constructed altar, and this they did at once.

The next morning, Cortés ordered two of our carpenters, named Alonzo Yañez and Alvaro López, to make a very tall cross.

When all this had been settled Cortés asked the Caciques what was their reason for attacking us three times when we had asked them to keep the peace; the chief replied that he had already asked pardon for their acts and had been forgiven, that the Cacique of Champoton, his brother, had advised it, and that he feared to be accused of cowardice, for he had already been reproached and dishonoured for not having attacked the other captain who had come with four ships (he must have meant Juan de Grijalva) and he also said that the Indian whom we had brought as an Interpreter, who escaped in the night, had advised them to attack us both by day and night.

Cortés then ordered this man to be brought before him with

out fail, but they replied that when he saw that the battle was going against them, he had taken to flight, and they knew not where he was although search had been made for him; but we came to know that they had offered him as a sacrifice because his counsel had cost them so dear.

Cortés also asked them where they procured their gold and jewels, and they replied, from the direction of the setting sun, and said "Culua" and "Mexico," and as we did not know what Mexico and Culua meant we paid little attention to it.

Then we brought another interpreter named Francisco, whom we had captured during Grijalva's expedition, who has already been mentioned by me but he understood nothing of the Tabasco language only that of Culua which is the Mexican tongue. By means of signs he told Cortés that Culua was far ahead, and he repeated "Mexico" which we did not understand.

So the talk ceased until the next day when the sacred image of Our Lady and the Cross were set up on the altar and we all paid reverence to them, and Padre Fray Bartolomé de Olmedo said mass and all the Caciques and chiefs were present and we gave the name of Santa Maria de la Victoria to the town, and by this name the town of Tabasco is now called. The same friar, with Aguilar as interpreter, preached many good things about our holy faith to the twenty Indian women who had been given us, and immediately afterwards they were baptized. One Indian lady, who was given to us here was christened Doña Marina, and she was truly a great chieftainess and the daughter of great Caciques and the mistress of vassals, and this her appearance clearly showed. Later on I will relate why it was and in what manner she was brought here.

Cortés allotted one of the women to each of his captains and Doña Marina, as she was good looking and intelligent and without embarrassment, he gave to Alonzo Hernández Puertocarrero. When Puertocarrero went to Spain, Doña Marina lived with Cortés, and bore him a son named Don Martin Cortés.

We remained five days in this town, to look after the wounded and those who were suffering from pain in the loins, from which they all recovered. Furthermore, Cortés drew the Caciques to him by kindly converse, and told them how our master the Emperor, whose vassals we were, had under his orders many great lords, and that it would be well for them also to render him obedience, and that then, whatever they might be in need of, whether it was our protection or any other necessity, if they would make it known to him, no matter where he might be, he would come to their assistance.

The Caciques all thanked him for this, and thereupon all declared themselves the vassals of our great Emperor. These were the first vassals to render submission to His Majesty in New Spain.

Cortés then ordered the Caciques to come with their women and children early the next day, which was Palm Sunday, to the altar, to pay homage to the holy image of Our Lady and to the Cross, and at the same time Cortés ordered them to send six Indian carpenters to accompany our carpenters to the town of Cintla, there to cut a cross on a great tree called a Ceiba, which grew there, and they did it so that it might last a long time, for as the bark is renewed the cross will show there for ever. When this was done he ordered the Indians to get ready all the canoes that they owned to help us to embark, for we wished to set sail on that holy day because the pilots had come to tell Cortés that the ships ran a great risk from a *Norther* which is a dangerous gale.

The next day, early in the morning, all the Caciques and chiefs came in their canoes with all their women and children and stood in the court where we had placed the church and cross, and many branches of trees had already been cut ready to be carried in the procession. Then the Caciques beheld us all, Cortés, as well as the captains, and every one of us marching together with the greatest reverence in a devout procession, and the Padre de la Merced and the priest Juan Díaz, clad in their vestments, said mass, and we paid reverence to and kissed the Holy Cross, while the Caciques and Indians stood looking on at us.

When our solemn festival was over the chiefs approached and offered Cortés ten fowls and baked fish and vegetables, and we took leave of them, and Cortés again commended to their care the Holy image and the sacred crosses and told them always to keep the place clean and well swept, and to deck the cross with garlands and to reverence it and then they would enjoy good health and bountiful harvests.

It was growing late when we got on board ship and the next

day, Monday, we set sail in the morning and with a fair wind
laid our course for San Juan de Ulúa, keeping close in shore all
the time.

As we sailed along in fine weather, we soldiers who knew
the coast would say to Cortés, "Señor, over there is La Rambla,
which the Indians call Ayagualulco," and soon afterwards we
arrived off Tonalá which we called San Antonio, and we
pointed it out to him. Further on we showed him the great
river of Coatzacoalcos, and he saw the lofty snow capped
mountains, and then the Sierra of San Martin, and further on
we pointed out the split rock, which is a great rock standing
out in the sea with a mark on the top of it which gives it the
appearance of a seat. Again further on we showed him the Rio
de Alvarado, which Pedro de Alvarado entered when we were
with Grijalva, and then we came in sight of the Rio de Banderas, where we had gained in barter the sixteen thousand dollars, then we showed him the Isla Blanca, and told him where
lay the Isla Verde, and close in shore we saw the Isla de Sacrificios, where we found the altars and the Indian victims in
Grijalva's time; and at last our good fortune brought us to San
Juan de Ulúa soon after midday on Holy Thursday.

† xxiii

Before telling about the great Montezuma and his famous City
of Mexico and the Mexicans, I wish to give some account of
Doña Marina, who from her childhood had been the mistress
and Cacica of towns and vassals. It happened in this way:

Her father and mother were chiefs and Caciques of a town
called Paynala, which had other towns subject to it, and stood
about eight leagues from the town of Coatzacoalcos. Her father
died while she was still a little child, and her mother married
another Cacique, a young man, and bore him a son. It seems
that the father and mother had a great affection for this son
and it was agreed between them that he should succeed to their
honours when their days were done. So that there should be no
impediment to this, they gave the little girl, Doña Marina, to
some Indians from Xicalango, and this they did by night so as
to escape observation, and they then spread the report that she
had died, and as it happened at this time that a child of one of

their Indian slaves died they gave out that it was their daughter and the heiress who was dead.

The Indians of Xicalango gave the child to the people of Tabasco and the Tabasco people gave her to Cortés. I myself knew her mother, and the old woman's son and her half-brother, when he was already grown up and ruled the town jointly with his mother, for the second husband of the old lady was dead. When they became Christians, the old lady was called Marta and the son Lázaro. I knew all this very well because in the year 1523 after the conquest of Mexico and the other provinces, when Cristóbal de Olid revolted in Honduras, and Cortés was on his way there, he passed through Coatzacoalcos and I and the greater number of the settlers of that town accompanied him on that expedition as I shall relate in the proper time and place. As Doña Marina proved herself such an excellent woman and good interpreter throughout the wars in New Spain, Tlaxcala and Mexico (as I shall show later on) Cortés always took her with him, and during that expedition she was married to a gentleman named Juan Jaramillo at the town of Orizaba.

Doña Marina was a person of the greatest importance and was obeyed without question by the Indians throughout New Spain.

When Cortés was in the town of Coatzacoalcos he sent to summon to his presence all the Caciques of that province in order to make them a speech about our holy religion, and about their good treatment, and among the Caciques who assembled was the mother of Doña Marina and her half-brother, Lázaro.

Some time before this Doña Marina had told me that she belonged to that province and that she was the mistress of vassals, and Cortés also knew it well, as did Aguilar, the interpreter. In such a manner it was that mother, daughter and son came together, and it was easy enough to see that she was the daughter from the strong likeness she bore to her mother.

These relations were in great fear of Doña Marina, for they thought that she had sent for them to put them to death, and they were weeping.

When Doña Marina saw them in tears, she consoled them and told them to have no fear, that when they had given her over to the men from Xicalango, they knew not what they were doing, and she forgave them for doing it, and she gave them many jewels of gold and raiment, and told them to return to their town, and said that God had been very gracious to her in freeing her from the worship of idols and making her a Christian, and letting her bear a son to her lord and master Cortés and in marrying her to such a gentleman as Juan Jaramillo, who was now her husband. That she would rather serve her husband and Cortés than anything else in the world, and would not exchange her place to be Cacica of all the provinces in New Spain.

Doña Marina knew the language of Coatzacoalcos, which is that common to Mexico, and she knew the language of Tabasco, as did also Jerónimo de Aguilar, who spoke the language of Yucatan and Tabasco, which is one and the same. So that these two could understand one another clearly, and Aguilar translated into Castilian for Cortés.

This was the great beginning of our conquests and thus, thanks be to God, things prospered with us. I have made a point of explaining this matter, because without the help of Doña Marina we could not have understood the language of New Spain and Mexico.

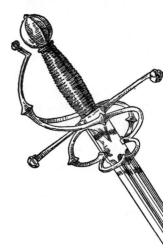

II

The March Inland

On Holy Thursday, in the year 1519, we arrived with all the fleet at the Port of San Juan de Ulúa, and as the Pilot Alaminos knew the place well from having come there with Juan de Grijalva he at once ordered the vessels to drop anchor where they would be safe from the northerly gales. The flagship hoisted her royal standards and pennants, and within half an hour of anchoring, two large canoes came out to us, full of Mexican Indians. Seeing the big ship with the standards flying they knew that it was there they must go to speak with the captain; so they went direct to the flagship and going on board asked who was the Tatuan[1] which in their language means the chief. Doña Marina, who understood the language well, pointed him out. Then the Indians paid many marks of respect to Cortés, according to their usage, and bade him welcome, and said that their lord, a servant of the great Montezuma, had sent them to ask what kind of men we were, and of what we were in search, and added that if we were in need of anything for ourselves or the ships, that we should tell them and they would supply it. Our Cortés thanked them through the two interpreters, Aguilar and Doña Marina, and ordered food and wine to be given them and some blue beads, and after they had drunk he told them that we came to see them and to trade with them and that our arrival in their country should cause them no uneasiness but be looked on by them as

[1] Tlatoan.

fortunate. The messengers returned on shore well content, and the next day, which was Good Friday, we disembarked with the horses and guns, on some sand hills which rise to a considerable height, for there was no level land, nothing but sand dunes; and the artilleryman Mesa placed the guns in position to the best of his judgment. Then we set up an altar where mass was said and we made huts and shelters for Cortés and the captains, and three hundred of the soldiers brought wood and made huts for themselves and we placed the horses where they would be safe and in this way was Good Friday passed.

The next day, Saturday, Easter Eve, many Indians arrived sent by a chief who was a governor under Montezuma, named Pitalpitoque[1] (whom we afterwards called Ovandillo), and they brought axes and dressed wood for the huts of the Captain Cortés and the other ranchos near to it, and covered them with large cloths on account of the strength of the sun, for the heat was very great—and they brought fowls, and maize cakes and plums, which were then in season, and I think that they brought some gold jewels, and they presented all these things to Cortés; and said that the next day a governor would come and would bring more food. Cortés thanked them heartily and ordered them to be given certain articles in exchange with which they went away well content. The next day, Easter Sunday, the governor whom they spoke of arrived. His name was Tendile,[2] a man of affairs, and he brought with him Pitalpitoque who was also a man of importance amongst the natives and there followed them many Indians with presents of fowls and vegetables. Tendile ordered these people to stand aside on a hillock and with much humility he made three obeisances to Cortés according to their customs, and then to all the soldiers who were standing around. Cortés bade them welcome through our interpreters and embraced them and asked them to wait, as he wished presently to speak to them. Meanwhile he ordered an altar to be made as well as it could be done in the time, and Fray Bartolomé de Olmedo, who was a fine singer, chanted Mass, and Padre Juan Díaz assisted, and the two governors and the other chiefs who were with them looked on. When Mass was over, Cortés and some of our captains and the

---

[1] Pitalpitoque = Cuitlalpitoc.
[2] Teuhtlilli.

two Indian Officers of the great Montezuma dined together. When the tables had been cleared away—Cortés went aside with the two Caciques and our two interpreters and explained to them that we were Christians and vassals of the greatest lord on earth who had many great princes as his vassals and servants, and that it was at his orders that we had come to this country, because for many years he had heard rumours about the country and the great prince who ruled it. That he wished to be friends with this prince and to tell him many things in the name of the Emperor which things, when he knew and understood them, would please him greatly. Moreover, he wished to trade with their prince and his Indians in good friendship, and he wanted to know where this prince would wish that they should meet so that they might confer together. Tendile replied somewhat proudly, and said:—"You have only just now arrived and you already ask to speak with our prince; accept now this present which we give you in his name, and afterwards you will tell me what you think fitting." With that he took out a *petaca*—which is a sort of chest, many articles of gold beautifully and richly worked and ordered ten loads of white cloth made of cotton and feathers to be brought, wonderful things to see, besides quantities of food. Cortés received it all with smiles in a gracious manner and gave in return, beads of twisted glass and other small beads from Spain, and he begged them to send to their towns to ask the people to come and trade with us as he had brought many beads to exchange for gold, and they replied that they would do as he asked. Cortés then ordered his servants to bring an arm-chair, richly carved and inlaid and some *margaritas,* stones with many [intricate] designs in them, and a string of twisted glass beads packed in cotton scented with musk and a crimson cap with a golden medal engraved with a figure of St. George on horseback, lance in hand, slaying the dragon, and he told Tendile that he should send the chair to his prince Montezuma, so that he could be seated in it when he, Cortés, came to see and speak with him, and that he should place the cap on his head, and that the stones and all the other things were presents from our lord the King, as a sign of his friendship, for he was aware that Montezuma was a great prince, and Cortés asked that a day and a place might be named where he could go to see Montezuma. Tendile received the present and said that his lord Montezuma was such a great prince that it would please him to know our great King, and that he would carry the present to him at once and bring back a reply.

It appears that Tendile brought with him some clever painters such as they had in Mexico and ordered them to make pictures true to nature of the face and body of Cortés and all his captains, and of the soldiers, ships, sails and horses, and of Doña Marina and Aguilar, even of the two greyhounds, and the cannon and cannon balls, and all of the army we had brought with us, and he carried the pictures to his master. Cortés ordered our gunners to load the lombards with a great charge of powder so that they should make a great noise when they were fired off, and he told Pedro de Alvarado that he and all the horsemen should get ready so that these servants of Montezuma might see them gallop and told them to attach little bells to the horses' breastplates. Cortés also mounted his horse and said: "It would be well if we could gallop on these sand dunes but they will observe that even when on foot we get stuck in the sand—let us go out to the beach when the tide is low and gallop two and two"—and to Pedro de Alvarado whose sorrel coloured mare was a great galloper, and very handy, he gave charge of all the horsemen.

All this was carried out in the presence of the two ambassadors, and so that they should see the cannon fired, Cortés made as though he wished again to speak to them and a number of other chieftains, and the lombards were fired off, and as it was quite still at that moment, the stones went flying through the forest resounding with a great din, and the two governors and all the other Indians were frightened by things so new to them, and ordered the painters to record them so that Montezuma might see. It happened that one of the soldiers had a helmet half gilt but somewhat rusty, and this Tendile noticed, for he was the more forward of the two ambassadors, and said that he wished to see it as it was like one that they possessed which had been left to them by their ancestors of the race from which they had sprung, and that it had been placed on the head of their god—Huichilobos,[1] and that their prince Montezuma would like to see this helmet. So it was given to him, and Cortés said to them that as he wished to know whether the gold of this country was the same as that we find

[1] Huitzilopochtli.

in our rivers, they could return the helmet filled with grains of gold so that he could send it to our great Emperor. After this, Tendile bade farewell to Cortés and to all of us and after many expressions of regard from Cortés he took leave of him and said he would return with a reply without delay. After Tendile had departed we found out that besides being an Indian employed in matters of great importance, Tendile was the most active of the servants whom his master, Montezuma, had in his employ, and he went with all haste and narrated everything to his prince, and showed him the pictures which had been painted and the present which Cortés had sent. When the great Montezuma gazed on it he was struck with admiration and received it on his part with satisfaction. When he examined the helmet and that which was on his Huichilobos, he felt convinced that we belonged to the race which, as his forefathers had foretold would come to rule over that land.

† xxv

When Tendile departed the other governor, Pitalpitoque, stayed in our camp and occupied some huts a little distance from ours, and they brought Indian women there to make maize bread, and brought fowls and fruit and fish, and supplied Cortés and the captains who fed with him. As for us soldiers, if we did not hunt for shell fish on the beach, or go out fishing, we did not get anything.

About that time, many Indians came from the towns and some of them brought gold and jewels of little value, and fowls to exchange with us for our goods, which consisted of green beads and clear glass beads and other articles, and with this we managed to supply ourselves with food. Almost all the soldiers had brought things for barter, as we learnt in Grijalva's time that it was a good thing to bring beads—and in this manner six or seven days passed by.

Then one morning, Tendile arrived with more than one hundred laden Indians, accompanied by a great Mexican Cacique, who in his face, features and appearance bore a strong likeness to our Captain Cortés and the great Montezuma had sent him purposely, for it is said that when Tendile brought the portrait of Cortés all the chiefs who were in Montezuma's company said that a great chief named Quintalbor looked exactly like Cortés and that was the name of the Cacique, who now arrived with Tendile; and as he was so like Cortés, we called them in camp "our Cortés" and "the other Cortés." To go back to my story, when these people arrived and came before our Captain they first of all kissed the earth and then fumigated him and all the soldiers who were standing around him, with incense which they brought in braziers of pottery. Cortés received them affectionately and seated them near himself, and that chief who came with the present had been appointed spokesman together with Tendile. After welcoming us to the country and after many courteous speeches had passed he ordered the presents which he had brought to be displayed, and they were placed on mats over which were spread cotton cloths. The first article presented was a wheel like a sun, as big as a cartwheel, with many sorts of pictures on it, the whole of fine gold, and a wonderful thing to behold, which those who afterwards weighed it said was worth more than ten thousand dollars. Then another wheel was presented of greater size made of silver of great brilliancy in imitation of the moon with other figures shown on it, and this was of great value as it was very heavy—and the chief brought back the helmet full of fine grains of gold, just as they are got out of the mines, and this was worth three thousand dollars. This gold in the helmet was worth more to us than if it had contained twenty thousand dollars, because it showed us that there were good mines there. Then were brought twenty golden ducks, beautifully worked and very natural looking, and some [ornaments] like dogs, and many articles of gold worked in the shape of tigers and lions and monkeys, and ten collars beautifully worked and other necklaces; and twelve arrows and a bow with its string, and two rods like staffs of justice, five palms long, all in beautiful hollow work of fine gold. Then there were presented crests of gold and plumes of rich green feathers, and others of silver, and fans of the same materials, and deer copied in hollow gold and many other things that I cannot remember for it all happened so many years ago. And then over thirty loads of beautiful cotton cloth were brought worked with many patterns and decorated with many coloured feathers, and so many other things were there that it is useless my trying to describe them for I know not how to do it. When all these things had been presented, this great Cacique Quintalbor and Tendile asked Cortés to accept this present with the same willingness with which his prince had sent it, and divide it among the *teules* and men who accompanied him. Cortés received the present with delight and then the ambassadors told Cortés that they wished to repeat what their prince, Montezuma, had sent them to say. First of all they told him that he was pleased that such valiant men, as he had heard that we were, should come to his country, for he knew all about what we had done at Tabasco, and that he would much like to see our great emperor who was such a mighty prince and whose fame was spread over so many lands, and that he would send him a present of precious stones; and that meanwhile we should stay in that port; that if he could assist us in any way he would do so with the greatest pleasure; but as to the interview, they should not worry about it; that there was no need for it and they (the ambassadors) urged many objections. Cortés kept a good countenance, and returned his thanks to them, and with many flattering expressions gave each of the ambassadors two holland shirts and some blue glass beads and other things, and begged them to go back as his ambassadors to Mexico and to tell their prince, the great Montezuma, that as we had come across so many seas and had journeyed from such distant lands solely to see and speak with him in person, that if we should return thus, that our great king and lord would not receive us well, and that wherever their prince Montezuma might be we wished to go and see him and do what he might order us to do. The ambassadors replied that they would go back and give this message to their prince, but as to the question of the desired interview—they considered it superfluous. By these ambassadors Cortés sent what our poverty could afford as a gift to Montezuma; a glass cup of Florentine ware, engraved with trees and hunting scenes and gilt, and three holland shirts and other things, and he charged the messengers to bring a reply. The two governors set out and Pitalpitoque remained in camp; for it seems that the other servants of Montezuma had given him orders to see that food was brought to us from the neighbouring towns.

As soon as the messengers had been sent off to Mexico, Cortés despatched two ships to explore the coast further along, and to seek out a safe harbour, and search for lands where we could settle, for it was clear that we could not settle on those sand dunes, both on account of the mosquitoes and the distance from other towns. They did as they were told and arrived at the Rio Grande, which is close to Panuco. They were not able to proceed any further on account of the strong currents. Seeing how difficult the navigation had become, they turned round and made for San Juan de Ulúa, without having made any further progress.

I must now go back to say that the Indian Pitalpitoque, who remained behind to look after the food, slackened his efforts to such an extent that no provisions reached the camp and we were greatly in need of food, for the cassava turned sour from the damp and rotted and became foul with weevils and if we had not gone hunting for shell fish we should have had nothing to eat. The Indians who used to come bringing gold and fowls for barter, did not come in such numbers as on our first arrival, and those who did come were very shy and cautious and we began to count the hours that must elapse before the return of the messengers who had gone to Mexico. We were thus waiting when Tendile returned accompanied by many Indians, and after having paid their respects in the usual manner by fumigating Cortés and the rest of us with incense, he presented ten loads of fine rich feather cloth, and four chalchihuites, which are green stones of very great value, and held in the greatest esteem among the Indians, more than emeralds are by us, and certain other gold articles. Not counting the chalchihuites, the gold alone was said to be worth three thousand dollars. Then Tendile and Pitalpitoque went aside with Cortés and Doña Marina and Aguilar, and reported that their prince Montezuma had accepted the present and was greatly pleased with it, but as to an interview, that no more should be said about it; that these rich stones of chalchihuite should be sent to the great Emperor as they were of the highest value, each one being worth more and being esteemed more highly than a great load of gold, and that it was not worth while to send any more messengers to Mexico. Cortés thanked the messengers and gave them presents, but it was certainly a disappointment to him to be told so distinctly that we could not see Monte-zuma, and he said to some soldiers who happened to be stand-ing near: "Surely this must be a great and rich prince, and some day, please God, we must go and see him"—and the sol-diers answered: "We wish that we were already living with him!"

Let us now leave this question of visits and relate that it was now the time of the Ave Maria, and at the sound of a bell which we had in the camp we all fell on our knees before a cross placed on a sand hill and said our prayers of the Ave Maria before the cross. When Tendile and Pitalpitoque saw us thus kneeling as they were very intelligent, they asked what was the reason that we humbled ourselves before a tree cut in that particular way. As Cortés heard this remark he said to the Padre de la Merced who was present: "It is a good opportu-nity, father, as we have good material at hand, to explain through our interpreters matters touching our holy faith." And then he delivered a discourse to the Caciques so fitting to the occasion that no good theologian could have bettered it. Cortés said many things very well expressed, which they thoroughly understood, and they replied that they would report them to their prince Montezuma. Cortés also told them that one of the objects for which our great Emperor had sent us to their coun-tries was to abolish human sacrifices, and the other evil rites which they practised and to see that they did not rob one an-other, or worship those cursèd images. And Cortés prayed them to set up in their city, in the temples where they kept the idols which they believed to be gods, a cross like the one they saw before them, and to set up in the same place an image of Our Lady, which he would give them, with her precious son in her arms, and they would see how well it would go with them, and what our God would do for them. I recall to mind that on this latest visit many Indians came with Tendile who were wishing to barter articles of gold, which, however, were of no great value. So all the soldiers set about bartering, and the gold which we gained by this barter we gave to the sailors who were out fishing in exchange for their fish so as to get something to eat, for otherwise we often underwent great privations through hunger. Cortés was pleased at this, although he pretended not to see what was going on.

† xxvii

When the friends of Diego Velásquez saw that some of us soldiers were bartering for gold, they asked Cortés why he permitted it, and said that Diego Velásquez did not send out the expedition in order that the soldiers should carry off most of the gold, and that it would be as well to issue an order that for the future no gold should be bartered for by anyone but Cortés himself and that all the gold already obtained should be displayed so that the royal fifth might be taken from it, and that some suitable person should be placed in charge of the treasury.

To all this Cortés replied that all they said was good, and that they themselves should name that person, and they chose Gonzalo Mejia. When this had been done, Cortés turned to them with angry mien and said: "Observe, gentlemen, that our companions are suffering great hardships from want of food, and it is for this reason that we ought to overlook things, so that they may all find something to eat; all the more so as the amount of gold they bargain for is but a trifle—and God willing, we are going to obtain a large amount of it. However, there are two sides to everything; the order has been issued that bartering for gold shall cease, as you desired; we shall see next what we will get to eat."

I will go on to relate how, one morning, we woke up to find not a single Indian in any of their huts, neither those who used to bring the food, nor those who came to trade, nor Pitalpitoque himself; they had all fled without saying a word. The cause of this, as we afterwards learned, was that Montezuma had sent orders to avoid further conversation with Cortés and those in his company; for it appears that Montezuma was very much devoted to his idols, named Tezcatepuca, and Huichilobos, the latter the god of war, and Tezcatepuca the god of hell; and daily he sacrificed youths to them so as to get an answer from the gods as to what he should do about us; for Montezuma had already formed a plan, if we did not go off

in the ships, to get us all into his power, and to raise a breed
of us and also to keep us for sacrifice. As we afterwards found
out, the reply given by the gods was that he should not listen
to Cortés, nor to the message which he sent about setting up a
cross and an image of Our Lady, and that such things should
not be brought to the city. This was the reason why the Indians left our camp without warning. When we heard the news
we thought that they meant to make war on us, and we were
very much on the alert. One day, as I and another soldier were
stationed on some sand dunes keeping a look out, we saw five
Indians coming along the beach, and so as not to raise a scare
in camp over so small a matter, we permitted them to approach. When they came up to us with smiling countenances
they paid us homage according to their custom, and made signs
that we should take them into camp. I told my companion to
remain where he was and I would accompany the Indians, for
at that time my feet were not as heavy as they are now that I
am old, and when we came before Cortés the Indians paid him
every mark of respect and said: *Lope luzio, lope luzio*—which
in the Totonac language means: "prince and great lord." These
men had large holes in their lower lips, some with stone
disks in them spotted with blue, and others with thin leaves of
gold. They also had their ears pierced with large holes in
which were placed disks of stone or gold, and in their dress
and speech they differed greatly from the Mexicans who had
been staying with us. When Doña Marina and Aguilar, the interpreters, heard the words *Lope luzio* they did not understand
it, and Doña Marina asked in Mexican if there were not among
them *Nahuatatos,* that is, interpreters of the Mexican language,
and two of the five answered yes, that they understood and
spoke it, and they bade us welcome and said that their chief
had sent them to ask who we might be, and that it would
please him to be of service to such valiant men, for it appeared
that they knew about our doings at Tabasco and Champoton,
and they added that they would have come to see us before but
for fear of the people of Culua who had been with us (by
Culua they meant Mexicans) and that they knew that three
days ago they had fled back to their own country, and in the
course of their talk Cortés found out that Montezuma had opponents and enemies, which he was delighted to hear, and after
flattering these five messengers and giving them presents he

bade them farewell, asking them to tell their chief that he
would very soon come and pay them a visit. From this time on
we called those Indians the *Lope luzios*. I must leave them now
and go on to say that in those sand dunes, where we were
camped there were always many mosquitos, both long-legged
ones and small ones which are called *xexenes* which are worse
than the large ones, and we could get no sleep on account of
them. We were very short of food and the cassava bread was
disappearing, and what there was of it was very damp and foul
with weevils. Some of the soldiers who possessed Indians in the
Island of Cuba were continually sighing for their homes, especially the friends and servants of Diego Velásquez. When
Cortés noted the state of affairs and the wishes of these men he
gave orders that we should go to the fortified town which had
been seen by Montejo and the pilot, Alaminos, named Quiahuitztlan where the ships would be under the protection of the
rock which I have mentioned. When arrangements were being
made for us to start, all the friends, relations and servants of
Diego Velásquez asked Cortés why he wanted to make that
journey without having any provisions, seeing that there was
no possibility of going on any further and that over thirty-five
soldiers had already died in camp from wounds inflicted at
Tabasco, and from sickness and hunger; that the country we
were in was a great one and the settlements very thickly populated and that any day they might make war on us; that it
would be much better to return to Cuba and account to Diego
Velásquez for the gold gained in barter, which already
amounted to a large sum, and the great presents from Montezuma, the sun and the silver moon and the helmet full of
golden grains from the mines, and all the cloths and jewels
already mentioned by me. Cortés replied to them that it was
not good advice to recommend our going back without reason;
that hitherto we could not complain of our fortune, and should
give thanks to God who was helping us in everything, and as
for those who had died, that that always happened in wars and
under hardships; that it would be as well to find out what the
country contained; that meanwhile we could eat the maize and
other food held by the Indians and by the neighbouring towns,
unless our hands had lost their cunning. With this reply, the
partisans of Diego Velásquez were somewhat, but not wholly

appeased, for there were already cliques formed in camp who discussed the return to Cuba.

† xxviii

It appears that Cortés had already talked the matter over with Alonzo Hernández Puertocarrero, and Pedro de Alvarado and his four brothers, Jorge, Gonzalo, Gómez, and Juan, and with Cristóbal de Olid, Alonzo de Ávila, Juan de Escalante, Francisco de Lugo, and with me and other gentlemen and captains, and suggested that we should beg of him to be our captain. Francisco de Montejo understood what was going on and was on the watch. One night, after midnight, Alonzo Hernández Puertocarrero, Juan de Escalante and Francisco de Lugo, came to my hut. Francisco de Lugo and I came from the same country and were distant kinsmen. They said to me: "Señor Bernal Díaz, come out with your arms and go the rounds; we will accompany Cortés who is just now going the rounds." When I was a little distance from the hut they said to me: "Look to it, sir, that you keep secret for a time what we wish to tell you, for it is a matter of importance, and see that your companions in your hut know nothing about it, for they are of the party of Diego Velásquez." What they said to me was: "Sir, does it seem to you to be right that Hernando Cortés should have deceived us all in bringing us here, he having proclaimed in Cuba that he was coming to settle, and now we find out that he has no power to do so, but only to trade, and they want us to return to Santiago de Cuba with all the gold that has been collected, and we shall lose our all, for will not Diego Velásquez take all the gold as he did before? Look, sir, counting this present expedition, you have already come to this country three times, spending your own property and contracting debts and risking your life many times with the wounds you have received. Many of us gentlemen who know that we are your honour's friends wish you to understand that this must not go on; that this land must be settled in the name of His Majesty, and by Hernando Cortés in His Majesty's name, while we await the opportunity to make it known to our lord the King in Spain. Be sure sir, to cast your vote so that all of us unanimously and

willingly choose him captain, for it will be a service to God
and our lord the King." I replied that it was not a wise decision to return to Cuba and that it would be a good thing for
the country to be settled, and that we should choose Cortés as
General and Chief Justice until His Majesty should order otherwise. This agreement passed from soldier to soldier and the
friends and relations of Diego Velásquez, who were more numerous than we were, got to know of it, and with overbold
words asked Cortés why he was craftily arranging to remain in
this country instead of returning to render an account of his
doings to the man who had sent him as captain, and they told
him that Diego Velásquez would not approve of it, and that
the sooner we embarked the better; that there was no use in
his subterfuges and secret meetings with the soldiers, for we
had neither supplies nor men, nor any possibility of founding a
settlement. Cortés answered without a sign of anger, and said
that he agreed with them; that he would not go against the instructions and notes which he had received from Diego Velásquez, and he issued an order for us all to embark on the following day, each one in the ship in which he had come. We
who had made the agreement answered that it was not fair to
deceive us so, that in Cuba he had proclaimed that he was coming to make a settlement, whereas he had only come to trade;
and we demanded on behalf of our Lord God and of His Majesty that he should at once form a settlement and give up any
other plan, because that would be of the greatest benefit and
service to God and the King; and they placed many other well-
reasoned arguments before him saying that the natives would
never let us land again as they had done this time, and that as
soon as a settlement was made in the country soldiers would
gather in from all the islands to give us help and that Velásquez had ruined us all by stating publicly that he had received
a decree from His Majesty to form a settlement, the contrary
being the case; that we wished to form a settlement, and to let
those depart who desired to return to Cuba. So Cortés agreed
to it, although he pretended to need much begging, as the saying goes: "You are very pressing, and I want to do it"—and he
stipulated that we should make him Chief Justice and Captain
General, and the worst of all that we conceded was that we
should give him a fifth of all the gold which should be obtained, after the royal fifth had been deducted, and then we

gave him the very fullest powers in the presence of the King's Notary, Diego de Godoy, embracing all that I have here stated. We at once set to work to found and settle a town, which was called the "Villa Rica de la Vera Cruz" because we arrived on Thursday of the (last) supper and landed on "Holy Friday of the Cross" and "rich" because of what that gentleman said, who approached Cortés and said to him: "Behold rich lands! May you know how to govern them well!"—and what he wanted to say was: "May you remain as their Captain General." That gentleman was Alonzo Hernández Puertocarrero.

To go back to my story: as soon as the town was founded we appointed alcaldes and regidores; the former were Alonzo Hernández Puertocarrero and Francisco Montejo. In the case of Montejo, it was because he was not on very good terms with Cortés that Cortés ordered him to be named as Alcalde, so as to place him in the highest position. I need not give the names of the Regidores, for it is no use naming only a few of them; but I must mention the fact that a pillory was placed in the Plaza and a gallows set up outside the town. We chose Pedro de Alvarado as captain of expeditions and Cristóbal de Olid as Maestro de Campo.[1] Juan de Escalante was chosen chief Alguacil,[2] Gonzalo Mejia, treasurer, and Alonzo de Ávila accountant. A certain Corral was named as Ensign, because Villaroel who had been Ensign was dismissed from the post on account of some offence he had given Cortés about an Indian woman from Cuba. Ochoa, a Biscayan, and Alonzo Romero were appointed Alguaciles of the Camp.[3]

It will be said that I have made no mention of the Captain Gonzalo de Sandoval. I say this was because at that time he was a youth, and we did not take such count of him and of other valiant captains until we saw him grow in worth in such a way that Cortés and all the soldiers held him in the same esteem as Cortés himself, as I shall tell later on.

When the partisans of Diego Velásquez realized the fact that we had chosen Cortés for our Captain and Chief Justice, and had founded a town and chosen Alcaldes and Regidores, and had done all that I have narrated, they were angry and furious and they began to excite factions and meetings and to use abu-

---

[1] *Maestro de Campo* = Quartermaster.
[2] *Alguacil Mayor* = High Constable.
[3] *Alguacil del Real* = Constables and storekeepers.

sive language about Cortés and those of us who had elected
him, saying that it was not right to do these things unless all
the captains and soldiers who had come on the expedition had
been parties to it; that Diego Velásquez had given Cortés no
such powers, only authority to trade, and that we partisans of
Cortés should take care that our insolence did not so increase
as to bring us to blows. Then Cortés secretly told Juan de Escalante that we should make him produce the instructions
given him by Diego Velásquez. Upon this Cortés drew them
from his bosom and gave them to the King's scribe to read
aloud. In these instructions were the words: "As soon as you
have gained all you can by trading, you will return," and the
document was signed by Diego Velásquez and countersigned
by his Secretary, Andrés de Duero. We begged Cortés to cause
this document to be attached to the deed recording the power
we had given him, as well as the proclamation which he issued
in the Island of Cuba. And this was done so that His Majesty in
Spain should know that all that we did was done in his royal
service, and that they should not bring against us anything but
the truth.

After this was done, these same friends and dependents of
Diego Velásquez returned to Cortés to say that they did not
wish to remain under his command, but to return at once to
the Island of Cuba. Cortés replied that he would detain no one
by force, and that to anyone who came to ask leave to return,
he would willingly grant it, even although he were left alone.
With this some of them were quieted, but not Juan Velásquez
de Leon, and Diego de Ordás, and Escobar, and other friends
of Diego Velásquez; and it came to this, that they refused all
obedience to Cortés. With our assistance, Cortés determined to
make prisoners of Juan Velásquez de Leon and Diego de Ordás, and Escobar and Pedro Escudero and we took care that
the others should create no disturbance. These men remained
prisoners for some days, in chains and under guard.

† xxix

When all that I have related had been settled and done with, it
was arranged that Pedro de Alvarado should go inland to some
towns which we had been told were near by and see what the

country was like and bring back maize and some sort of supplies, for there was a great want of food in camp. Alvarado took one hundred soldiers with him, among them fifteen crossbowmen and six musketeers. More than half his soldiers were partisans of Diego Velásquez. All Cortés' party remained with him for fear there should be any further disturbance or tricks played or any rising against him, until things became more settled.

Alvarado went first to some small towns subject to another town called Cotaxtla, where the language of Culua was spoken. This name, Culua, means the common language of Mexico.

When Pedro de Alvarado reached these towns he found that they had all been deserted that same day, and he found in the *cues* bodies of men and boys who had been sacrificed, and the walls and altars stained with blood and the hearts placed as offerings before the Idols. He also found the stones on which the sacrifices were made and the stone knives with which to open the chest so as to take out the heart.

Pedro de Alvarado said that he found most of the bodies without arms or legs, and that he was told by some Indians that they had been carried off to be eaten, and our soldiers were astounded at such great cruelty. I will not say any more of the number of sacrifices, although we found the same thing in every town we afterwards entered. Alvarado found the towns well provisioned but deserted that very day by their inhabitants, so that he could not find more than two Indians to carry maize, and each soldier had to load himself with poultry and vegetables, and he returned to camp without doing any other damage (although he had good opportunity for doing it) because Cortés had given orders to that effect, so that there should be no repetition of what happened in Cozumel.

We were pleased enough in camp even with the little food that had been brought, for all evils and hardships disappear when there is plenty to eat.

To go back to my story: As Cortés was most energetic in every direction, he managed to make friends with the partisans of Diego Velásquez, for, with that solvent of hardness, presents of gold from our store to some, and promises to others, he brought them over to his side, and took them out of prison; all except Juan Velásquez de Leon and Diego de Ordás, who were in irons on board ship. These, too, he let out of prison after a few days, and made good and true friends of them as will be seen further on—and all through gold which is such a pacifier!

When everything had been settled, we arranged to go to the fortified town already mentioned by me, which was called Quiahuitztlan. The ships were to go to the rock and harbour which was opposite that town, about a league distant from it. I remember that as we marched along the coast we killed a large fish which had been thrown up high and dry by the sea. When we arrived at the river where Vera Cruz is now situated [1] we found the water to be deep, and we crossed over it in some broken canoes like troughs, and others crossed by swimming or on rafts.

Then we came on some towns subject to the large town named Cempoala, whence came the five Indians with the golden labrets, who came as messengers to Cortés at the sand dunes. We found some idol houses and places of sacrifice, and blood splashed about, and incense used for fumigation and other things belonging to the idols, and stones with which they made the sacrifices, and parrots' feathers and many paper books doubled together in folds like Spanish cloth; but we found no Indians, they having already fled, for as they had never before seen men like us, nor horses, they were afraid.

We slept there that night, and went without supper, and next day, leaving the coast, we continued our march inland towards the west, without knowing the road we were taking, and we came on some good meadows called *savannas* where deer were grazing, and Pedro de Alvarado rode after one on his sorrel mare and struck at it with his lance and wounded it, but it got away into the woods and could not be caught.

While this was happening we saw twelve Indians approaching, inhabitants of the farms where we had passed the night. They came straight from their Cacique, and brought fowls and maize cakes, and they said to Cortés through our interpreters, that their chief had sent the fowls for us to eat, and begged us to come to his town, which was, according to the signs they made, distant one sun's (that is one day's) march.

Cortés thanked them and made much of them, and we continued our march and slept in another small town, where also

[1] The third site, now known as La Antigua.

many sacrifices had been made, but as many readers will be tired of hearing of the great number of Indian men and women whom we found sacrificed in all the towns and roads we passed, I shall go on with my story without stopping to say any more about them.

They gave us supper at the little town and we learnt that the road to Quiahuitztlan, which I have already said is a fortress, passed by Cempoala.

† xxx

We slept at the little town where the twelve Indians I have mentioned had prepared quarters for us, and after being well informed about the road which we had to take to reach the town on the hill, very early in the morning we sent word to the Caciques of Cempoala that we were coming to their town and that we hoped they would approve. Cortés sent six of the Indians with this message and kept the other six as guides. He also ordered the guns, muskets, and crossbows to be kept ready for use, and sent scouts on ahead on the look out, and the horsemen and all the rest of us were kept on the alert, and in this way we marched to within a league of the town. As we approached, twenty Indian chieftains came out to receive us in the name of the Cacique, and brought some cones made of the roses of the country with a delicious scent, which they gave to Cortés and those on horseback with every sign of friendliness, and they told Cortés that their Lord was awaiting us at our apartments, for, as he was a very stout and heavy man, he could not come out to receive us himself. Cortés thanked them and we continued our march, and as we got among the houses and saw what a large town it was, larger than any we had yet seen, we were struck with admiration. It looked like a garden with luxuriant vegetation, and the streets were so full of men and women who had come to see us, that we gave thanks to God at having discovered such a country.

Our scouts, who were on horseback, reached a great plaza with courts, where they had prepared our quarters, and it seems that during the last few days they had been whitewashed and burnished, a thing they knew well how to do, and it seemed to one of the scouts that this white surface which shone so

brightly must be silver and he came back at full speed to tell
Cortés that the walls of the houses were made of silver! Doña
Marina and Aguilar said that it must be plaster or lime and
we had a good laugh over the man's silver and excitement and
always afterwards we told him that everything white looked to
him like silver. I will leave our jokes and say that we reached
the buildings, and the fat Cacique came out to receive us in
the court. He was so fat that I shall call him by this name;
and he made deep obeisance to Cortés and fumigated him, as is
their custom, and Cortés embraced him and we were lodged in
fine and large apartments that held us all, and they gave us
food and brought some baskets of plums which were very
plentiful at that season, and maize cakes, and as we arrived
ravenous and had not seen so much food for a long time, we
called the town Villa Viciosa.

Cortés gave orders that none of the soldiers should leave the
plaza and that on no account should they give any offence to
the Indians. When the fat Cacique heard that we had finished
eating he sent to tell Cortés that he wished to come and visit
him; and he came in company with a great number of Indian chieftains, all wearing large gold labrets and rich mantles.
Cortés left his quarters to go out and meet them, and embraced the Cacique with great show of caressing and flattery,
and the fat Cacique ordered a present to be brought which he
had prepared, consisting of gold, jewels and cloths; but although it did not amount to much and was of little value he
said to Cortés: "*Lope luzio, Lope luzio,* accept this in good
part; if I had more I would give it to you!"

Cortés replied through Doña Marina and Aguilar that he
would pay for the gift in good works, and that if the Cacique
would tell him what he wanted to be done that he would do
it for them for we were the vassals of a great prince, the
Emperor Don Carlos, who had sent us to redress grievances
and punish evil doers, and to put an end to human sacrifices.
And he explained to them many things touching our holy
religion. When the fat Cacique heard this, he sighed, and complained bitterly of the great Montezuma and his governors saying that he had recently been brought under his yoke; that all
his golden jewels had been carried off, and he and his people
were so grievously oppressed, that they dared do nothing without Montezuma's orders, for he was the Lord over many cities

and countries and ruled over countless vassals and armies of warriors.

As Cortés knew that he could not attend at that time to the complaints which they made, he replied that he would see to it that they were relieved of their burdens, that he was now on the way to visit his *Acales* (for so they call the ships in the Indian language) and take up his residence and make his headquarters in the town of Quiahuitztlan, and that as soon as he was settled there he would consider the matter more thoroughly. To this the fat Cacique replied that he was quite satisfied that it should be so.

The next morning we left Cempoala, and there were await-ing our orders over four hundred Indian carriers, who carry fifty pounds weight on their backs and march five leagues with it. When we saw so many Indians to carry burdens we rejoiced, as before this, those of us who had not brought Indians with us from Cuba had to carry knapsacks on our own backs. And only six or seven Cubans had been brought in the fleet. Doña Marina and Aguilar told us that in these parts in times of peace the Caciques are bound to furnish *tamenes* to carry bur-dens, as a matter of course, and from this time forward wher-ever we went we asked for Indians to carry loads.

Cortés took leave of the fat Cacique, and on the following day we set out on our march and slept at a little town which had been deserted near to Quiahuitztlan, and the people of Cempoala brought us food.

†   xxxi

The next day about ten o'clock we reached the fortified town called Quiahuitztlan, which stands amid great rocks and lofty cliffs and if there had been any resistance it would have been very difficult to capture it. Expecting that there would be fight-ing we kept a good formation with the artillery in front and marched up to the fortress in such a manner that if anything had happened we could have done our duty.

We went half way through the town without meeting a sin-gle Indian to speak to, at which we were very much surprised, for they had fled in fear that very day when they had seen us climbing up to their houses. When we had reached the top

of the fortress in the plaza near by where they had their *cues*
and great idol houses, we saw fifteen Indians awaiting us all
clad in good mantles, and each one with a brazier in his hand
containing incense, and they came to where Cortés was standing and fumigated him and all the soldiers who were standing
near and with deep obeisances they asked pardon for not coming out to meet us, and assured us that we were welcome
and asked us to rest. And they said that they had fled and
kept out of the way until they could see what sort of things
we were, for they were afraid of us and of our horses, but
that night they would order all the people to come back to
the town.

Cortés displayed much friendship toward them, and he gave
them some green beads and other trifles from Spain; and they
brought fowls and maize cakes. While we were talking, someone came to tell Cortés that the fat Cacique from Cempoala
was coming in a litter carried on the shoulders of many Indian chieftains. When the fat Cacique arrived he, together with
the Cacique and chiefs of the town, addressed Cortés, relating
their many causes of complaint against Montezuma and telling
him of his great power, and this they did with such signs and
tears that Cortés and those who were standing with him were
moved to pity. Besides relating the way that they had been
brought into subjection, they told us that every year many of
their sons and daughters were demanded of them for sacrifice,
and others for service in the houses and plantations of their
conquerors; and they made other complaints which were so
numerous that I do not remember them all; but they said
that Montezuma's tax-gatherers carried off their wives and
daughters if they were handsome, and ravished them, and this
they did throughout the land where the Totonac language was
spoken, which contained over thirty towns.

Cortés consoled them as well as he was able through our interpreters and said he would help them all he could, and
would prevent these robberies and offences, as it was for that
our lord the Emperor had sent us to these parts, and that they
should have no anxiety, for they would soon see what we would
do in the matter; and they seemed to gather some satisfaction
from this assurance but their hearts were not eased on account of the great fear they had of the Mexicans.

While this conversation was going on, some Indians from the

town came in great haste to tell the Caciques who were talking
to Cortés, that five Mexicans, who were Montezuma's tax-
gatherers, had just arrived. When they heard the news they
turned pale and trembled with fear, and leaving Cortés alone
they went off to receive the Mexicans, and in the shortest
possible time they had decked a room with flowers, and had
food cooked for the Mexicans to eat, and prepared plenty of
cacao, which is the best thing they have to drink.

When these five Indians entered the town, they came to the
place where we were assembled, where were the houses of the
Cacique and our quarters, and approaching us with the utmost
assurance and arrogance without speaking to Cortés, or to any
of us, they passed us by. Their cloaks and loin-cloths were
richly embroidered, and their shining hair was gathered up as
though tied on their heads, and each one was smelling the
roses that he carried, and each had a crooked staff in his hand.
Their Indian servants carried fly-whisks and they were accompanied by many of the chief men of the other Totonac
towns, who until they had shown them to their lodgings and
brought them food of the best, never left them.

As soon as they had dined they sent to summon the fat
Cacique and the other chiefs, and scolded them for entertaining us in their houses, for now they would have to speak and
deal with us which would not please their lord Montezuma;
for without his permission and orders they should not have
sheltered us, nor given us presents of golden jewels, and on
this subject they uttered many threats against the fat Cacique
and the other chiefs and ordered them at once to provide
twenty Indians, men and women, to appease their gods for
the wrong that had been done.

When he saw what was going on, Cortés asked our interpreters, Doña Marina and Jerónimo de Aguilar why the Caciques were so agitated since the arrival of those Indians, and
who they were. Doña Marina who understood full well what
had happened, told him what was going on; and then Cortés
summoned the fat Cacique and the other chiefs, and asked
them who these Indians were, and why they made such a
fuss about them. They replied that they were the tax-gatherers
of the great Montezuma and that they had come to inquire
why they had received us in their town without the permission
of their lord, and that they now demanded twenty men and

women to sacrifice to their god, Huichilobos, so that he would
give them victory over us, for they [the tax-gatherers] said that
Montezuma had declared that he intended to capture and make
slaves of us.

Cortés reassured them and bade them have no fear for he
was here with all of us in his company and that he would
chastise the tax-gatherers.

† xxxii

As soon as Cortés understood what the chiefs were telling him,
he said that he had already explained to them that our lord
the King had sent him to chastise evil doers and that he would
not permit either sacrifice or robbery, and that as these tax-
gatherers had made this demand, he ordered them to make
prisoners of them at once and to hold them in custody until
their lord Montezuma should be told the reason, namely, how
they had come to rob them and carry off their wives and
children as slaves and commit other violence. When the Caciques heard this they were thunderstruck at such daring.
What!—to order the messengers of the great Montezuma to be
maltreated? They said that they were too much afraid, and
did not dare to do it. But Cortés went on impressing on them
that the messengers should be thrown into prison at once, and
so it was done, and in such a way that with some long poles
and collars (such as are in use among them) they secured
them so that they could not escape, and they flogged one of
them who would not allow himself to be bound. Then Cortés
ordered all the Caciques to pay no more tribute or obedience
to Montezuma, and to make proclamation to that effect in all
their friendly and allied towns, and if any tax-gatherers came
to their other towns, to inform him of it, and he would send
for them. So the news was known throughout that province,
for the fat Cacique promptly sent messengers to spread the
tidings, and the chiefs who had come in company with the
tax-gatherers as soon as they had seen them taken prisoners,
noised it abroad, for each one returned to his own town to
deliver the order and relate what had happened.

When they witnessed deeds so marvellous and of such importance to themselves they said that no human beings would dare to do such things, and that it was the work of Teules, for so they call the idols which they worship, and for this reason from that time forth, they called us Teules, which, is as much as to say that we were either gods or demons.

I must go back and tell about the prisoners. It was the advice of all the Caciques that they should be sacrificed so that none of them could return to Mexico to tell the story; but when Cortés heard this he said that they should not be killed, and that he would take charge of them, and he set some of our soldiers to guard them. At midnight, Cortés sent for these soldiers who were in charge and said to them: "See to it that two of the prisoners are loosened, the two that appear to you the most intelligent, in such a way that the Indians of this town shall know nothing about it." And he told them to bring the prisoners to his lodging. When the prisoners came before him, he asked them through our interpreters, why they were prisoners and what country they came from, as though he knew nothing about them. They replied that the Caciques of Cempoala and of this town, with the aid of their followers and ours, had imprisoned them, and Cortés answered that he knew nothing about it, and was sorry for it, and he ordered food to be brought them and talked in a very friendly manner to them, and told them to return at once to their lord Montezuma, and tell him that we were all his good friends and entirely at his service, and that lest any harm should happen to them he had taken them from their prison, and had quarrelled with the Caciques who had seized them and that anything he could do to serve them he would do with the greatest good will, and that he would order the three Indians their companions who were still held prisoners to be freed and protected. That they two should go away at once and not turn back to be captured and killed.

The two prisoners replied that they valued his mercy and said they still had fear of falling into the hands of their enemies, as they were obliged to pass through their territory. So Cortés ordered six sailors to take them in a boat during the night a distance of four leagues and set them on friendly ground beyond the frontier of Cempoala. When the morning came and the Caciques of the town and the fat Cacique found that the two prisoners were missing they were all the more intent on sacrificing those that remained, if Cortés had not put it out of their power and pretended to be enraged at the loss of the two who had escaped. He ordered a chain to be brought from the ships and bound the prisoners to it, and then ordered them to be taken on board ship, saying that he himself would guard them, as such bad watch had been kept over the others. When they were once on board he ordered them to be freed from their chains and with friendly words he told them that he would soon send them back to Mexico.

Then all the Caciques of this town and of Cempoala, and all the other Totonac chiefs who had assembled, asked Cortés what was to be done, for all the force of the great Montezuma and of Mexico would descend upon them and they could not escape death and destruction.

Cortés replied with the most cheerful countenance that he and his brothers who were here with him would defend them and would kill anyone who wished to molest them. Then the Caciques and other townsmen vowed one and all that they would stand by us in everything we ordered them to do and would join their forces with ours against Montezuma and all his allies. Then, in the presence of Diego de Godoy, the scribe, they pledged obedience to His Majesty and messengers were sent to relate all that had happened to the other towns in that province. And as they no longer paid any tribute and no more tax-gatherers appeared there was no end to the rejoicing at being rid of that tyranny.

† xxxiii

As soon as we had made this federation and friendship with more than twenty of the hill towns, known as the towns of the Totonacs, which at this time rebelled against the great Montezuma, and gave their allegiance to His Majesty, and offered to serve us—we determined with their ready help at once to found the Villa Rica de la Vera Cruz on a plain half a league from this fortresslike town, called Quiahuitztlan, and we laid out plans of a church, market-place and arsenals, and all those things that are needed for a town, and we built a fort, and from the laying of the foundations until the walls were high enough to receive the woodwork, loopholes, watch-towers, and barbicans, we worked with the greatest haste.

Cortés himself was the first to set to work to carry out the earth and stone on his back, and to dig foundations, and all his captains and soldiers followed his example; and we kept on labouring without pause so as to finish the work quickly, some of us digging foundations and others building walls, carrying water, working in the lime kilns, making bricks and tiles, or seeking for food. Others worked at the timber, and the blacksmiths, for we had two blacksmiths with us, made nails. In this way we all laboured without ceasing, from the highest to the lowest; the Indians helping us, so that the church and some of the houses were soon built and the fort almost finished.

While we were thus at work it seems that the great Monte-zuma heard the news in Mexico about the capture of his tax-gatherers and the rebellion against his rule, and how the Totonac towns had withdrawn their allegiance and risen in revolt. He showed much anger against Cortés and all of us, and had already ordered a great army of warriors to make war on the people who had rebelled against him, and not to leave a single one of them alive. He was also getting ready to come against us with a great army with many companies.

Just at this moment there arrived two Indian prisoners whom Cortés had ordered to be set free, and when Montezuma knew that it was Cortés who had taken them out of prison, and had sent them to Mexico—and when he heard the words and promises which he had sent them to report, it pleased our Lord God that his anger was appeased, and he resolved to send and gather news of us. For this purpose he despatched his two young nephews under the charge of four old men who were Caciques of high rank, and sent with them a present of gold and cloth, and told his messengers to give thanks to Cortés for freeing his servants.

On the other hand, he sent many complaints saying that it was owing to our protection that those towns had dared to commit such a great treason as to refuse to pay him tribute and to renounce their allegiance to him, and that now, having respect for what he knew to be true—that we were those whom his ancestors had foretold were to come to their country, and must therefore be of his own lineage, how was it that we were living in the houses of these traitors? He did not at once send to destroy them, but the time would come when they would not brag of such acts of treason.

Cortés accepted the gold and the cloth, which was worth more than two thousand dollars, and he embraced the envoys and gave as an excuse that he and all of us were very good friends of the Lord Montezuma, and that it was as his servant that he still kept guard over the three tax-gatherers, and he sent at once to have them brought from the ships—where they had been well treated and well clothed, and he delivered them up to the messengers.

Then Cortés, on his part, complained greatly of Montezuma, and told the envoys how the Governor, Pitalpitoque, had left the camp one night without giving him notice, which was not well done and that he believed and felt certain that the Lord Montezuma had not authorized any such meanness, and that it was on account of this that we had come to these towns where we were now residing and where we had been well treated by the inhabitants. And he prayed him to pardon the disrespect of which the people had been guilty. As to what he said about the people no longer paying tribute, they could not serve two masters and during the time we had been there they had rendered service to us in the name of our Lord and King; but as he, Cortés, and all his brethren were on their way to visit him, and place themselves at his service, that when we were once there, then his commands would be attended to.

When this conversation and more of the same nature was over, Cortés ordered blue and green glass beads to be given to the two youths, who were Caciques of high rank, and to the four old men who had come in charge of them, who were also chieftains of importance, and paid them every sign of honour. And as there were some good meadows in the neighbourhood, Cortés ordered Pedro de Alvarado who had a good and very handy sorrel mare, and some of the other horsemen, to gallop and skirmish before the Caciques, who were delighted at the sight of their galloping, and they then took leave of Cortés and of all of us well contented, and returned to Mexico.

About this time Cortés' horse died, and he bought or was given another called "El Arriero," a dark chestnut which belonged to Ortiz, the musician, and Bartolomé García, the miner; it was one of the best of the horses that came in the fleet.

I must stop talking about this, and relate that as these towns of the sierra, our allies, and the town of Cempoala had hitherto been very much afraid of the Mexicans, believing that the great Montezuma would send his great army of warriors to destroy them, when they saw the kinsmen of the great Montezuma arriving with the presents I have mentioned, and paying such marked respect to Cortés and to all of us, they were fairly astounded and the Caciques said to one another that we must be Teules for Montezuma had fear of us, and had sent us presents of gold. If we already had reputation for valour, from this time forth it was greatly increased.

† xxxiv

As soon as the Mexican messengers had departed, the fat Cacique with many other friendly chieftains came to beg Cortés to go at once to a town named Cingapacinga,[1] two days' journey from Cempoala (that is about eight or nine leagues)—as there were many warriors of the Mexicans, assembled there, who were destroying their crops and plantations and were waylaying and ill-treating their vassals, and doing other injuries. Cortés believed the story as they told it so earnestly. He had promised that he would help them, and would destroy the Culuas and other Indians who might annoy them, and noting with what importunity they pressed their complaints, he did not know what to answer them, unless it were to say that he would willingly go, or send some soldiers under one of us, to turn these Mexicans out. As he stood there thinking the matter over he said laughingly to some of us companions who were with him: "Do you know, gentlemen, that it seems to me that we have already gained a great reputation for valour throughout this country, and that from what they saw us do in the matter of Montezuma's tax-gatherers, the people here take us for gods or beings like their idols. I am thinking that so as to make them believe that one of us is enough to defeat those Indian warriors, their enemies, who they say are occupy-

[1] Not marked on the modern maps.

ing the town with the fortress, that we will send Heredia
against them." Now, this old man was a Biscayan musketeer
who had a bad twitch in his face, a big beard, a face covered
with scars, and was blind of one eye and lame of one leg.

Cortés sent for him and said: "Go with these Caciques to
the river which is a quarter of a league distant, and when you
get there, stop to drink and wash your hands, and fire a shot
from your musket, and then I will send to call you back. I
want this to be done because the people here think that we
are gods, or at least they have given us that name and reputation, and as you are ugly enough, they will believe that you
are an idol." Heredia did what he was told, for he was an intelligent and clever man who had been a soldier in Italy, and
Cortés sent for the fat Cacique and the other chieftains who
were waiting for his help and assistance, and said to them: "I
am sending this brother of mine with you to kill or expel
all the Culuas from this town you speak of, and to bring me
here as prisoners all who refuse to leave." The Caciques were
surprised when they heard this and did not know whether
to believe it or not, but seeing that Cortés never changed his
face, they believed that what he told them was true. So old
Heredia shouldered his musket and set out with them, and he
fired shots into the air as he went through the forest so that
the Indians might see and hear him. And the Caciques sent
word to the other towns that they were bringing along a
Teule to kill all the Mexicans who were in Cingapacinga. I tell
this story here merely as a laughable incident, and to show the
wiles of Cortés. When Cortés knew that Heredia had reached
the river that he had been told about, he sent in haste to call
him back, and when old Heredia and the Caciques had returned, he told them that on account of the good will he
bore them that he, Cortés himself, would go in person with
some of his brethren to afford them the help they needed and
visit the country and fortress; and he ordered them at once to
bring one hundred Indian carriers to transport the *tepusques,*
that is, the cannon, and they came early the next morning,
and we set out that same day with four hundred men and
fourteen horsemen, and crossbowmen and musketeers who
were all ready.

When the officers went to warn certain soldiers of the party
of Diego Velásquez to go with us, and those who had them

to bring their horses, they answered haughtily that they did not want to go on any expedition but back to their farms and estates in Cuba; that they had already lost enough through Cortés having enticed them from their homes, and that he had promised them on the sand dunes that whosoever might wish to leave, that he would give them permission to do so and a ship and stores for the voyage; and for that reason there were now seven soldiers all ready to return to Cuba. When Cortés heard this he sent to summon these men before him, and when he asked them why they were doing such a mean thing they replied somewhat indignantly and said that they wondered at his honour, with so few soldiers under his command, wishing to settle in a place where there were reported to be such thousands of Indians and such great towns; that as for themselves, they were invalids and could hardly crawl from one place to another, and that they wished to return to their homes and estates in Cuba, and they asked him to grant them leave to depart as he had promised that he would do. Cortés answered them gently that it was true that he had promised it, but that they were not doing their duty in deserting from their captain's flag. And then he ordered them to embark at once without delay and assigned a ship to them and ordered them to be furnished with cassava bread and a jar of oil and such other supplies as we possessed.

When these people were ready to set sail, all of us comrades, and the Alcaldes and Regidores of our town of Villa Rica, went and begged Cortés on no account to allow anyone to leave the country, for, in the interest of the service of our Lord God and His Majesty any person asking for such permission should be considered as deserving the punishment of death, in accordance with military law, as a deserter from his captain and his flag in time of war and peril, especially in this case, when, as they had stated, we were surrounded by such a great number of towns peopled by Indian warriors.

Cortés acted as though he wished to give them leave to depart, but in the end he revoked the permission and they remained baffled, and even ashamed of themselves.

† xxxv

We set out on our expedition to Cingapacinga and slept that
night at the town of Cempoala. Two thousand Indian warriors
divided into four commands, were all ready to accompany us,
and on the first day we marched five leagues in good order.
The next day, a little after dusk we arrived at some farms near
the town of Cingapacinga, and the natives of the town heard
the news of our coming. When we had already begun the
ascent to the fortress and houses which stood amid great cliffs
and crags, eight Indian chieftains and priests came out to meet
us peacefully and asked Cortés with tears, why he wished to
kill and destroy them when they had done nothing to deserve
it; that we had the reputation of doing good to all and of re-
lieving those who had been robbed, and we had imprisoned
the tax-gatherers of Montezuma; that these Cempoala Indians
who accompanied us were hostile to them on account of old
enmities over the land claims and boundaries, and under our
protection they had come to kill and rob them. It was true,
they said, that there was formerly a Mexican garrison in the
town, but that they had left for their own country a few days
earlier when they heard that we had taken the other tax-
gatherers prisoner, and they prayed us not to let the matter go
any further, but to grant them protection. When Cortés thoroughly understood what they had said through Doña Marina
and Aguilar, without delay he ordered Captain Pedro de
Alvarado, and the quartermaster Cristóbal de Olid, and all of
us comrades who were with him, to restrain the Indians of
Cempoala and prevent them from advancing; and this we did.
But although we made haste to stop them, they had already
begun to loot the farms. This made Cortés very angry and he
sent for the captains who had command of the Cempoala warriors, and with angry words and serious threats, he ordered
them to bring the Indian men and women and cloths and
poultry that they had stolen from the farms, and forbade any
Cempoala Indian to enter the town, and said that for having
lied and for having come under our protection merely to rob
and sacrifice their neighbours, they were deserving of death,
they should keep their eyes wide open in order that such a
thing did not happen again, otherwise he would not leave one

of them alive. Then the caciques and captains of the Cempoalans brought to Cortés everything they had seized, both Indian men and women and poultry, and he gave them all back to their owners and with a face full of wrath he turned to the Cempoalans and ordered them to retire and sleep in the fields—and this they did.

When the caciques and priests[1] of that town saw how just we were in our dealings and heard the affectionate words that Cortés spoke to them through our interpreters, including matters concerning our holy religion, which it was always our custom to explain, and his advice to them to give up human sacrifices and robbing one another, and the worship of their curséd Idols, and much other good counsel which he gave them, they showed such good will towards us that they at once sent to call together the people of the neighbouring towns, and all gave their fealty to His Majesty.

They soon began to utter many complaints against Montezuma just as the people of Cempoala had done. On the next morning Cortés sent to summon the captains and caciques of Cempoala, who were waiting in the fields to know what we should order them to do, and still in terror of Cortés on account of the lies they had told him. When they came before him he made them make friends with the people of the town, a pact which was never broken by any of them.

Then we set out for Cempoala by another road and passed through two towns friendly to Cingapacinga, where we rested, for the sun was very hot and we were wearied with carrying our arms on our backs. A soldier took two chickens from an Indian house in one of the towns, and Cortés who happened to see it, was so enraged at that soldier for stealing chickens in a friendly town before his very eyes that he immediately ordered a halter to be put around his neck, and he would have been hanged there if Pedro de Alvarado, who chanced to be near Cortés, had not cut the halter with his sword when the poor soldier was half dead.

When we had left those towns in peace and continued our march towards Cempoala, we met the fat cacique and other chiefs waiting for us in some huts with food, for although they were Indians, they saw and understood that justice is good and sacred, and that the words Cortés had spoken to them, that

[1] *Papas*.

we had come to right wrongs and abolish tyranny, were in conformity with what had happened on that expedition, and they were better affected towards us than ever before.

We slept the night in those huts, and all the caciques bore us company all the way to our quarters in their town. They were really anxious that we should not leave their country, as they were fearful that Montezuma would send his warriors against them, and they said to Cortés that as we were already their friends, they would like to have us for brothers, and that it would be well that we should take from their daughters, so as to have children by them; and to cement our friendship, they brought eight damsels, all of them daughters of caciques, and gave one of these cacicas, who was the niece of the fat cacique, to Cortés; and one who was the daughter of another great cacique was given to Alonzo Hernández Puertocarrero. All eight of them were clothed in the rich garments of the country, beautifully ornamented as is their custom. Each one of them had a golden collar around her neck and golden ear-rings in her ears, and they came accompanied by other Indian girls who were to serve as their maids. When the fat cacique presented them, he said to Cortés: "Tecle (which in their language means Lord)—these seven women are for your captains, and this one, who is my niece, is for you, and she is the señora of towns and vassals." Cortés received them with a cheerful countenance, and thanked the caciques for the gifts, but he said that before we could accept them and become brothers, they must get rid of those idols which they believed in and worshipped, and which kept them in darkness, and must no longer offer sacrifices to them, and that when he could see those cursed things thrown to the ground and an end put to sacrifices that then our bonds of brotherhood would be most firmly tied. He added that these damsels must become Christians before we could receive them. Every day we saw sacrificed before us three, four or five Indians whose hearts were offered to the idols and their blood plastered on the walls, and the feet, arms and legs of the victims were cut off and eaten, just as in our country we eat beef brought from the butchers. I even believe that they sell it by retail in the *tianguez* as they call their markets. Cortés told them that if they gave up these evil deeds and no longer practised them, not only would we be their friends, but we would make them lords over other provinces. All the caciques, priests and chiefs replied that it did not seem to them good to give up their idols and sacrifices and that these gods of theirs gave them health and good harvests and everything of which they had need.

When Cortés and all of us who had seen so many cruelties and infamies which I have mentioned heard that disrespectful answer, we could not stand it, and Cortés spoke to us about it and reminded us of certain good and holy doctrines and said: "How can we ever accomplish anything worth doing if for the honour of God we do not first abolish these sacrifices made to idols?" and he told us to be all ready to fight should the Indians try to prevent us; but even if it cost us our lives the idols must come to the ground that very day. We were all armed ready for a fight as it was ever our custom to be so, and Cortés told the caciques that the idols must be overthrown. When they saw that we were in earnest, the fat cacique and his captains told all the warriors to get ready to defend their idols, and when they saw that we intended to ascend a lofty *cue*—which stood high and was approached by many steps—the fat cacique and the other chieftains were beside themselves with fury and called out to Cortés to know why he wanted to destroy their idols, for if we dishonoured them and overthrew them, that they would all perish and we along with them. Cortés answered them in an angry tone, that he had already told them that they should offer no more sacrifices to those evil images; that our reason for removing them was that they should no longer be deluded, and that either they, themselves, must remove the idols at once, or we should throw them out and roll them down the steps, and he added that we were no longer their friends, but their mortal enemies, for he had given them good advice which they would not believe; besides he had seen their companies come armed for battle and he was angry with them and would make them pay for it by taking their lives.

When the Indians saw Cortés uttering these threats, and our interpreter Doña Marina knew well how to make them understood, and even threatened them with the power of Montezuma which might fall on them any day, out of fear of all this they replied that they were not worthy to approach their gods, and that if we wished to overthrow them it was not with their consent, but that we could overthrow them and do what we chose.

The words were hardly out of their mouths before more than fifty of us soldiers had clambered up [to the temple] and had thrown down their idols which came rolling down the steps shattered to pieces. The idols looked like fearsome dragons, as big as calves, and there were other figures half men and half great dogs of hideous appearance. When they saw their idols broken to pieces the caciques and priests who were with them wept and covered their eyes, and in the Totonac tongue they prayed their gods to pardon them, saying that the matter was no longer in their hands and they were not to blame, but these Teules who had overthrown them, and that they did not attack us on account of the fear of the Mexicans.

When this was over the captains of the Indian warriors who, as I have said, had come ready to attack us, began to prepare to shoot arrows at us, and when we saw this, we laid our hands on the fat cacique and the six priests and some other chiefs, and Cortés cried out that on the least sign of hostility they would all be killed. Then the fat cacique commanded his men to retire from our front and not attempt to fight.

† xxxvi

When the Caciques, priests, and chieftains were silenced, Cortés ordered all the idols which we had overthrown and broken to pieces to be taken out of sight and burned. Then eight priests who had charge of the idols came out of a chamber and carried them back to the house whence they had come, and burned them. These priests wore black cloaks like cassocks and long gowns reaching to their feet, and some had hoods like those worn by canons, and others had smaller hoods like those worn by Dominicans, and they wore their hair very long, down to the waist, with some even reaching down to the feet, covered with blood and so matted together that it could not be separated, and their ears were cut to pieces by way of sacrifice, and they stank like sulphur, and they had another bad smell like carrion, and as they said, and we learnt that it was true, these priests were the sons of chiefs and they abstained from women, and they fasted on certain days, and what I saw them eat was the pith of seeds of cotton when the cotton was being cleaned, but they may have eaten other things which I did not see.

Cortés made them a good speech through our interpreters, and told them that now we would treat them as brothers and would help them all we could against Montezuma and his Mexicans, and we had already sent to tell him not to make war on them or levy tribute, and that as now they were not to have any more idols in their lofty temples, he wished to leave with them a great lady who was the Mother of our Lord Jesus Christ whom we believe in and worship. He told them many things about our holy religion as well stated as only a priest could do it nowadays, so that it was listened to with good will. Then he ordered all the Indian masons in the town to bring plenty of lime so as to clean the place and clear away the blood which encrusted the cues and to clean them thoroughly. The next day when they were whitewashed, an altar was set up, and he told the people to adorn the altar with garlands and always keep the place swept and clean. He then ordered four of the priests to have their hair shorn, and to change their garments and clothe themselves in white, and always keep themselves clean, and he placed them in charge of the altar and of that sacred image of Our Lady. So that it should be well looked after, he left there as hermit one of our soldiers named Juan de Torres de Córdoba, who was old and lame. He ordered our carpenters to make a cross and place it on a stone support which we had already built and plastered over.

The next morning, mass was celebrated at the altar by Padre Fray Bartolomé de Olmedo, and then an order was given to fumigate the holy image of Our Lady and the sacred cross with the incense of the country, and we showed them how to make candles of the native wax and ordered these candles always to be kept burning on the altar, for up to that time they did not know how to use the wax. The most important chieftains of that town and of others who had come together, were present at the Mass.

At the same time the eight Indian damsels were brought to be made Christians, for they were still in the charge of their parents and uncles. And they were admonished about many things touching our holy religion and were then baptized. The niece of the fat Cacique was named Doña Catalina, and she was very ugly; she was led by the hand and given to Cortés who received her and tried to look pleased. The daughter of the great Cacique, Cuesco, was named Doña Francisca, she was very beautiful for an Indian, and Cortés gave her to Alonzo Hernández Puertocarrero. I cannot now recall to mind the names of the other six, but I know that Cortés gave them to different soldiers. When this had been done, we took leave of all the Caciques and chieftains, who from that time forward always showed us good will, especially when they saw that Cortés received their daughters and that we took them away with us, and after Cortés had repeated his promises of assistance against their enemies we set out for our town of Villa Rica.

† xxxvii

After we had finished our expedition and the people of Cempoala and Cingapacinga had been reconciled to one another, and had given their fealty to His Majesty, and all the other things that I have told about had happened, we returned to our settlement, and took with us certain chieftains from Cempoala. On the day of our arrival there came into port a ship from the Island of Cuba, under the command of Francisco de Saucedo.

At the same time there arrived Luis Marin (a man of great merit) and ten soldiers. Saucedo brought a horse, and Luis Marin a mare; and they brought from Cuba the news that the decree had reached Diego Velásquez from Spain giving him authority to trade and found settlements, at which his friends were greatly rejoiced, all the more when they learned that he had received his commission appointing him Adelantado of Cuba.

Being in that town without any plans beyond finishing the fort, for we were still at work on it, most of us soldiers suggested to Cortés to let the fort stand as it was, for a memorial (it was just ready to be roofed), for we had already been over three months in the country, and it seemed to us better to go and see what this great Montezuma might be like and to earn an honest living and make our fortune; but that before we started on our journey we should send out salutations to His Majesty the Emperor, and give him an account of all that had happened since we left the Island of Cuba. It also began to be debated whether we should send to His Majesty all the gold that we had received, both what we had got from barter, as well as the presents that Montezuma had sent us. Cortés replied that it was a very wise decision and that he had already talked to some of the gentlemen about it, and that as perchance in this matter of the gold there might be some soldiers who wished to keep their shares, and if it were divided up there would be very little to send, that for this reason he had appointed Diego de Ordás and Francisco de Montejo who were good men of business, to go from soldier to soldier among those whom it was suspected would demand their share of the gold, and say these words: "Sirs, you already know that we wish to send His Majesty a present of the gold which we have obtained here, and as it is the first [treasure] that we are sending from this land it ought to be much greater; it seems to us that we should all place at his service the portions that fall to our share. We gentlemen and soldiers who have here written our names have signed as not wishing to take anything, but to give it all voluntarily to His Majesty, so that he may bestow favours on us. If anyone wishes for his share it will not be refused him, but whoever renounces it let him do as we have all done, and sign here."

In this way they all signed to a man. When this was settled, Alonzo Hernández Puertocarrero and Francisco de Montejo were chosen as proctors to go to Spain, for Cortés had already given them over two thousand dollars to keep them in his interest. The best ship in the fleet was got ready, and two pilots were appointed, one of them being Anton de Alaminos, who knew the passage through the Bahama Channel, for he was the first man to sail through it, and fifteen sailors were told off, and a full supply of ship's stores given to them. When everything was ready, we agreed to write to tell His Majesty all that had happened. Cortés wrote on his own account, so he told us, an accurate narrative of the events, but we did not see his letter.

The Cabildo[1] wrote a letter jointly with ten of the soldiers from among those who wished to settle in the land and had

[1] Cabildo—Municipality, the alguaciles, etc., already mentioned.

appointed Cortés as their general, and the letter was drawn up with great accuracy so that nothing was omitted, and I put my signature to it; and besides these letters and narratives, all the captains and soldiers together wrote another letter.

Besides these narratives, we begged His Majesty until he be pleased to order otherwise, to grant the government to Hernando Cortés, with the greatest respect and humility as well as we were able and as was proper.

† xxxviii

Within four days of the departure of our proctors to present themselves before our Lord the Emperor, some of the friends and dependents of Diego Velásquez, named Pedro Escudero, Juan Cermeño, and Gonzalo de Umbria a pilot, and a priest named Juan Díaz, and certain sailors who called themselves Peñates,[1] who bore Cortés ill will, determined to seize a small ship and sail her to Cuba to give notice to Diego Velásquez and advise him how he might have an opportunity of capturing our proctors with all the gold and the messages. These men had already got their stores in the ship, and made other preparations, and the time being past midnight, were ready to embark, when one of them seems to have repented of his wish to return to Cuba, and went to report the matter to Cortés. When Cortés heard of it and learned how many there were and why they wished to get away, and who had given counsel and held the threads of the plot, he ordered the sails, compass and rudder to be removed at once from the ship, and had the men arrested, and their confessions taken down. They all told the truth, and their confessions involved in their guilt others who were remaining with us, but Cortés kept this quiet at the time as there was no other course open to him. The sentence which Cortés delivered was that Pedro Escudero and Juan Cermeño should be hanged; that the pilot Gonzalo de Umbria, should have his feet cut off, and the sailors, Peñates, should receive two hundred lashes each, and Father Juan Díaz, but for the honour of the church, would have been punished as well; as it was he gave him a great fright. I remember that when Cortés signed that sentence, he said with great grief and

[1] *Peñates* = rockmen.

sighs: "Would that I did not know how to write, so as not to have to sign away men's lives!"

As soon as the sentence was carried out,[1] Cortés rode off at break-neck speed for Cempoala which was five leagues distant, and ordered two hundred of us soldiers, and all the horsemen to follow him.

Being in Cempoala, as I have stated, and discussing with Cortés questions of warfare, and our advance into the country, and going on from one thing to another, we, who were his friends, counselled him, although others opposed it, not to leave a single ship in the port, but to destroy them all at once, so as to leave no source of trouble behind, lest, when we were inland, others of our people should rebel like the last; besides, we should gain much additional strength from the masters, pilots and sailors who numbered nearly one hundred men, and they would be better employed helping us to watch and fight than remaining in port.

As far as I can make out, this matter of destroying the ships which we suggested to Cortés during our conversation, had already been decided on by him, but he wished it to appear as though it came from us, so that if any one should ask him to pay for the ships, he could say that he had acted on our advice and we would all be concerned in their payment. Then he sent Juan de Escalante to Villa Rica with orders to bring on shore all the anchors, cables, sails, and everything else on board which might prove useful, and then to destroy the ships and preserve nothing but the boats, and that the pilots, sailing masters and sailors, who were old and no use for war, should stay at the town, and with the two nets they possessed should undertake the fishing, for there was always fish in that harbour, although they were not very plentiful. Juan de Escalante did all that he was told to do, and soon after arrived at Cempoala with a company of sailors, whom he had brought from the ships, and some of them turned out to be very good soldiers.

When this was done, Cortés sent to summon all the Caciques of the hill towns who were allied to us and in rebellion against Montezuma, and told them how they must give their service to the Spaniards who remained in Villa Rica, to finish building the church, fortress and houses, and Cortés took Juan de

---

[1] As the signature of Juan Cermeño is attached to the letter written by the army in 1520, it looks as though the sentence was not executed.

Escalante by the hand before them all, and said to them: "This is my brother," and told them to do whatever he should order them, and that should they need protection or assistance against the Mexicans, they should go to him and he would come in person to their assistance.

All the Caciques willingly promised to do what might be asked of them, and I remember that they at once fumigated Juan de Escalante with incense, although he did not wish it done. Escalante was a man well qualified for any post and a great friend of Cortés, so he could place him in command of the town and harbour with confidence, so that if Diego Velásquez should send an expedition there, it would meet with resistance.

† xxxix

When the ships had been destroyed, with our full knowledge, one morning after we had heard mass, when all the captains and soldiers were assembled and were talking to Cortés about military matters, he begged us to listen to him, and argued with us as follows:

"We all understood what was the work that lay before us, and that with the help of our Lord Jesus Christ we must conquer in all battles and encounters [that fell to our lot], and must be as ready for them as was befitting, for if we were anywhere defeated, which pray God would not happen, we could not raise our heads again, as we were so few in numbers, and we could look for no help or assistance, but that which came from God, for we no longer possessed ships in which to return to Cuba, but must rely on our own good swords and stout hearts"—and he went on to draw many comparisons and relate the heroic deeds of the Romans. One and all we answered him that we would obey his orders, that the die was cast for good fortune, as Cæsar said when he crossed the Rubicon, and that we were all of us ready to serve God and the King. After this excellent speech, which was delivered with more honied words and greater eloquence than I can express here, Cortés at once sent for the fat Cacique and reminded him that he should treat the church and cross with great reverence and keep them clean; and he also told him that he meant to depart at once for Mexico to order Montezuma not to rob or offer human sacrifices, and that he now had need of two hundred Indian carriers to transport his artillery. He also asked fifty of the leading warriors to go with us. Just as we were ready to set out, a soldier, whom Cortés had sent to Villa Rica with orders for some of the men remaining there to join him, returned from the town bearing a letter from Juan de Escalante, saying that there was a ship sailing along the coast, and that he had made smoke signals and others, and he believed that they had seen his signals, but that they did not wish to come into the harbour, and that he had sent some Spaniards to watch to what place the ships should go, and they had reported that the ship had dropped anchor near the mouth of a river distant about three leagues, and that he wished to know what he should do.

When Cortés had read the letter he at once ordered Pedro de Alvarado to take charge of all his army at Cempoala and with him Gonzalo de Sandoval. This was the first time that Sandoval was given a command.

Then Cortés rode off at once in company with four horsemen, leaving orders for fifty of the most active soldiers to follow him, and he named those of us who were to form this company and that same night we arrived at Villa Rica.

When we reached Villa Rica, Juan de Escalante came to speak to Cortés and said that it would be as well to go to the ship that night, lest she should set sail and depart, and that he would go and do this with twenty soldiers while Cortés rested himself. Cortés replied that he could not rest, that "a lame goat must not nap," that he would go in person with the soldiers he had brought with him. So before we could get a mouthful of food we started to march along the coast and on the road we came on four Spaniards who had come to take possession of the land in the name of Francisco de Garay, the governor of Jamaica.

When Cortés heard this and knew that de Garay was staying behind in Jamaica and sending captains to do the work, he asked by what right and title those captains came. The four men replied that in the year 1518 as the fame of the lands we had discovered had spread throughout the Islands, that then

Garay had information that he could beg from His Majesty the right to all the country he could discover from the Rio San Pedro and San Pablo towards the north.

As Garay had friends at Court who could support his petition, he hoped to obtain their assistance, and he sent his Mayordomo to negotiate the matter, and this man brought back a commission for him as Adelantado and Governor of all the land he could discover north of the Rio San Pedro and San Pablo. Under this commission he at once despatched three ships with about two hundred and seventy soldiers and supplies and horses under the captain Alonzo Álvarez Pinedo, who was settling on the Rio Panuco, about seventy leagues away; and these Spaniards said that they were merely doing what their captain told them to do, and were in no way to blame.

When Cortés had learned their business he cajoled them with many flattering speeches and asked them whether we could capture the ship. Guillen de la Loa, who was the leader of the four men, answered that they could wave to the ship and do what they could, but although they shouted and waved their cloaks and made signals, they would not come near, for, as those men said, their captain knew that the soldiers of Cortés were in the neighbourhood and had warned them to keep clear of us.

When we saw that they would not send a boat, we understood that they must have seen us from the ship as we came along the coast, and that unless we could trick them they would not send the boat ashore again. Cortés asked the four men to take off their clothes so that four of our men could put them on, and when this was done we returned along the coast the way we had come so that our return could be seen from the ship and those on board might think that we had really gone away. Four of our soldiers remained behind wearing the other men's clothes, and we remained hidden in the wood with Cortés until past midnight, and then when the moon set it was dark enough to return to the mouth of the creek but we kept well hidden so that only the four soldiers could be seen. When the dawn broke the four soldiers began to wave their cloaks to the ship, and six sailors put off from her in a boat. Two of the sailors jumped ashore to fill two jugs with water, and we who were with Cortés kept in hiding waiting for the other sailors to land; but they stayed where they were and our four soldiers who were wearing the clothes of Garay's people pretended that they were washing their hands and kept their faces hidden. The men in the boat cried out: "Come on board, what are you doing? Why don't you come?" One of our men answered: "Come on shore for a minute and you will see." As they did not know his voice, they pushed off with their boat, and although we shouted to them they would answer nothing. We wanted to shoot at them with muskets and cross bows, but Cortés would not allow it, and said: "Let them go in peace and report to their captain."

So six soldiers from that ship remained in our company, the four we had first captured, and the two sailors who had come ashore. And we returned to Villa Rica without having had anything to eat since we first started.

Introductory Note

THE MARCH FROM CEMPOALA TO TLAXCALA

The Spaniards left Cempoala on the 16th August and crossed the frontier into Tlaxcalan territory on the 31st August.

Bernal Díaz says that they reached Jalapa on the first day, but that is not probable. Between Jalapa and Ixtacmaxtitlan there is no name given by Bernal Díaz or Cortés which coincides with a name on the modern map, although the Socochima of the narrative is undoubtedly Xico Viejo, a few miles from the modern village of Xico. The ruins of Xico Viejo were recently visited by Dr J. W. Fewkes, who says that "the last half mile of the road is practically impassable for horses, and must be made on foot, justifying the statements of Gomara regarding the difficulties the horsemen of Cortés encountered in reaching the pueblo." (Twenty-fifth Annual Report, Bureau of American Ethnology, 1903–4.)

The Theuhixuacan mentioned by Gomara must be the Ixuacan of the modern map.

The Spaniards passed to the south of the great mountain mass of the Cofre de Perote (13,403 ft.) between that mountain and the snowcapped volcano of Orizaba (17,365 ft.) to the tableland of Tlaxcala.

There is a considerable rise between Cempoala and Jalapa, which stands at an elevation of 4,608 ft.

I am unable to ascertain the height of the pass between Perote and Orizaba, but it probably exceeds 10,000 ft., followed by a descent of about

3,000 ft. to the plains of Tlaxcala and Puebla which are 7,000 ft. to 8,000 ft. above sea level.

According to Bernal Díaz, the most difficult pass (Puerto de Nombre de Dios) was crossed before reaching the main divide.

After the passage between the mountains the Spaniards came to the salt lakes, marshes, and inhospitable stretches of sand and volcanic ash which extend along the western slope of the Cofre de Perote.

It is impossible to locate the exact route between the mountain pass and Zocotlan, as no names are given and part of the country is uninhabitable. Zocotlan itself was in all probability the Zautla of the modern map, but we are not on secure ground until the Spaniards reach Ixtacmaxtitlan, near the Tlaxcalan frontier. This frontier is still marked by the ruins of the wall built by the Tlaxcalans as a defence against their enemies, but the ruins are not marked on the Government map. However, the natural line of travel would be up stream from Ixtacmaxtitlan, and this would bring us to a place marked on the map Altlatlaya (no doubt *Atalaya*, which means *a watch tower*), and I have taken this to be the spot where the Spaniards passed the wall.

The march from Jalapa to Zocotlan must have been a most arduous one, and all the more difficult from the fact that it was undertaken in the middle of the rainy season. There is a much easier, although somewhat longer, route passing round the north of Cofre de Perote, but this was probably avoided by the Cempoalans as passing through too much of the enemies' country.

Appended is an Itinerary, with dates compiled from the writings of Bernal Díaz,[1] Cortés,[2] Gomara,[3] and Andrés de Tápia,[4] with the modern spelling of some of the names taken from Padre Augustin Rivera.[5]

AUGUST.

16. Leave Cempoala.

17.

18. Jalapa.

19. Xico (modern map), Cocochima (B. D.), Sienchimalen (C.), Sienchimatl (G.), Xicochimilco (R.).

20. A high pass and Tejutla (B. D.), Puerto de Nombre de Dios and Ceyconacan (C.), Theuhixuacan (G.), Ceycoccnacan, now Ishua-

[1] (B. D.)
[2] (C.)
[3] (G.)
[4] (T.)
[5] (R.)

†   XL

When our departure for Mexico had received full consideration, we sought advice as to the road we should take, and the chieftains of Cempoala were agreed that the best and most convenient road was through the province of Tlaxcala, for the Tlaxcalans were their allies and mortal enemies of the Mexicans.

Forty chieftains, all warriors, were already prepared to accompany us and were of great assistance to us on that journey; and they provided us as well with two hundred carriers to transport our artillery. We poor soldiers had no need of help, for at that time we had nothing to carry except our arms, lances, muskets, crossbows, shields, and the like, with which we both marched and slept, and we were shod with hempen shoes, and were always prepared for a fight.

In the middle of August, 1519, we set out from Cempoala, keeping always in good formation, with scouts and some of the most active soldiers in advance.

The first day we marched towards a town named Jalapa, and thence to Socochima, a strong place with a difficult approach, and inside there were many vines of the grapes of the country[1] on trellises. In both these towns, through our interpreters, all matters touching our holy religion were explained to the people, and that we were the vassals of the Emperor Don Carlos, who had sent us to put an end to human sacrifices and robbery. As they were friends of the Cempoalans and did not pay tribute to Montezuma, we found them very well disposed towards us, and they provided us with food. A cross was erected in each town and its meaning was explained to them and they were told to hold it in great reverence.

Beyond Socochima we crossed some high mountain ranges by a pass, and arrived at another town named Texutla, where we were also well received, for like the others they paid no tribute to Mexico. On leaving that town we finished the ascent of the mountains and entered an uninhabited country, and it was very cold and hail and rain fell that night. There was a great scarcity of food and a wind came down from the snowy hills on one side of us which made us shiver with cold. As we had come from the coast, which is very hot, and had nothing with which to cover ourselves, only our armour, we suffered from the frost, for we were not accustomed to a different temperature.

Then we entered another pass where there were some hamlets and large temples with idols, and they had great piles of firewood for the service of the idols which were kept in those temples; but still there was nothing to eat, and the cold was intense.

We next entered into the land belonging to the town of Xocotlan, and we sent two Cempoala Indians to advise the Cacique how we were faring so that the people might receive us favourably. This town was subject to Mexico so we always marched on the alert and in good order for we could see that

[1] These were probably *grenadillas*, the fruit of passion-flowers.

we were already in a different sort of country, and when we saw the white gleam of the roof tops and the houses of the Caciques and the cues and numerous oratories, which were very lofty and covered with white plaster, they looked very pleasing like a town in our own Spain, so we called the place Castil-blanco, and so it is called to this day. And when, through our messengers, they knew that we were approaching, the Cacique and other chieftains came out to meet us close by their houses. The name of the Cacique was Olintecle, and he conducted us to some lodgings and gave us food, but there was very little of it and it was given with ill will.

As soon as we had eaten, Cortés asked through our interpreters about their Lord Montezuma. The chief told us of his great strength in warriors, which he kept in all the provinces under his sway, without counting many other armies which were posted on the frontiers and in neighbouring provinces, and he [the chief] then spoke of the great fortress of Mexico, and how the houses were built in the water, and how one can only pass from one house to another by means of bridges, or canoes; and how all the houses have flat roofs, which, by raising breastworks when they are needed, can be turned into fortresses. That the city is entered by three causeways, each causeway having four or five openings in it through which the water can flow from one part to another, and each opening has a wooden bridge over it so that when any one of those bridges is raised no one can enter the city of Mexico. Then the chief told us of the great store of gold and silver, and chalchihuite stones and other riches which Montezuma, his lord, possessed, and he never ceased telling us how great a lord he was, so that Cortés and all of us marvelled at hearing him. The more he told us about the great fortress and bridges, of such stuff are we Spanish soldiers made, the more we wanted to try our luck against them, although it seemed a hopeless enterprise, judging from what Olintecle explained and told us. In reality Mexico was much stronger and had better munitions and defences than anything he told us about, for it is one thing to have seen the place itself and its strength, and quite another thing to describe it as I do. He added that Montezuma was so great a prince that he placed anything he chose under his rule, and that he did not know if he would be pleased when he heard of our stay in that town, and that we had been given lodgings and food without his permission.

Cortés replied through our interpreters:—"I would have you know that we have come from distant lands at the order of our lord and King, who has many and great princes as his vassals, and he sends us to command your great Prince Montezuma not to sacrifice or kill any more Indians, or to rob his vassals, or to seize any more lands, but to give his fealty to our lord the King. And now I say the same to you, Olintecle, and to all the other Caciques who are with you, desist from your sacrifices, and no longer eat the flesh of your own relations, and the other evil customs which you practise, for such is the will of our Lord God, whom we believe in and worship, the giver of life and death who will take us up to heaven." To all of which things they made no reply.

Cortés said to the soldiers who were present around him: "It seems to me, gentlemen, that there remains nothing for us to do but to set up a cross." But Padre Fray Bartolomé de Olmedo replied: "It seems to me, sir, that the time has not yet come to leave crosses in the charge of these people for they are somewhat shameless and without fear, and as they are vassals of Montezuma they may burn the crosses or do some other evil thing, and what you have said to them is enough until they know something more of our holy religion." So the matter was settled and no cross was set up. I will go on to say that we had with us a very large lurcher which belonged to Francisco de Lugo, which barked much of a night, and it seems that the Caciques of the town asked our friends whom we had brought from Cempoala, whether it was a tiger or a lion, or an animal with which to kill Indians, and they answered them: "They take it with them to kill anyone who annoys them."

They also asked what we did with the artillery we had brought with us, and the Cempoalans replied that with some stones which we put inside them we could kill anyone we wished to kill, and that the horses ran like deer and they would catch anyone we told them to run after. Then Olintecle said to the other chiefs: "Surely they must be Teules!" Our Indian friends replied: "So at last you have found it out! Take care not to do anything to annoy them, for they will know it at once; they even know one's thoughts. These Teules are those who captured the tax-gatherers of your great Montezuma and decreed that no more tribute should be paid throughout the sierras nor in our town of Cempoala; and they are the same who turned our Teules out of their temples and replaced them with their own gods and who have conquered the people of Tabasco and Champoton, and they are so good that they have made friendship between us and the people of Cingapacinga. In addition to this you have seen how the great Montezuma, notwithstanding all his power, has sent them gold and cloth, and now they have come to your town and we see that you have given them nothing—run at once and bring them a present!"

It seems that we had brought good advocates with us, for the townspeople soon brought us four pendants, and three necklaces, and some lizards, all made of gold, but all the gold was of poor quality; and they brought us four Indian women who were good for grinding maize for bread, and one load of cloth. Cortés received these things with a cheerful good will and with many expressions of thanks.

I remember that in the plaza where some of their oratories stood, there were piles of human skulls so regularly arranged that one could count them, and I estimated them at more than a hundred thousand. I repeat again that there were more than one hundred thousand of them. And in another part of the plaza there were so many piles of dead men's thigh bones that one could not count them; there was also a large number of skulls strung between beams of wood, and three priests who had charge of these bones and skulls were guarding them. We had occasion to see many such things later on as we penetrated into the country for the same custom was observed in all the towns, including those of Tlaxcala.

After all that I have related had happened, we determined to set out on the road to Tlaxcala which our friends told us was very near, and that the boundary was close by where some boundary stones were placed to mark it. So we asked the Cacique Olintecle, which was the best and most level road to Mexico, and he replied the road which passed by the large town named Cholula, and the Cempoalans said to Cortés: "Sir, do not go by Cholula for the people there are treacherous, and Montezuma always keeps a large garrison of warriors in that town"; and they advised us to go by way of Tlaxcala where the people were their friends and enemies of the Mexicans. So we agreed to take the advice of the Cempoalans, trusting that God would direct us.

Cortés demanded of Olintecle twenty warrior chiefs to go with us, and he gave them at once. The next morning we set out for Tlaxcala and arrived at a little town belonging to the people of Xalacingo.

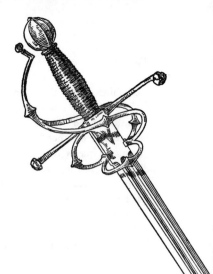

III

The War in Tlaxcala

Introductory Note

Between the 31st August when the Spaniards crossed the Tlaxcalan frontier and fought a skirmish with some Otomi-Tlaxcalan troops, and the 23rd September when they entered the Capital of Tlaxcala, only two dates are mentioned by Bernal Díaz. He gives the 2nd September (Gomara says the 1st September) as the date of the first great battle against the Tlaxcalan army under Xicotenga (Xicotencatl), and the name of the battlefield as Tehuacingo or Tehuacacingo, which cannot now be identified.

After the battle the Spaniards took shelter in a village with a temple on a hill; this hill is still pointed out by the natives as the site of Cortés' camp. Here the Spaniards formed a fortified camp, which continued to be their headquarters until the war was over, and they marched to the Capital of Tlaxcala.

Bernal Díaz tells us that this camp was near Cunpanzingo, probably the Tzompantzingo of the modern maps.

Bernal Díaz gives the 5th September as the date of the second great battle, which was fought close by the camp.

Although the accounts of the war in Tlaxcala given by Bernal Díaz and Cortés agree in the main points, they do not always give the events in the same order. It seems probable that Bernal Díaz places the night attack too early, and that it took place after Xicotenga had sent the spies to the Spanish camp.

The boundaries of the so-called Republic of Tlaxcala appear to have been almost identical with those of the modern state of the same name.

It has become a commonplace to describe the Tlaxcalans as hardy mountaineers and their form of Government as Republican, but such discrimination is misleading. Their country was no more mountainous than that of the Mexicans, and their form of Government was much the same as that of other Nahuá communities; but as they had achieved no foreign conquests, they were compelled to be self-supporting, and in that differed from the Mexicans, who were becoming a military caste, supported to a great extent by tribute from conquered tribes. Their country was fertile, and there must have been a large agricultural population, and all the men were inured to hardship and continual border warfare.

According to Andrés de Tápia the existence of the Tlaxcalans as an independent nation was owing to the forbearance of the Mexicans themselves, for when he asked why they had not been conquered, Montezuma himself answered: "We could easily do so, but then there would be nowhere for the young men to exercise themselves without going a long way off, and besides we always like to have people to sacrifice to our Gods."

† XLI

From the little town belonging to Xalacingo, where they gave us a golden necklace and some cloth and two Indian women, we sent two Cempoalan chieftains as messengers to Tlaxcala, with a letter, and a fluffy red Flemish hat, such as was then worn. We well knew that the Tlaxcalans could not read the letter, but we thought that when they saw paper different from their own, they would understand that it contained a message; and what we sent to them was that we were coming to their town, and hoped they would receive us well, as we came, not to do them harm, but to make them our friends. We did this because in this little town they assured us that the whole of Tlaxcala was up in arms against us, for it appears that they had already received news of our approach and that we were accompanied by many friends, both from Cempoala and Xocotlan, and other towns through which we had passed. As all these towns usually paid tribute to Montezuma, the Tlaxcalans took it for granted that we were coming to attack Tlaxcala, as their country had often been entered by craft and cunning and then laid waste, and they thought that this was another attempt to do so. So as soon as our two messengers arrived with the letter and the hat and began to deliver their message, they were seized as prisoners before their story was finished, and we waited all that day and the next for an answer and none arrived.

Then Cortés addressed the chiefs of the town where we had halted, and repeated all he was accustomed to tell the Indians about our holy religion, and many other things which we usually repeated in most of the towns we passed through, and after making them many promises of assistance, he asked for twenty Indian warriors of quality to accompany us on our march, and they were given us most willingly.

After commending ourselves to God, with a happy confidence we set out on the following day for Tlaxcala, and as we were marching along, we met our two messengers who had been taken prisoner. It seems that the Indians who guarded them were perplexed by the warlike preparations and had been careless of their charge, and in fact, had let them out of prison. They arrived in such a state of terror at what they had seen and heard that they could hardly succeed in expressing themselves.

According to their account, when they were prisoners the Tlaxcalans had threatened them, saying: "Now we are going to kill those whom you call Teules, and eat their flesh, and we will see whether they are as valiant as you announce; and we shall eat your flesh too, you who come here with treasons and lies from that traitor Montezuma!"—and for all that the messengers could say, that we were against the Mexicans, and wished to be brothers to the Tlaxcalans, they could not persuade them of its truth.

When Cortés and all of us heard those haughty words, and learned how they were prepared for war, although it gave us matter for serious thought, we all cried: "If this is so, forward —and good luck to us!" We commended ourselves to God and marched on, the Alferez, Corral, unfurling our banner and carrying it before us, for the people of the little town where we had slept, as well as the Cempoalans assured us that the Tlaxcalans would come out to meet us and resist our entry into their country.

In this way we marched about two leagues, when we came upon a fortress strongly built of stone and lime and some other cement, so strong that with iron pickaxes it was difficult to demolish it and it was constructed in such a way both for offence and defence, that it would be very difficult to capture. We halted to examine it, and Cortés asked the Indians from Xocotlan for what purpose the fortress had been built in such a way. They replied that, as war was always going on between the people of Tlaxcala and their lord Montezuma, the Tlaxcalans had built this fort so strong the better to defend their towns, for we were already in their territory. We rested awhile and this, our entry into the land of Tlaxcala and the fortress, gave us plenty to think about. Cortés said: "Sirs, let us follow our banner which bears the sign of the holy cross, and through it we shall conquer!" Then one and all we answered him: "May good fortune attend our advance, for in God lies the true strength." So we began our march again in the order I have already noted.

We had not gone far when our scouts observed about thirty Indians who were spying. These spies wore devices and feather head-dresses, and when our scouts observed them they came back to give us notice. Cortés then ordered the same scouts to follow the spies, and to try and capture one of them without hurting them; and then he sent five more mounted men as a support, in case there should be an ambush. Then all our army hastened on, for our Indian friends who were with us said that there was sure to be a large body of warriors waiting in ambush.

When the thirty Indian spies saw the horsemen coming towards them, and beckoning to them with their hands, they would not wait for them to come up and capture one of them; furthermore, they defended themselves so well, that with their swords and lances they wounded some of the horses.

When our men saw how fiercely the Indians fought and that their horses were wounded, they were obliged to kill five of the Indians. As soon as this happened, a squadron of Tlaxcalans, more than three thousand strong, which was lying in ambush, fell on them all of a sudden, with great fury and began to shower arrows on our horsemen who were now all together; and they made a good fight with their arrows and fire-hardened darts, and did wonders with their two-handed swords. At this moment we came up with our artillery, muskets and crossbows, and little by little the Indians gave way, but they had kept their ranks and fought well for a considerable time.

In this encounter, they wounded four of our men and I think that one of them died of his wounds a few days later.

As it was now late the Tlaxcalans beat a retreat and we did not pursue them; they left about seventeen dead on the field, and many wounded. Where these skirmishes took place the ground was level and there were many houses and plantations of maize and magueys, which is the plant from which they make their wine.

We slept near a stream, and with the grease from a fat Indian whom we had killed and cut open, we dressed our wounds, for we had no oil, and we supped very well on some dogs which the Indians breed [for food] for all the houses were abandoned and the provisions carried off, and they had even taken the dogs with them, but these came back to their homes in the night, and there we captured them, and they proved good enough food.

All night we were on the alert with watches and patrols and scouts, and the horses bitted and saddled, in fear lest the Indians would attack us.

† XLII

The next day, as we marched on, two armies of warriors approached to give us battle. They numbered six thousand men and they came on us with loud shouts and the din of drums and trumpets, as they shot their arrows and hurled their darts and acted like brave warriors. Cortés ordered us to halt, and sent forward the three prisoners whom we had captured the day before, to tell them not to make war on us as we wished to treat them as brothers. He also told one of our soldiers, named Diego de Godoy, who was a royal notary, to watch what took place so that he could bear witness if it should be necessary, so that at some future time we should not have to answer for the deaths and damages which were likely to take place, for we begged them to keep the peace.

When the three prisoners whom we had sent forward began to speak to the Indians, it only increased their fury and they made such an attack on us that we could not endure it. Then Cortés shouted:—"Santiago—and at them!" and we attacked them with such impetuosity that we killed and wounded many of them with our fire and among them three captains. They then began to retire towards some ravines, where over forty thousand warriors and their captain general, named Xicotenga, were lying in ambush, all wearing a red and white device for that was the badge and livery of Xicotenga.

As there was broken ground there we could make no use of the horses, but by careful manœuvring we got past it, but the passage was very perilous for they made play with their good archery, and with their lances and broadswords did us much hurt, and the hail of stones from their slings was even more damaging. When we reached the level ground with our horsemen and artillery, we paid them back and slew many of them, but we did not dare to break our formation, for any soldier who left the ranks to follow some of the Indian captains and swordsmen was at once wounded and ran great danger. As the battle went on they surrounded us on all sides and we could do little or nothing. We dared not charge them, unless we charged all together, lest they should break up our formation; and if we did charge them, as I have said, there were twenty squadrons ready to resist us, and our lives were in great danger for they were so numerous they could have blinded us with handfuls of earth, if God in his great mercy had not succoured us.

While we found ourselves in this conflict among these great warriors and their fearful broadswords, we noticed that many of the strongest among them crowded together to lay hands on a horse. They set to work with a furious attack, laying hands on a good mare known to be very handy either for sport or for charging. The rider, Pedro de Moron, was a very good horseman, and as he charged with three other horsemen into the ranks of the enemy the Indians seized hold of his lance and he was not able to drag it away, and others gave him cuts with their broadswords, and wounded him badly, and then they slashed at the mare, and cut her head off at the neck so that it hung by the skin, and she fell dead. If his mounted companions had not come at once to his rescue they would also have finished killing Pedro de Moron. We might possibly have helped him with our whole battalion, but I repeat again that we hardly dared to move from one place to another for fear that they would finally rout us, and we could not move one way or another; it was all we could do to hold our own and prevent ourselves from being defeated. However, we rushed to the conflict around the mare and managed to save Moron from the hands of the enemy who were already dragging him off half dead, and we cut the mare's girths, so as not to leave the saddle behind. In that act of rescue, ten of our men were wounded and I remember that at the same time we killed four of the (Indian) captains, for we were advancing in close order and we did great execution with our swords. When this had happened, the enemy began to retire, carrying the mare with them, and they cut her in pieces to exhibit in all the towns of Tlaxcala, and we learnt afterwards that they made an offering to their idols of the horseshoes, of the Flemish felt hat, and the two letters which we had sent them offering peace.

We were a full hour fighting in the fray and our shots must have done the enemy much damage for they were so numerous and in such close formation, that each shot must have hit many of them. Horsemen, musketeers, crossbowmen, swordsmen and those who used lance and shield, one and all, we fought like men to save our lives and to do our duty, for we were certainly in the greatest danger in which we had ever found ourselves. Later on they told us that we killed many Indians in this battle, and among them eight of their leading captains, sons of the old Caciques who lived in their principal towns, and for this reason they drew off in good order. We did not attempt to follow them, and we were not sorry for it as we were so tired out we could hardly stand, and we stayed where we were in that little town. All the country round was thickly peopled, and they even have some houses underground like caves in which many of the Indians live.

The place where this battle took place is called Tehuacingo, and it was fought on the 2nd day of the month of September in the year 1519. When we saw that victory was ours, we gave thanks to God who had delivered us from such great danger.

From the field of battle we withdrew the whole force to some Cues which were strong and lofty like a fortress. We dressed the wounded men, who numbered fifteen, with the fat of an Indian. One man died of his wounds. We also doctored four or five horses which had received wounds, and we rested and supped very well that night, for we found a good supply of poultry and little dogs in the houses. And taking every precaution by posting spies, patrols and scouts, we rested until the next morning.

In that battle we captured fifteen Indians, two of them chieftains. There was one peculiarity that the Tlaxcalans showed in this and all the other battles—that was to carry off any Indian as soon as he was wounded so that we should not be able to see their dead.

† XLIII

As we felt weary after the battles we had fought, and many of the soldiers and horses were wounded and some died there, and it was necessary to repair the crossbows and replenish our stock of darts, we passed one day without doing anything worthy of mention. The following morning Cortés said that it would be as well for all the horsemen who were fit for work to scour the country, so that the Tlaxcalans should not think that we had given up fighting on account of the last battle, and that they should see that we meant to follow them up; and it was better for us to go out and attack them than for them to come and attack us and thus find out our weakness. As the country was level and thickly populated, we set out with seven horsemen and a few musketeers and crossbowmen and about two hundred soldiers and our Indian allies, leaving the camp as well guarded as was possible. In the houses and towns through which we passed, we captured about twenty Indian men and women without doing them any hurt, but our allies, who are a cruel people, burnt many of the houses and carried off much poultry and many dogs for food. When we returned to the camp which was not far off, Cortés set the prisoners free, after giving them something to eat, and Doña Marina and Aguilar spoke kindly to them and gave them beads and told them not to be so mad any longer, but to make peace with us, as we wished to help them and treat them as brothers. Then we also released the two prisoners who were chieftains and they were given another letter, and were to tell the high Caciques who lived in the town—which was the capital of all the towns of the province—that we had not come to do them any harm or to annoy them, but to pass through their country on our way to Mexico to speak to Montezuma. The two messengers went to Xicotenga's camp which was distant about two leagues, and when they gave him the letter and our message the reply that their captain Xicotenga gave them was, that we might go to his town where his father was living; that there peace would be made by satiating themselves on our flesh, and honour paid to his gods with our hearts and blood, and that we should see his answer the very next day.

When Cortés and all of us heard that haughty message, as we were already tired out with the battles and encounters we had passed through, we certainly did not think that things looked well. So Cortés flattered the messengers with soft words for it seemed that they had lost all fear, and ordered them to be given some strings of beads, as he wished to send them back as messengers of peace.

Cortés then learned from them more fully all about the Captain Xicotenga, and what forces he had with him. They told him that Xicotenga had many more men with him now than he had when he attacked us before, for he had five captains with him and each captain had brought ten thousand warriors. This was the way in which the count was made: Of the followers of Xicotenga who was blind from age—the father of the captain of the same name—ten thousand; of the followers of another great chief named Mase Escasi, another ten thousand; of the followers of another great chief named Chichimecatecle the same number; of another great Cacique, lord of Topeyanco, named Tecapacaneca, another ten thousand; and of another great chief named Guaxoban, another ten thousand; so that there were in all fifty thousand. That their banner and standard had been brought out, which was a white bird with the appearance of an ostrich, with wings outstretched, as though it wished to fly, and that each company had its device and uniform, for each Cacique had a different one, as do our dukes and counts in our own Castile.

All that I have here said we accepted as perfectly true, for certain Indians among those whom we had captured and who were released that day, related it very clearly, although they were not then believed. When we knew this, as we were but human and feared death, many of us, indeed the majority of us, confessed to the Padre de la Merced and to the priest, Juan

Díaz, who were occupied all night in hearing our repentance
and commending us to God and praying that He would pardon us and save us from defeat.

† XLIV

The next morning, the 5th September, 1519, we mustered the
horses. There was not one of the wounded men who did not
come forward to join the ranks and give as much help as he
could. The crossbowmen were warned to use the store of darts
very cautiously, some of them loading while the others were
shooting, and the musketeers were to act in the same way, and
the men with sword and shield were instructed to aim their
cuts and thrusts at the bowels [of their enemies] so that they
would not dare to come as close to us as they did before. With
our banner unfurled, and four of our comrades guarding the
standard-bearer, Corral, we set out from our camp. We had
not marched half a quarter of a league before we began to see
the fields crowded with warriors with great feather crests and
distinguishing devices, and to hear the blare of horns and trumpets.

All the plain was swarming with warriors and we stood four
hundred men in number, and of those many sick and wounded.
And we knew for certain that this time our foe came with the
determination to leave none of us alive excepting those who
would be sacrificed to their idols.

How they began to charge on us! What a hail of stones sped
from their slings! As for their bowmen, the javelins lay like corn
on the threshing floor; all of them barbed and fire-hardened,
which would pierce any armour and would reach the vitals
where there is no protection; the men with swords and shields
and other arms larger than swords, such as broadswords, and
lances, how they pressed on us and with what valour and what
mighty shouts and yells they charged upon us! The steady
bearing of our artillery, musketeers and crossbowmen, was indeed a help to us, and we did the enemy much damage, and
those of them who came close to us with their swords and
broadswords met with such sword play from us that they were
forced back and they did not close in on us so often as in the
last battle. The horsemen were so skilful and bore themselves

so valiantly that, after God who protected us, they were our bulwark. However, I saw that our troops were in considerable confusion, so that neither the shouts of Cortés nor the other captains availed to make them close up their ranks, and so many Indians charged down on us that it was only by a miracle of sword play that we could make them give way so that our ranks could be reformed. One thing only saved our lives, and that was that the enemy were so numerous and so crowded one on another that the shots wrought havoc among them, and in addition to this they were not well commanded, for all the captains with their forces could not come into action and from what we knew, since the last battle had been fought, there had been disputes and quarrels between the Captain Xicotenga and another captain the son of Chichimecatecle, over what the one had said to the other, that he had not fought well in the previous battle; to this the son of Chichimecatecle replied that he had fought better than Xicotenga, and was ready to prove it by personal combat. So in this battle Chichimecatecle and his men would not help Xicotenga, and we knew for a certainty that he had also called on the company of Huexotzinco to abstain from fighting. Besides this, ever since the last battle they were afraid of the horses and the musketry, and the swords and crossbows, and our hard fighting; above all was the mercy of God which gave us strength to endure. So Xicotenga was not obeyed by two of the commanders, and we were doing great damage to his men, for we were killing many of them, and this they tried to conceal; for as they were so numerous, whenever one of their men was wounded, they immediately bound him up and carried him off on their shoulders, so that in this battle, as in the last, we never saw a dead man.

The enemy were already losing heart, and knowing that the followers of the other two captains whom I have already named, would not come to their assistance, they began to give way. It seems that in that battle we had killed one very important captain, and the enemy began to retreat in good order, our horsemen following them at a hard gallop for a short distance, for they could not sit their horses for fatigue, and when we found ourselves free from that multitude of warriors, we gave thanks to God.

In this engagement, one soldier was killed, and sixty were

wounded, and all the horses were wounded as well. They gave me two wounds, one in the head with a stone, and one in the thigh with an arrow; but this did not prevent me from fighting, and keeping watch, and helping our soldiers, and all the soldiers who were wounded did the same; for if the wounds were not very dangerous, we had to fight and keep guard, wounded as we were, for few of us remained unwounded.

Then we returned to our camp, well contented, and giving thanks to God. We buried the dead in one of those houses which the Indians had built underground, so that the enemy should not see that we were mortals, but should believe that, as they said, we were Teules. We threw much earth over the top of the house, so that they should not smell the bodies, then we doctored all the wounded with the fat of an Indian. It was cold comfort to be even without salt or oil with which to cure the wounded. There was another want from which we suffered, and it was a severe one—and that was clothes with which to cover ourselves, for such a cold wind came from the snow mountains, that it made us shiver, for our lances and muskets and crossbows made a poor covering. That night we slept with more tranquillity than on the night before, when we had so much duty to do, with scouting, spies, watchmen and patrols.

† XLV

After the battle which I have described was over, in which we had captured three Indian chieftains, our Captain Cortés sent them at once in company with the two others who were in our camp and who had already been sent as messengers and ordered them to go to the Caciques of Tlaxcala and tell them that we begged them to make peace and to grant us a passage through their country on our way to Mexico, and to say that if they did not now come to terms, we would slay all their people, but that as we were well disposed towards them we had no desire to annoy them, unless they gave us reason to do so; and he said many flattering things to them so as to make friends of them, and the messengers then set out eagerly for the capital of Tlaxcala and gave their message to all the Caciques already mentioned by me whom they found gathered in council with many other elders and priests. They were very sorrowful both over the want of success in the war and at the death of those captains, their sons and relations, who had fallen in battle. As they were not very willing to listen to the message, they decided to summon all the soothsayers, priests, and those others called *Tacal naguas,* and they told them to find out from their witchcraft, charms, and lots what people we were, and if by giving us battle day and night without ceasing we could be conquered, and to say if we were Teules, as the people of Cempoala asserted, and to tell them what things we ate, and ordered them to look into all these matters with the greatest care.

When the soothsayers and wizards and many priests had got together and made their prophecies and forecasts, and performed all the other rites according to their use, it seems that they said that by their divinations they had found out we were men of flesh and blood and ate poultry and dogs and bread and fruit, when we had them, and that we did not eat the flesh nor the hearts of the Indians whom we killed. It seems that our Indian friends whom we had brought from Cempoala had made them believe that we were Teules, and that we ate the hearts of Indians, and that the cannon shot forth lightning, such as falls from heaven and that the Lurcher, which was a sort of lion or tiger, and the horses, were used to catch Indians when we wanted to kill them, and much more nonsense of the same sort.

The worst of all that the priests and wizards told the Caciques was, that it was not during the day, but only at night that we could be defeated, for as night fell, all our strength left us. When the Caciques heard this, and they were quite convinced of it, they sent to tell their captain general Xicotenga that as soon as it was possible he should come and attack us in great force by night. On receiving this order Xicotenga assembled ten thousand of the bravest of his Indians and came to our camp, and from three sides they began alternately to shoot arrows and throw single pointed javelins from their spear throwers, and from the fourth side the swordsmen and those armed with macanas and broadswords approached so suddenly that they felt sure that they would carry some of us off to be sacrificed. Our Lord God provided otherwise, for secretly as they approached, they found us well on the alert, and as soon as our outposts and spies perceived the great noise of their movement, they ran at breakneck speed to give the alarm, and as we were all accustomed to sleep ready shod, with our arms on us and our horses bitted and saddled, and with all our arms ready for use, we defended ourselves with guns, crossbows and sword play so that they soon turned their backs. As the ground was level and there was a moon the horsemen followed them a little way, and in the morning we found lying on the plain about twenty of them dead and wounded. So they went back with great loss and sorely repenting this night expedition, and I have heard it said, that as what the priests and wizards had advised did not turn out well they sacrificed two of them.

That night, one of our Indian friends from Cempoala was killed and two of our soldiers were wounded and one horse, and we captured four of the enemy. When we found that we had escaped from that impetuous attack we gave thanks to God, and we buried our Cempoala friend and tended the wounded and the horse, and slept the rest of the night after taking every precaution to protect the camp as was our custom.

When we awoke and saw how all of us were wounded, even with two or three wounds, and how weary we were and how others were sick and clothed in rags, and knew that Xicotenga was always after us, and already over forty-five of our soldiers had been killed in battle, or succumbed to disease and chills, and another dozen of them were ill, and our Captain Cortés himself was suffering from fever as well as the Padre de la Merced, and what with our labours and the weight of our arms which we always carried on our backs, and other hardships from chills and the want of salt, for we could never find any to eat, we began to wonder what would be the outcome of all this fighting, and what we should do and where we should go when it was finished. To march into Mexico we thought too arduous an undertaking because of its great armies, and we said to one another that if those Tlaxcalans, which our Cempoalan friends had led us to believe were peacefully disposed, could reduce us to these straits, what would happen when we found ourselves at war with the great forces of Montezuma? In addition to this we had heard nothing from the Spaniards whom we had left settled in Villa Rica, nor they of us. As there were among us very excellent gentlemen and soldiers, steady and valiant men of good counsel, Cortés never said or did anything [important] without first asking advice, and acting in concert with us.

One and all we put heart into Cortés, and told him that he must get well again and reckon upon us, and that as with the help of God we had escaped from such perilous battles, our Lord Jesus Christ must have preserved us for some good end; that he [Cortés] should at once set our prisoners free and send them to the head Caciques, so as to bring them to peace, when all that had taken place would be pardoned, including the death of the mare.

Let us leave this and say how Doña Marina who, although a native woman, possessed such manly valour that, although she had heard every day how the Indians were going to kill us and eat our flesh with chili, and had seen us surrounded in the late battles, and knew that all of us were wounded and sick, yet never allowed us to see any sign of fear in her, only a courage passing that of woman. So Doña Marina and Jerónimo de Aguilar spoke to the messengers whom we were now sending and told them that they must come and make peace at once, and that if it was not concluded within two days we should go and kill them all and destroy their country and would come to seek them in their city, and with these brave words they were despatched to the capital where Xicotenga the elder and Mase Escasi were residing.

† XLVI

When the messengers arrived at Tlaxcala, they found the two principal Caciques in consultation, namely: Mase Escasi and Xicotenga, the elder (the father of the Captain General Xicotenga). When they had heard the embassy, they were undecided and kept silence for a few moments, and it pleased God to guide their thoughts towards making peace with us; and they sent at once to summon all the other Caciques and captains who were in their towns, and those of a neighbouring province called Huexotzingo who were their friends and allies, and when all had come together Mase Escasi and Xicotenga, the elder, who were very wise men, made them a speech, as we afterwards learned, to the following effect, if not exactly in these words:

"Brothers and friends, you have already seen how many times these Teules who are in this country expecting to be attacked, have sent us messengers asking us to make peace, saying that they come to assist us and adopt us as brothers; and you have also seen how many times they have taken prisoners numbers of our vassals to whom they do no harm, and whom they quickly set free. You well know how we have three times attacked them with all our forces, both by day and by night, and have failed to conquer them, and that they have killed during the attacks we made on them, many of our people, and of our sons, relations and captains. Now, again, they have sent to ask us to make peace and the people of Cempoala whom they are bringing in their company say that they are the enemies of Montezuma and his Mexicans, and have ordered the towns of the Totonac sierra and those of Cempoala no longer to pay tribute to Montezuma. You will remember well enough that the Mexicans make war on us every year, and have done so for more than a hundred years, and you can readily see that we are hemmed in in our own lands, so that we do not dare to go outside even to seek for salt, so that we have none to eat, and we have no cotton, and bring in very little cotton cloth, and if some of our people go out or have gone out to seek for it, few of them return alive, for those traitorous Mexicans and their allies kill them or make slaves of them. Our wizards[1] and soothsayers and priests have told us what they think about the persons of these Teules, and that they are very valiant. It seems to me that we should seek to be friends with them, and in either case, whether they be men or Teules, that we should make them welcome, and that four of our chieftains should set out at once and take them plenty to eat, and should offer them friendship and peace, so that they should assist us and defend us against our enemies, and let us bring them here to us, and give them women, so that we may have relationship with their offspring, for the ambassadors whom they have sent to treat for peace, tell us that they have some women with them."

When they had listened to this discourse, all the Caciques and chiefs approved of it and said that it was a wise decision and that peace should be made at once, and that notice should be sent to the Captain Xicotenga and the other captains who

[1] *Tacal naguas.*

were with him to return at once and not to attack again, and that they should be told that peace was already made, and messengers were immediately sent off to announce it. However, the Captain Xicotenga the younger would not listen to the four chiefs, and got very angry and used abusive language against them, and said he was not for peace, for he had already killed many of the Teules and a mare, and that he wished to attack us again by night and completely conquer us and slay us.

When his father, Xicotenga the elder, and Mase Escasi and the other Caciques heard this reply they were very angry and sent orders at once to the captains and to all the army that they should not join Xicotenga in attacking us again, and should not obey him in anything that he ordered unless it was in making peace. And even so he would not obey, and when they [the Caciques] saw the disobedience of their captain, they at once sent the same four chieftains whom they had sent before, to bring food to our camp and treat for peace in the name of all Tlaxcala and Huexotzingo, but, from fear of Xicotenga the younger, the four old men did not come at that time.

† XLVII

As two days had passed without our doing anything worthy of record, we suggested to Cortés, and it was agreed to, that as there was a town about one league distant from our camp, which had sent no reply when summoned to make peace, that we should march against it by night and take it by surprise, not with intent to do it any harm, I mean not to kill or wound its inhabitants, or take them prisoners, but to carry off food and to frighten or talk them into making peace, according to the way they might act.

This town was called Tzumpantzingo, and was the capital of many other small towns, and the township where our camp was placed was subject to it, and all round about it was thickly peopled.

So one night, long before the approach of dawn, we rose early to go to that town with six of the best horsemen and the healthiest of the soldiers and ten crossbowmen and eight musketeers, with Cortés as our captain, although he was suffering

from tertian fever, and we left the camp as well guarded as
was possible. We started on our march two hours before dawn
came, and there was such a cold wind that morning blowing
down from the snowy mountains that it made us shiver and
shake, and the horses we had with us felt it keenly, for two of
them were seized with colic and were trembling all over,
which worried us a good deal as we feared that they would
die. Cortés ordered their owners to take them back to the
camp and try to cure them.

As the town was not far off we arrived there before daylight,
and when the natives perceived our approach, they fled from
their houses shouting to one another to look out for the Teules
who were coming to kill them, and the parents, in their panic,
did not even wait to look after their children. When we saw
what was happening, we halted in a court until it was daylight, so as not to do the people any harm. As soon as the
priests who were in the temples, the elders of the town and
some of the old chieftains saw that we stood there without doing any harm, they came to Cortés and asked his pardon for
not coming to our camp peacefully and bringing food when we
had summoned them to do so, the reason being that the captain Xicotenga, who was in the neighbourhood, had sent to
them to say that they should not give us any, because his camp
was supplied from that town and from many others, and he had
with him as warriors the sons of the people of that town and
from all the territory of Tlaxcala. Cortés told them through
Doña Marina and Aguilar, who always went with us on every
expedition—even when it took place at night—to have no fear,
but to go at once to the Caciques at the capital and tell them
to come and make peace, for the war was disastrous to them,
and he [Cortés] sent those [same] priests [as messengers], for,
by the other messengers whom we had sent we had so far received no reply whatever.

These priests of the town quickly searched for more than
forty cocks and hens and two women to grind tortillas, and
brought them to us, and Cortés thanked them for it, and ordered them at once to send twenty Indians to our camp, and
they came with the food without any fear whatever and stayed
in the camp until the afternoon, and they were given little
beads with which they returned well contented to their homes,

and in all the small hamlets in our neighbourhood they spread word that we were good because we caused them no annoyance, and the priests and elders sent notice to the captain Xicotenga and told him how they had given us the food and the women, and he rated them severely, and they went at once to the capital to make it known to the old Caciques. As soon as they heard that we had not done the people any harm, although we might have killed many of them that night, and that we were sending them to treat for peace, they were greatly pleased, and ordered that we should be supplied every day with all that we needed; and they again ordered the four Caciques, whom they had before charged with the mission of peace, to depart instantly for our camp, and carry with them all the food that had been prepared. We then returned to our camp with our supplies of food and the Indian women, all of us well contented.

However, on our return, we found that there had been meetings and discussions in camp about the very great danger we were running day by day during this war, and on our arrival the discussion grew most lively. Those who talked most and were most persistent, were those who had left houses and assignments of Indians behind them in Cuba, and as many as seven of these men (whose names I will not mention so as to save their honour) met together and went to the hut where Cortés was lodging, and one of them who spoke for all, for he was very fluent of speech and knew very well what they had come to propose, said, as though he were giving advice to Cortés, that if he should wish to preserve his life and the lives of us all, that we should at once return to Villa Rica as the country there was at peace; that we ought not to wait for another battle like the last; and they said more to the same effect.

Cortés noticing that they spoke somewhat haughtily, considering that their words took the form of unasked advice, answered them very gently.

It is true enough that they grumbled at Cortés and cursed him, and even at us who had advised him, and at the Cempoalans who had brought us here, and said other unworthy things, but in such times they were overlooked. Finally all were fairly obedient.

† XLVIII

When Mase Escasi and Xicotenga the elder, and the greater
number of the Caciques of the capital of Tlaxcala sent four
times to tell their captain not to attack us but to go and treat
for peace, he was very close to our camp, and they sent to the
other captains who were with him and told them not to follow
him unless it was to accompany him when he went to see us
peacefully.

As Xicotenga was bad tempered and obstinate and proud,
he decided to send forty Indians with food, poultry, bread and
fruit and four miserable looking old Indian women, and much
copal and many parrots' feathers. From their appearance we
thought that the Indians who brought this present came with
peaceful intentions, and when they reached our camp they
fumigated Cortés with incense without doing him reverence, as
was usually their custom. They said: "The Captain Xicotenga
sends you all this so that you can eat. If you are savage Teules,
as the Cempoalans say you are, and if you wish for a sacrifice,
take these four women and sacrifice them and you can eat
their flesh and hearts, but as we do not know your manner of
doing it, we have not sacrificed them now before you; but if
you are men, eat the poultry and the bread and fruit, and if
you are tame Teules we have brought you copal and parrots'
feathers; make your sacrifice with that."

Cortés answered through our interpreters that he had already sent to them to say that he desired peace and had not
come to make war, but had come to entreat them and make
clear to them that they should not kill or sacrifice anyone as
was their custom to do. That we were all men of bone and
flesh just as they were, and not Teules but Christians, and that
it was not the custom to kill anyone; that had we wished to
kill people, many opportunities of perpetrating cruelties had
occurred during the frequent attacks they had made on us,
both by day and night. That for the food they had brought he
gave them thanks, and that they were not to be as foolish as
they had been, but should now make peace.

It seems that these Indians whom Xicotenga had sent with
the food were spies. They remained with us that day and the
following night, and some of them went with messages to Xico-

tenga and others arrived. Our friends from Cempoala were sure that they were spies, and were the more suspicious of them in that they had been told that Xicotenga was all ready with a large number of warriors to attack our camp by night, and the Cempoalans at that time took it for a joke or bravado, and not believing it they had said nothing to Cortés; but Doña Marina heard of it at once and she repeated it to Cortés.

So as to learn the truth, Cortés had two of the most honest looking of the Tlaxcalans taken apart from the others, and they confessed that they were spies; then two others were taken and they also confessed and added that their Captain Xicotenga was awaiting their report to attack us that night with all his companies. When Cortés heard this he let it be known throughout the camp that we were to keep on the alert. Then he had seventeen of those spies captured and cut off the hands of some and the thumbs of others and sent them to the Captain Xicotenga to tell him that he had had them thus punished for daring to come in such a way, and to tell him that he might come when he chose by day or by night, for we should await him here two days, and that if he did not come within those two days that we would go and look for him in his camp, and that we would already have gone to attack them and kill them, were it not for the liking we had for them, and that now they should quit their foolishness and make peace.

They say that it was at the very moment that those Indians set out with their hands and thumbs cut off, that Xicotenga wished to set out from his camp with all his forces to attack us by night as had been arranged; but when he saw his spies returning in this manner he wondered greatly and asked the reason of it, and they told him all that had happened, and from this time forward he lost his courage and pride, and in addition to this one of his commanders with whom he had wrangles and disagreements during the battles which had been fought, had left the camp with all his men.

† XLIX

While we were in camp and were busy polishing our arms and making arrows, each one of us doing what was necessary to prepare for battle, at that moment one of our scouts came hurrying in to say that many Indian men and women with loads were coming along the high road from Tlaxcala, and were making for our camp. Cortés and all of us were delighted at this news, for we believed that it meant peace, as in fact it did, and Cortés ordered us to make no display of alarm and not to show any concern, but to stay hidden in our huts. Then, from out of all those people who came bearing loads, the four chieftains advanced who were charged to treat for peace, according to the instructions given by the old Caciques. Making signs of peace by bowing the head, they came straight to the hut where Cortés was lodging and placed one hand on the ground and kissed the earth and three times made obeisance and burnt copal, and said that all the Caciques of Tlaxcala and their allies and vassals, friends and confederates, were come to place themselves under the friendship and peace of Cortés and of his brethren the Teules who accompanied him. They asked his pardon for not having met us peacefully, and for the war which they had waged on us, for they had believed and held for certain that we were friends of Montezuma and his Mexicans, who have been their mortal enemies from times long past, for they saw that many of his vassals who paid him tribute had come in our company, and they believed that they were endeavouring to gain an entry into their country by guile and treachery, as was their custom to do, so as to rob them of their women and children; and this was the reason why they did not believe the messengers whom we had sent to them; that now they came to beg pardon for their audacity, and had brought us food, and that every day they would bring more and trusted that we would receive it with the friendly feeling with which it was sent; that within two days the captain Xicotenga would come with other Caciques and give a further account of the sincere wish of all Tlaxcala to enjoy our friendship.

As soon as they had finished their discourse they bowed their heads and placed their hands on the ground and kissed the earth. Then Cortés spoke to them through our interpreters very seriously, pretending he was angry, and said that there were reasons why we should not listen to them and should reject their friendship, for as soon as we had entered their country we sent to them offering peace and had told them that we wished to assist them against their enemies, the Mexicans, and they would not believe it and wished to kill our ambassadors; and not content with that, they had attacked us three times both by day and by night, and had spied on us and held us under observation; and in the attacks which they made on us we might have killed many of their vassals, but he would not, and he grieved for those who were killed; but it was their own fault and he had made up his mind to go to the place where the old chiefs were living and to attack them; but as they had now sought peace in the name of that province, he would receive them in the name of our lord the King and thank them for the food they had brought. He told them to go at once to their chieftains and tell them to come or send to treat for peace with fuller powers, and that if they did not come we would go to their town and attack them.

He ordered them to be given some blue beads to be handed to their Caciques as a sign of peace, and he warned them that when they came to our camp it should be by day and not by night, lest we should kill them.

Then those four messengers departed, and left in some Indian houses a little apart from our camp, the Indian women whom they had brought to make bread, some poultry, and all the necessaries for service, and twenty Indians to bring wood and water. From now on they brought us plenty to eat, and when we saw this and believed that peace was a reality, we gave great thanks to God for it. It had come in the nick of time, for we were already lean and worn out and discontented with the war, not knowing or being able to forecast what would be the end of it.

As our Lord God, through his great loving kindness, was pleased to give us victory in those battles in Tlaxcala, our fame spread throughout the surrounding country, and reached the ears of the great Montezuma in the great City of Mexico; and if hitherto they took us for Teules, from now on they held us in even greater respect as valiant warriors, and terror fell on the whole country at learning how, being so few in number and the Tlaxcalans in such great force, we had conquered them and that they had sued us for peace. So that now Montezuma, the great Prince of Mexico, powerful as he was, was in fear of our going to his city, and sent five chieftains, men of much importance, to our camp at Tlaxcala to bid us welcome, and say that he was rejoiced at our great victory against so many squadrons of warriors, and he sent a present, a matter of a thousand dollars' worth of gold, in very rich jewelled ornaments, worked in various shapes, and twenty loads of fine cotton cloth, and he sent word that he wished to become the vassal of our great Emperor, and that he was pleased that we were already near his city, on account of the good will that he bore Cortés and all his brothers, the Teules, who were with him and that he [Cortés] should decide how much tribute he wished for every year for our great Emperor, and that he [Montezuma] would give it in gold and silver, cloth and chalchihuites, provided we would not come to Mexico. This was not because he would not receive us with the greatest willingness, but because the land was rough and sterile, and he would regret to see us undergo such hardships which perchance he might not be able to alleviate as well as he could wish. Cortés answered by saying that he highly appreciated the good will shown us, and the present which had been sent, and the offer to pay tribute to His Majesty, and he begged the messengers not to depart until he went to the capital of Tlaxcala, as he would despatch them from that place, for they could then see how that war ended.

† L

While Cortés was talking to the ambassadors of Montezuma, and he wanted to take some rest, for he was ill with fever, they came to tell him that the Captain Xicotenga was arriving with many other Caciques and Captains, all clothed in white and red cloaks, half of the cloak was white and the other half red, for this was the device and livery of Xicotenga [who was approaching] in a very peaceful manner, and was bringing with him in his company about fifty chieftains.

When Xicotenga reached Cortés' quarters he paid him the greatest respect by his obeisance, and ordered much copal to be burned. Cortés, with the greatest show of affection, seated him by his side and Xicotenga said that he came on behalf of his father and of Mase Escasi and all the Caciques, and Commonwealth of Tlaxcala to pray Cortés to admit them to our friendship, and that he came to render obedience to our King and Lord, and to ask pardon for having taken up arms and made war upon us. That this had been done because they did not know who we were, and they had taken it for certain that we had come on behalf of their enemy Montezuma, and for that reason had endeavoured to defend themselves and their country, and were obliged to show fight. He said that they were a very poor people who possessed neither gold, nor silver, nor precious stones, nor cotton cloth, nor even salt to eat, because Montezuma gave them no opportunity to go out and search for it, and that although their ancestors possessed some gold and precious stones, they had been given to Montezuma on former occasions when, to save themselves from destruction, they had made peace or a truce, and this had been in times long past; so that if they had nothing to give now, we must pardon them for it, for poverty and not the want of good will was the cause of it. He made many complaints of Montezuma and his allies who were all hostile to them and made war on them, but they had defended themselves very well. Now they had thought to do the same against us, but they could not do it although they had gathered against us three times with all their warriors, and we must be invincible, and when they found this out about our persons they wished to become friends with us and the vassals of the great prince the Emperor Don Carlos, for they felt sure that in our company they and their women and children would be guarded and protected, and would not live in dread of the Mexican traitors, and he said many other words placing themselves and their city at our disposal.

Xicotenga was tall, broad shouldered and well made; his face was long, pockmarked and coarse, he was about thirty-five years old and of a dignified deportment.

Cortés thanked him very courteously, in a most flattering manner, and said that he would accept them as vassals of our King and Lord, and as our own friends. Then Xicotenga begged us to come to his city, for all the Caciques, elders and priests were waiting to receive us with great rejoicing. Cortés replied that he would go there promptly, and would start at once, were it not for some negotiations which he was carrying on with the great Montezuma, and that he would come after he had despatched the messengers. Then Cortés spoke somewhat more sharply and severely about the attacks they had made on us both by day and night, adding that as it could not now be amended he would pardon it. Let them see to it that the peace we now were granting them was an enduring one, without any change, for otherwise he would kill them and destroy their city and that he [Xicotenga] should not expect further talk about peace, but only of war.

When Xicotenga and all the chieftains who had come with him heard these words they answered one and all, that the peace would be firm and true, and that to prove it they would all remain with us as hostages.

The Mexican Ambassadors were present during all these discussions and heard all the promises that were made, and the conclusion of peace weighed on them heavily, for they fully understood that it boded them no good. And when Xicotenga had taken his leave these Ambassadors of Montezuma half laughingly asked Cortés whether he believed any of those promises which were made on behalf of all Tlaxcala [alleging] that it was all a trick which deserved no credence, and the words were those of traitors and deceivers; that their object was to attack and kill us as soon as they had us within their city in a place where they could do so in safety; that we should bear in mind how often they had put forth all their strength to destroy us and had failed to do so, and had lost many killed and wounded, and that now they offered a sham peace so as to avenge themselves. Cortés answered them, with a brave face, that their alleged belief that such was the case did not trouble him, for even if it were true he would be glad of it so as to punish them [the Tlaxcalans] by taking their lives, that it did not matter to him whether they attacked him by day or by night, in the city or in the open, he did not mind one way or the other, and it was for the purpose of seeing whether they were telling the truth that he was determined to go to their city.

The Ambassadors seeing that he had made up his mind begged him to wait six days in our camp as they wished to send two of their companions with a message to their Lord Montezuma, and said that they would return with a reply within six days. To this Cortés agreed, on the one hand because, as I have said he was suffering from fever, and on the other because, although when the Ambassadors had made these statements he had appeared to attach no importance to them, he thought that there was a chance of their being true, and that until there was greater certainty of peace, they were of a nature requiring much consideration.

As at the time that this peace was made the towns all along the road that we had traversed from our Villa Rica de Vera Cruz were allied to us and friendly, Cortés wrote to Juan de Escalante who, as I have said, remained in the town to finish building the fort, and had under his command the sixty old or sick soldiers who had been left behind. In these letters he told them of the great mercies which our Lord Jesus Christ had vouchsafed to us in the victories which we had gained in our battles and encounters since we had entered the province of Tlaxcala, which had now sued for peace with us, and asked that all of them would give thanks to God for it. He also told them to see to it that they always kept on good terms with our friends in the towns of the Totonacs, and he told him to send at once two jars of wine which had been left behind, buried in a certain marked place in his lodgings, and some sacred wafers for the Mass, which had been brought from the Island of Cuba for those which we had brought on this expedition were already finished.

These letters were most welcome, and Escalante wrote in reply to say what had happened in the town, and all that was asked for arrived very quickly.

About this time we set up a tall and sumptuous cross in our camp, and Cortés ordered the Indians of Tzumpantzingo and those who dwelt in the houses near our camp to whitewash it, and it was beautifully finished.

I must cease writing about this and return to our new friends the Caciques of Tlaxcala, who when they saw that we did not go to their city, came themselves to our camp and brought poultry and tunas,[1] which were then in season, each one brought some of the food which he had in his house and gave it to us with the greatest good will without asking anything in return, and they always begged Cortés to come with them soon to their city. As we had promised to wait six days for the return of the Mexicans, Cortés put off the Tlaxcalans with fair speeches. When the time expired, according to their word, six chieftains, men of great importance, arrived from Mexico, and brought a rich present from the great Montezuma consisting of valuable gold jewels wrought in various shapes worth three

[1] *Tuna* = the prickly pear, the fruit of the *Nopal Cactus* (*Opuntia*).

thousand pesos in gold, and two hundred pieces of cloth, richly worked with feathers and other patterns. When they offered this present the Chieftains said to Cortés that their Lord Montezuma was delighted to hear of our success, but that he prayed him most earnestly on no account to go with the people of Tlaxcala to their town, nor to place any confidence in them, that they wished to get him there to rob him of his gold and cloth, for they were very poor, and did not possess a decent cotton cloak among them, and that the knowledge that Montezuma looked on us as friends, and was sending us gold and jewels and cloth, would still more induce the Tlaxcalans to rob us.

Cortés received the present with delight, and said that he thanked them for it, and would repay their Lord Montezuma with good works, and if he should perceive that the Tlaxcalans had that in mind against which Montezuma had sent them to warn him, they would pay for it by having all their lives taken, but he felt sure they would be guilty of no such villainy, and he still meant to go and see what they would do.

Cortés begged the Mexican Ambassadors to wait for three days for the reply to their prince, as he had at present to deliberate and decide about the past hostilities and the peace which was now offered, and the Ambassadors said that they would wait.

† ᴸᴵ

When the old Caciques from all Tlaxcala saw that we did not come to their city, they decided to come to us, some in litters, others in hammocks or carried on men's backs, and others on foot. These were the Caciques already mentioned by me, named Mase Escasi, Xicotenga the elder, Guaxolocingo, Chichimecatecle, and Tecapaneca of Topeyanco. They arrived at our camp with a great company of chieftains, and with every sign of respect made three obeisances to Cortés and to all of us, and they burnt copal and touched the ground with their hands and kissed it, and Xicotenga the elder began to address Cortés in the following words:

"Malinche, Malinche, we have sent many times to implore you to pardon us for having attacked you and to state our excuse, that we did it to defend ourselves from the hostility of Montezuma and his powerful forces, for we believed that you belonged to his party and were allied to him. If we had known what we now know, we should not only have gone out to receive you on the roads with supplies of food, but would even have had them swept for you, and we would even have gone to you to the sea where you keep your *acales* (which are the ships). Now that you have pardoned us, what I and all these Caciques have come to request is, that you will come at once with us to our City, where we will give you of all that we possess and will serve you with our persons and property. Look to it Malinche that you do not decide otherwise or we will leave you at once, for we fear that perchance these Mexicans may have told you some of the falsehoods and lies that they are used to tell about us. Do not believe them nor listen to them, for they are false in everything, and we well know that it is on their account that you have not wished to come to our City."

Cortés answered them with cheerful mien and said, that it was well known, many years before we had come to these countries, what a good people they were and that it was on this account that he wondered at their attacking us.

He said that the Mexicans who were there were [merely] awaiting a reply which he was sending to their Lord Montezuma.

He thanked them heartily for what they said about our going at once to their City and for the food which they were continually sending and for their other civilities, and he would repay them by good deeds. He said that he would already have set out for their City if he had had anyone to carry the *tepuzques* (that is, the cannon). As soon as they heard these words the Tlaxcalans were so pleased that one could see it in their faces, and they said: "So this is the reason why you have delayed, and never mentioned it." And in less than half an hour they provided over five hundred Indian carriers.

The next day, early in the morning we began our march along the road to the Capital of Tlaxcala.

The messengers of Montezuma had already begged Cortés that they might go with us to see how affairs were settled at Tlaxcala and that he would despatch them from there, and that they should be quartered in his own lodgings so as not to receive any insults, for, as they said, they feared such from the Tlaxcalans.

Before going on any further I wish to say that in all the towns we had passed through, and in others where they had heard of us, Cortés was called Malinche, and so I will call him Malinche from now henceforth in all the accounts of conversations which were held with any of the Indians.

The reason why he was given this name is that Doña Marina, our interpreter, was always in his company, particularly when any Ambassadors arrived, and she spoke to them in the Mexican language. So that they gave Cortés the name of "Marina's Captain" and for short Malinche.

I also wish to say that from the time we entered the territory of Tlaxcala until we set out for the city, twenty-four days had elapsed, and we entered the city on the 23rd September, 1519.

When the Caciques saw that our baggage was on the way to their city, they at once went on ahead to see that everything was ready for our reception and that our quarters were decked with garlands.

When we arrived within a quarter of a league of the city, these same Caciques who had gone on ahead came out to receive us, and brought with them their sons and nephews and many of the leading inhabitants, each group of kindred and clan and party by itself. There were four parties in Tlaxcala, without counting that of Tecapaneca the lord of Topeyanco which made five. Their followers also came from all parts of the country wearing their different liveries, and although they were made of henequen, for there was no cotton to be obtained, they were very fine and beautifully embroidered and painted. Then came the priests from all parts of the province, and they were very numerous on account of the great oratories which they possess, the places where they keep their idols and offer sacrifices. These priests carried braziers with live coals and incense and fumigated all of us, and some of them were clothed in very long garments like fur cloaks and these were white, and they wore hoods over them which looked like those used by canons, and their hair was very long and tangled so that it could not be parted unless it were cut, and it was clotted with blood which oozed from their ears, which on that day they had cut by way of sacrifice; and they lowered their heads as a sign of humility when they saw us.

The nails on their fingers were very long, and we heard it said that these priests were very pious and led good lives.

Many of the chieftains came near to Cortés and accompanied him, and when we entered the town there was not space in the streets and on the roofs for all the Indian men and women with happy faces who came out to see us. They brought us about twenty cones made of sweet scented native roses of various colours, and gave them to Cortés and to the other soldiers whom they thought were Captains, especially to the horsemen. When we arrived at some fine courts where our quarters were, Xicotenga the elder and Mase Escasi took Cortés by the hand and led him into his lodging. For each one of us had been prepared a bed of matting such as they use, and sheets of henequen. Our friends whom we had brought from Cempoala and Xocotlan were lodged near to us, and Cortés asked that the messengers from the great Montezuma might also be given quarters close to his lodging.

Although we could see clearly that we were in a land where they were well disposed towards us, and were quite at peace, we did not cease to be very much on the alert as was always our custom, and it appears that one captain whose duty it was to station the scouts and spies and watchmen said to Cortés, "It seems, sir, that the people are very peaceful and we do not need so many guards, nor to be so circumspect as we are accustomed to be." Cortés replied, "Well, gentlemen, I can myself see all that you have brought to my notice, but it is a good custom always to be prepared, and although these may be very good people, we must not trust to their peacefulness, but must be as alert as we should be if they intended to make war on us and we saw them coming on to the attack, and whether it was done in good faith or bad, we must remember that the great Montezuma has sent to warn us." Xicotenga the elder and Mase Escasi were greatly annoyed with Cortés, and said to him through our interpreters: "Malinche, either you take us for enemies or you show signs in what we see you doing that you have no confidence in us or in the peace which you promised to us and we promised to you, and we say this to you because we see that you keep watch, and travelled along the

road all ready for action in the same way as when you attacked our squadrons, and we believe that you, Malinche, do
this on account of the treasons and abominations which the
Mexicans had told you in secret so as to turn you against us.
See to it that you do not believe them, for you are established
here, and we will give you all that you desire, even ourselves
and our children, and we are ready to die for you, so you can
demand as hostages whatever you may wish."

Cortés and all of us marvelled at the courtesy and affection
with which they spoke, and Cortés answered them that he had
always believed them, and there was no need of hostages, it
was enough to note their good will, and that as to being on the
alert, it was always our custom, and they must not be offended
at it. When this conversation was over, other chiefs arrived
with a great supply of poultry and maize bread, and tunas and
other fruits and vegetables which the country produced, and
supplied the camp very liberally, and during the twenty days
that we stayed there there was always more than enough to
eat.

† LII

Early next day Cortés ordered an Altar to be put up and Mass
to be said, for now we had both the wine and the sacred
wafers.

It was the priest Juan Díaz who said the Mass, for the
Padre de la Merced was ill with fever and very feeble. There
were present Mase Escasi and Xicotenga the elder and other
Caciques. When Mass was over Cortés entered his lodging
with some of us soldiers who usually accompanied him, and
the two old Caciques, and Xicotenga said to him that they
wished to bring him a present, and Cortés showed much affection to them, and said that they should bring it whenever they
wished, so some mats were at once spread out and covered
with a cloth, and they brought six or seven trifles of gold, and
some stones of small value, and some loads of henequen cloth;
it was all very poor and not even worth twenty dollars and
when it had been presented, those Caciques said, laughing:
"Malinche, we know well enough that as what we have to give
is so small you will not receive it with good grace. We have

already sent to tell you that we are poor and that we own neither gold nor riches, and the reason of it is that these traitorous and evil Mexicans and Montezuma, who is now their Lord, have taken all that we once possessed, when we asked them for peace or a truce, to prevent their making war on us, so do not consider the small value of the gift, but accept it with a good grace as the gift of friends and servants which we will be to you." Then they brought, separately, a large supply of food.

Cortés accepted it most cheerfully, and said to them that he valued it more as coming from their hands with the good will with which it was offered, than he would a house full of grains of gold brought by others, and it was in this spirit that he accepted it, and he displayed much affection towards them.

It appears that it had been arranged among all the Caciques to give us from among their daughters and nieces the most beautiful of the maidens who were ready for marriage, and Xicotenga the elder said: "Malinche, so that you may know more clearly our good will towards you and our desire to content you in everything, we wish to give you our daughters, to be your wives, so that you may have children by them, for we wish to consider you as brothers as you are so good and valiant. I have a very beautiful daughter who has not been married, and I wish to give her to you," so also Mase Escasi and all the other Caciques said that they would bring their daughters, and that we should accept them as wives, and they made many other speeches and promises. Throughout the day Mase Escasi and Xicotenga the elder never left Cortés' immediate neighbourhood. As Xicotenga the elder was blind from old age, he felt Cortés all over his head and face and beard and over all his body.

Cortés replied to them that, as to the gift of the women, he and all of us were very grateful and would repay them with good deeds as time went on. The Padre de la Merced was present and Cortés said to him: "Señor Padre, it seems to me that this would be a good time to make an attempt to induce these Caciques to give up their Idols and their sacrifices, for they will do anything we tell them to do on account of the great fear they have of the Mexicans." The friar replied: "Sir, that is true, but let us leave the matter until they bring their daughters and then there will be material to work upon, and your honour can say that you do not wish to accept them until they give up sacrifices—if that succeeds, good, if not we shall do our duty."

The next day the same old Caciques came and brought with them five beautiful Indian maidens, and for Indians they were very good looking and well adorned, and each of the Indian maidens brought another Indian girl as her servant, and all were the daughters of Caciques, and Xicotenga said to Cortés: "Malinche, this is my daughter who has never been married and is a maiden, take her for your own," and he gave her to him by the hand, "and let the others be given to the captains." Cortés expressed his thanks, and with every appearance of gratification said that he accepted them and took them as our own, but that for the present they should remain in the care of their parents. The Chiefs asked him why he would not take them now, and Cortés replied that he wished first to do the will of God our Lord, and that for which our Lord the King had sent us, which was to induce them to do away with their Idols, and no longer to kill and sacrifice human beings, and to lead them to believe in that which we believed, that is in one true God, and he told them much more touching our holy faith, and in truth he expressed it very well, for Doña Marina and Aguilar, our interpreters, were already so expert at it that they explained it very clearly. He also told them that if they wished to be our brothers and to have true friendship with us, so that we should willingly accept their daughters and take them, as they said, for our wives, that they should at once give up their evil Idols and believe in and worship our Lord God and things would prosper with them, and when they died their souls would go to Heaven to enjoy glory everlasting; but that if they went on making sacrifices as they were accustomed to do to their Idols, they would be led to Hell where they would burn for ever in live flames, and what they replied to it all is as follows:

"Malinche, we have already understood from you before now, and we thoroughly believe that this God of yours and this great Lady are very good, but look you, you have only just come to our homes, as time goes on we shall understand your beliefs much more clearly, and see what they are, and will do what is right. But how can you ask us to give up our Teules which for many years our ancestors have held to be gods and have made sacrifices to them and have worshipped them? Even if we, who are old men, might wish to do it to please you, what would our priests say, and all our neighbours, and the youths and children throughout the province? They would rise against us, especially as the priests have already consulted the greatest of our Teules, and he told them not to forget the sacrifice of men and all the rites they were used to practise, otherwise the gods would destroy the whole province with famine, pestilence and war." Thus they spoke and gave as their answer that we should not trouble to talk of them on that subject again for they were not going to leave off making sacrifices even if they were killed for it.

When we heard that reply which they gave so honestly and without fear, the Padre de la Merced, who was a wise man, and a theologian, said: "Sir, do not attempt to press them further on this subject, for it is not just to make them Christians by force, and I would not wish that you should do what we did in Cempoala, that is, destroy their Idols, until they have some knowledge of our Holy Faith." Furthermore two gentlemen, namely Juan Velásquez de Leon and Francisco de Lugo, spoke to Cortés and said: "The Padre is right in what he says, you have fulfilled your duty with what you have done, and do not touch again on this matter when speaking to these Caciques," and so the subject dropped. What we induced the Caciques to do, by entreaty, was at once to clear out one of the cues, which was close by and had been recently built, and after removing the Idols, to clean it and whitewash it so that we could place a cross in it and the image of Our Lady, and this they promptly did. Then Mass was said there and the Cacicas were baptized. The daughter of the blind Xicotenga was given the name of Doña Luisa, and Cortés took her by the hand and gave her to Pedro de Alvarado, and said to Xicotenga that he to whom he gave her was his brother and his Captain, and that he should be pleased at it as she would be well treated by him, and Xicotenga was contented that it should be so. The daughter or niece of Mase Escasi was named Doña Elvira and she was very beautiful and it seems to me that she was given to Juan Velásquez de Leon. The others were given baptismal names, always with the title of nobility (doña) and Cortés gave them to Gonzalo de Sandoval and Cristóbal de Olid and Alonzo de Ávila. When this had been done Cortés told them the reason why he put up two crosses, and that it was because their Idols were afraid of them, and that wherever we were encamped or wherever we slept they were placed in the roads; and at all this they were quite content.

Before I go on any further I wish to say about the Cacica the daughter of Xicotenga, who was named Doña Luisa and was given to Pedro de Alvarado, that when they gave her to him all the greater part of Tlaxcala paid reverence to her, and gave her presents, and looked on her as their mistress, and Pedro de Alvarado, who was then a bachelor, had a son by her named Don Pedro and a daughter named Doña Leonor, who is now the wife of Don Francisco de la Cueva, a nobleman, and a cousin of the Duke of Alburquerque, who had by her four or five sons, very good gentlemen.

† LIII

Cortés then took those Caciques aside and questioned them very fully about Mexican affairs. Xicotenga, as he was the best informed and a great chieftain, took the lead in talking, and from time to time he was helped by Mase Escasi who was also a great chief.

He said that Montezuma had such great strength in warriors that when he wished to capture a great city or make a raid on a province, he could place a hundred and fifty thousand men in the field, and this they knew well from the experience of the wars and hostilities they had had with them for more than a hundred years past.

Cortés asked them how it was that with so many warriors as they said came down on them they had never been entirely conquered. They answered that although the Mexicans sometimes defeated them and killed them, and carried off many of their vassals for sacrifice, many of the enemy were also left dead on the field and others were made prisoners, and that they never could come so secretly that they did not get some warning, and that when they knew of their approach they mustered all their forces and with the help of the people of Huexotzingo they defended themselves and made counter attacks. That as all the provinces which had been raided by Montezuma and placed under his rule were ill disposed towards the Mexicans, and that as their inhabitants were carried off by force to the wars, they did not fight with good will; indeed, it was from these very men that they received warnings, and for this reason they had defended their country to the best of their ability.

The place from which the most continuous trouble came to them was a very great city a day's march distant, which is called Cholula, whose inhabitants were most treacherous. It was there that Montezuma secretly mustered his companies and, as it was near by, they made their raids by night. Moreover, Mase Escasi said that Montezuma kept garrisons of many warriors stationed in all the provinces in addition to the great force he could bring from the city, and that all the provinces paid tribute of gold and silver, feathers, stones, cloth and cotton, and Indian men and women for sacrifice and others for servants, that he [Montezuma] was such a great prince that he possessed everything he could desire, that the houses where he dwelt were full of riches and [precious] stones and chalchihuites which he had robbed and taken by force from those who would not give them willingly, and that all the wealth of the country was in his hands.

Then they spoke of the great fortifications of the city, and what the lake was like, and the depth of water, and about the causeways that gave access to the city, and the wooden bridges in each causeway, and how one can go in and out [by water] through the opening that there is in each bridge, and how when the bridges are raised one can be cut off between bridge and bridge and not be able to reach the city. How the greater part of the city was built in the lake, and that one could not pass from house to house except by draw-bridges and canoes which they had ready. That all the houses were flat-roofed and all the roofs were provided with parapets so that they could fight from them.

They brought us pictures of the battles they had fought with the Mexicans painted on large henequen cloths, showing their manner of fighting.

As our captain and all of us had already heard about all that these Caciques were telling us, we changed the subject, and started them on another more profound, which was, how was it that they came to inhabit that land, and from what direction had they come? and how was it that they differed so much from and were so hostile to the Mexicans, seeing that their countries were so close to one another?

They said that their ancestors had told them, that in times past there had lived among them men and women of giant size with huge bones, and because they were very bad people of evil manners that they had fought with them and killed them, and those of them who remained died off. So that we could see how huge and tall these people had been they brought us a leg bone of one of them which was very thick and the height of a man of ordinary stature, and that was the bone from the hip to the knee. I measured myself against it and it was as tall as I am although I am of fair size. They brought other pieces of bone like the first but they were already eaten away and destroyed by the soil. We were all amazed at seeing those bones and felt sure that there must have been giants in this country, and our Captain Cortés said to us that it would be well to send that great bone to Castile so that His Majesty might see it, so we sent it with the first of our agents who went there.

These Caciques also told us that they had learnt from their forefathers that one of their Idols, to which they paid the greatest devotion, had told them that men would come from distant lands in the direction of the rising sun to subjugate them and govern them, and that if we were those men, they were rejoiced at it, as we were so good and brave, and that when they made peace with us they had borne in mind what their Idols had said, and for this reason they had given us their daughters so as to obtain relations who would defend them against the Mexicans.

When they had finished their discourse we were all astounded and said can they possibly have spoken the truth? Then our Captain Cortés replied to them and said that certainly we came from the direction of the sunrise and that our Lord the King had sent us for this very purpose that we should become as brothers to them; for he had heard of them, and that he prayed God to give us grace, so that by our hands and our intercession they would be saved, and we all said Amen.

I feel bound to dwell on one other thing which they discussed with us, and that is the volcano near Huexotzingo which at the time we were in Tlaxcala was throwing out much fire, much more than usual. Our Captain Cortés and all of us were greatly astonished as we had never seen such a thing before. One of our Captains named Diego de Ordás was very anxious to go and see what sort of a thing it was, and asked leave of the general to ascend the mountain, and leave was given,[1] and he even expressly ordered him to do it. He took with him two of our soldiers and certain Indian chiefs from Huexotzingo, and the chiefs that he took with him frightened him by saying that when one was half way up Popocatepetl, for so the volcano is called, one could not endure the shaking of the ground and the flames and stones and ashes which were thrown out of the mountain, and that they would not dare to ascend further than where stood the cues of the Idols which are called the Teules of Popocatepetl. Nevertheless Diego de Ordás and his two companions went on up until they reached the summit, and the Indians who had accompanied them remained below and did not dare to make the ascent. It appears from what Ordás and the two soldiers said afterwards, that, as they ascended, the volcano began to throw out great tongues of flame, and half burnt stones of little weight and a great quantity of ashes, and that the whole of the mountain range where the volcano stands was shaken, and that they stopped still without taking a step in advance for more than an hour, when they thought that the outburst had passed and not so much smoke and ashes were being thrown out; then they climbed up to the mouth which was very wide and round, and opened to the width of a quarter of a league. From this summit could be seen the great city of Mexico, and the whole of the lake, and all the towns which were built in it. This volcano is distant twelve or thirteen leagues from Mexico.

Ordás was delighted and astonished at the sight of Mexico and its cities and after having had a good look at the view he returned to Tlaxcala with his companions, and the Indians of Huexotzingo and of Tlaxcala looked on it as a deed of great daring. When he told his story to Captain Cortés and all of us, we were greatly astonished at it, for at that time we had not

---

[1] This account of the ascent of Popocatepetl appears to be given in the wrong place by Bernal Díaz: it probably took place when the Spaniards left Cholula. See Cortés' Second Letter.

seen nor heard of such things as we have to-day, when we know all about it, and many Spaniards and even some Franciscan friars have made the ascent to the crater.

When Diego de Ordás went to Castile he asked the King for it [the mountain] as his [coat of] arms and his nephew who lives at Puebla, now bears them.

Since we have been settled in this land we have never known the volcano to throw out so much fire or make such a noise as it did when we first arrived, and it has even remained some years without throwing out any fire, up to the year 1539 when it threw up great flames and stones and ashes.

I must tell how in this town of Tlaxcala we found wooden houses furnished with gratings, full of Indian men and women imprisoned in them, being fed up until they were fat enough to be sacrificed and eaten. These prisons we broke open and destroyed, and set free the prisoners who were in them, and these poor Indians did not dare to go in any direction, only to stay there with us and thus escape with their lives. From now on, in all the towns that we entered, the first thing our Captain ordered us to do was to break open these prisons and set free the prisoners.

These prisons are common throughout the land and when Cortés and all of us saw such great cruelty, he showed that he was very angry with the Caciques of Tlaxcala, and they promised that from that time forth they would not kill and eat any more Indians in that way. I said [to myself] of what benefit were all those promises, for as soon as we turned our heads they would commit the same cruelties.

† LIV

When our Captain remembered that we had already been resting in Tlaxcala for seventeen days, and that we had heard so much said about the great wealth of Montezuma and his flourishing city, he arranged to take counsel with all those among our captains and soldiers whom he could depend on as wishing to advance, and it was decided that our departure should take place without delay, but there was a good deal of dissent expressed in camp about this decision, for some soldiers said that it was a very rash thing to go and enter into such a strong city, as we were so few in number, and they spoke of the very great strength of Montezuma. Our Captain Cortés replied that there was now no other course open to us, for we had constantly asserted and proclaimed that we were going to see Montezuma, so that other counsels were useless.

When Xicotenga and Mase Escasi, the lords of Tlaxcala, saw that we were determined to go to Mexico, their spirits were weighed down, and they were constantly with Cortés advising him not to enter on such an undertaking.

Our captain said to them that he thanked the Caciques for their good counsel, and he showed them much affection, and made them many promises, and he gave as presents to Xicotenga the elder, and to Mase Escasi and most of the other Caciques a great part of the fine cloth which Montezuma had presented, and told them that it would be a good thing to make peace between them and the Mexicans, so that they should become friends and they could then obtain salt and cotton and other merchandise. Xicotenga replied that peace was useless, and that enmity was deeply rooted in their hearts, for such were the Mexicans that, under cover of peace, they would only be guilty of greater treachery, for they never told the truth in anything that they promised, and that he was not to trouble about saying more on the subject, and that they could only again implore us to take care not to fall into the hands of such bad people.

We went on to talk about the road which we should take to reach Mexico, for the ambassadors from Montezuma, who remained with us and were to be our guides, said that the most level and the best road was by the city of Cholula, where the people were vassals of Montezuma and there we should receive proper attention. To all of us this appeared to be good advice, that we should go by that city. When however the Caciques of Tlaxcala heard that we wished to go by a road which the Mexicans were choosing for us, they became very sorrowful, and begged us in any case to go by Huexotzingo, where the people were their relations and our friends, and not by way of Cholula, for in Cholula Montezuma always kept his double dealings concealed.

For all that they talked and advised us not to enter into that city, our Captain (in accordance with our counsel which had been well talked over) still determined to go by Cholula, on the one hand, because all agreed that it was a large town, and well furnished with towers, and fine and tall cues, and situated on a beautiful plain, and on the other hand, because it was almost surrounded by other considerable towns and could provide ample supplies, and our friends of Tlaxcala were near at hand. We intended to stay there until we could decide how to get to Mexico without having to fight for it, for the great power of the Mexicans was a thing to be feared, and unless God our Lord, by His Divine mercy which always helped us and gave us strength, should first of all so provide, we could not enter Mexico in any other manner.

After much discussion it was settled that we should take the road by Cholula, and Cortés at once sent messengers to ask the people of Cholula how it happened that being so near to us they had not come to visit us, and pay that respect which was due to us as the messengers of so great a prince as the King who had sent us to the country to tell them of their salvation. He then requested all the Caciques and priests of that city to come and see us and give their fealty to our Lord and King, and if they did not come he would look upon them as ill disposed towards us.

† LV

While Cortés was talking to us all and to the Caciques of Tlaxcala about our departure and about warfare, they came to tell him that four Ambassadors, all four chieftains who were bringing presents, had arrived in the town.

Cortés ordered them to be called, and when they came before him they paid the greatest reverence to him and to all of us soldiers who were there with him, and presented their gift of rich jewels of gold and many sorts of workmanship, well worth two thousand dollars, and ten loads of cloth beautifully embroidered with feathers.

Cortés received them most graciously, and the Ambassadors said, on behalf of their Lord Montezuma, that he greatly wondered that we should stay so many days among a people who were so poor and so ill bred, who were so wicked, and such traitors and thieves that they were not fit even to be slaves,

and that when either by day or by night we were most off our
guard they would kill us in order to rob us. That he begged us
to come at once to his city, and he would give us of all that he
possessed, although it would not be as much as we deserved
or he would like to give, and that although all the supplies had
to be carried into the city, he would provide for us as well as
he was able.

Montezuma did this so as to get us out of Tlaxcala, for he
knew of the friendship we had made, and how, to perfect it,
the Tlaxcalans had given their daughters to Malinche, and the
Mexicans fully understood that our confederation could bring
no good to them.

Cortés thanked the messengers with many caressing expressions and signs of affection, and gave as his answer that he
would go very soon to see their Lord Montezuma, and he
begged them to remain a few days with us.

At that time Cortés decided that two of our Captains should
go and see and speak to the great Montezuma, and see the
great city of Mexico and Pedro de Alvarado and Bernaldino
Vásquez de Tápia had already set out on the journey, accompanied by some of the ambassadors of the great Montezuma
who were used to being with us, and the four ambassadors
who had brought the present remained with us as hostages.
However, we did not think it well advised, so he wrote to
them telling them to return at once.

The ambassadors with whom they had been traveling gave
an account of their doings to Montezuma, and he asked them
what sort of faces and general appearance had these two
Teules who were coming to Mexico, and whether they were
Captains, and it seems that they replied that Pedro de
Alvarado was of very perfect grace both in face and person,
that he looked like the Sun, and that he was a Captain, and in
addition to this they brought with them a picture of him with
his face very naturally portrayed, and from that time forth
they gave him the name of Tonatio, which means the Sun or
the child of the Sun, and so they called him ever after. Of
Bernaldino Vásquez de Tápia, they said that he was a robust
man, and of a very pleasant disposition, and that he also was a
captain, and Montezuma was much disappointed that they had
turned back again.

I have already said how our Captain sent messengers to Cholula to tell the Caciques of that City to come and see us at Tlaxcala. When the Caciques understood what Cortés ordered them to do, they thought that it would be sufficient to send four unimportant Indians to make their excuses. The Caciques of Tlaxcala were present when these messengers arrived, and they said to our Captain that the people of Cholula had sent those Indians to make a mock of him and of all of us, for they were only commoners of no standing; so Cortés at once sent them back with four other Cempoala Indians to tell the people of Cholula that they must send some chieftains, and as the distance was only five leagues that they must arrive within three days, otherwise he should look on them as rebels; that when they came he wished to receive them as friends and brothers as he had received their neighbours and people of Tlaxcala, and that if they did not wish for our friendship that we should take measures which would displease them and anger them.

When the Caciques of Cholula had listened to that embassy they answered that they were not coming to Tlaxcala, for the Tlaxcalans were their enemies, and they knew that they [the Tlaxcalans] had said many evil things about them and about their Lord Montezuma; that it was for us to come to their city and to leave the confines to Tlaxcala, and that then if they did not do what they ought to do we could treat them as such as we had sent to say they were.

When our Captain saw that the excuse that they made was a just one we resolved to go to Cholula, and as soon as the Caciques of Tlaxcala perceived that we were determined to go there, they said to Cortés: "So you wish to trust to the Mexicans and not to us who are your friends, we have already told you many times that you must beware of the people of Cholula and of the power of Mexico, and so that you can receive all the support possible from us, we have got ready ten thousand warriors to accompany you." Cortés thanked them very heartily for this, but after consultation with all of us it was agreed that it would not be advisable to take so many warriors to a country in which we were seeking friends, and that it would be better to take only one thousand, and this number we asked of the Tlaxcalans and said that the rest should remain in their houses.

Padre Sahagun, in his history of the Conquest, states that the first presents sent by Montezuma to Cortés were the ornaments of the Temple of Quetzalcoatl. Montezuma is reported to have said to his messengers: "Our Lord Quetzalcoatl has arrived, go and receive him and listen to what he says with great attention, see to it that you do not forget anything that he may say, you see that these jewels that you are presenting to him on my behalf, are all the priestly ornaments that belong to him." Then follows a detailed description of the ornaments of the deity beginning with "A mask worked in a mosaic of turquoise; this mask has a double and twisted snake worked in the same stones whose fold was (on) the projection of the nose, then the tail was parted from the head and the head with part of the body went above one of the eyes so that it formed an eyebrow, and the tail with a part of the body went over the other eye to form the other eyebrow. This mask was decked with a great and lofty crown, full of rich feathers, very long and beautiful, so that on placing the crown on the head, the mask was placed over the face," etc. The messengers also carried for presentation to Cortés "The ornaments or finery with which Tezcatlipoca was decorated," and "the ornaments and finery of the God called Tlalocantecutli" (Tlaloc). Also other ornaments of the same Quetzalcoatl, a mitre of tigerskins, etc.

It is interesting to know that the masks belonging to these four costumes and adornments of the Gods are still in existence, and that three of them can be seen in the room devoted to American Antiquities in the British Museum.

The mask of Quetzalcoatl with the folds of the snake's body forming the eyebrows is easily identified, and the mask with the eyes of pyrites and the bands across the face is probably the mask of the God Tezcatlipoca.

The presents sent by Cortés to Charles V were conveyed to Spain in the charge of Alonzo Hernández Puertocarrero and Francisco de Montejo, who sailed from Villa Rica in July, 1519, and reached Valladolid probably in October of the same year, where they awaited the arrival of the Emperor. Bernal Díaz says that Charles V was in Flanders when the presents arrived in Spain, but this is not correct; the Emperor was in Catalonia and did not return to Valladolid until some time in 1520, when he was on his way to Coruña, whence he sailed for Flanders in May, 1520.

It is, however, remarkable that these masks and ornaments of the Gods do not appear in the list of the presents, signed by Puertocarrero and

Montejo, which accompanied the letter from the Municipality of Vera Cruz, dated 10th July, 1519, nor in the *Manual del Tesorero de la Casa de Contratacion de Sevilla,* both of which documents were published in the *Documentos Ineditos para la historia de España,* Madrid, 1842. A note to the former document states that the gifts and the letter from the Municipality were received by the King, Don Carlos, in Valladolid during Holy Week, in the beginning of April, 1520.

As, however, this note mentions the letter from the Municipality only (*con la carta y relacion de suso dicha que et concejo de la Vera Cruz envió*), and makes no mention of the first letter sent to the Emperor by Cortés himself, which letter has never yet been found, it is possible that the masks and ornaments of the Gods were sent separately with Cortés' first letter, and were therefore not included in the list of gifts sent by Cortés in conjunction with the Municipality.

Las Casas (*Hist. de las Indias,* chap. cxxi), writing about these presents, which included two great discs, one of gold and the other of silver, says: "These wheels were certainly wonderful things to behold. I saw them and all the rest (of the presents) in the year 1520 at Valladolid, on the day that the emperor saw them, for they arrived there then sent by Cortés."

There is a tradition that Charles V presented these gifts to the Pope (a Medici) for the family Museum, which is well known to have existed, and of which the present Museum of Natural History at Florence is an outcome. If these gifts were sent to Rome, as is probable, soon after their arrival in Spain, they must have been sent to Leo X (Giovanni de Medici), who died in 1521. If they were not sent before the death of Leo X, it is not likely that they were sent to Italy during the troublous years that followed, but they may have been taken to Spain by Cortés himself when he returned in 1528 and have been given to Clement VII (Giulio de Medici) when Charles V was crowned by him as King of the Romans at Bologna in 1529–30.

However that may be, I have the authority of Professor H. Giglioli, the Director of the Museum of Natural History in Florence, for stating that nearly all the known group of objects—namely, mosaic masks, mosaic decorated knife-handles, gold-plated and figured atlatls (spear throwers), etc.—were at one time in Florence. At the end of the sixteenth century, when Aldrovandi, who was a friend of the Medici, founded his celebrated Museum at Bologna, he was given some of these articles from the Medici Collection at Florence; and these, with the exception of the turquoise mosaic mask mentioned below, were discovered by Professor L. Pigorini in the attics of the Bologna University and transferred to the Ethnographic Museum in Rome, which he was then forming, and which now contains perhaps the finest collection of these relics. However, the greater number of them up to the years 1819–21 were registered in the Florentine Museum under the title of *Maschere e strumenti de popoli barbari,* and were partly sent thence to the *Officina delle pietre dure* in that city to be broken up and used for mosaic work, being *Maschere di cattivi turchesi!*

The last turquoise mosaic mask (now in Rome) was found a few years ago by Professor Luigi Pigorini in the store-room of the *pietre dure* laboratory, labelled with an inventory value of two francs and a half! As this mask shows the remains of tusk-like teeth, it is probably the Mask of Tlaloc.

Five years ago two magnificent plated atlatls[1] were found in the garret of a nobleman's palace in Florence, and sold by a dealer to the Ethnographical Museum in that city, for 500 *lire,* as "Indian Sceptres"; they were in a leathern case, stamped with the Medici arms. One of them is double-grooved, for throwing two darts at a time.

The whole number of known examples of this class of Mexican work did not exceed twenty in 1893, and of these eight are now in the British Museum. Many of them were bought by Mr Christy and Sir Augustus Franks in Northern Italy, where they had been scattered after the dispersal of the Medicean Collection.

A full account of these interesting objects, by Mr C. H. Read, is given, with illustrations, in *Archæologia,* vol. liv, 1895. Professor Pigorini published, in 1885, a full account, with coloured plates, of the collection in the Ethnographical Museum at Rome, in the *Memorie* of the R. Academia dei Lincei at Rome. Another interesting paper on the subject was published by Dr W. Lehmann in *Globus* (Bd. 91, No. 21), 6th June, 1907.

[1] Described and figured in the *American Anthropologist* (N.S.), vol. vii, No. 2, April–June, 1905.

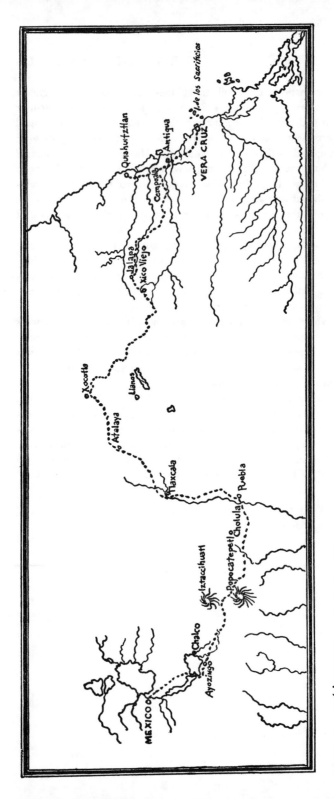

ROUTE OF CORTÉS' EXPEDITION TO MEXICO CITY

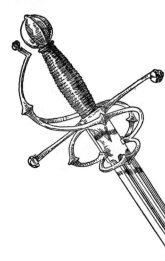

IV

The March to Mexico

One morning we started on our march to the city of Cholula
and that day we went on to sleep at a river which runs within
a short league of the city, and there they put up for us some
huts and ranchos. This same night the Caciques of Cholula
sent some chieftains to bid us welcome to their country, and
they brought supplies of poultry and maize bread, and said
that in the morning all the Caciques and priests would come
out to receive us, and they asked us to forgive their not having
come sooner. Cortés thanked them both for the food they had
brought and for the good will which they showed us.

At dawn we began to march and the Caciques and priests
and many other Indians came out to receive us, most of them
were clothed in cotton garments made like tunics. They came
in a most peaceful manner and willingly, and the priests carried braziers containing incense with which they fumigated
our Captain and us soldiers who were standing near him. When
these priests and chiefs saw the Tlaxcalan Indians who came
with us, they asked Doña Marina to tell the General that it was
not right that their enemies with arms in their hands should
enter their city in that manner. When our Captain understood
this, he ordered the soldiers and the baggage to halt, and,
when he saw us all together and that no one was moving, he
said: "It seems to me, Sirs, that before we enter Cholula these
Caciques and priests should be put to the proof with a friendly
speech, so that we can see what their wishes may be; for they

come complaining of our friends the Tlaxcalans and they have much cause for what they say, and I want to make them understand in fair words the reason why we come to their city, and as you gentlemen already know, the Tlaxcalans have told us that the Cholulans are a turbulent people, and, as it would be a good thing that by fair means they should render their obedience to His Majesty, this appears to me to be the proper thing to do."

Then he told Doña Marina to call up the Caciques and priests to where he was stationed on horseback with all of us around him, and three chieftains and two priests came at once, and they said: "Malinche, forgive us for not coming to Tlaxcala to see you and to bring food, it was not for want of good will but because Mase Escasi and Xicotenga and all Tlaxcala are our enemies, and have said many evil things of us and of the Great Montezuma our Prince, and as though what they said were not enough, they now have the boldness, under your protection, to come armed into our city, and we beg you as a favour to order them to return to their own country, or at least to stay outside in the fields and not to enter our city in such a manner." But as for us they said that we were very welcome.

As our Captain saw that what they said was reasonable, he at once sent Pedro de Alvarado and Cristóbal de Olid to ask the Tlaxcalans to put up their huts and ranchos there in the fields, and not to enter the city with us, excepting those who were carrying the cannon, and our friends from Cempoala, and he told them to explain to the Tlaxcalans that the reason why he asked them to do so was that all the Caciques and priests were afraid of them, and that when we left Cholula on our way to Mexico we would send to summon them, and that they were not to be annoyed at what he was doing. When the people of Cholula knew what Cortés had done, they appeared to be much more at ease.

Then Cortés began to make a speech to them, saying that our Lord and King had sent us to these countries to give them warning and command them not to worship Idols, nor sacrifice human beings, or eat their flesh, and as the road to Mexico, whither we were going to speak with the Great Montezuma, passed by there, and there was no other shorter road, we had come to visit their city and to treat them as brothers. As other great Caciques had given their obedience to His Majesty, it would be well that they should give theirs as the others had done.

They replied that we had hardly entered into their country, yet we already ordered them to give up their Teules, and that they could not do it. As to giving their obedience to our King they were content to do so. And thus they pledged their word, but it was not done before a notary. When this was over we at once began our march towards the City, and so great was the number of people who came out to see us that both the streets and house tops were crowded, and I do not wonder at this for they had never seen men such as we are, nor had they ever seen horses.

They lodged us in some large rooms where we were all together with our friends from Cempoala and the Tlaxcalans who carried the baggage, and they fed us on that day and the next very well and abundantly.

† LVII

After the people of Cholula had received us in the festive manner already described, and most certainly with a show of good will, it presently appeared that Montezuma sent orders to his ambassadors, who were still in our company, to negotiate with the Cholulans that an army of 20,000 men which Montezuma had sent and equipped should, on entering the city, join with them in attacking us by night or by day, get us into a hopeless plight and bring all of us that they could capture bound to Mexico. And he sent many presents of jewels and cloths, also a golden drum, and he also sent word to the priests of the city that they were to retain twenty of us to sacrifice to their idols.

The warriors whom Montezuma sent were stationed in some ranchos and some rocky thickets about half a league from Cholula and some were already posted within the houses.

They fed us very well for the first two days, but on the third day they neither gave us anything to eat nor did any of the Caciques or priests make their appearance, and if any Indians came to look at us, they did not approach us, but remained some distance off, laughing at us as though mocking us. When our Captain saw this, he told our interpreters to tell the Ambassadors of the Great Montezuma to order the Caciques to bring some food, but all they brought was water and fire wood, and the old men who brought it said there was no more maize.

That same day other Ambassadors arrived from Montezuma, and joined those who were already with us and they said to Cortés, very impudently, that their Prince had sent them to say that we were not to go by his city because he had nothing to give us to eat, and that they wished at once to return to Mexico with our reply. When Cortés saw that their speech was unfriendly, he replied to the Ambassadors in the blandest manner, that he marvelled how such a great Prince as Montezuma should be so vacillating, and he begged them not to return to Mexico, for he wished to start himself on the next day, to see their Prince, and act according to his orders, and I believe that he gave the Ambassadors some strings of beads and they agreed to stay.

When this had been done, our Captain called us together, and said to us: "I see that these people are very much disturbed, and it behoves us to keep on the alert, in case some trouble is brewing among them," and he at once sent for the principal Cacique, telling him either to come himself or to send some other chieftains. The Cacique replied that he was ill and could not come.

When our Captain heard this, he ordered us to bring before him, with kindly persuasion, two of the numerous priests who were in the great Cue near our quarters. We brought two of them, without doing them any disrespect, and Cortés ordered each of them to be given a Chalchihuite, and addressing them with friendly words he asked them what was the reason that the Cacique and chieftains and most of the priests were frightened, for he had sent to summon them and they did not want to come. It seems that one of these priests was a very important personage among them, who had charge of or command over all the Cues in the City, and was a sort of Bishop among the priests and was held in great respect. He replied that they, who were priests, had no fear of us, and if the Cacique and chieftain did not wish to come, he would go himself and summon them, and that if he spoke to them he believed they would do as he told them and would come.

Cortés at once told him to go, and that his companion should await his return. So the priest departed and summoned the Cacique and chieftains who returned in his company to Cortés' quarters. Cortés asked them what it was they were afraid of, and why they had not given us anything to eat, and said that if our presence in their city were an annoyance to them, we wished to leave the next day for Mexico to see and speak to the Lord Montezuma, and he asked them to provide carriers for the transport of the baggage and *tepusques* and to send us some food at once.

The Cacique was so embarrassed that he could hardly speak, he said that they would look for the food, but their Lord Montezuma had sent to tell them not to give us any, and was not willing that we should proceed any further.

While this conversation was taking place, three of our friends, the Cempoala Indians, came in and said secretly to Cortés, that close by where we were quartered they had found holes dug in the streets, covered over with wood and earth, so that without careful examination, one could not see them, that they had removed the earth from above one of the holes and found it full of sharp pointed stakes to kill the horses when they galloped, and that the *Azoteas* had breastworks of *adobes*[1] and were piled up with stones, and certainly this was not done with good intent for they also found barricades of thick timbers in another street. At this moment eight Tlaxcalans arrived, from the Indians whom we had left outside in the fields with orders that they were not to enter Cholula, and they said to Cortés: "Take heed, Malinche, for this City is ill disposed, and we know that this night they have sacrificed to their Idol, which is the God of War, seven persons, five of them children, so that the God may give them victory over you, and we have further seen that they are moving all their baggage and women and children out of the city." When Cortés heard this, he immediately sent these Tlaxcalans back to their Captains, with orders to be fully prepared if we should send to summon them, and he turned to speak to the Caciques, priests and chieftains of Cholula and told them to have no fear and show no alarm, but to remember the obedience which they had promised to him, and not to swerve from it, lest he should have to chastise them. That he had already told them that we wished to set out on the morrow and that he had need of two thousand warriors

[1] Sun-dried bricks.

from the city to accompany us, just as the Tlaxcalans had provided them, for they were necessary on the road. They replied
that the men would be given, and asked leave to go at once to
get them ready, and they went away very well contented, for
they thought that between the warriors with whom they were
to supply us, and the regiments sent by Montezuma, which
were hidden in the rocky thickets and barrancas, we could not
escape death or capture, for the horses would not be able to
charge on account of certain breastworks and barricades which
they immediately advised the troops to construct, so that only a
narrow lane would be left through which it would be impossible for us to pass. They warned the Mexicans to be in readiness
as we intended to start on the next day and told them that our
capture would be sure, for they had made sacrifices to their
War Idols who had promised them victory.

As our Captain wished to be more thoroughly informed
about the plot and all that was happening, he told Doña Marina to take more chalchihuites to the two priests who had
been the first to speak, for they were not afraid, and to tell
them with friendly words that Malinche wished them to come
back and speak to him, and to bring them back with her. Doña
Marina went and spoke to the priests in the manner she knew
so well how to use, and thanks to the presents they at once accompanied her. Cortés addressed them and asked them to say
truly what they knew, for they were the priests of Idols and
chieftains and ought not to lie, and that what they should say
would not be disclosed in any manner, for we were going to
leave the next morning, and he would give them a large
quantity of cloth. They said the truth was that their Lord
Montezuma knew that we were coming to their city, and that
every day he was of many minds and could not come to any decision on the matter, that sometimes he sent orders to pay us
much respect when we arrived and to guide us on the way to
his city, and at other times he would send word that it was not
his wish that we should go to Mexico, and now recently his
Gods Tescatepuca and Huichilobos, to whom he paid great devotion, had counselled him that we should either be killed here
in Cholula or should be sent, bound, to Mexico. That the day
before he had sent out twenty thousand warriors, and half of
them were already within this city, and the other half were stationed near by in some gullies, and that they already knew that

we were about to start to-morrow; they also told us about the barricades which they had ordered to be made and the two thousand warriors that were to be given to us, and how it had already been agreed that twenty of us were to be kept to be sacrificed to the Idols of Cholula.

Cortés ordered these men to be given a present of richly embroidered cloth, and told them not to say anything about the information they had given us for, if they disclosed it, on our return from Mexico we would kill them. He also told them that we should start early the next morning, and he asked them to summon all the Caciques to come then so that he might speak to them.

That night Cortés took counsel of us as to what should be done, for he had very able men with him whose advice was worth having, but as in such cases frequently happens, some said that it would be advisable to change our course and go by Huexotzingo, others that we must manage to preserve the peace by every possible means and that it would be better to return to Tlaxcala, others of us gave our opinion that if we allowed such treachery to pass unpunished, wherever we went we should be treated to worse treachery, and that being there in the town, with ample provisions, we ought to make an attack, for the Indians would feel the effect of it more in their own homes than they would in the open, and that we should at once warn the Tlaxcalans so that they might join in it. All thought well of this last advice. As Cortés had already told them that we were going to set out on the following day, for this reason we should make a show of tying together our baggage, which was little enough, and then in the large courts with high walls, where we were lodged, we should fall on the Indian warriors, who well deserved their fate. As regards the Ambassadors of Montezuma, we should dissemble and tell them that the evil-minded Cholulans had intended treachery and had attempted to put the blame for it on their Lord Montezuma, and on themselves as his Ambassadors, but we did not believe Montezuma had given any such orders, and we begged them to stay in their apartments and not have any further converse with the people of the city, so that we should not have reason to think they were in league with them in their treachery, and we asked them to go with us as our guides to Mexico.

They replied that neither they themselves nor their Lord Montezuma knew anything about that which we were telling them. Although they did not like it, we placed guards over the Ambassadors, so that they could not go out without our permission.

All that night we were on the alert and under arms with the horses saddled and bridled, for we thought that for certain all the companies of the Mexicans as well as the Cholulans would attack us during the night.

There was an old Indian woman, the wife of a Cacique, who knew all about the plot and trap which had been arranged, and she had come secretly to Doña Marina, having noticed that she was young and good looking and rich, and advised her, if she wanted to escape with her life, to come with her to her house, for it was certain that on that night or during the next day we were all going to be killed. Because she knew of this, and on account of the compassion she felt for Doña Marina, she had come to tell her that she had better get all her possessions together and come with her to her house, and she would there marry her to her son, the brother of a youth who accompanied her.

When Doña Marina understood this (as she was always very shrewd) she said to her: "O mother, thank you much for this that you have told me, I would go with you at once but that I have no one here whom I can trust to carry my clothes and jewels of gold of which I have many, for goodness sake, mother, wait here a little while, you and your son, and to-night we will set out, for now, as you can see, these Teules are on the watch and will hear us."

The old woman believed what she said, and remained chatting with her, and Doña Marina asked her how they were going to kill us all, and how and when and where the plot was made. The old woman told her neither more nor less than what the two priests had already stated, and Doña Marina replied: "If this affair is such a secret, how is it that you came to know about it?" and the old woman replied that her husband had told her, for he was a captain of one of the parties in the city; as to the plot she had known about it for three days, for a gilded drum had been sent to her husband from Mexico, and rich cloaks and jewels of gold had been sent to three other cap-

tains to induce them to bring us bound to their Lord Montezuma.

When Doña Marina heard this she deceived the old woman
and said: "How delighted I am to hear that your son to whom
you wish to marry me is a man of distinction. We have already
talked a good deal, and I do not want them to notice us, so
Mother you wait here while I begin to bring my property, for
I cannot bring it all at once, and you and your son, my brother,
will take care of it, and then we shall be able to go." The old
woman believed all that was told her, and she and her son sat
down to rest. Then Doña Marina went swiftly to the Captain
and told him all that had passed with the Indian woman.
Cortés at once ordered her to be brought before him, and questioned her about these treasons and plots, and she told him neither more nor less than the priests had already said, so he
placed a guard over the woman so that she could not escape.

† LVIII

When dawn broke it was a sight to see the haste with which
the Caciques and priests brought in the warriors, laughing and
contented as though they had already caught us in their traps
and nets, and they brought more Indian warriors than we had
asked for, and large as they are (for they still stand as a memorial of the past) the courtyards would not hold them all.

We were already quite prepared for what had to be done.
The soldiers with swords and shields were stationed at the gate
of the great court so as not to let a single armed Indian pass out.
Our Captain was mounted on horseback with many soldiers
round him, as a guard, and when he saw how very early the
Caciques and priests and warriors had arrived, he said: "How
these traitors long to see us among the barrancas so as to gorge
on our flesh, but Our Lord will do better for us." Then he
asked for the two priests who had let out the secret, and he sent
our interpreter, Aguilar, to tell them to go to their houses, for
he had no need of their presence now. This was in order that,
as they had done us a good turn, they should not suffer for it,
and should not get killed. Cortés was on horseback and Doña
Marina near to him, and he asked the Caciques why was it, as

we had done them no harm whatever, that they had wished to kill us, and why should they turn traitors against us, when all we had said or done was to warn them against certain things of which we had already warned all the towns that we had passed through, and to tell them about matters concerning our holy faith, and this without compulsion of any kind? To what purpose then had they quite recently prepared many long and strong poles with collars and cords and placed them in a house near to the Great Temple, and why for the last three days had they been building barricades and digging holes in the streets and raising breastworks on the roofs of the houses, and why had they removed their children and wives and property from the city? Their ill will however had been plainly shown, and they had not been able to hide their treason. They had not even given us food to eat, and as a mockery had brought us firewood and water, and said that there was no maize. He knew well that in the barrancas near by, there were many companies of warriors lying in wait for us, ready to carry out their treacherous plans, thinking that we should pass along that road towards Mexico. So in return for our having come to treat them like brothers and to tell them what Our Lord God and the King have ordained, they wished to kill us and eat our flesh, and had already prepared the pots with salt and peppers and tomatoes. If this was what they wanted it would have been better for them to make war on us in the open field like good and valiant warriors, as did their neighbours the Tlaxcalans. He knew for certain all that had been planned in the city and that they had even promised to their Idol, that twenty of us should be sacrificed before it, and that three nights ago they had sacrificed seven Indians to it so as to ensure victory, which was promised them; but as the Idol was both evil and false, it neither had, nor would have power against us, and all these evil and traitorous designs which they had planned and put into effect were about to recoil on themselves. Doña Marina told all this to them, and made them understand it very clearly, and when the priests, Caciques, and captains had heard it, they said that what had been stated was true but that they were not to blame for it, for the Ambassadors of Montezuma had ordered it at the command of their Prince.

Then Cortés told them that the royal laws decreed that such treasons as those should not remain unpunished and that for their crime they must die. Then he ordered a musket to be fired, which was the signal that we had agreed upon for that purpose, and a blow was given to them which they will remember for ever, for we killed many of them, so that they gained nothing from the promises of their false idols.

Not two hours had passed before our allies, the Tlaxcalans, arrived, and they had fought very fiercely where the Cholulans had posted other companies to defend the streets and prevent their being entered, but these were soon defeated. The Tlax-calans went about the city, plundering and making prisoners and we could not stop them, and the next day more companies from the Tlaxcalan towns arrived, and did great damage, for they were very hostile to the people of Cholula, and when we saw this, both Cortés and the captains and the soldiers, on account of the compassion that we had felt, restrained the Tlax-calans from doing further damage, and Cortés ordered Cristó-bal de Olid to bring him all the Tlaxcalan captains together so that he could speak to them, and they did not delay in coming; then he ordered them to gather together all their men and go and camp in the fields, and this they did, and only the men from Cempoala remained with us.

Just then certain Caciques and priests of Cholula who belonged to other districts of the town, and said that they were not concerned in the treasons against us (for it is a large city and they have parties and factions among themselves), asked Cortés and all of us to pardon the provocation of the treachery that had been plotted against us, for the traitors had already paid with their lives. Then there came the two priests who were our friends and had disclosed the secret to us, and the old woman, the wife of the captain, who wanted to be the mother-in-law of Doña Marina, and all prayed Cortés for pardon.

When they spoke to him, Cortés made a show of great anger and ordered the Ambassadors of Montezuma, who were detained in our company, to be summoned. He then said that the whole city deserved to be destroyed, but that out of respect for their Lord Montezuma, whose vassals they were, he would pardon them, and that from now on they must be well behaved, and let them beware of such affairs as the last happening again, lest they should die for it.

Then, he ordered the Chiefs of Tlaxcala, who were in the

fields, to be summoned, and told them to return the men and women whom they had taken prisoners, for the damage they had done was sufficient. Giving up the prisoners went against the grain with the Tlaxcalans, and they said that the Cholulans had deserved far greater punishment for the many treacheries they had constantly received at their hands. Nevertheless as Cortés ordered it, they gave back many persons, but they still remained rich, both in gold and mantles, cotton cloth, salt and slaves. Besides this Cortés made them and the people of Cholula friends, and, from what I have since seen and ascertained, that friendship has never been broken.

Furthermore, Cortés ordered all the priests and Caciques to bring back the people to the city, and to hold their markets and fairs, and not to have any fear, for no harm would be done to them. They replied that within five days the city would be fully peopled again, for at that time nearly all the inhabitants were in hiding. They said it was necessary that Cortés should appoint a Cacique for them, for their ruler was one of those who had died in the Court, so he asked them to whom the office ought to go, and they said to the brother of the late Cacique, so Cortés at once appointed him to be Governor.

In addition to this, as soon as he saw the city was reinhabited, and their markets were carried on in safety, he ordered all the priests, captains and other chieftains of that city to assemble, and explained to them very clearly all the matters concerning our holy faith, and told them that they could see how their Idols had deceived them, and were evil things not speaking the truth; he begged them to destroy the Idols and break them in pieces. That if they did not wish to do it themselves we would do it for them. He also ordered them to whitewash a temple, so that we might set up a cross there.

They immediately did what we asked them in the matter of the cross, and they said that they would remove their Idols, but although they were many times ordered to do it, they delayed. Then the Padre de la Merced said to Cortés that it was going too far, in the beginning, to take away their Idols until they should understand things better, and should see how our expedition to Mexico would turn out, and time would show us what we ought to do in the matter, that for the present the warnings we had given them were sufficient, together with the setting up of the Cross.

The city is situated on a plain, in a locality where there were many neighbouring towns, and it is a land fruitful in maize and other vegetables, and much Chili pepper, and the land is full of Magueys from which they make their wine. They make very good pottery in the city of red and black and white clay with various designs, and with it supply Mexico and all the neighbouring provinces. At that time there were many high towers in the city where the Idols stood, especially the Great Cue which was higher than that of Mexico, although the Mexican Cue was very lofty and magnificent.

As soon as the Squadrons sent by the Great Montezuma, which were already stationed in the ravines near Cholula, learned what had taken place they returned, faster than at a walk, to Mexico and told Montezuma how it all happened. But fast as they went the news had already reached him, through the two Chieftains who had been with us and who went to him post-haste. We learned on good authority that when Montezuma heard the news he was greatly grieved and very angry, and at once sacrificed some Indians to his Idol Huichilobos, whom they looked on as the God of War, so that he might tell him what was to be the result of our going to Mexico, or if he should permit us to enter the city. We even knew that he was shut in at his devotions and sacrifices for two days in company with ten of the Chief Priests, and that a reply came from those Idols which was, that they advised him to send messengers to us to disclaim all blame for the Cholulan affair, and that with demonstrations of peace we should be allowed to enter into Mexico, and that when we were inside, by depriving us of food and water, or by raising some of the bridges, they would kill us.

This affair and punishment at Cholula became known throughout the provinces of New Spain and if we had a reputation for valour before, from now on they took us for sorcerers, and said that no evil that was planned against us could be so hidden from us that it did not come to our knowledge, and on this account they showed us good will.

I think that the curious reader must be already satiated hearing this story about Cholula and I wish that I had finished writing about it, but I cannot avoid calling to mind the prisons of thick wooden beams which we found in the city, which were full of Indians and boys being fattened so that they could be sacrificed and their flesh eaten. We broke open all these prisons, and Cortés ordered all the Indian prisoners that were confined within them to return to their native countries, and with threats he ordered the Caciques and captains and priests of the city not to imprison any more Indians in that way, and not to eat human flesh. They promised not to do so, but what use were such promises? as they never kept them.

† LIX

Fourteen days had already passed since we had come to Cholula and we had nothing more to do there, for we saw that the city was again fully peopled, and we had established friendship between them and the people of Tlaxcala. But as we knew that the Great Montezuma was secretly sending spies to our camp to enquire and find out what our plans were, our Captain determined to take counsel of certain captains and soldiers, whom he knew to be well disposed towards him, because he never did anything without first asking our advice about it. It was agreed that we should send to tell the Great Montezuma, gently and amicably, that in order to carry out the purpose for which our Lord and King had sent us to these parts, we had crossed many seas and distant lands, and that while we were marching towards his city, his ambassadors had guided us by way of Cholula, where the people had plotted a treason with the intention of killing us, and we had punished some of those who intended to carry out the plot. As our Captain knew that the Cholulans were his subjects, it was only out of respect for his person, and on account of our great friendship, that he refrained from destroying and killing all those who were concerned in the treason. However, the worst of it all is that the priests and Caciques say it was done on his advice and command. This of course we never believed, that such a great prince as he is could issue such orders, especially as he had declared himself our friend, and we had inferred from his character that since his Idols had put such an evil thought as making war on us into his head, he would surely fight us in the open field. But as we look upon him as our great friend and wish to see and speak to him, we are setting

out at once for his city to give him a more complete account
of what Our Lord the King had commanded us to do.

When Montezuma heard this message and learned through
the people of Cholula that we did not lay all the blame on him,
we heard it said that he returned again with his priests to fast
and make sacrifices to his Idols, to know if they would again
repeat their permission to allow us to enter into the city or no,
and whether they would reiterate the commands they had already given him. The answer which they gave was the same as
the first, that he should allow us to enter and that once inside
the city he could kill us when he chose. His captains and priests
also advised him that if he should place obstacles in the way of
our entry, we would make war on him through his subject
towns, seeing that we had as our friends the Tlaxcalans, and
all the Totonacs of the hills, and other towns which had accepted our alliance, and to avoid these evils the best and most
sensible advice was that which Huichilobos had given.

When Montezuma heard the message which we sent to him
concerning our friendship and the other fearless remarks, after
much deliberation he despatched six chieftains with a present
of gold and jewels of a variety of shapes which were estimated
to be worth over two thousand pesos, and he sent certain loads
of very rich mantles beautifully worked.

When the Chiefs came before Cortés with the present they
touched the ground with their hands and with great reverence,
such as they use among themselves, they said: "Malinche, Our
Lord the Great Montezuma, sends thee this present, and asks
thee to accept it with the great affection which he has for thee
and all thy brethren, and he says that the annoyance that the
people of Cholula have caused him weighs heavily on him,
and he wishes to punish them more in their persons, for they
are an evil and a lying people in that they have thrown the
blame of the wickedness which they wished to commit upon
him and his ambassadors," that we might take it as very certain
that he was our friend, and that we could go to his City whenever we liked, for he wished to do us every honour as very valiant men, and the messengers of such a great King. But because he had nothing to give us to eat, for everything has to be
carried into the city by carriers as it is built on the lake, he
could not entertain us very satisfactorily, but he would endeav-

our to do us all the honour that was possible, and he had ordered all the towns through which we had to pass to give us what we might need. Cortés received the present with demonstrations of affection and embraced the messengers, and ordered them to be given certain twisted cut glass beads.

Cortés gave the ambassadors a suitable and affectionate reply and ordered the messengers who had come with the present to remain with us as guides and the other three to return with the answer to their Prince, and to advise him that we were already on the road.

When the Chief Caciques of Tlaxcala understood that we were going, their souls were afflicted and they sent to say to Cortés that they had already warned him many times that he should be careful what he was about, and should refrain from entering such a strong city where there was so much war-like preparation and such a multitude of warriors, for one day or the other we would be attacked, and they feared that we would not escape alive, and on account of the good will that they bore us, they wished to send ten thousand men under brave captains to go with us and carry food for the journey.

Cortés thanked them heartily for their good wishes and told them that it was not just to enter into Mexico with such a host of warriors, especially when one party was so hostile to the other, that he only had need of one thousand men to carry the tepusques and the baggage, and to clear some of the roads, and they at once sent us the thousand Indians very well equipped.

Just as we were ready to set out, there came to Cortés all the Caciques and all the principal warriors whom we had brought from Cempoala, who had marched in our company and served us well and loyally, and said that they wanted to go back to Cempoala and not to proceed beyond Cholula in the direction of Mexico, for they felt certain that if they went there it would be for them and for us to go to our deaths. The Great Montezuma would order them to be killed because they had broken their fealty by refusing to pay him tribute and by imprisoning his tax-gatherers.

When Cortés observed the determination with which they demanded permission, he answered that they need not have the slightest fear that they would come to any harm, for, as they would go in our company, who would dare to annoy either them or us? and he begged them to change their minds and stay with us, and he promised to make them rich. Although Cortés pressed them to stay, and Doña Marina put it in the most warm-hearted manner, they never wished to stay, but only to return to their homes. When Cortés perceived this he said: "God forbid that these Indians who have served us so well should be forced to go," and he sent for many loads of rich mantles and divided them among them, and he also sent to our friend the fat Cacique two loads of mantles for himself and for his nephew the other great Cacique named Cuesco.

† LX

We set out from Cholula in carefully arranged order as we were always accustomed to do, and arrived that day at some ranchos standing on a hill about four leagues from Cholula, they are peopled from Huexotzingo, and I think they are called the Ranchos of Yscalpan. To this place soon came the Caciques and priests of the towns of Huexotzingo which were near by, and people from other small towns, which stand on the slopes of the volcano near their boundary line, who brought us food and a present of golden jewels of small value, and they asked Cortés to accept them and not consider the insignificance of the gift but the good will with which it was offered. They advised him not to go to Mexico as it was a very strong city and full of warriors, where we should run much risk. They also told us to look out, if we had decided upon going, for when we had ascended to the pass we should find two broad roads, one leading to a town named Chalco, and the other to another town called Tlamanalco,[1] both of them subject to Mexico; that the one road was well swept and cleared so as to induce us to take it, and that the other road had been closed up and many great pines and other trees had been cut down so that horses could not use it and we could not march along it. That a little way down the side of the mountain along the road that had been cleared, the Mexicans (thinking that we must take that road) had cut away a piece of the hill side, and had made ditches and barricades, and that certain squadrons of Mexicans had waited at that point so as to kill us there. So they counselled us not to go by the road which was clear, but by the road

[1] B. D. writes Tlamanalco in error—Cortés says it was Amecameca.

where the felled trees were, saying that they would send many men with us to clear it.

Cortés thanked them for the counsel they had given him, and said that with God's help he would not abandon his march but would go the way they advised him. Early the next morning we began our march, and it was nearly midday when we arrived at the ridge of the mountain where we found the roads just as the people of Huexotzingo had said. There we rested a little and began to think about the Mexican squadrons on the intrenched hillside where the earth works were that they had told us about.

Then Cortés ordered the Ambassadors of the great Montezuma who came in our company to be summoned, and he asked them how it was that those two roads were in that condition, one very clean and swept and the other covered with newly-felled trees. They replied that it was done so that we should go by the cleared road which led to a city named Chalco, where the people would give us a good reception, for it belonged to their Prince Montezuma, and that they had cut the trees and closed up the other road to prevent our going by it, for there were bad passes on it, and it went somewhat round about before going to Mexico, and came out at another town which was not as large as Chalco. Then Cortés said that he wished to go by the blocked up road, and we began to ascend the mountain with the greatest caution, our allies moving aside the huge thick tree trunks with great labour, and some of them still lie by the roadside to this very day. As we rose higher it began to snow and the snow caked on the ground. Then we descended the hill and went to sleep at a group of houses which they build like inns or hostels where the Indian traders lodge, and we supped well, but the cold was intense, and we posted our watchmen, sentinels, and patrols and even sent out scouts. The next day we set out on our march, and, about the hour of high mass, arrived at a town (Amecameca), where they received us well and where there was no scarcity of food.

When the other towns in the neighbourhood heard of our arrival, people soon came from Chalco and from Chimaloacan and from Ayotzingo, where the canoes are, for it is their port. All of them together brought a present of gold and two loads of mantles and eight Indian women and the gold was worth over one hundred and fifty pesos and they said: "Malinche, accept these presents which we give you and look on us in the future as your friends." Cortés received them with great good will and promised to help them in whatever they needed and when he saw them together he told the Padre de la Merced to counsel them regarding matters touching our holy faith, and that they should give up their Idols. Cortés also explained to them about the great power of our Lord, the Emperor, and how we had come to right wrongs and to stop robbery.

When they heard this, all these towns that I have named, secretly, so that the Mexican Ambassadors should not hear them, made great complaints about Montezuma, and his tax-gatherers, who robbed them of all they possessed, and carried off their wives and daughters, and made the men work as though they were slaves, and made them carry pine timber and stone and firewood and maize either in their canoes or over land, and many other services such as planting cornfields, and they took their lands for the service of the Idols.

Cortés comforted them with kindly words which he knew well how to say to them through Doña Marina, but added that at the present moment he could not undertake to see justice done them and they must bear it awhile and he would presently free them from that rule. The Caciques replied: "We are of opinion that you should stay here with us, and we will give you what we possess, and that you should give up going to Mexico, as we know for certain it is very strong and full of warriors, and they will not spare your lives."

Cortés replied to them, with a cheerful mien, that we had no fear that the Mexicans, or any other nation, could destroy us and, as we wished to start at once, he asked them to give him twenty of their principal men to go in his company, and they brought us the twenty Indians.

† LXI

Just as we were starting on our march to Mexico there came before Cortés four Mexican chiefs sent by Montezuma who brought a present of gold and cloths. After they had made obeisance according to their custom, they said: "Malinche, our Lord the Great Montezuma sends you this present and says that he is greatly concerned for the hardships you have endured in coming from such a distant land in order to see him, and that he has already sent to tell you that he will give you much gold and silver and chalchihuites as tribute for your Emperor and for yourself and the other Teules in your company, provided you do not come to Mexico, and now again he begs as a favour, that you will not advance any further but return whence you have come, and he promises to send you to the port a great quantity of gold and silver and rich stones for that King of yours, and, as for you, he will give you four loads of gold and for each of your brothers one load, but as for going on to Mexico your entrance into it is forbidden, for all his vassals have risen in arms to prevent your entry, and besides this there is no road thither, only a very narrow one, and there is no food for you to eat." And he used many other arguments about the difficulties to the end that we should advance no further.

Cortés with much show of affection embraced the Ambassadors, although the message grieved him, and he accepted the present, and said that he marvelled how the Lord Montezuma, having given himself out as our friend, and being such a great Prince, should be so inconstant; that one time he says one thing and another time sends to order the contrary, and regarding what he says about giving gold to our Lord the Emperor and to ourselves, he is grateful to him for it, and what he sends him now he will pay for in good works as time goes on. How can he deem it befitting that being so near to his city, we should think it right to return on our road without carrying through what our Prince has commanded us to do? If the Lord Montezuma had sent his messengers and ambassadors to some great prince such as he is himself, and if, after nearly reaching his house, those messengers whom he sent should turn back without speaking to the Prince about that which they were sent to say, when they came back into his [Montezuma's] presence with such a story, what favour would he show them? He would merely treat them as cowards of little worth; and this is what our Emperor would do with us, so that in one way or another we were determined to enter his city, and from this time forth he must not send any more excuses on the subject, for he [Cortés] was bound to see him, and talk to him and explain the whole purpose for which we had come, and this he must do to him personally. Then after he understood it all, if our presence in the city did not seem good to him, we would

return whence we had come. As for what he said about there
being little or no food, not enough to support us, we were men
who could get along even if we have but little to eat, and we
were already on the way to his city, so let him take our coming in good part.

As soon as the messengers had been despatched, we set out
for Mexico, and as the people of Huexotzingo and Chalco had
told us that Montezuma had held consultations with his Idols
and priests, who had said he was to allow us to enter and that
then he could kill us, and as we are but human and feared
death, we never ceased thinking about it. As that country is
very thickly peopled we made short marches, and commended
ourselves to God and to Our Lady his blessed Mother, and
talked about how and by what means we could enter the City,
and it put courage into our hearts to think that as our Lord
Jesus Christ had vouchsafed us protection through past dangers, he would likewise guard us from the power of the Mexicans.

We went to sleep at a town called Iztapalatengo[1] where half
the houses are in the water and the other half on dry land, and
there they gave us a good supper.

The Great Montezuma, when he heard the reply which
Cortés had sent to him, at once determined to send his nephew
named Cacamatzin, the Lord of Texcoco, with great pomp to
bid welcome to Cortés and to all of us, and one of our scouts
came in to tell us that a large crowd of friendly Mexicans was
coming along the road clad in rich mantles. It was very early
in the morning when this happened, and we were ready to
start, and Cortés ordered us to wait in our quarters until he
could see what the matter was.

At that moment four chieftains arrived, who made deep
obeisance to Cortés and said that close by there was approaching Cacamatzin, the great Lord of Texcoco, a nephew of the
Great Montezuma, and he begged us to have the goodness to
wait until he arrived.

He did not tarry long, for he soon arrived with greater pomp
and splendour than we had ever beheld in a Mexican Prince,
for he came in a litter richly worked in green feathers, with
many silver borderings, and rich stones set in bosses made out
of the finest gold. Eight Chieftains, who, it was said were all

[1] This is clearly a mistake; the town was Ayotzingo.

Lords of Towns, bore the litter on their shoulders. When they
came near to the house where Cortés was quartered, the Chieftains assisted Cacamatzin to descend from the litter, and they
swept the ground, and removed the straws where he had to
pass, and when they came before our Captain they made him a
deep reverence, and Cacamatzin said:

"Malinche, here we have come, I and these Chieftains to
place ourselves at your service, and to give you all that you may
need for yourself and your companions and to place you in
your home, which is our city, for so the Great Montezuma our
Prince has ordered us to do, and he asks your pardon that he
did not come with us himself, but it is on account of ill-health
that he did not do so, and not from want of very good will
which he bears towards you."

When our Captain and all of us beheld such pomp and majesty in those chiefs, especially in the nephew of Montezuma,
we considered it a matter of the greatest importance, and said
among ourselves, if this Cacique bears himself with such dignity, what will the Great Montezuma do?

When Cacamatzin had delivered his speech, Cortés embraced him, and gave many caresses to him and all the other
Chieftains, and gave him three stones which are called Margaritas, which have within them many markings of different
colours, and to the other Chieftains he gave blue glass beads,
and he told them that he thanked them and when he was able
he would repay the Lord Montezuma for all the favours which
every day he was granting us.

As soon as the speech-making was over, we at once set out,
and as the Caciques whom I have spoken about brought many
followers with them, and as many people came out to see us
from the neighbouring towns, all the roads were full of them.

During the morning, we arrived at a broad Causeway[1] and
continued our march towards Iztapalapa, and when we saw so
many cities and villages built in the water and other great
towns on dry land and that straight and level Causeway going
towards Mexico, we were amazed and said that it was like the
enchantments they tell of in the legend of Amadis, on account
of the great towers and cues and buildings rising from the water, and all built of masonry. And some of our soldiers even

[1] The Causeway of Cuitlahuac separating the lake of Chalco from the lake of
Xochimilco.

asked whether the things that we saw were not a dream. It is not to be wondered at that I here write it down in this manner, for there is so much to think over that I do not know how to describe it, seeing things as we did that had never been heard of or seen before, not even dreamed about.

Thus, we arrived near Iztapalapa, to behold the splendour of the other Caciques who came out to meet us, who were the Lord of the town named Cuitlahuac, and the Lord of Culuacan, both of them near relations of Montezuma. And then when we entered the city of Iztapalapa, the appearance of the palaces in which they lodged us! How spacious and well built they were, of beautiful stone work and cedar wood, and the wood of other sweet scented trees, with great rooms and courts, wonderful to behold, covered with awnings of cotton cloth.

When we had looked well at all of this, we went to the orchard and garden, which was such a wonderful thing to see and walk in, that I was never tired of looking at the diversity of the trees, and noting the scent which each one had, and the paths full of roses and flowers, and the many fruit trees and native roses, and the pond of fresh water. There was another thing to observe, that great canoes were able to pass into the garden from the lake through an opening that had been made so that there was no need for their occupants to land. And all was cemented and very splendid with many kinds of stone [monuments] with pictures on them, which gave much to think about. Then the birds of many kinds and breeds which came into the pond. I say again that I stood looking at it and thought that never in the world would there be discovered other lands such as these, for at that time there was no Peru, nor any thought of it. Of all these wonders that I then beheld to-day all is overthrown and lost, nothing left standing.

Let us go on, and I will relate that the Caciques of that town and of Coyoacan brought us a present of gold, worth more than two thousand pesos.

†   LXII

Early next day we left Iztapalapa with a large escort of those great Caciques whom I have already mentioned. We proceeded along the Causeway which is here eight paces in width and runs so straight to the City of Mexico that it does not seem to me to turn either much or little, but, broad as it is, it was so crowded with people that there was hardly room for them all, some of them going to and others returning from Mexico, besides those who had come out to see us, so that we were hardly able to pass by the crowds of them that came; and the towers and cues were full of people as well as the canoes from all parts of the lake. It was not to be wondered at, for they had never before seen horses or men such as we are.

Gazing on such wonderful sights, we did not know what to say, or whether what appeared before us was real, for on one side, on the land, there were great cities, and in the lake ever so many more, and the lake itself was crowded with canoes, and in the Causeway were many bridges at intervals, and in front of us stood the great City of Mexico, and we—we did not even number four hundred soldiers! and we well remembered the words and warnings given us by the people of Huexotzingo and Tlaxcala, and the many other warnings that had been given that we should beware of entering Mexico, where they would kill us, as soon as they had us inside.

Let the curious readers consider whether there is not much to ponder over in this that I am writing. What men have there been in the world who have shown such daring? But let us get on, and march along the Causeway. When we arrived where another small causeway branches off[1] [leading to Coyoacan, which is another city] where there were some buildings like towers, which are their oratories, many more chieftains and Caciques approached clad in very rich mantles, the brilliant liveries of one chieftain differing from those of another, and the causeways were crowded with them. The Great Montezuma had sent these great Caciques in advance to receive us, and when they came before Cortés they bade us welcome in their language, and as a sign of peace, they touched their hands against the ground, and kissed the ground with the hand.

There we halted for a good while, and Cacamatzin, the Lord of Texcoco, and the Lord of Iztapalapa and the Lord of Tacuba and the Lord of Coyoacan went on in advance to meet the Great Montezuma, who was approaching in a rich litter accompanied by other great Lords and Caciques, who owned vassals. When we arrived near to Mexico, where there were some

[1] Acachinango.

other small towers, the Great Montezuma got down from his litter, and those great Caciques supported him with their arms beneath a marvellously rich canopy of green coloured feathers with much gold and silver embroidery and with pearls and chalchihuites suspended from a sort of bordering, which was wonderful to look at. The Great Montezuma was richly attired according to his usage, and he was shod with sandals, the soles were of gold and the upper part adorned with precious stones. The four Chieftains who supported his arms were also richly clothed according to their usage, in garments which were apparently held ready for them on the road to enable them to accompany their prince, for they did not appear in such attire when they came to receive us. Besides these four Chieftains, there were four other great Caciques who supported the canopy over their heads, and many other Lords who walked before the Great Montezuma, sweeping the ground where he would tread and spreading cloths on it, so that he should not tread on the earth. Not one of these Chieftains dared even to think of looking him in the face, but kept their eyes lowered with great reverence, except those four relations, his nephews, who supported him with their arms.

When Cortés was told that the Great Montezuma was approaching, and he saw him coming, he dismounted from his horse, and when he was near Montezuma, they simultaneously paid great reverence to one another. Montezuma bade him welcome and our Cortés replied through Doña Marina wishing him very good health. And it seems to me that Cortés, through Doña Marina, offered him his right hand, and Montezuma did not wish to take it, but he did give his hand to Cortés and then Cortés brought out a necklace which he had ready at hand, made of glass stones, which I have already said are called Margaritas, which have within them many patterns of diverse colours, these were strung on a cord of gold and with musk so that it should have a sweet scent, and he placed it round the neck of the Great Montezuma and when he had so placed it he was going to embrace him, and those great Princes who accompanied Montezuma held back Cortés by the arm so that he should not embrace him, for they considered it an indignity.

Then Cortés through the mouth of Doña Marina told him that now his heart rejoiced at having seen such a great Prince, and that he took it as a great honour that he had come in person to meet him and had frequently shown him such favour.

Then Montezuma spoke other words of politeness to him, and told two of his nephews who supported his arms, the Lord of Texcoco and the Lord of Coyoacan, to go with us and show us to our quarters, and Montezuma with his other two relations, the Lord of Cuitlahuac and the Lord of Tacuba who accompanied him, returned to the city, and all those grand companies of Caciques and chieftains who had come with him returned in his train. As they turned back after their Prince we stood watching them and observed how they all marched with their eyes fixed on the ground without looking at him, keeping close to the wall, following him with great reverence. Thus space was made for us to enter the streets of Mexico, without being so much crowded. But who could now count the multitude of men and women and boys who were in the streets and on the azoteas, and in canoes on the canals, who had come out to see us. It was indeed wonderful, and, now that I am writing about it, it all comes before my eyes as though it had happened but yesterday. Coming to think it over it seems to be a great mercy that our Lord Jesus Christ was pleased to give us grace and courage to dare to enter into such a city; and for the many times He has saved me from danger of death, as will be seen later on, I give Him sincere thanks, and in that He has preserved me to write about it, although I cannot do it as fully as is fitting or the subject needs. Let us make no words about it, for deeds are the best witnesses to what I say here and elsewhere.

Let us return to our entry to Mexico. They took us to lodge in some large houses, where there were apartments for all of us, for they had belonged to the father of the Great Montezuma, who was named Axayaca, and at that time Montezuma kept there the great oratories for his idols, and a secret chamber where he kept bars and jewels of gold, which was the treasure that he had inherited from his father Axayaca, and he never disturbed it. They took us to lodge in that house, because they called us Teules, and took us for such, so that we should be with the Idols or Teules which were kept there. However, for one reason or another, it was there they took us, where there were great halls and chambers canopied with the cloth of the country for our Captain, and for every one of us beds of matting

with canopies above, and no better bed is given, however great the chief may be, for they are not used. And all these palaces were coated with shining cement and swept and garlanded.

As soon as we arrived and entered into the great court, the Great Montezuma took our Captain by the hand, for he was there awaiting him, and led him to the apartment and saloon where he was to lodge, which was very richly adorned according to their usage, and he had at hand a very rich necklace made of golden crabs, a marvellous piece of work, and Montezuma himself placed it round the neck of our Captain Cortés, and greatly astonished his [own] Captains by the great honour that he was bestowing on him. When the necklace had been fastened, Cortés thanked Montezuma through our interpreters, and Montezuma replied—"Malinche, you and your brethren are in your own house, rest awhile," and then he went to his palaces, which were not far away, and we divided our lodgings by companies, and placed the artillery pointing in a convenient direction, and the order which we had to keep was clearly explained to us, and that we were to be much on the alert, both the cavalry and all of us soldiers. A sumptuous dinner was provided for us according to their use and custom, and we ate it at once. So this was our lucky and daring entry into the great city of Tenochtitlan Mexico on the 8th day of November the year of our Saviour Jesus Christ, 1519.

Thanks to our Lord Jesus Christ for it all. And if I have not said anything that I ought to have said, may your honours pardon me, for I do not know now even at the present time how better to express it.

Let us leave this talk and go back to our story of what else happened to us, which I will go on to relate.

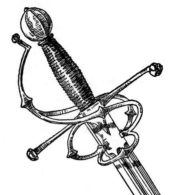

V

The Stay in Mexico

Introductory Notes

THE VALLEY OF MEXICO

The Valley of Mexico is a level plain about 7,244 feet above the sea, completely surrounded by mountains which leave no exit for the escape of the water from a fairly abundant rainfall, and as a consequence the whole valley at one period must have formed one vast lake, whose volume was limited only by soakage and the very rapid evaporation due to a tropical sun. At the time of the Conquest the area of the surface of the lakes was (very roughly) 442 square miles.

The mountains surrounding the valley may be roughly divided into three ranges. To the East the Sierra Nevada, with the great peaks of Popocatepetl (17,887 ft.) and Ixtaccihuatl (17,342 ft.) capped with perpetual snow, and the three lower peaks to the North, Papayo, Telapon and Tlaloc; to the South lies the great volcanic barrier of Ajusco, to the West the range of Las Cruces, and to the North that of Pachuca.

Although the lakes have received different names, the water surface must have been continuous until separated by the earthworks of the Indians. Starting from the North the lakes are named Zumpango, Xaltocan, Texcoco, Xochimilco and Chalco. All these lakes were very shallow.

The site of the City was originally, in all probability, two reed-covered mud banks or islands, which may have been cultivated in much the same manner as were the *chinampas* or floating gardens at the time of the Conquest, or as the chinampas of Xochimilco are at the present day, and these two islands became respectively the sites of the towns of Tlatelolco and Tenochtitlan, and the space between them was eventually reduced to a rather broad canal.

The chinampas were formed by heaping up the soft mud from the lake on to wattles in order to form seed beds for flowers and vegetables, and these floating gardens gradually increased in size and became more compact from the growth of the interlacing roots of the willows and other water-loving plants until they may have supported a small hut for the owner and his family, and the lengthening roots eventually anchored them on the shallow margin of the lake.

These gardens are divided into long narrow strips with canals running between just wide enough for the passage of a dug-out canoe. The Indian cultivator poles his canoe along the narrow channels and scoops up the soft mud from the bottom to spread it over the land, and splashes the water over the growing plants with his paddle. It was probably this method of cultivation which gave the mainly rectangular arrangement of the streets of the City of Mexico, the more unsymmetrical canals showing the original water-ways between the mud banks, while the aggregation of chinampas may have left an irregular margin of outlying houses and gardens.

The very slight difference in level between the Lake of Texcoco and the site of the City made the latter liable to frequent inundations, and this difficulty was met by the inhabitants by engineering works of considerable importance. A causeway was built passing through the island town of Tlahuac, dividing the Lake of Chalco from that of Xochimilco, and a second causeway separated the waters of Xochimilco from those of Texcoco. The City of Mexico had probably already been joined to the mainland, for purposes of communication, by the causeways of Tlacopan (Tacuba) and Tepeyac (Guadalupe), and a third and longer causeway was added by connecting the City with the barrier holding back the waters of Xochimilco; this third causeway was known as the causeway of Iztapalapa. The lakes of Zumpango and Xaltocan were also traversed by causeways, but it is not now possible to locate their position.

These various causeways did much to control the movement of the waters of the lakes during the rainy season, but they were not sufficient to prevent serious inundations, and native tradition and a picture in a Mexican codex[1] go to prove that during the reign of Motecuhzoma (Montezuma) Illhuicamina, between the years 1440 and 1450, a very wet season caused the waters of Lake Texcoco to rise so much that the City was almost destroyed and the inhabitants had to take refuge in their canoes and piraguas. Montezuma applied for assistance and advice to his friend Netzahualcoyotl the King of Texcoco, and under his sage direction a great dyke was constructed, known as the "Albarradon of Nezhualcoyotl."

[1] *Codex Telleriano Remeusio.*

"This gigantic dyke started from Atzacualco on the North and followed a straight line to the South as far as Ixtapalapa at the foot of the hill called la Estrella. This great work, which was sixteen kilometres[1] in length, was constructed of stone and clay and crowned with a strong wall of rubble masonry, and was protected on both sides by a strong stockade which broke the force of the waves.

"The dyke divided the lake into two parts, the larger to the East was known as the Lake of Texcoco, from the city situated on its shores, the lesser to the West was called the Lake of Mexico because the capital was surrounded by its waters on all sides. From this arrangement Mexico derived an aggregate of inestimable benefits. The great lake, like all lakes having no outlet for their waters, was salt, notwithstanding the volume of all the rivers which flowed into it, for in fact it owed its saltness to this very flow which carried in its current the soluble salts which the falling rain has robbed from the land. The salt water saturating the soil has little by little rendered it sterile, and in addition, the carbonate of soda and the thousand other impurities with which it is charged are hostile to animal life to such an extent that fishes could not live in it, neither to-day nor at the time of the Conquest, as was stated by the writers at that epoch, although the water was then less salt than it is at the present. As the lakes of fresh water to the south poured their surplus water into the lake of Mexico through the narrows of Culhuacan and Mexicaltzingo, those waters spread through the western lake, the Lake of Mexico, and completely filled it, separated as it was from the salt lake by the dyke of Netzahualcoyotl. In this way the basin of fresh water was converted into a fish pond and a home for all sorts of aquatic fowl. Chinampas covered its surface, separated by limpid spaces which were furrowed by swift canoes, and all the suburbs of this enchanting capital became flowery orchards." [2]

The great dyke was provided with numerous openings for the passage of canoes, but these openings were furnished with sluicegates, which could be closed during the rainy season when the water of Texcoco rose and threatened to flood the City, and could be opened again to let out the fresh water from Mexico when the rapid evaporation during the summer months had lowered the level of Texcoco.

There must have been one or more springs on the site of the City which supplied its earliest inhabitants with drinking water, although in

[1] Ten Miles.
[2] Francisco de Garay, *El valle de Mexico, apuntes historicos sobre su hidrographia*, pp. 13 and 14.

later Indian times the supply was brought in an aqueduct from a fine spring near Chapultepec.

"The population of Tenochtitlan (the City of Mexico) at the time of the conquest is variously stated. No contemporary writer estimates it at less than sixty thousand houses, which by the ordinary rules of reckoning would give three hundred thousand souls. If a dwelling often contained, as it asserted, several families, it would swell the amount considerably higher." [1]

The supply of food for such a population must have been a matter of no little difficulty, for the soil on the hill-sides is scanty, many of the slopes are composed of *tepetatle,* a mixture of volcanic ash and scoria fit only for growing Maguey,[2] and considerable surfaces are covered with lava and carry no loam at all. The scarcity of good soil must have led to an intensive cultivation, and this is also shown by the care with which manure was collected as is the case of China and Japan to-day.

Food must have been brought from very considerable distances, and the want of sufficient supply from the near neighbourhood must have had much to do with the predatory nature of the Aztec dominion.

The lakes of Xaltocan and Zumpango are now almost dry during the summer months. The Lake of Chalco has been drained dry, excepting the southern edge round Mixcuic, and is now one vast maize field.

Xochimilco is reduced to a swamp traversed by many water-ways and the water from its springs is being utilized for the supply of drinking water to the City. Texcoco alone remains, in a shrunken condition, and no further drainage of its waters is contemplated, as the evaporation from its surface is one of the main factors contributing to the equable climate of the valley.

THE CITY OF MEXICO

The two towns of Tenochtitlan and Tlaltelolco appear to have risen side by side, each retaining control of its own local affairs, until the time of Axayacatl, the sixth ruler of Tenochtitlan (1473), when, after a fierce battle in the streets of the City, Tlaltelolco was conquered, its chiefs killed, and it became a part of the City of Tenochtitlan. It is, however, this growth of the City in two distinct parts that accounts for the existence of the two centres of religious worship, the great teocalli of Tenochtitlan with its surrounding courts and temples (where the Cathedral of Mexico now stands), and the still larger and more important teocalli of

[1] Prescott, *Conquest of Mexico.*
[2] The American aloe, *Agave americana,* from which pulque is made.

Tlaltelolco and the adjacent temples, courts, and priests' houses, etc., which are so fully described by Bernal Díaz in the text.

The following quotation is from the writings of the "Anonymous Conqueror" who himself beheld Mexico in the days of Montezuma:—"The great city of Temistan (Tenochtitlan) Mexico, has and had many wide and handsome streets; of these two or three are the principal streets, and all the others are formed half of hard earth like a brick pavement, and the other half of water, so that they can go out along the land or by water in the boats and canoes which are made of hollowed wood, and some are large enough to hold five persons. The inhabitants go abroad some by water in these boats and others by land, and they can talk to one another as they go. There are other principal streets in addition, entirely of water which can only be traversed by boats and canoes, as it their wont, as I have already said, for without these boats they could neither go in nor out of their houses."

Cortés in his second letter to the Emperor says:

"There are many very large and fine houses in this City, and the reason of there being so many important houses is that all the Lords of the land who are vassals of the said Montezuma have houses in this City and reside therein for a certain time of the year, and in addition to this there are many rich Citizens who also possess very fine houses. All these houses in addition to having very fine and large dwelling rooms, have very exquisite flower gardens both on the upper apartments as well as down below." [1]

"The principal houses were of two stories, but the greater number of houses were of one storey only. The materials, according to the importance of the buildings, were tezontli[2] and lime, adobes[3] formed the walls plastered with lime, and in the suburbs and shores of the island (the houses were constructed) of reeds and straw, appropriate for the fisher men and the lower classes." [4]

Of the external ornament or decoration of the more important houses or palaces we know nothing, as the destruction of the City was complete If the ornamentation was elaborate we hear nothing about it from the conquerors, and it must in any case have been of plaster or some perishable material, otherwise some fragments of it would have survived. It seems therefore probable that the architectural decoration of the houses was of a very simple character, and that the more elaborate stone work was reserved for the teocallis and temples of their gods.

[1] Cortés' Second Letter.
[2] Tezontli, a volcanic stone, easily worked, of a beautiful dull-red colour.
[3] *Adobes,* sun-dried bricks.
[4] Orozco y Berra, *Hist. de Mexico,* vol. iv, p. 281.

Notwithstanding the above qualifications, the ancient City of Tenochtitlan must have been a place of much beauty and even of considerable
magnificence, and it could not have failed to make a vivid impression
on the Spaniards, who, it must be remembered, until they set foot in
Yucatan, two years earlier, had seen nothing better during the twenty-five
years of exploration of America than the houses of poles and thatch of
Indian tribes, none of whom had risen above a state of barbarism. Much
no doubt was due to the natural surroundings; the white City with its
numerous teocallis was embowered in trees and surrounded by the blue
waters of the lake sparkling under a tropical sun, a lake that was alive
with a multitude of canoes passing and repassing to the other white
cities on its shores, and in every direction the horizon was closed with
a splendid panorama of forest-covered hills, while to the south-east the
eye always rested with delight on the beautiful slopes and snow-covered
peaks of the two great volcanoes. It is an enchanting scene to-day, in
spite of the shrinkage of the lakes, the smoke from factory chimneys, and
the somewhat squalid surroundings of a modern city, and but little effort
of imagination is needed to appreciate the charm that it must have exercised in the days of Montezuma.

Gardens and groves were evidently numerous in the City itself; the
Mexicans were distinguished for their love of flowers, and there is no
climate where gardening is more remunerative than in these tropical
highlands when water is plentiful. The flowering plants cultivated on
the roofs of the houses must have added greatly to the picturesque aspect
of the streets and canals.

Bernal Díaz tells us how clean the surroundings of the great temple
were kept, where not a straw or a spot of dust could be seen (filth seems
to have been confined to the temples themselves where the horrid rites
of their religion were performed) and this cleanliness probably extended
to the City itself, for it will be observed by any traveller in Mexico or
Central America that the purely Indian villages of considerable size are
almost always kept swept and tidy, while this is not the case in the towns
and villages inhabited by the mixed race.

† LXIII

When the Great Montezuma had dined and he knew that some
time had passed since our Captain and all of us had done the
same, he came in the greatest state to our quarters with a numerous company of chieftains, all of them his kinsmen. When

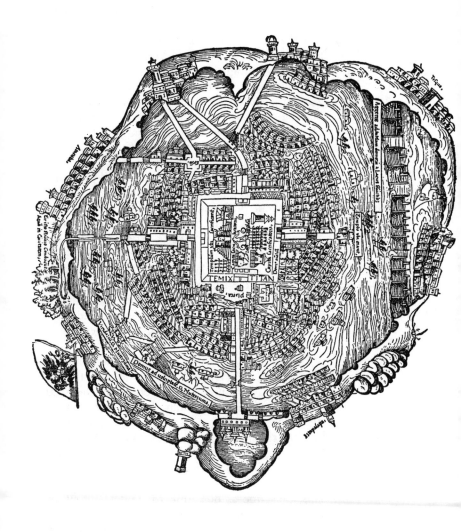

MAP OF MEXICO CITY FROM CORTÉS' SECOND LETTER TO CHARLES **V**

Cortés was told that he was approaching he came out to the middle of the Hall to receive him, and Montezuma took him by the hand, and they brought some seats, made according to their usage and very richly decorated and embroidered with gold in many designs, and Montezuma asked our Captain to be seated, and both of them sat down each on his chair. Then Montezuma began a very good speech, saying that he was greatly rejoiced to have in his house and his kingdom such valiant gentlemen as were Cortés and all of us. That two years ago he had received news of another Captain who came to Champoton and likewise last year they had brought him news of another Captain who came with four ships, and that each time he had wished to see them, and now that he had us with him he was at our service, and would give us of all that he possessed; that it must indeed be true that we were those of whom his ancestors in years long past had spoken, saying that men would come from where the sun rose to rule over these lands, and that we must be those men, as we had fought so valiantly in the affairs at Champoton and Tabasco and against the Tlaxcalans; for they had brought him pictures of the battles true to life.

Cortés answered him through our interpreters who always accompanied him, especially Doña Marina, and said to him that he and all of us did not know how to repay him the great favours we received from him every day. It was true that we came from where the sun rose, and were the vassals and servants of a great Prince called the Emperor Don Carlos, who held beneath his sway many and great princes, and that the Emperor having heard of him and what a great prince he was, had sent us to these parts to see him, and to beg them to become Christians, the same as our Emperor and all of us, so that his soul and those of all his vassals might be saved. Later on he would further explain how and in what manner this should be done, and how we worship one only true God, and who He is, and many other good things which he should listen to, such as he had already told to his ambassadors Tendile and Pitalpitoque and Quintalbor when we were on the sand dunes. When this conference was over, the Great Montezuma had already at hand some very rich golden jewels, of many patterns, which he gave to our Captain, and in the same manner to each one of our Captains he gave trifles of gold, and three loads of mantles of rich feather work, and to the soldiers also he gave to each one two loads of mantles, and he did it cheerfully and in every way he seemed to be a great Prince. When these things had been distributed, he asked Cortés if we were all brethren and vassals of our great Emperor, and Cortés replied yes, we were brothers in affection and friendship, and persons of great distinction, and servants of our great King and Prince. Further polite speeches passed between Montezuma and Cortés, and as this was the first time he had come to visit us, and so as not to be wearisome, they ceased talking. Montezuma had ordered his stewards that, according to our own use and customs in all things, we should be provided with maize and grinding stones, and women to make bread, and fowls and fruit, and much fodder for the horses. Then Montezuma took leave of our Captain and all of us with the greatest courtesy, and we went out with him as far as the street. Cortés ordered us not to go far from our quarters for the present, until we knew better what was expedient.

The next day Cortés decided to go to Montezuma's palace, and he first sent to find out what he intended doing and to let him know that we were coming. He took with him four captains, namely Pedro de Alvarado, Juan Velásquez de Leon, Diego de Ordás, and Gonzalo de Sandoval, and five of us soldiers also went with him.

When Montezuma knew of our coming he advanced to the middle of the hall to receive us, accompanied by many of his nephews, for no other chiefs were permitted to enter or hold communication with Montezuma where he then was, unless it were on important business. Cortés and he paid the greatest reverence to each other and then they took one another by the hand and Montezuma made him sit down on his couch on his right hand, and he also bade all of us to be seated on seats which he ordered to be brought.

Then Cortés began to make an explanation through Doña Marina and Aguilar, and said that he and all of us were rested, and that in coming to see and converse with such a great prince as he was, we had completed the journey and fulfilled the command which our great King and Prince had laid on us. But what he chiefly came to say on behalf of our Lord God had already been brought to his [Montezuma's] knowledge through his ambassadors, Tendile, Pitalpitoque, and Quintalbor, at the

time when he did us the favour to send the golden sun and
moon to the sand dunes; for we told them then that we were
Christians and worshipped one true and only God, that we believe in Him and worship Him, but that those whom they
look upon as gods are not so, but are devils, which are evil
things, and if their looks are bad their deeds are worse, and
they could see that they were evil and of little worth, for where
we had set up crosses such as those his ambassadors had seen,
they dared not appear before them, through fear of them, and
that as time went on they would notice this.

He also told them that, in course of time, our Lord and King
would send some men who among us lead very holy lives,
much better than we do, who will explain to them all about it,
for at present we merely came to give them due warning, and
so he prayed him to do what he was asked and carry it into
effect.

As Montezuma appeared to wish to reply, Cortés broke off
his argument, and to all of us who were with him he said:
"With this we have done our duty considering it is the first attempt."

Montezuma replied: "Señor Malinche, I have understood
your words and arguments very well before now, from what
you said to my servants at the sand dunes, this about three Gods
and the Cross, and all those things that you have preached in
the towns through which you have come. We have not made
any answer to it because here throughout all time we have worshipped our own gods, and thought they were good, as no
doubt yours are, so do not trouble to speak to us any more
about them at present. Regarding the creation of the world, we
have held the same belief for ages past, and for this reason we
take it for certain that you are those whom our ancestors pre-
dicted would come from the direction of the sunrise. As for
your great King, I feel that I am indebted to him, and I will
give him of what I possess, for as I have already said, two years
ago I heard of the Captains who came in ships from the direction in which you came, and they said that they were the servants of this your great King, and I wish to know if you are all
one and the same."

Cortés replied: Yes, that we were all brethren and servants
of our Emperor, and that those men came to examine the way
and the seas and the ports so as to know them well in order

that we might follow as we had done. Montezuma was referring to the expeditions of Francisco Hernández de Córdova and of Grijalva, and he said that ever since that time he had wished to capture some of those men who had come so as to keep them in his kingdoms and cities and to do them honour, and his gods had now fulfilled his desires, for now that we were in his home, which we might call our own, we should rejoice and take our rest, for there we should be well treated. And if he had on other occasions sent to say that we should not enter his city, it was not of his free will, but because his vassals were afraid, for they said that we shot our flashes of lightning, and killed many Indians with our horses, and that we were angry Teules, and other childish stories, and now that he had seen our persons and knew we were of flesh and bone, and had sound sense, and that we were very valiant, for these reasons he held us in much higher regard than he did from their reports, and he would share his possessions with us. Then Cortés and all of us answered that we thanked him sincerely for such signal good will, and Montezuma said, laughing, for he was very merry in his princely way of speaking: "Malinche, I know very well that these people of Tlaxcala with whom you are such good friends have told you that I am a sort of God or Teule, and that everything in my houses is made of gold and silver and precious stones, I know well enough that you are wise and did not believe it but took it as a joke. Behold now, Señor Malinche, my body is of flesh and bone like yours, my houses and palaces of stone and wood and lime; that I am a great king and inherit the riches of my ancestors is true, but not all the nonsense and lies that they have told you about me, although of course you treated it as a joke, as I did your thunder and lightning."

Cortés answered him, also laughing, and said that opponents and enemies always say evil things, without truth in them, of those whom they hate, and that he well knew that he could not hope to find another Prince more magnificent in these countries, and that not without reason had he been so vaunted to our Emperor.

While this conversation was going on, Montezuma secretly sent a great Cacique, one of his nephews who was in his company, to order his stewards to bring certain pieces of gold, which it seems must have been put apart to give to Cortés,

and ten loads of fine cloth, which he apportioned, the gold and
mantles between Cortés and the four captains, and to each of
us soldiers he gave two golden necklaces, each necklace being
worth ten pesos, and two loads of mantles. The gold that he
then gave us was worth in all more than a thousand pesos and
he gave it all cheerfully and with the air of a great and valiant
prince. As it was now past midday, so as not to appear impor-
tunate, Cortés said to him: "Señor Montezuma, you always
have the habit of heaping load upon load in every day conferring favours on us, and it is already your dinner time." Montezuma replied that he thanked us for coming to see him, and
then we took our leave with the greatest courtesy and we went
to our lodgings.

And as we went along we spoke of the good manners and
breeding which he showed in everything, and that we should
show him in all ways the greatest respect, doffing our quilted
caps when we passed before him, and this we always did.

† LXIV

The Great Montezuma was about forty years old, of good
height and well proportioned, slender and spare of flesh, not
very swarthy, but of the natural colour and shade of an Indian.
He did not wear his hair long, but so as just to cover his ears,
his scanty black beard was well shaped and thin. His face was
somewhat long, but cheerful, and he had good eyes and
showed in his appearance and manner both tenderness and,
when necessary, gravity. He was very neat and clean and
bathed once every day in the afternoon. He had many women
as mistresses, daughters of Chieftains, and he had two great
Cacicas as his legitimate wives. He was free from unnatural
offences. The clothes that he wore one day, he did not put on
again until four days later. He had over two hundred Chieftains
in his guard, in other rooms close to his own, not that all were
meant to converse with him, but only one or another, and
when they went to speak to him they were obliged to take off
their rich mantles and put on others of little worth, but they
had to be clean, and they had to enter barefoot with their eyes
lowered to the ground, and not to look up in his face. And they
made him three obeisances, and said: "Lord, my Lord, my

Great Lord," before they came up to him, and then they made their report and with a few words he dismissed them, and on taking leave they did not turn their backs, but kept their faces towards him with their eyes to the ground, and they did not turn their backs until they left the room. I noticed another thing, that when other great chiefs came from distant lands about disputes or business, when they reached the apartments of the Great Montezuma, they had to come barefoot and with poor mantles, and they might not enter directly into the Palace, but had to loiter about a little on one side of the Palace door, for to enter hurriedly was considered to be disrespectful.

For each meal, over thirty different dishes were prepared by his cooks according to their ways and usage, and they placed small pottery braziers beneath the dishes so that they should not get cold. They prepared more than three hundred plates of the food that Montezuma was going to eat, and more than a thousand for the guard. When he was going to eat, Montezuma would sometimes go out with his chiefs and stewards, and they would point out to him which dish was best, and of what birds and other things it was composed, and as they advised him, so he would eat, but it was not often that he would go out to see the food, and then merely as a pastime.

I have heard it said that they were wont to cook for him the flesh of young boys, but as he had such a variety of dishes, made of so many things, we could not succeed in seeing if they were of human flesh or of other things, for they daily cooked fowls, turkeys, pheasants, native partridges, quail, tame and wild ducks, venison, wild boar, reed birds, pigeons, hares and rabbits, and many sorts of birds and other things which are bred in this country, and they are so numerous that I cannot finish naming them in a hurry; so we had no insight into it, but I know for certain that after our Captain censured the sacrifice of human beings, and the eating of their flesh, he ordered that such food should not be prepared for him thenceforth.

Let us cease speaking of this and return to the way things were served to him at meal times. It was in this way: if it was cold they made up a large fire of live coals of a firewood made from the bark of trees which did not give off any smoke, and the scent of the bark from which the fire was made was very fragrant, and so that it should not give off more heat than he required, they placed in front of it a sort of screen adorned with figures of idols worked in gold. He was seated on a low stool, soft and richly worked, and the table, which was also low, was made in the same style as the seats, and on it they placed the table cloths of white cloth and some rather long napkins of the same material. Four very beautiful cleanly women brought water for his hands in a sort of deep basin which they call *xicales*,[1] and they held others like plates below to catch the water, and they brought him towels. And two other women brought him tortilla bread, and as soon as he began to eat they placed before him a sort of wooden screen painted over with gold, so that no one should watch him eating. Then the four women stood aside, and four great chieftains who were old men came and stood beside them, and with these Montezuma now and then conversed, and asked them questions, and as a great favour he would give to each of these elders a dish of what to him tasted best. They say that these elders were his near relations, and were his counsellors and judges of law suits, and the dishes and food which Montezuma gave them they ate standing up with much reverence and without looking at his face. He was served on Cholula earthenware either red or black. While he was at his meal the men of his guard who were in the rooms near to that of Montezuma, never dreamed of making any noise or speaking aloud. They brought him fruit of all the different kinds that the land produced, but he ate very little of it. From time to time they brought him, in cup-shaped vessels of pure gold, a certain drink made from cacao, and the women served this drink to him with great reverence.

Sometimes at meal-times there were present some very ugly humpbacks, very small of stature and their bodies almost broken in half, who are their jesters, and other Indians, who must have been buffoons, who told him witty sayings, and others who sang and danced, for Montezuma was fond of pleasure and song, and to these he ordered to be given what was left of the food and the jugs of cacao. Then the same four women removed the table cloths, and with much ceremony they brought water for his hands. And Montezuma talked with those four old chieftains about things that interested him, and they took leave of him with the great reverence in which they held him, and he remained to repose.

As soon as the Great Montezuma had dined, all the men of

Gourds.

the Guard had their meal and as many more of the other house servants, and it seems to me that they brought out over a thousand dishes of the food of which I have spoken, and then over two thousand jugs of cacao all frothed up, as they make it in Mexico, and a limitless quantity of fruit, so that with his women and female servants and bread makers and cacao makers his expenses must have been very great.

Let us cease talking about the expenses and the food for his household and let us speak of the Stewards and the Treasures and the stores and pantries and of those who had charge of the houses where the maize was stored. I say that there would be so much to write about, each thing by itself, that I should not know where to begin, but we stood astonished at the excellent arrangements and the great abundance of provisions that he had in all, but I must add what I had forgotten, for it is as well to go back and relate it, and that is, that while Montezuma was at table eating, as I have described, there were waiting on him two other graceful women to bring him tortillas, kneaded with eggs and other sustaining ingredients, and these tortillas were very white, and they were brought on plates covered with clean napkins, and they also brought him another kind of bread, like long balls kneaded with other kinds of sustaining food, and *pan pachol,* for so they call it in this country, which is a sort of wafer. There were also placed on the table three tubes much painted and gilded, which held *liquidambar* mixed with certain herbs which they call *tabaco,* and when he had finished eating, after they had danced before him and sung and the table was removed, he inhaled the smoke from one of those tubes, but he took very little of it and with that he fell asleep.

I remember that at that time his steward was a great Cacique to whom we gave the name of Tápia, and he kept the accounts of all the revenue that was brought to Montezuma, in his books which were made of paper which they call *amal,* and he had a great house full of these books. Now we must leave the books and the accounts for it is outside our story, and say how Montezuma had two houses full of every sort of arms, many of them richly adorned with gold and precious stones. There were shields great and small, and a sort of broad-swords, and others like two-handed swords set with stone knives which cut much better than our swords, and lances longer than ours are, with a fathom of blade with many knives set in it, which

even when they are driven into a buckler or shield do not
come out, in fact they, cut like razors so that they can shave
their heads with them. There were very good bows and arrows
and double-pointed lances and others with one point, as well as
their throwing sticks, and many slings and round stones shaped
by hand, and some sort of artful shields which are so made that
they can be rolled up, so as not to be in the way when they
are not fighting, and when they are needed for fighting they
let them fall down, and they cover the body from top to toe.
There was also much quilted cotton armour, richly ornamented on the outside with many coloured feathers, used as
devices and distinguishing marks, and there were casques or
helmets made of wood and bone, also highly decorated with
feathers on the outside, and there were other arms of other
makes which, so as to avoid prolixity, I will not describe, and
there were artisans who were skilled in such things and worked
at them, and stewards who had charge of the arms.

Let us leave this and proceed to the Aviary, and I am forced
to abstain from enumerating every kind of bird that was there
and its peculiarity, for there was everything from the Royal
Eagle and other smaller eagles, and many other birds of great
size, down to tiny birds of many-coloured plumage, also the
birds from which they take the rich plumage which they use
in their green feather work. The birds which have these feathers are about the size of the magpies in Spain, they are called
in this country *Quezales*,[1] and there are other birds which have
feathers of five colours—green, red, white, yellow and blue; I
don't remember what they are called; then there were parrots
of many different colours, and there are so many of them that
I forget their names, not to mention the beautifully marked
ducks and other larger ones like them. From all these birds
they plucked the feathers when the time was right to do so,
and the feathers grew again. All the birds that I have spoken
about breed in these houses, and in the setting season certain
Indian men and women who look after the birds, place the
eggs under them and clean the nests and feed them, so that
each kind of bird has its proper food. In this house that I have
spoken of there is a great tank of fresh water and in it there are
other sorts of birds with long stilted legs, with body, wings and

[1] *Trogon resplendens.*

tail all red; I don't know their names, but in the Island of Cuba they are called *Ypiris,* and there are others something like them, and there are also in that tank many other kinds of birds which always live in the water.

Let us leave this and go on to another great house, where they keep many Idols, and they say that they are their fierce gods, and with them many kinds of carnivorous beasts of prey, tigers and two kinds of lions, and animals something like wolves and foxes, and other smaller carnivorous animals, and all these carnivores they feed with flesh, and the greater number of them breed in the house. They give them as food deer and fowls, dogs and other things which they are used to hunt, and I have heard it said that they feed them on the bodies of the Indians who have been sacrificed. It is in this way: you have already heard me say that when they sacrifice a wretched Indian they saw open the chest with stone knives and hasten to tear out the palpitating heart and blood, and offer it to their Idols, in whose name the sacrifice is made. Then they cut off the thighs, arms and head and eat the former at feasts and banquets, and the head they hang up on some beams, and the body of the man sacrificed is not eaten but given to these fierce animals. They also have in that cursed house many vipers and poisonous snakes which carry on their tails things that sound like bells. These are the worst vipers of all, and they keep them in jars and great pottery vessels with many feathers, and there they lay their eggs and rear their young, and they give them to eat the bodies of the Indians who have been sacrificed, and the flesh of dogs which they are in the habit of breeding.

Let me speak now of the infernal noise when the lions and tigers roared and the jackals and foxes howled and the serpents hissed, it was horrible to listen to and it seemed like a hell. Let us go on and speak of the skilled workman Montezuma employed in every craft that was practised among them. We will begin with lapidaries and workers in gold and silver and all the hollow work, which even the great goldsmiths in Spain were forced to admire, and of these there were a great number of the best in a town named Atzcapotzalco, a league from Mexico. Then for working precious stones and chalchihuites, which are like emeralds, there were other great artists.

Let us go on to the great craftsmen in feather work, and painters and sculptors who were most refined; then to the Indian women who did the weaving and the washing, who made such an immense quantity of fine fabrics with wonderful feather work designs; the greater part of it was brought daily from some towns of the province on the north coast near Vera Cruz called Cotaxtla.

In the house of the great Montezuma himself, all the daughters of chieftains whom he had as mistresses always wore beautiful things, and there were many daughters of Mexican citizens who lived in retirement and wished to appear to be like nuns, who also did weaving but it was wholly of feather work. These nuns had their houses near the great Cue of Huichilobos and out of devotion to it, or to another idol, that of a woman who was said to be their mediatrix in the matter of marriage, their fathers placed them in that religious retirement until they married, and they were only taken out thence to be married.

Let us go on and tell about the great number of dancers kept by the Great Montezuma for his amusement, and others who used stilts on their feet, and others who flew when they danced up in the air, and others like Merry-Andrews, and I may say that there was a district full of these people who had no other occupation. Let us go on and speak of the workmen that he had as stone cutters, masons and carpenters, all of whom attended to the work of his houses, I say that he had as many as he wished for. We must not forget the gardens of flowers and sweet-scented trees, and the many kinds that there were of them, and the arrangement of them and the walks, and the ponds and tanks of fresh water where the water entered at one end and flowed out of the other; and the baths which he had there, and the variety of small birds that nested in the branches, and the medicinal and useful herbs that were in the gardens. It was a wonder to see, and to take care of it there were many gardeners. Everything was made in masonry and well cemented, baths and walks and closets, and apartments like summer houses where they danced and sang. There was as much to be seen in these gardens as there was everywhere else, and we could not tire of witnessing his great power. Thus as a consequence of so many crafts being practised among them, a large number of skilled Indians were employed.

† LXV

As we had already been four days in Mexico and neither the Captain nor any of us had left our lodgings except to go to the houses and gardens, Cortés said to us that it would be well to go to the great Plaza of Tlaltelolco and see the great Temple of Huichilobos, and that he wished to consult the Great Montezuma and have his approval. For this purpose he sent Jerónimo de Aguilar and the Doña Marina as messengers, and with them went our Captain's small page named Orteguilla, who already understood something of the language. When Montezuma knew his wishes he sent to say that we were welcome to go; on the other hand, as he was afraid that we might do some dishonour to his Idols, he determined to go with us himself with many of his chieftains. He came out from his Palace in his rich litter, but when half the distance had been traversed and he was near some oratories, he stepped out of the litter, for he thought it a great affront to his idols to go to their house and temple in that manner. Some of the great chieftains supported him with their arms, and the tribal lords went in front of him carrying two staves like sceptres held on high, which was the sign that the Great Montezuma was coming. (When he went in his litter he carried a wand half of gold and half of wood, which was held up like a wand of justice.) So he went on and ascended the great Cue accompanied by many priests, and he began to burn incense and perform other ceremonies to Huichilobos.

Our Captain and all of those who had horses went to Tlaltelolco on horseback, and nearly all of us soldiers were fully equipped, and many Caciques whom Montezuma had sent for that purpose went in our company. When we arrived at the great market place, called Tlaltelolco, we were astounded at the number of people and the quantity of merchandise that it contained, and at the good order and control that was maintained, for we had never seen such a thing before. The chieftains who accompanied us acted as guides. Each kind of merchandise was kept by itself and had its fixed place marked out. Let us begin with the dealers in gold, silver, and precious stones, feathers, mantles, and embroidered goods. Then there were other wares consisting of Indian slaves both men and women;

and I say that they bring as many of them to that great
market for sale as the Portuguese bring negroes from Guinea;
and they brought them along tied to long poles, with collars
round their necks so that they could not escape, and others
they left free. Next there were other traders who sold great
pieces of cloth and cotton, and articles of twisted thread, and
there were *cacahuateros* who sold cacao. In this way one could
see every sort of merchandise that is to be found in the whole
of New Spain. There were those who sold cloths of henequen
and ropes and the sandals with which they are shod, which
are made from the same plant, and sweet cooked roots, and
other tubers which they get from this plant, all were kept in
one part of the market in the place assigned to them. In another part there were skins of tigers and lions, of otters and
jackals, deer and other animals and badgers and mountain
cats, some tanned and others untanned, and other classes of
merchandise.

Let us go on and speak of those who sold beans and sage
and other vegetables and herbs in another part, and to those
who sold fowls, cocks with wattles, rabbits, hares, deer, mal-
lards, young dogs and other things of that sort in their part of
the market, and let us also mention the fruiterers, and the
women who sold cooked food, dough and tripe in their own
part of the market; then every sort of pottery made in a thousand different forms from great water jars to little jugs, these
also had a place to themselves; then those who sold honey and
honey paste and other dainties like nut paste, and those who
sold lumber, boards, cradles, beams, blocks and benches, each
article by itself, and the vendors of *ocote*[1] firewood, and other
things of a similar nature. But why do I waste so many words
in recounting what they sell in that great market?—for I shall
never finish if I tell it all in detail. Paper, which in this country is called *amal,* and reeds scented with *liquidambar,* and full
of tobacco, and yellow ointments and things of that sort are
sold by themselves, and much cochineal is sold under the
arcades which are in that great market place, and there are
many vendors of herbs and other sorts of trades. There are also
buildings where three magistrates sit in judgment, and there
are executive officers like *Alguacils* who inspect the merchandise. I am forgetting those who sell salt, and those who make

[1] Pitch-pine for torches.

the stone knives, and how they split them off the stone itself; and the fisherwomen and others who sell some small cakes made from a sort of ooze which they get out of the great lake, which curdles, and from this they make a bread having a flavour something like cheese. There are for sale axes of brass and copper and tin, and gourds and gaily painted jars made of wood. I could wish that I had finished telling of all the things which are sold there, but they are so numerous and of such different quality and the great market place with its surrounding arcades was so crowded with people, that one would not have been able to see and inquire about it all in two days.

Then we went to the great Cue, and when we were already approaching its great courts, before leaving the market place itself, there were many more merchants, who, as I was told, brought gold for sale in grains, just as it is taken from the mines. The gold is placed in thin quills of the geese of the country, white quills, so that the gold can be seen through, and according to the length and thickness of the quills they arrange their accounts with one another, how much so many mantles or so many gourds full of cacao were worth, or how many slaves, or whatever other thing they were exchanging.

Before reaching the great Cue there is a great enclosure of courts, it seems to me larger than the plaza of Salamanca, with two walls of masonry surrounding it, and the court itself all paved with very smooth great white flagstones. And where there were not these stones it was cemented and burnished and all very clean, so that one could not find any dust or a straw in the whole place.

When we arrived near the Great Cue and before we had ascended a single step of it, the Great Montezuma sent down from above, where he was making his sacrifices, six priests and two chieftains to accompany our Captain. On ascending the steps, which are one hundred and fourteen in number, they attempted to take him by the arms so as to help him to ascend (thinking that he would get tired) as they were accustomed to assist their lord Montezuma, but Cortés would not allow them to come near him. When we got to the top of the great Cue, on a small plaza which has been made on the top where there was a space like a platform with some large stones placed on it, on which they put the poor Indians for sacrifice, there was a bulky image like a dragon and other evil figures and much blood shed that very day.

When we arrived there Montezuma came out of an oratory where his cursed idols were, at the summit of the great Cue, and two priests came with him, and after paying great reverence to Cortés and to all of us he said: "You must be tired, Señor Malinche, from ascending this our great Cue," and Cortés replied through our interpreters who were with us that he and his companions were never tired by anything. Then Montezuma took him by the hand and told him to look at his great city and all the other cities that were standing in the water, and the many other towns on the land round the lake, and that if he had not seen the great market place well, that from where they were they could see it better.

So we stood looking about us, for that huge and cursed temple stood so high that from it one could see over everything very well, and we saw the three causeways which led into Mexico, that is the causeway of Iztapalapa by which we had entered four days before, and that of Tacuba, and that of Tepeaquilla,[1] and we saw the fresh water that comes from Chapultepec which supplies the city, and we saw the bridges on the three causeways which were built at certain distances apart through which the water of the lake flowed in and out from one side to the other, and we beheld on that great lake a great multitude of canoes, some coming with supplies of food and others returning loaded with cargoes of merchandise; and we saw that from every house of that great city and of all the other cities that were built in the water it was impossible to pass from house to house, except by drawbridges which were made of wood or in canoes; and we saw in those cities Cues and oratories like towers and fortresses and all gleaming white, and it was a wonderful thing to behold; then the houses with flat roofs, and on the causeways other small towers and oratories which were like fortresses.

After having examined and considered all that we had seen we turned to look at the great market place and the crowds of people that were in it, some buying and others selling, so that the murmur and hum of their voices and words that they used could be heard more than a league off. Some of the soldiers among us who had been in many parts of the world, in Con-

[1] Guadelupe.

stantinople, and all over Italy, and in Rome, said that so large a market place and so full of people, and so well regulated and arranged, they had never beheld before.

Let us leave this, and return to our Captain, who said to Fray Bartolomé de Olmedo, who happened to be near by him: "It seems to me, Señor Padre, that it would be a good thing to throw out a feeler to Montezuma, as to whether he would allow us to build our church here"; and the Padre replied that it would be a good thing if it were successful, but it seemed to him that it was not quite a suitable time to speak about it, for Montezuma did not appear to be inclined to do such a thing.

Then our Cortés said to Montezuma: "Your Highness is indeed a very great prince and worthy of even greater things. We are rejoiced to see your cities, and as we are here in your temple, what I now beg as a favour is that you will show us your gods and Teules." Montezuma replied that he must first speak with his high priests, and when he had spoken to them he said that we might enter into a small tower and apartment, a sort of hall, where there were two altars, with very richly carved boardings on the top of the roof. On each altar were two figures, like giants with very tall bodies and very fat, and the first which stood on the right hand they said was the figure of Huichilobos their god of War; it had a very broad face and monstrous and terrible eyes, and the whole of his body was covered with precious stones, and gold and pearls, and with seed pearls stuck on with a paste that they make in this country out of a sort of root, and all the body and head was covered with it, and the body was girdled by great snakes made of gold and precious stones, and in one hand he held a bow and in the other some arrows. And another small idol that stood by him, they said was his page, and he held a short lance and a shield richly decorated with gold and stones. Huichilobos had round his neck some Indians' faces and other things like hearts of Indians, the former made of gold and the latter of silver, with many precious blue stones.

There were some braziers with incense which they call copal, and in them they were burning the hearts of the three Indians whom they had sacrificed that day, and they had made the sacrifice with smoke and copal. All the walls of the oratory were so splashed and encrusted with blood that they were black, the floor was the same and the whole place stank vilely. Then we saw on the other side on the left hand there stood the other great image the same height as Huichilobos, and it had a face like a bear and eyes that shone, made of their mirrors which they call *Tezcat,* and the body plastered with precious stones like that of Huichilobos, for they say that the two are brothers; and this Tezcatepuca was the god of Hell and had charge of the souls of the Mexicans, and his body was girt with figures like little devils with snakes' tails. The walls were so clotted with blood and the soil so bathed with it that in the slaughter houses of Spain there is not such another stench.

They had offered to this Idol five hearts from the day's sacrifices. In the highest part of the Cue there was a recess of which the woodwork was very richly worked, and in it was another image half man and half lizard, with precious stones all over it, and half the body was covered with a mantle. They say that the body of this figure is full of the seeds that there are in the world, and they say that it is the god of seed time and harvest, but I do not remember its name, and everything was covered with blood, both walls and altar, and the stench was such that we could hardly wait the moment to get out of it.

They had an exceedingly large drum there, and when they beat it the sound of it was so dismal and like, so to say, an instrument of the infernal regions, that one could hear it a distance of two leagues, and they said that the skins it was covered with were those of great snakes. In that small place there were many diabolical things to be seen, bugles and trumpets and knives, and many hearts of Indians that they had burned in fumigating their idols, and everything was so clotted with blood, and there was so much of it, that I curse the whole of it, and as it stank like a slaughter house we hastened to clear out of such a bad stench and worse sight. Our Captains said to Montezuma through our interpreter, half laughing: "Señor Montezuma, I do not understand how such a great Prince and wise man as you are has not come to the conclusion, in your mind, that these idols of yours are not gods, but evil things that are called devils, and so that you may know it and all your priests may see it clearly, do me the favour to approve of my placing a cross here on the top of this tower, and that in one part of these oratories where your Huichilobos and Tezcatepuca stand we may divide off a space where we can set up an image of Our Lady (an image which Montezuma had already seen) and you will see by the fear in which these Idols hold it that they are deceiving you."

Montezuma replied half angrily (and the two priests who were with him showed great annoyance), and said: "Señor Malinche, if I had known that you would have said such defamatory things I would not have shown you my gods, we consider them to be very good, for they give us health and rains and good seed times and seasons and as many victories as we desire, and we are obliged to worship them and make sacrifices, and I pray you not to say another word to their dishonour."

When our Captain heard that and noted the angry looks he did not refer again to the subject, but said with a cheerful manner: "It is time for your Excellency and for us to return," and Montezuma replied that it was well, but that he had to pray and offer certain sacrifices on account of the great *tatacul,* that is to say sin, which he had committed in allowing us to ascend his great Cue, and being the cause of our being permitted to see his gods, and of our dishonouring them by speaking evil of them, so that before he left he must pray and worship.

Then Cortés said: "I ask your pardon if it be so," and then we went down the steps, and as they numbered one hundred and fourteen, and as some of our soldiers were suffering from tumours and abscesses, their legs were tired by the descent.

† LXVI

I will leave off talking about the oratory, and I will give my impressions of its surroundings, and if I do not describe it as accurately as I should do, do not wonder at it, for at that time I had other things to think about, regarding what we had on hand, that is to say my soldier's duties and what my Captain ordered me to do, and not about telling stories. To go back to the facts, it seems to me that the circuit of the great Cue was equal to that of six large sites,[1] such as they measure in this

---

[1] *Solares.* Solar is a town lot for house-building.

country, and from below up to where a small tower stood, where they kept their idols, it narrowed, and in the middle of the lofty Cue up to its highest point, there were five hollows like barbicans, but open, without screens, and as there are many Cues painted on the banners of the conquerors, and on one which I possess, any one who has seen them can infer what they looked like from outside, better than I myself saw and understood it. There was a report that at the time they began to build that great Cue, all the inhabitants of that mighty city had placed as offerings in the foundations, gold and silver and pearls and precious stones, and had bathed them with the blood of the many Indian prisoners of war who were sacrificed, and had placed there every sort and kind of seed that the land produces, so that their Idols should give them victories and riches, and large crops. Some of my inquisitive readers will ask, how could we come to know that into the foundations of that great Cue they cast gold and silver and precious chalchihuites and seeds, and watered them with the human blood of the Indians whom they sacrificed, when it was more than a thousand years ago that they built and made it? The answer I give to this is that after we took that great and strong city, and the sites were apportioned, it was then proposed that in the place of that great Cue we should build a church to our patron and guide Señor Santiago, and a great part of the site of the great temple of Huichilobos was occupied by the site of the holy church, and when they opened the foundations in order to strengthen them, they found much gold and silver and chalchihuites and pearls and seed pearls and other stones. And a settler in Mexico who occupied another part of the same site found the same things, and the officers of His Majesty's treasury demanded them saying that they belonged by right to His Majesty, and there was a lawsuit about it. I do not remember what happened except that they sought information from the Caciques and Chieftains of Mexico, and from Guatémoc, who was then alive, and they said that it was true that all the inhabitants of Mexico at that time cast into the foundations those jewels and all the rest of the things, and that so it was noted in their books and pictures of ancient things, and from this cause those riches were preserved for the building of the holy church of Santiago.

Let us leave this and speak of the great and splendid Courts which were in front of the temple of Huichilobos, where now stands the church of Señor Santiago, which was called Tlaltelolco, for so they were accustomed to call it.

I have already said that there were two walls of masonry which had to be passed before entering, and that the court was paved with white stones, like flagstones, carefully whitewashed and burnished and clean, and it was as large and as broad as the plaza of Salamanca. A little way apart from the great Cue there was another small tower which was also an Idol house, or a true hell, for it had at the opening of one gate a most terrible mouth such as they depict, saying that such there are in hell. The mouth was open with great fangs to devour souls, and here too were some groups of devils and bodies of serpents close to the door, and a little way off was a place of sacrifice all blood-stained and black with smoke, and encrusted with blood, and there were many great ollas and cántaros and tinajas[1] of water inside the house, for it was here that they cooked the flesh of the unfortunate Indians who were sacrificed, which was eaten by the priests. There were also near the place of sacrifice many large knives and chopping blocks, such as those on which they cut up meat in the slaughter houses. Then behind that cursed house, some distance away from it, were some great piles of firewood, and not far from them a large tank of water which rises and falls, the water coming through a tube from the covered channel which enters the city from Chapultepec. I always called that house "the Infernal Regions."

Let us go on beyond the court to another Cue where the great Mexican princes were buried, where also there were many Idols, and all was full of blood and smoke, and it had other doorways with hellish figures, and then near that Cue was another full of skulls and large bones arranged in perfect order, which one could look at but could not count, for there were too many of them. The skulls were by themselves and the bones in separate piles. In that place there were other Idols, and in every house or Cue or oratory that I have mentioned there were priests with long robes of black cloth and long hoods like those of the Dominicans and slightly resembling those of the Canons. The hair of these priests was very long and so matted that it could not be separated or disentangled, and most of

[1] Names of various large pottery vessels for holding water and cooking.

them had their ears scarified, and their hair was clotted with blood. Let us go on; there were other Cues, a little way from where the skulls were, which contained other Idols and places of sacrifice decorated with other evil paintings. And they said that those idols were intercessors in the marriages of men. I do not want to delay any longer telling about idols, but will only add that all round that great court there were many houses, not lofty, used and occupied by the priests and other Indians who had charge of the Idols. On one side of the great Cue there was another much larger pond or tank of very clear water dedicated solely to the service of Huichilobos and Tezcatepuca, and the water entered that pond through covered pipes which came from Chapultepec. Near to this were other large buildings such as a sort of nunnery where many of the daughters of the inhabitants of Mexico were sheltered like nuns up to the time they were married, and there stood two Idols with the figures of women, which were the intercessors in the marriages of women, and women made sacrifices to them and held festivals so that they should give them good husbands.

I have spent a long time talking about this great Cue of Tlaltelolco and its Courts, but I say that it was the greatest temple in the whole of Mexico although there were many others, very splendid. Four or five parishes or districts possessed, between them, an oratory with its Idols, and as they were very numerous I have not kept count of them all. I will go on and say that the great oratory that they had in Cholula was higher than that of Mexico, for it had one hundred and twenty steps, and according to what they say they held the Idol of Cholula to be good, and they went to it on pilgrimages from all parts of New Spain to obtain absolution, and for this reason they built for it such a splendid Cue; but it is of another form from that of Mexico although the courts are the same, very large with a double wall. I may add that the Cue in the City of Texcoco was very lofty, having one hundred and seventeen steps, and the Courts were broad and fine, shaped in a different form from the others. It is a laughable matter that every province had its Idols and those of one province or city were of no use to the others, thus they had an infinite number of Idols and they made sacrifices to them all.

After our Captain and all of us were tired of walking about and seeing such a diversity of Idols and their sacrifices, we returned to our quarters, all the time accompanied by many Caciques and chieftains whom Montezuma sent with us.

† LXVII

When our Captain and the Friar of the Order of Mercy saw that Montezuma was not willing that we should set up a cross on the Temple of Huichilobos nor build a church there, and because, ever since we entered this city of Mexico, when Mass was said, we had to place an altar on tables and then to dismantle it again, it was decided that we should ask Montezuma's stewards for masons so that we could make a church in our quarters.

The stewards said that they would tell Montezuma of our wishes, and Montezuma gave his permission and ordered us to be supplied with all the material we needed. In two days we had our church finished and the holy cross set up in front of our apartments, and Mass was said there every day until the wine gave out. As Cortés and some of the other Captains and the Friar had been ill during the war in Tlaxcala, they made the wine that we had for Mass go too fast, but after it was all finished we still went to the church daily and prayed on our knees before the altar and images, for one reason, because we were obliged to do so as Christians and it was a good habit, and for another reason, in order that Montezuma and all his Captains should observe it, and should witness our adoration and see us on our knees before the Cross, especially when we intoned the Ave Maria, so that it might incline them towards it.

When we were all assembled in those chambers, as it was our habit to inquire into and want to know everything while we were looking for the best and most convenient site to place the altar, two of our soldiers, one of whom was a carpenter named Alonzo Yañes, noticed on one of the walls marks showing that there had been a door there, and that it had been closed up and carefully plastered over and burnished. Now as there was a rumour and we had heard the story that Montezuma kept the treasure of his father Axayaca in that building, it was suspected that it might be in this chamber which had been closed up and cemented only a few days before. Yañes spoke about it to Juan Velásquez de Leon and Francisco de Lugo, and those Captains told the story to Cortés, and the door was secretly opened. When it was opened Cortés and some of his Captains went in first, and they saw such a number of jewels and slabs and plates of gold and chalchihuites and other great riches, that they were quite carried away and did not know what to say about such wealth. The news soon spread among all the other Captains and soldiers, and very secretly we went in to see it. When I saw it I marvelled, and as at that time I was a youth and had never seen such riches as those in my life before, I took it for certain that there could not be another such store of wealth in the whole world. It was decided by all our captains and soldiers, that we should not dream of touching a particle of it, but that the stones should immediately be put back in the doorway and it should be sealed up and cemented just as we found it, and that it should not be spoken about, lest it should reach Montezuma's ears, until times should alter.

Let us leave this about the riches, and say that four of our captains took Cortés aside in the church, with a dozen soldiers in whom he trusted and confided, and I was one of them, and we asked him to look at the net and trap in which we found ourselves, and to consider the great strength of that city, and observe the causeways and bridges, and to think over the words of warning that we had been given in all the towns we had passed through, that Montezuma had been advised by his Huichilobos to allow us to enter into the city, and when we were there, to kill us. That he [Cortés] should remember that the hearts of the men are very changeable, especially those of Indians, and he should not repose trust in the good will and affection that Montezuma was showing us, for at some time or other, when the wish occurred to him, he would order us to be attacked, and by the stoppage of our supplies of food or of water, or by the raising of any of the bridges, we should be rendered helpless. Then, considering the great multitude of Indian warriors that Montezuma had as his guard, what should we be able to do either in offence or defence? and as all the houses were built in the water, how could our friends the Tlaxcalans enter and come to our aid? He should think over all this that we had said, and if we wished to safeguard our lives, that we should at once, without further delay, seize

Montezuma and should not wait until next day to do it. He should also remember that all the gold that Montezuma had given us and all that we had seen in the treasury of his father Axayaca, and all the food which we ate, all would be turned to arsenic poison in our bodies, for we could neither sleep by night nor day nor rest ourselves while these thoughts were in our minds, and that if any of our soldiers should give him other advice short of this, they would be senseless beasts who were dazed by the gold, incapable of looking death in the face.

When Cortés heard this he replied: "Don't you imagine, gentlemen, that I am asleep, or that I am free from the same anxiety, you must have felt that it is so with me; but what possibility is there of our doing a deed of such great daring as to seize such a great prince in his own palace, surrounded as he is by his own guards and warriors, by what scheme or artifice can we carry it out, so that he should not call on his warriors to attack us at once?" Our Captains replied (that is Juan Velásquez de Leon and Diego de Ordás, Gonzalo de Sandoval and Pedro de Alvarado) that with smooth speeches he should be got out of his halls and brought to our quarters, and should be told that he must remain a prisoner, and if he made a disturbance or cried out, that he would pay for it with his life; that if Cortés did not want to do this at once, he should give them permission to do it, as they were ready for the work, for, between the two great dangers in which we found ourselves, it was better and more to the purpose to seize Montezuma than to wait until he attacked us; for if he began the attack, what chance should we have? Some of us soldiers also told Cortés that it seemed to us that Montezuma's stewards, who were employed in providing us with food, were insolent and did not bring it courteously as during the first days. Also two of our Allies the Tlaxcalan Indians said secretly to Jerónimo de Aguilar, our interpreter, that the Mexicans had not appeared to be well disposed towards us during the last two days. So we stayed a good hour discussing the question whether or not we should take Montezuma prisoner, and how it was to be done, and to our Captain this last advice seemed opportune, that in any case we should take him prisoner, and we left it until the next day. All that night we were praying to God that our plan might tend to His Holy service.

The next morning after these consultations, there arrived,

very secretly, two Tlaxcalan Indians with letters from Villa
Rica and what they contained was the news that Juan de
Escalante, who had remained there as Chief Alguacil, and six
of our soldiers had been killed in a battle against the Mexicans,
that his horse had also been slain, and many Totonacs who
were in his company. Moreover, all the towns of the Sierra
and Cempoala and its subject towns were in revolt, and refused
to bring food or serve in the fort. They [the Spaniards] did
not know what to do, for as formerly they had been taken to
be Teules, that now after this disaster, both the Totonacs and
Mexicans were like wild animals, and they could hold them to
nothing, and did not know what steps to take.

When we heard this news, God knows what sorrow affected
us all, for this was the first disaster we had suffered in New
Spain.

† LXVIII

As we had determined the day before to seize Montezuma, we
were praying to God all that night that it would turn out in a
manner redounding to His Holy service, and the next morning the way it should be done was settled.

Cortés took with him five captains who were Pedro de
Alvarado, Gonzalo de Sandoval, Juan Velásquez de Leon,
Francisco de Lugo and Alonzo de Ávila, and he took me and
our interpreters Doña Marina and Aguilar, and he told us all
to keep on the alert, and the horsemen to have their horses
saddled and bridled. As for our arms I need not call them to
mind, for by day or night we always went armed and with
our sandals on our feet, for at that time such was our foot-
gear, and Montezuma had always seen us armed in that way
when we went to speak to him, so did not take it as anything
new, nor was he disturbed at all.

When we were all ready, our Captain sent to tell Montezuma
that we were coming to his Palace, for this had always been
our custom, and so that he should not be alarmed by our
arriving suddenly.

Montezuma understood more or less that Cortés was coming
because he was annoyed about the Villa Rica affair, and he was

afraid of him, but sent word for him to come and that he would be welcome.

When Cortés entered, after having made his usual salutations, he said to him through our interpreters: "Señor Montezuma, I am very much astonished that you, who are such a valiant Prince, after having declared that you are our friend, should order your Captains, whom you have stationed on the coast near to Tuxpan, to take arms against my Spaniards, and that they should dare to rob the towns which are in the keeping and under the protection of our King and master and to demand of them Indian men and women for sacrifice, and should kill a Spaniard, one of my brothers, and a horse." (He did not wish to speak of the Captain nor of the six soldiers who died as soon as they arrived at Villa Rica, for Montezuma did not know about it, nor did the Indian Captains who had attacked them), and Cortés went on to say: "Being such a friend of yours I ordered my Captains to do all that was possible to help and serve you, and you have done exactly the contrary to us. Also in the affair at Cholula your Captains and a large force of warriors had received your own commands to kill us. I forgave it at the time out of my great regard for you, but now again your vassals and Captains have become insolent, and hold secret consultations stating that you wish us to be killed. I do not wish to begin a war on this account nor to destroy this city, I am willing to forgive it all, if silently and without raising any disturbance you will come with us to our quarters, where you will be as well served and attended to as though you were in your own house, but if you cry out or make any disturbance you will immediately be killed by these my Captains, whom I brought solely for this purpose." When Montezuma heard this he was terrified and dumbfounded, and replied that he had never ordered his people to take arms against us, and that he would at once send to summon his Captains so that the truth should be known, and he would chastise them, and at that very moment he took from his arm and wrist the sign and seal of Huichilobos, which was only done when he gave an important and weighty command which was to be carried out at once. With regard to being taken prisoner and leaving his Palace against his will, he said that he was not the person to whom such an order could be given, and that he would not go. Cortés replied to him with very good arguments and Montezuma answered him with even better, showing that he ought not to leave his house. In this way more than half an hour was spent over talk, and when Juan Velásquez de Leon and the other Captains saw that they were wasting time over it and could not longer await the moment when they should remove him from his house and hold him a prisoner, they spoke to Cortés somewhat angrily and said: "What is the good of your making so many words, let us either take him prisoner, or stab him, tell him once more that if he cries out or makes an uproar we will kill him, for it is better at once to save our lives or to lose them," and as Juan Velásquez said this with a loud and rather terrifying voice, for such was his way of speaking, Montezuma, who saw that our Captains were angered, asked Doña Marina what they were saying in such loud tones. As Doña Marina was very clever, she said: "Señor Montezuma, what I counsel you, is to go at once to their quarters without any disturbance at all, for I know that they will pay you much honour as a great Prince such as you are, otherwise you will remain here a dead man, but in their quarters you will learn the truth." Then Montezuma said to Cortés: "Señor Malinche, if this is what you desire, I have a son and two legitimate daughters, take them as hostages, and do not put this affront on me, what will my chieftains say if they see me taken off as a prisoner?" Cortés replied to him that he must come with them himself and there was no alternative. At the end of much more discussion that took place, Montezuma said that he would go willingly, and then Cortés and our Captains bestowed many caresses on him and told him that they begged him not to be annoyed, and to tell his captains and the men of his guard that he was going of his own free will, because he had spoken to his Idol Huichilobos and the priests who attended him, and that it was beneficial for his health and the safety of his life that he should be with us. His rich litter, in which he was used to go out with all the Captains who accompanied him was promptly brought, and he went to our quarters where we placed guards and watchmen over him.

All the attentions and amusements which it was possible for him to have, both Cortés and all of us did our best to afford him, and he was not put under any personal restraint, and soon all the principal Mexican Chieftains, and his nephews came to talk with him, and to learn the reason of his seizure, and whether he wished them to attack us. Montezuma answered them, that he was delighted to be here some days with us of his own free will and not by force, and that when he wished for anything he would tell them so, and that they must not excite themselves nor the City, nor were they to take it to heart, for what had happened about his being there was agreeable to his Huichilobos, and certain priests who knew had told him so, for they had spoken to the Idol about it. In this way which I have now related the capture of the Great Montezuma was effected.

There, where he remained, he had his service and his women and his baths in which he bathed himself, and twenty great chiefs always stayed in his company holding their ancient offices, as well as his councillors and captains, and he stayed there a prisoner without showing any anger at it, and Ambassadors from distant lands came there with their suites, and brought him his tribute, and he carried on his important business.

I will not say anything more at present about this imprisonment, and will relate how the messengers whom Montezuma sent with his sign and seal to summon the Captains who had killed our soldiers, brought them before him as prisoners and what he said to them I do not know, but he sent them on to Cortés, so that he might do justice to them, and their confession was taken when Montezuma was not present and they confessed that what I have already stated was true, that their Prince had ordered them to wage war and to extract tribute, and that if any Teules should appear in defence of the towns, they too should be attacked or killed. When Cortés heard this confession he sent to inform Montezuma how it implicated him in the affair, and Montezuma made all the excuses he could, and our captain sent him word that he believed the confession himself, but that although Montezuma deserved punishment in conformity with the ordinances of our King, to the effect that any person causing others, whether guilty or innocent, to be killed, shall die for it, yet he was so fond of him and wished him so well, that even if that crime lay at his door, he, Cortés, would pay the penalty with his own life sooner than allow Montezuma's to pass away. With all this that

Cortés sent to tell him, Montezuma felt anxious, and without any further discussion Cortés sentenced those captains to death and to be burned in front of Montezuma's palace. This sentence was promptly carried out, and, so that there could be no obstruction while they were being burned, Cortés ordered shackles to be put on Montezuma himself, and when this was done Montezuma roared with rage, and if before this he was scared, he was then much more so. After the burning was over our Cortés with five of our captains went to Montezuma's apartment and Cortés himself took off the fetters, and he spoke such loving words to him that his anger soon passed off, for our Cortés told him that he not only regarded him as a brother, but much more, and that, as he was already Lord and King of so many towns and provinces, if it were possible he would make him Lord of many more countries as time went on, such as he had not been able to subdue, and which did not now obey him, and he told him that if he now wished to go to his Palace, that he would give him leave to go. Cortés told him this through our interpreters and while Cortés was saying it the tears apparently sprang to Montezuma's eyes. He answered with great courtesy, that he thanked him for it (but he well knew that Cortés' speech was mere words), and that now at present it was better for him to stay there a prisoner, for there was danger, as his chieftains were numerous, and his nephews and relations came every day to him to say that it would be a good thing to attack us and free him from prison, that as soon as they saw him outside they might drive him to it. He did not wish to see revolutions in his city, but if he did not comply with their wishes possibly they would want to set up another Prince in his place. And so he was putting those thoughts out of their heads by saying that Huichilobos had sent him word that he should remain a prisoner. (From what we understood, and there is no doubt about it, Cortés had told Aguilar to tell Montezuma secretly, that although Malinche wished to release him from his imprisonment, that the rest of our captains and soldiers would not agree to it.) When he heard this reply, Cortés threw his arms round him and embraced him and said: "It is not in vain Señor Montezuma that I care for you as I care for myself." Then Montezuma asked Cortés that a Spanish page named Orteguilla who already knew something of his language might attend on him, and this was very advantageous

both for Montezuma and for us, for through this page Montezuma asked and learned many things about Spain, and we
learned what his captains said to him, and in truth this page
was so serviceable that Montezuma got to like him very much.

Let us cease talking about how Montezuma became fairly
contented with the great flattery and attention he received and
the conversation that he had with us, and whenever we passed
before him, even if it was Cortés himself, we doffed our mailed
caps or helmets, for we always went armed, and he treated us
all with politeness. The name of the principal captain who
was punished by being burned was Quetzalpopoca. I may say
that when the news of this punishment spread about throughout the provinces of New Spain, they were terrified, and the
towns of the Coast, where they had killed our soldiers, returned
again and rendered good service to the settlers who remained
in Villa Rica.

† LXIX

After justice had been done on Quetzalpopoca and his captains
and the Great Montezuma had been tamed, our Captain decided to send to Villa Rica, as his lieutenant, a soldier named
Alonzo de Grado, for he was a very prudent man of good
address and presence, and a musician and a great writer.

This Alonzo de Grado was one of those who were always
in opposition of our Cortés about going to Mexico, and wished
us to go back to Villa Rica. And when at the time of the
Tlaxcala affair there were certain meetings of the discontented,
it was always Alonzo de Grado who agitated. Had he been as
good a man of war as he was a man of good manners, it
would have been to his advantage. I say this because when
Cortés gave him this appointment, as he was not a bold man,
he was facetious in his remarks, and said to him: "Here,
Señor Alonzo de Grado, you have your wish fulfilled, for you
are going now to Villa Rica as you have wished, and you will
take charge of the fortress, and take care that you don't go
out on any expeditions and get killed as Juan de Escalante did."
And when he was saying this to him Cortés winked his eye,
so that we soldiers who were standing round might see it, and
we knew why he said this, for it was well known of Alonzo de

Grado that he would not go on such an expedition even if he were ordered to do so with threats. Cortés charged him to look well after the settlers and to see that he caused no annoyance to our Indian Allies and should take nothing from them by force.

When Alonzo de Grado arrived at the town he gave himself great importance towards the settlers, and wished to make them do him service as a great Lord, and to the allied towns which numbered more than thirty, he sent to demand jewels of gold and pretty Indian women, and he paid no attention at all to the fortress. How he spent his time was in feeding well and in gambling, and what was worse than all this, he secretly called together his friends, and even some who were not his friends and suggested that if Diego Velásquez or any of his captains should come from Cuba to that country, that they should join him and give up the land to him. All this news was at once sent in haste by letter to Cortés in Mexico, and it seemed to Cortés advisable to send some man whom he could trust to the port and town, so he sent Gonzalo de Sandoval.

When Gonzalo de Sandoval arrived at Villa Rica he sent Alonzo de Grado as a prisoner to Mexico under a guard of Indians, for so Cortés had told him to do.

When Alonzo de Grado reached Mexico, Cortés would not allow him to be brought before him but ordered him to be imprisoned in some wooden stocks which had just been newly made, and he remained a prisoner for two days.

As Alonzo de Grado was very plausible and a man of many expedients, he made many promises to Cortés that he would be his humble servant and loyal to him in all things, and gave so many indications of his desire to serve him that at length he convinced him, and he gained his release. I must not forget to say that when Cortés sent Gonzalo de Sandoval to Villa Rica he had ordered him, as soon as he arrived, to send two blacksmiths, with all their apparatus of bellows and tools and much iron from the ships which we had destroyed, and two great iron chains which were already made, and he told him to send also sails and tackle, and pitch and tow and a mariner's compass, and everything else that was needed to build two sloops to sail on the lake of Mexico. These things Sandoval sent at once following in every particular the orders he had received.

As our captain was careful in all things, and seeing that Montezuma was a prisoner, and fearing that he might become depressed at being shut in and confined, he endeavoured every day, after prayers (for we had no wine for Mass) to go and pay court to him, and he went accompanied by four Captains, usually by Pedro de Alvarado, Juan Velásquez and Diego de Ordás, and with much reverence they asked Montezuma how he was, and that he should issue his orders and they would all be carried out, so that he should not be weary of his confinement. He answered that on the contrary, being a prisoner rested him, and this was because our gods gave us power to confine him or his Huichilobos permitted it, and in one conversation after another they gave him to understand more fully the things about our holy faith, and the great power of the Emperor our Lord.

Then sometimes Montezuma and Cortés would play at Totoloque, which is the name they give to a game played with some very smooth small pellets made of gold for this game, and they toss these pellets to some distance as well as some little slabs which were also made of gold, and in five strokes [tries] they gained or lost certain pieces of gold or rich jewels that they staked. I remember that Pedro de Alvarado was keeping the score for Cortés, and one of his nephews, a great cacique, was marking for Montezuma, and Pedro de Alvarado always marked one point more than Cortés gained, and when Montezuma saw it he said courteously and laughingly that he did not like Tonatio (for so they called Pedro de Alvarado) to keep the score for Cortés, because he made so much *yxoxol* in what he marked, which in their language means to say that he cheated, in that he always marked one point too many. Cortés and all of us soldiers who were on guard at the time, could not restrain our laughter at what the great Montezuma said, because Pedro de Alvarado, although he was so handsome and well mannered, had a mania for excessive talking, and we knew his temperament. To return to the game, if Cortés won, he gave the jewels to those nephews and favourites of Montezuma who attended on him, and if Montezuma won he divided them among us soldiers on guard,

and in addition to what he gave us from the game, he never
omitted giving us every day presents of gold and cloth, both
to us and to the captain of the Guard, who, at that time, was
Juan Velásquez de Leon, who showed himself in every way to
be the friend and servant of Montezuma.

A soldier named Pedro López was placed as sentinel over
Montezuma, and on the question whether it was time to
change the watch during the night, he had words with an
officer and said, "Oh! curse this dog, I am sick to death of
keeping constant guard over him." Montezuma heard the expression, and weighed it in his mind, and when Cortés came
to pay his court to him, he heard of it, and was so angry about
it, that he had Pedro López, good soldier as he was, flogged
in our quarters, and from that time on all the soldiers who
came on guard, went through their watch in silence and good
manners. However it was not necessary to give orders to many
of us who stood guard over him about the civility that we
ought to show to this great cacique; he knew each one of
us and even knew our names and our characters and he was
so kind that to all of us he gave jewels and to some mantles,
and handsome Indian women. As I was a young man in those
days, whenever I was on guard, or passed in front of him, I
doffed my headpiece with the greatest respect, and the page
Orteguilla had told him that I had been on two expeditions to
discover New Spain before the time of Cortés, so I asked
Orteguilla to beg Montezuma to do me the favour of giving me
a very pretty Indian woman, and when Montezuma heard
this he told them to call me, and he said to me: "Bernal
Díaz del Castillo, they tell me that you have quantities of
cloth and gold, and I will order them to give you to-day a
pretty maid. Treat her very well for she is the daughter of a
chieftain, and they will also give you gold and mantles," and I
answered him with much reverence, that I kissed his hands
for his great favour, and might God our Lord prosper him, and
it seems that he asked the page what I had replied to him,
and he told him; and Montezuma said to him: "Bernal Díaz
seems to me to be a gentleman," for as I have said, he knew
all our names, and he told them to give me three small slabs
of gold and two loads of mantles.

Let us stop talking of this and tell how of a morning after
saying his prayers and making sacrifices to his idols, he took

his breakfast, which was a small matter, for he ate no meat, only chili peppers, then he was occupied for an hour in hearing suits from many parts brought by Caciques who came to him from distant lands.

† LXX

As all the materials for building the two sloops had arrived, Cortés at once went to tell the great Montezuma that he wished to build two small ships so as to take pleasure trips on the lake, and asked him to send his carpenters to cut the wood, together with our experts in boat-building, who were named Martin López and Andrés Nuñez. As the oak timber was distant about four leagues, it was soon brought and shaped, and as there were many Indian carpenters, the boats were soon built and caulked and tarred, and their rigging was set up and their sails cut to the right size and measurement, and an awning provided for each one, and they turned out to be as good and fast as though they had taken a month to set up the models, for Martin López was a past master of the art.

Let us leave this and say that Montezuma told Cortés that he wished to go to his temples and make sacrifices, and pay the devotion to his gods that it was his duty to do, so that his Captains and chieftains might observe it, especially certain nephews of his, who came every day to tell him that they wished to free him and to attack us, and he answered them, that it pleased him to be with us, so they should think it was as he had told them, that his God Huichilobos had commanded him to stay with us, as he had made them believe before. Cortés replied that as to this permission he asked for, he should beware not to do anything for which he might lose his life, and so as to prevent any disorders, or commands to his Captains or priests either to release him, or attack us, he would send Captains and soldiers with him who would immediately stab him to death, should any change be noticed in his bearing. He might go and welcome, but must not sacrifice any human beings, for that was a great offence against the true God, that was to the God we were preaching to him about, and there stood our altars and the image of Our Lady, before whom he could pray. Montezuma said that he would not sacrifice a single human being, and he set off in his rich litter in great state with many great Caciques in his company as was his custom, and they carried his insignia in front of him in the form of a sort of staff or rod, which was the sign that his royal presence was going that way (just as they do now to the Viceroys of New Spain). There went with him as a guard four of our Captains, and one hundred and fifty soldiers, and the Padre de la Merced also went with us to stop the sacrifice if he should offer human beings. So we went to the Cue of Huichilobos and when we came near to that cursed temple, Montezuma ordered them to take him from his litter and he was carried on the shoulders of his nephews and of other Caciques until he arrived at the temple; as I have already stated, as he went through the streets all the chieftains cast down their eyes and never looked at his face. When we arrived at the foot of the steps leading to the oratory there were many priests waiting to help him with their arms in the ascent.

There had already been sacrificed the night before four Indians, and in spite of what our Captain said and the dissuasions of the Padre de la Merced, he paid no heed but persisted in killing men and boys to accomplish his sacrifice, and we could do nothing at that time only pretend not to notice it, for Mexico and the other great cities were very ready to rebel under the nephews of Montezuma, as I shall explain further on. When Montezuma had completed his sacrifices, and he did not tarry much in making them, we returned with him to our quarters, and he was very cheerful, and gave presents of golden jewels to us soldiers who had accompanied him.

When the two sloops were finished building and had been launched and the masts and rigging had been set up and adorned with the Royal and Imperial banners, and the sailors had been got ready to navigate them, they went out in them both rowing and sailing, and they sailed very well. When Montezuma heard of it, he said to Cortés that he wished to go hunting on a rocky Island,[1] standing in the lake which was preserved so that no one dared to hunt there, however great a chief he might be, under pain of death. Cortés replied that he was very welcome to go, but he must remember what he had told him on the former occasion when he went to visit his Idols, that to raise any disturbances was more than his life was

[1] The *Peñon de Tepepolco* or *del Marques*.

worth; moreover, he could go in the sloops, as it was better sailing in them than in the canoes and pirogues however large they might be. Montezuma said that he would be delighted to sail in the sloop that was the swiftest, and he took with him many lords and chieftains, and advised his huntsmen to follow in canoes and pirogues. A son of Montezuma and many Caciques went in the other sloop. Then Cortés ordered Velásquez de Leon who was captain of the Guard and Pedro de Alvarado and Cristóbal de Olid, Alonzo de Ávila with two hundred soldiers, to accompany Montezuma, and to remember the great responsibility he was placing on them in looking after him, and as all those Captains whom I have named were very alert, they took on board all the soldiers I have spoken about, and four bronze cannon and all the powder that we possessed, and our gunners, and they put up a highly decorated awning as a protection from the weather, and Montezuma and his chieftains went under it. As at that time there was a strong breeze blowing, and the sailors were delighted to please and content Montezuma, they worked the sails so well that they went flying along, and the canoes which held his huntsmen and chieftains were left far behind in spite of the large number of rowers they carried. Montezuma was charmed, and said that it was a great art this of combining sails and oars together. So he arrived at the Peñol, which was not very far off, and Montezuma killed all the game he wanted, deer and hares and rabbits, and returned very contented to the city. When we arrived near Mexico, Pedro de Alvarado and Juan Velásquez de Leon and the other Captains ordered the cannon to be discharged, and this delighted Montezuma, and as we saw him so frank and kind, we treated him with the respect in which the Kings of these countries are held, and he behaved in the same manner to us. If I were to relate the traits and qualities that he showed as a great Prince, and the reverence and service that all the Lords of New Spain paid to him, I should never come to an end. There was not a thing that he ordered to be brought that was not immediately there.

As Cacamatzin, lord of the City of Texcoco, which after Mexico is the largest and most important city that there is in New Spain, knew that his uncle, Montezuma, had been imprisoned for many days, and that we were taking the upper hand in every way that was possible, and also got to know that we had opened the chamber where the great treasure of his grandfather Axayaca was kept, but had not taken anything from it, he determined, before we could take possession of the treasure, to call together all the Lords of Texcoco, who were his vassals, and the lord of Coyoacan, who was his cousin and Montezuma's nephew, and the lord of Tacuba, and the lord of Iztapalapa, and another great Cacique who was lord of Matalçingo, who was very nearly related to Montezuma and of whom it was even said that he was the rightful heir to the kingdom and lordship of Mexico, and who was a chieftain known among the Indians for his personal bravery. While Cacamatzin continued to negotiate with these and other Mexican chieftains that on a given day they should come with all their forces and attack us, it seems that the Cacique whom I have said was known for his personal bravery (whose name I do not know) said that if Cacamatzin would assure to him the Kingship of Mexico, to which he was the rightful heir, that he and all his relations, and the people of the province called Matalçingo, would be the first to take up arms and turn us out of Mexico, or not leave anyone of us alive. It appears that Cacamatzin replied that the Chieftainship of Mexico belonged to him and that he himself must be King; for he was the nephew of Montezuma; and that if the Lord of Matalçingo did not wish to come, that they would make war on us without his help or that of his people, for it seems that Cacamatzin had got ready all the Lords and towns already named by me, and had already arranged the day on which they were to fall on Mexico, and that the chieftains of his faction who were then in the city would facilitate their entry.

While these negotiations were going on, Montezuma knew all about them from the lord of Matalçingo, and to be more sure of it, Montezuma sent to summon all the Caciques and chieftains of Texcoco, and they told him how Cacamatzin was going about persuading them all with words and gifts to join him in an attack on us, and to free his uncle. As Montezuma was prudent and did not wish to see his city rise up in arms or riots, he told Cortés what was happening. Our Captain and all of us soldiers knew a good deal about this disturbance, but not so fully as Montezuma now detailed it. The advice that Cortés now gave him was that he should give us his Mexican followers and we would fall on Texcoco and capture or destroy that city and its neighbourhood. As that advice did not suit Montezuma, Cortés sent to tell Cacamatzin that he should cease his preparations for war, which would be the means of his destruction, for he wished to have him as a friend. Now Cacamatzin was a young man who found many others, who shared his opinions, ready to support him in the war, so he sent to tell Cortés, that he understood his flatteries and did not want to hear any more of them. Cortés again sent to tell him that he should beware not to do an ill turn to our King and Lord, for he would pay for it with his person, and lose his life for it. He replied that he knew no King and wished he had never known Cortés, who, for all his fair words, had imprisoned his uncle.

As Montezuma had both great Caciques and kinsmen in Texcoco who were not friendly with Cacamatzin (who was very haughty and much disliked) and as he had with him there in Mexico a brother of this same Cacamatzin, a youth of a good disposition, who had fled from his own brother to escape being killed by him (for after Cacamatzin he was the heir to the kingdom of Texcoco) our captain implored Montezuma to concert measures with his people in Texcoco to seize Cacamatzin, or to send secretly to summon him to come to Mexico, and if he did come, to lay hands on him and keep him in his power until he had quieted down and later on should promote this other nephew to be the Lord of Texcoco and take the chieftainship from Cacamatzin.

Montezuma said that he would at once send to summon Cacamatzin, but he did not think he would come, and that if he did not come he would make arrangements with his Captains and relations to seize him.

Cortés thanked him heartily for this, and even said: "Señor Montezuma, you may indeed believe me that if you wish to go to your Palace, you are free to do so, for since I understand that you are well disposed towards me, I am so devoted to you, that were I not in such a difficult position, I would not even insist upon accompanying you when you proceed to your palace with all your nobility. If I have failed to carry out such a plan, it is on account of my Captains who went to seize you, for they are not willing that I should set you free, and also because you say that you prefer to stay in confinement so as to avoid the disturbances through which your nephews would attempt to obtain power over this City of yours, and deprive you of your rule."

Montezuma thanked him, and as he began to understand Cortés' flattering speeches and saw that he made them, not with any intention of setting him free, but only to test his good will, he added that it was as well for him to remain a prisoner until he could see whither the treachery of his nephews would lead. Moreover he would immediately send messengers to Cacamatzin, begging him to appear before him, as he wished to speak to him about friendship between him and us. Montezuma sent the same message to the Captains of Texcoco, telling them that he was sending to summon his nephew to make friends, adding that they should beware how that youth turned their brains so that they would take up arms against us.

Cacamatzin took counsel with his chiefs as to what should be done, and began to bluster and say that he would kill us all within four days, and that his uncle was a chicken not to attack us when he advised him to do so.

Cacamatzin promised his followers there and then, that if the Lordship of Mexico should fall to him, he would make them great chieftains, and he also gave them many golden jewels, and told them that he had already made arrangements with his cousins, the lords of Coyoacan and Iztapalapa and Tacuba and other relations, to help him, and there were other chieftains in Mexico itself who would assist him and let him into the city at whatever hour he might choose. He said that some of them might go along the causeway and all the rest could go across the lake in their pirogues and small canoes, and they would enter the city without meeting opponents to defend it, for his uncle was a prisoner, and they need have no fear of us, for they knew that only a few days ago, in the affair of Almeria, his uncle's Captains had killed many Teules and a horse, and they had seen the head of the Teule and the body of the horse; that they could kill us all in an hour and could have feasts and stuff themselves with our bodies.

When this speech was finished, they say that the Captains looked at one another, waiting for those who usually spoke first in councils of war, and that four or five of these Captains replied to him how was it possible for them to go without the permission of their great prince Montezuma, and wage war in his very house and city? that they should first send to let him know about it, and if he consented, they would accompany Cacamatzin with the greatest good will; but otherwise they did not wish to turn traitors. It seems that Cacamatzin was angered with the Captains and ordered three of those who gave that reply to be imprisoned. As there were present at that meeting and council others, who were his relations, who were longing for a riot, they said that they would aid him to the death. So he decided to send to his uncle the great Montezuma to say that he ought to be ashamed of sending him word to come and make friends with those who had done him such harm and dishonour in holding him a prisoner, that such a thing was only possible because we were wizards and had stolen away all his great strength and bravery with our witchcraft, and that our gods and this great lady from Castile, whom we said was our Counsellor, had given us the great power to do what we had done. The gist of his message was, that he would come in spite of us and of his uncle to speak to us and to kill us.

When the great Montezuma heard that insolent reply, he was greatly angered, and at once sent to summon six of his most trusted captains. And he gave them his seal, and ordered them to go to Texcoco and secretly to show that seal to certain Captains and relations of his, who were on bad terms with Cacamatzin on account of his haughtiness, and so to manage that they should make prisoners of Cacamatzin and those who were in his confidence, and bring them before him at once. When those Captains had departed, and it was understood in Texcoco what it was that Montezuma had ordered, as Cacamatzin was greatly disliked, he was taken prisoner in his own palace while he was discussing the subject of the war with his confederates, and they brought five of them as prisoners in his company.

As that city stands close to the lake, they got ready a great pirogue with awnings, and they placed Cacamatzin and the other prisoners in it and with a great crew of rowers they brought them to Mexico. When they had disembarked, they placed Cacamatzin in a richly adorned litter fit for a king such as he was, and with the greatest show of respect they brought him before Montezuma.

It seems that in his interview with Montezuma, he was even more insolent than he had been before, and if Montezuma was angry with his nephew before, he was now doubly so, and he promptly sent him to our Captain to be held as a prisoner, and the other prisoners he ordered to be set free.

Cortés went at once to the palace to Montezuma's chamber to thank him for so great a favour and the order was given that the youth, who was in Montezuma's company, who was also his nephew and the brother of Cacamatzin, should be raised to the Kingship of Texcoco.

So as to make the appointment with all solemnity and with the consent of all the city, Montezuma summoned before him the principal chieftains of the whole province and after fully discussing the matter, they elected him as King and Lord of that great city, and he was named Don Carlos.

After all this was over, when the Caciques and Kinglets, nephews of the great Montezuma, namely the Lord of Coyoacan, and the Lord of Iztapalapa, and he of Tacuba saw and heard of the imprisonment of Cacamatzin, and learnt that the great Montezuma knew that they had joined in the conspiracy to deprive him of his kingdom, and give it to Cacamatzin, they were frightened and did not come to pay their court to Montezuma as they were used to do. So with the consent of Cortés, who clamoured and persuaded him to order them to be seized, within eight days they were all in prison and attached to the great chain, and our Captain and all of us felt not a little relieved.

†   LXXII

When Captain Cortés saw that those kinglets named by me were prisoners, and that all the cities were at peace, he said to Montezuma that, before we had entered Mexico, he [Montezuma] had twice sent to say that he wished to pay tribute to

His Majesty, and that as he now understood about the great power of our Lord and King, to whom many lands pay tribute and taxes and many great kings are subject, it would be well for him and all his vassals to give him their fealty, for such is the custom, first to give fealty and then to give tribute and taxes. Montezuma replied that he would gather his vassals together, and talk to them about it. And within ten days nearly all the Caciques of that territory assembled together, but that Cacique who was most nearly related to Montezuma did not come, and said that he would neither come, nor pay taxes, for he was not able to keep himself with the income from his provinces. Montezuma was very angry at this reply, and at once sent some Captains to take him prisoner, but as he was a great Lord, and had many relations, he was warned of this and withdrew to his province where they were not then able to catch him.

I must leave him now and state how, in the discussion that Montezuma held with the Caciques of all the territory whom he had called together, after he had made a speech without Cortés or any of us, excepting Orteguilla the page, being present, it was reported that he had told them to consider how for many years past they had known for certain, through the traditions of their ancestors, which they had noted down in their books of records, that men would come from the direction of the sunrise to rule these lands, and that then the lordship and kingdom of the Mexicans would come to an end. Now he believed, from what his Gods had told him, that we were these men, and the priests had consulted Huichilobos about it and offered up sacrifices, but their Gods would no longer answer them as they had been accustomed to do.

All that Huichilobos would give them to understand was that what he had told them before he now again gave as his reply, and they were not to ask him again, so that they took it to mean that they should give their fealty to the King of Spain whose vassals these Teules say that they are. He went on to say: "As for the present it does not imply anything, and as in time to come we shall see whether we receive another and better reply from our Gods, so we will act according to the time. For the present, what I order and beg you all to do with good will is to give and contribute some sign of vassalage, and I will soon tell you what is most suitable, and as just now I am importuned about it by Malinche, I beg that no one will refuse it. During the eighteen years that I have been your Prince, you have always been very loyal to me, and I have enriched you and have broadened your lands, and have given you power and wealth, and if at this present time, our Gods permit me to be held captive here, it would not have happened, unless, as I have told you many times, my great Huichilobos had commanded it."

When they heard these arguments, all of them gave as an answer that they would do as he had ordered them, and they said it with many tears and sighs, and Montezuma more tearful than any of them. Then he sent a chieftain to say that on the following day they would give their fealty and vassalage to His Majesty.

Montezuma returned after this to talk about the matter with his Caciques, and in the presence of Cortés and our Captains and many of our soldiers, and of Pedro Hernández, Cortés' secretary, they gave their fealty to His Majesty, and they showed much emotion in doing so, and Montezuma could not keep back his tears. He was so dear to us, and we were so much affected at seeing him weep, that our own eyes were softened and one soldier wept as much as Montezuma, such was the affection we had for him. I will leave off here, and say that Cortés and the Fraile de la Merced, who was very wise, were constantly in Montezuma's palace, trying to amuse him and to persuade him to give up his Idols.

† LXXIII

As Captain Diego de Ordás and the other soldiers [who had been sent by Cortés on an exploring expedition] arrived with samples of gold and the report that all the land was rich, Cortés by the advice of Ordás and the other Captains and soldiers, decided to speak to, and demand of Montezuma, that all the Caciques and towns of the land should pay tribute to His Majesty, and that he himself as the greatest Chieftain, should also contribute from his treasure. Montezuma replied that he would send to all his towns to ask for gold, but that many of them did not possess any, only some jewels of little worth which had come to them from their ancestors. He at once despatched chieftains to the places where there were mines and ordered each town to give so many ingots of fine gold, of the same size and thickness as others that they were used to pay as tribute, and the messengers carried with them as samples two small ingots. From other parts they only brought small jewels of little worth.

He also sent to the province whose Cacique and Lord was that near kinsman of his who would not obey him. This province was distant from Mexico about twelve leagues, and the reply the messengers brought back was to the effect that neither would he give any gold nor obey Montezuma, that he also was Lord of Mexico, and that the dominion belonged to him as much as to Montezuma himself, who was sending to ask him to pay tribute.

When Montezuma heard this he was so enraged that he immediately sent his seal and sign by some faithful captains with orders to bring him as a prisoner. When this kinsman was brought into Montezuma's presence he spoke to him very disrespectfully, and without any fear, and very valiantly, and they say, that he had intervals of madness, for he was as though thunderstruck. Cortés came to know all about this, and he sent to beg Montezuma as a favour, to give this man to him as he wished to place a guard over him, for he had been told that Montezuma had ordered him to be killed. When the Cacique was brought before him Cortés spoke to him in a most amiable manner and told him not to act like a madman against his prince, and wished to set him free. However, when Montezuma heard this he said that he should not be set free but should be attached to the great chain like the other Kinglets already named by me.

Let us go back to say that within twenty days all the chieftains whom Montezuma had sent to collect the tribute of gold, came back again. And as they arrived Montezuma sent to summon Cortés and our captains and certain soldiers whom he knew, who belonged to his guard, and said these formal words, or others of like meaning:—

"I wish you to know, Señor Malinche and Señores Captains and soldiers, that I am indebted to your great King, and I bear him good will both for being such a great Prince and for having sent to such distant lands to make inquiries about me; and the thought that most impresses me is that he must be the one who is to rule over us, as our ancestors have told us, and as even our gods have given us to understand in the answers we have received from them. Take this gold which has been collected; on account of haste no more has been brought. That which I have got ready for the emperor is the whole of the Treasure which I have received from my father, which is in your possession and in your apartments.

"I know well enough that as soon as you came here you opened the chamber and beheld it all, and that you sealed it up again as it was before. When you send it to him, tell him in your papers and letters, 'This is sent to you by your true vassal Montezuma.' I will also give you some very valuable stones which you will send to him in my name; they are Chalchihuites, and are not to be given to any one else but only to him, your Great Prince. Each stone is worth two loads of gold. I also wish to send him three blow guns with their bags and pellet moulds for they have such good jewelwork on them that he will be pleased to see them, and I also wish to give him of what I possess although it is but little, for all the rest of the gold and jewels that I possessed I have given you from time to time."

When Cortés and all of us heard this we stood amazed at the great goodness and liberality of the Great Montezuma, and with much reverence we all doffed our helmets, and returned him our thanks, and with words of the greatest affection Cortés promised him that we would write to His Majesty of the magnificence and liberality of this gift of gold which he gave us in his own royal name. After some more polite conversation Montezuma at once sent his Mayordomos to hand over all the treasure and gold and wealth that was in that plastered chamber, and in looking it over and taking off all the embroidery with which it was set, we were occupied for three days, and to assist us in undoing it and taking it to pieces, there came Montezuma's goldsmiths from the town named Azcapotzalco, and I say that there was so much, that after it was taken to pieces there were three heaps of gold, and they weighed more than six hundred thousand pesos, as I shall tell further on, without the silver and many other rich things, and not counting in this the ingots and slabs of gold, and the gold in grains from the mines. We began to melt it down with the help of the Indian goldsmiths, and they made broad bars of it, each bar measuring three fingers of the hand across. When it was already melted and made into bars, they brought another present separately which the Grand Montezuma had said that he would give, and it was a wonderful thing to behold the wealth of gold and the richness of the other jewels that were brought, for some of the Chalchihuites were so fine that among these Caciques they were worth a vast quantity of gold. The three blow guns with their pellet moulds, and their coverings of jewels and pearls, and pictures in feathers of little birds covered with pearlshell and other birds, all were of great value. I will not speak of the plumes and feathers and other rich things for I shall never finish calling them to mind.

The gold I have spoken about was marked with an iron stamp, and the stamp was the royal arms. The mark was not put on the rich jewels which it did not seem to us should be taken to pieces.

As we had neither marked weights nor scales, some iron weights were made, some as much as an arroba,[1] others of half an arroba, two pounds, one pound and half a pound, and of four ounces, not that they would turn out very exact, but within half an ounce more or less in each lot that was weighed.

After the weight was taken the officers of the King said that there was gold worth more than six hundred thousand pesos, and this was without counting the silver and many other jewels which were not yet valued.

Some soldiers said that there was more. As there was now nothing more to do than to take out the royal fifth, and to give to each captain and soldier his share, and to set aside the shares of those who remained at the port of Villa Rica, it seems that Cortés endeavoured not to have it divided up so soon, but to wait until there was more gold, and there were good weights, and proper accounts of how it turned out. But most of us captains and soldiers said that it should be divided up at once, for we had seen that at the time when the pieces were given out of the Treasury of Montezuma, there was much more gold in the heaps, and that a third part of it was missing, which they had taken and hidden both on behalf of Cortés, as well as of the Captains and the Fraile de la Merced, and it went on diminishing. The next day they were to distribute the shares, and I will tell how it was divided, and the greater part remained with

[1] An *arroba* = 25 lbs.

Captain Cortés and other persons, and what was done about it I will go on to relate.

First of all the royal fifth was taken out, then Cortés said that they should take out for him another fifth, the same as for His Majesty, for we had promised it to him at the sand dunes when we elected him Captain General and Chief Justice. After that, he said that he had been put to certain expenses in the Island of Cuba and that what he had spent on the expedition should be taken from the heap, and in addition to this that there should be taken from the same heap the expenses incurred by Diego Velásquez in the ships which we had destroyed, and we all agreed to it, and beside this the expenses of the procurators who were sent to Spain. Then there were the shares of those who remained in Villa Rica, and there were seventy of them, and for his horse that had died, and for the mare which had belonged to Juan Sedeño which the Tlaxcalans had killed with a sword cut; then for the Fraile de la Merced, and the priest Juan Díaz and the Captains and for those who had brought horses, double shares, and for musketeers and crossbowmen the same, and other trickeries, so that very little was left to each as a share, and it was so little that many of the soldiers did not want to take it, and Cortés was left with it all. At that time we could do nothing but hold our tongues, for to ask for justice in the matter was useless. There were other soldiers who took their shares at the rate of one hundred pesos and clamoured for the rest, and to content them Cortés secretly gave to one and the other, apparently bestowing favours so as to satisfy them, and with the smooth speeches that he made to them they put up with it.

At that time many of our Captains ordered very large golden chains to be made by the Great Montezuma's goldsmiths. Cortés, too, ordered many jewels to be made, and a great service of plate. Some of our soldiers had their hands so full, that many ingots of gold, marked and unmarked, and jewels of a great diversity of patterns were openly in circulation. Heavy gaming was always going on with some playing cards which were made from drum skins by Pedro Valenciano and were as well made and painted as the originals. So this was the condition we were in, but let us stop talking of the gold and of the bad way it was divided, and worse way in which it was spent.

As Cortés heard that many of the soldiers were discontented

over their share of the gold and the way the heaps had been robbed, he determined to make a speech to them all with honeyed words, and he said that all he owned was for us, and he did not want the fifth but only the share that came to him as Captain General, and that if any one had need of anything he would give it to him, and that the gold we had collected was but a breath of air, that we should observe what great cities there were there and rich mines, and that we should be lords of them all and very prosperous and rich, and he used other arguments very well expressed which he knew well how to employ.

† LXXIV

One day Montezuma said: "Look here, Malinche, I love you so much that I want to give you one of my daughters, who is very beautiful, so that you can marry her and treat her as your legitimate wife"; Cortés doffed his cap in thanks, and said that it was a great favour that Montezuma was conferring on him, but that he was already married and had a wife, and that among us we were not permitted to have more than one wife, he would however, keep her [Montezuma's daughter] in the rank to which the daughter of so great a prince was entitled, but that first of all he desired her to become a Christian, as other ladies, the daughters of Chieftains, already were; and to this Montezuma consented.

The Great Montezuma always showed good will to us, but he never ceased his sacrifices at which human beings were killed, and Cortés tried to dissuade him from this but met with no success. So Cortés took counsel with his captains as to what should be done in the matter, for he did not dare to put an end to it for fear of a rising in the City and of the priests who were in charge of Huichilobos. On the advice of his Captains, Cortés went to the Palace where Montezuma was imprisoned and took seven captains and soldiers with him, and said to Montezuma: "Señor, I have often asked you not to sacrifice any more human beings to your gods who are deceiving you, and you will not cease doing it, I wish you to know that all my companions and these captains who are with me have come to beg you to give them leave to remove the gods from your temple and put our Lady Santa Maria and a Cross in their place, and, if you will not give them leave now, they will go and remove them, and I would not like them to kill any priests."

When Montezuma heard those words, and saw that the Captains were rather angry, he said: "Oh! Malinche, how can you wish to destroy the city entirely! for our gods are very angry with us, and I do not know that they will stop even at your lives, what I pray you to do for the present is to be patient, and I will send to summon all the priests and I will see their reply." When Cortés heard this he made a sign that he wished to speak quite privately to Montezuma. When they were left alone he said to Montezuma, that in order to prevent this affair from becoming known and causing a disturbance and becoming an offence to the priests on account of their Idols being overturned, that he would arrange with these Captains to the effect that they should do nothing of the sort, provided they were given an apartment in the Great Cue where they might make an altar on which to place the Image of Our Lady and set up a Cross. Then Montezuma, with sighs and a very sorrowful countenance, said that he would confer with his priests. After much discussion had taken place, it was agreed to, and our altars and an image of Our Lady and a Cross were set up, apart from their curséd Idols, with great reverence and with thanks to God from all of us, and the Padre de la Merced chanted Mass assisted by the priest Juan Díaz and many of our soldiers. Our Captain ordered an old soldier to be stationed there as guardian, and begged Montezuma to order the priests not to touch the altar, but only to keep it swept and to burn incense and keep wax candles burning there by day and night, and to decorate it with branches and flowers.

There was never a time when we were not subject to surprises of such a kind, that had our Lord God not assisted us, they would have cost us our lives. Thus as soon as we had placed the image of Our Lady and the Cross on the Altar which we had made on the Great Cue and the Holy Gospel had been preached and Mass said, it seems that Huichilobos and Tezcatepuca spoke to the priests, and told them that they wished to leave their country as they were so badly treated by the Teules, and they did not wish to stay where those figures and the Cross had been placed, nor would they remain there unless we were killed, and this was their answer and they need not expect any other, and they should inform Montezuma and all his Captains, so that they might at once go to war and kill us. The Idols further told them that they could see how all the gold that used to be kept for their honour, had been broken up by us and made into ingots, and let them beware how we were making ourselves lords over the country, and were holding five great Caciques prisoners, and they told them of other misdeeds so as to induce them to attack us. In order that Cortés and all of us should know about this, the Great Montezuma sent word to tell Cortés that he wished to speak to him on very important matters, and the page Orteguilla came and said to him that Montezuma was very sad and much disturbed, and that during the previous night and part of the day many priests and leading Captains had been with him and had said things to him privately that he [the page] could not understand.

When Cortés heard this he went in haste to the palace where Montezuma was staying and took with him Cristóbal de Olid, who was Captain of the Guard, and four other Captains and Doña Marina and Jerónimo de Aguilar, and, after they had paid much respect to him, Montezuma said: "Oh! Señor Malinche and Captains, how distressed I am at the reply and command which our Teules have given to our priests and to me and all my Captains, which is that we should make war on you and kill you, and drive you back across the sea. I have thought it over, and what seems to me best is that you should at once leave this city before you are attacked, and that not one of you should remain here. This, Señor Malinche, I say that you should not fail to do, for it is to your interest, if not you will be killed, remember it is a question of your lives." Cortés and our Captains felt grief at what he said and were even a good deal disquieted, and it was not to be wondered at, the affair coming so suddenly and with such insistence that our lives were at once placed in the greatest danger by it, for the warning was given us with the greatest urgency. Cortés replied that he thanked Montezuma sincerely for the warning, and that at the present time there were two things that troubled him, one was that he had no vessels in which to sail, for he had ordered those in which he had come to be broken up, and the other was that Montezuma would be forced to come with us so that our great Emperor might see him, and that he begged as a favour that he would place restraint on his priests and captains while three ships were being built at the sand dunes, as it would be more advantageous to them, for if they began the war they would all of them be killed.

He also asked, so that Montezuma might see that he wished to carry out what he had said without delay, that carpenters might be sent with two of our soldiers who were great experts in ship building, to cut wood near the sand dunes.

Montezuma was even more sorrowful than before because Cortés told him that he would have to come with us before the Emperor; he said that he would send the carpenters, and that they should hurry and not waste time in talk, but work, and that meanwhile he would command the priests and captains not to ferment disturbances in the city and he would order Huichilobos to be appeased with sacrifices, but not of human lives. After this exciting conversation Cortés and his captains took leave of Montezuma, and we were all in the greatest anxiety wondering when they would begin the attack.

Then Cortés ordered Martin López, the ship carpenter, to be summoned and Andrés Nuñez, and the Indian carpenters whom the Great Montezuma had given him and after some discussion as to the size of the three vessels to be built he ordered him at once to set about the work and to get them ready, for in Villa Rica there was everything necessary in the way of iron and blacksmiths, tackle, tow, and calkers and pitch. So they set out and cut the wood on the coast near Villa Rica, and in haste began to build ships.

Let us leave him building the ships and say how we all went about in that city very much depressed, fearing that at any moment they might attack us; and our friends from Tlaxcala and Doña Marina also told the captain that an attack was probable, and Orteguilla, Montezuma's page, was always in tears. We all kept on the alert and placed a strong Guard over Montezuma, and we slept shod and armed and with all our weapons to hand, and our horses stood saddled and bridled all day long. There is another thing I must say, but not with the intention of boasting about it, that I grew so accustomed to go about armed, and to sleep in the way I have said, that after the conquest of New Spain I kept to the habit of sleeping in my clothes and without a bed, and I slept thus better than on a mattress.

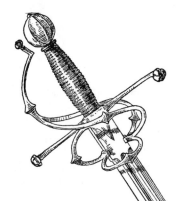

VI

The Expedition under Narvaez

We must now go a little way back in our story so that what I am about to relate may be clearly understood. Diego Valás- quez, the Governor of Cuba, knew that we had sent our Proc- tors to His Majesty, with all the gold that we had obtained, and that we were not asking his assistance about anything. He also knew that Don Juan Rodríguez de Fonseca, Bishop of Burgos and President of the Indies, had everything absolutely under his authority, because His Majesty was in Flanders, and that the Bishop had treated our Proctors very badly. They say that the Bishop advised Diego Velásquez to have us captured, and that he, from Spain, would afford him full support for so doing. So Diego Velásquez got together a fleet of nineteen ships and fourteen hundred soldiers, and they brought with them over twenty cannon and much powder and all sorts of stores of stones and balls, and two gunners, eighty horsemen and ninety crossbowmen and seventy musketeers. Diego Velás- quez, although he was very fat and heavy, himself went about from village to village, and from town to town, provisioning the fleet and inviting the settlers who had Indians, as well as his relations and friends, to go with Pánfilo Narvaez to capture Cortés and use his Captains and soldiers, or at least not to leave any of us alive, and he went about so incensed and angry and with such energy, that he got as far as Guaniguanico which is seventy leagues beyond Havana. It seems that when the Royal Audiencia of Santo Domingo got to hear of it, they decided to send a Licentiate named Lucas Vásquez de Ayllon, who was Oidor of this same Royal Audiencia, to stop this fleet of Diego Velásquez and not to let it sail, under pain of heavy penalties, but all the injunctions and penalties that the Oidor proclaimed were of no avail, and when the Oidor saw this he himself accompanied Narvaez so as to keep the peace and to promote agreement between Cortés and Narvaez.

As Pánfilo de Narvaez came across the sea with all his fleet of nineteen ships, it appears that on nearing the Sierra of San Martin, he was struck by a north wind, which is a head wind on that coast, and during the night he lost one ship of small burden which foundered; her Captain and a number of other persons were drowned. All the rest of the fleet arrived at San Juan de Ulúa.

When the arrival of this great fleet came to the ears of those soldiers whom Cortés had sent to look for mines, these three men came to the ships of Narvaez. When they found themselves safe on board ship and in Narvaez's Company, it is said that they raised their hands to God who had delivered them from the power of Cortés and got them out of the great City of Mexico where every day they expected to be killed. When they had eaten with Narvaez and drunk wine, and were satiated with too much drink, they kept saying to one another before the General himself: "See here, is it not better to be here drinking wine than to be unhappy in the power of Cortés who made such slaves of us night and day that we hardly dared to speak, expecting from day to day to meet death staring us in the face." And one of them named Cervantes, who was a buffoon, even said by way of pleasantry: "Oh, Narvaez, Narvaez, how fortunate you are to have come at this time, for this traitor of a Cortés has got together more than seven hundred thousand dollars of gold, and all the soldiers are very discontented with him because he has taken a great part of their share of the gold, and they do not want to accept what he is giving them." So those soldiers who had deserted from us as they were mean and worthless, told Narvaez much more that he wanted to know. They also informed him that eight leagues distant from where he was, a town had been founded named Villa Rica de la Vera Cruz and that Gonzalo de Sandoval was in command of it with seventy soldiers, all of them old and invalid, and that if he should send some fighting men there at once, they would surrender to him, and they told him many other things.

Now the great Montezuma soon got to know that there were ships anchored in the port with many captains and soldiers on board, and he secretly sent some of his chiefs, without Cortés knowing anything about it, and ordered the Spaniards in the ships to be given food, gold and cloth, and the neighbouring villages were told to furnish them with supplies of food. Narvaez sent to tell Montezuma many abusive and many uncivil things about Cortés and all of us, such as that we were bad men and thieves who had fled from Castile without the permission of our Lord and King, and that when our Lord the King had heard that we were in this country, and knew about the evil deeds and robberies we had committed and that we had taken Montezuma prisoner, he had ordered Narvaez to set out at once with all these ships and soldiers and horses, to put an end to such evils and to free him [Montezuma] from his prison, and either to kill Cortés and all of us evil-doers, or to capture us and send us back to Spain in these same ships, and that when we arrived there we should be condemned to death; and he sent to tell him much more nonsense. The interpreters who explained all this to the Indians were the three soldiers who already understood the language. In addition to these messages, Narvaez also sent some gifts of things from Spain.

When Montezuma heard all this he was very well satisfied with the news, for he believed that they would take us prisoner. In addition to this when his chieftains saw our three soldiers with Narvaez and perceived that they said much evil of Cortés, they accepted as the truth all that Narvaez had told them to say. They brought with them a picture of the fleet painted quite correctly on some cloths. Then Montezuma sent Narvaez much more gold and cloths and ordered all the towns in his neighbourhood to take them plenty to eat, and for three days Montezuma was in possession of this news and Cortés knew nothing at all.

One day when our Captain went to see Montezuma and to pay him court, after the usual civilities had passed between them, it seemed to Captain Cortés that Montezuma was looking very cheerful and happy, and he asked him how he felt, and Montezuma replied that he was better. When Montezuma

saw that he came to visit him twice in one day, he was afraid
that Cortés knew about the ships, and so as to get ahead of
him and to avoid suspicion, he said to him: "Señor Malinche,
only just now messengers have come to tell me that at the port
where you landed there have arrived eighteen more ships and
many people and horses, and they have brought it all to me
painted on some cloths, and as you came twice to visit me to-day
I thought that you must have come to bring me this news; now
you will have no need to build ships. Because you did not tell
me about it, on the one hand I was annoyed with you for keeping me in ignorance, and on the other hand I was delighted
at the arrival of your brothers, for now you can all return to
Spain and there need be no further excuse."

When Cortés heard about the ships and saw the picture on
the cloth, he rejoiced greatly and said: "Thank God! who at
the right moment provides for us," and we soldiers were so delighted that we could not keep quiet, and the horsemen rode
skirmishing round about and we fired off shots. But Cortés was
very thoughtful, for he well understood that that fleet was sent
by Diego Velásquez the Governor of Cuba against him and
against all of us, and, wise man as he was, he said what he felt
about it to all of us captains and soldiers, and by great gifts of
gold to us, and promises to make us rich, he induced us all to
stand by him. He did not know who had come in command of
the fleet, but we were greatly rejoiced at the news, and at the
gold that Cortés had given us by the way of gratuity, as if he
had taken it from his own property and not from that which
should have been our share.

†   LXXVI

As those three scoundrelly soldiers of ours had gone over to
Narvaez, and had given him news of all the things that Cortés
and all of us had done since we entered New Spain, and had
told him that Captain Gonzalo de Sandoval was about eight
leagues distant at Vera Cruz, and that he had with him seventy
settlers nearly all of them old or invalids, Narvaez determined
to send to the town a priest named Guevara, who had good
address, and another man of considerable importance named
Amaya, a relation of Diego Velásquez of Cuba, and a notary

named Vergara, and three witnesses whose names I do not remember. He sent them to give notice to Sandoval to surrender at once to Narvaez, and for this purpose they said that they brought copies of the decrees. It is said that Gonzalo de Sandoval had already received news from some Indians about the ships and the great number of persons that had come in them, and as he was very much of a man, he always had everything in readiness and his soldiers armed, and as he suspected that that fleet came from Diego Velásquez and that some of the crew would be sent to that town to take possession of it, and so as not to be hampered by his old and invalid soldiers, he sent them off at once to an Indian town named Papalote, and kept with himself the healthy ones.

Sandoval called his soldiers together and impressed on them that if Diego Velásquez or any one else should come, they must not surrender the town to him, and all the soldiers answered that they would do as he wished; he furthermore ordered a gallows to be set up on a hill. The spies whom he had posted on the road hurried in to give him notice that six Spaniards and some Cuban Indians were approaching the town, and Sandoval awaited them in his house, for he would not go out to receive them, and he had already ordered that none of his soldiers should leave their houses or speak to them. When the priest and those whom he had brought in his company met with no Spanish settlers to speak to but only Indians who were working at the fort and did not understand them, they entered the town, and went to the church to say their prayers, and then went to the house of Sandoval, as it seemed to them to be the largest in the place. After giving Sandoval a friendly salutation to which he replied, they say that the priest commenced a speech saying that Diego Velásquez, the Governor of Cuba, had spent much money on the fleet, and that Cortés and all the others whom he had brought in his company had been traitors to him, and that they had come to give notice that they must go at once and give their obedience to Señor Pánfilo de Narvaez who came as Captain General on behalf of Diego Velásquez. When Sandoval heard these words and the rudeness with which the Padre Guevara spoke, he was biting his lips with annoyance at what he heard, and said: "Señor Padre, you are speaking very maliciously, in using these words about traitors—we are here all better servants of His Majesty than

Diego Velásquez—but that you are a priest I would chastise you as you deserve for your bad manners. Be off with you and go to Mexico, where you will find Cortés who is Captain General and Chief Justice of this New Spain, and he will give you your answer, here you need say no more."

Then the priest in a blustering way told the notary named Vergara whom he had brought with him, to take out at once the decrees that he carried in his bosom to notify Sandoval and the settlers who were with him, but Sandoval told the notary that he should not read a single paper, that he did not care whether they were decrees or any other documents. While they were disputing, the notary began to take out from his bosom the documents he had brought, and Sandoval said to him: "Look here, Vergara, I have already told you not to read any papers here, but to go to Mexico, and I promise you that if you do read them I will have you given a hundred lashes, for we do not know whether you are a king's notary or not; show us your title, and if you have got that, read it; nor do we know if these decrees are the originals or copies or other documents." The priest who was a very haughty man, exclaimed: "How are you dealing with these traitors? Bring out the decrees and notify them," and he said this with much anger. When Sandoval heard that expression he told him that he lied like a vile priest, and at once ordered his soldiers to take them all prisoner to Mexico. He had hardly uttered the words when a number of the Indians who were at work at the fort, snatched them up in net hammocks like sinful souls, and carried them off on their backs, and in four days arrived with them close to Mexico, for they travelled day and night with relays of Indians. They were indeed frightened when they saw so many cities and large towns, and food was brought to them, and one party dropped them and another carried them on their way, and it is said that they were wondering whether it was all witchcraft or a dream.

Sandoval wrote in haste to Cortés to tell him who was Captain of the fleet, and all that had happened. As soon as Cortés knew that the prisoners were close to Mexico, he sent out horses for the three principal persons and ordered them at once to be released from their confinement and wrote to them that he regretted that Sandoval should have treated them so disrespectfully, as he would have wished him to do them much honour, and when they arrived at Mexico he went out to meet them, and brought them very honourably into the city. When the priest and his companions saw how great a city was Mexico and the wealth of gold that we possessed, and the many other cities in the waters of the lake, and all us captains and soldiers, and the frank open-heartedness of Cortés, they were amazed, and by the end of the two days they stayed with us, Cortés had talked to them in such a way with promises and flattery and even by greasing their palms with little ingots and jewels of gold, that when he sent them back to their Narvaez with food for the road, although they had set out as fierce lions, they returned thoroughly tamed, and offered themselves to Cortés as his servants. So when they returned to Cempoala to report to their Captain, they began to persuade all the camp of Narvaez to come over to our side.

† LXXVII

As Cortés always exercised great care and forethought and no matter escaped him that he did not try and put right, and as I have often said before, he had trustworthy and good captains and soldiers who, besides being very valiant, gave him good advice—it was agreed to by all of us that he should at once write and send the letters by Indians post haste to Narvaez, before the priest Guevara could arrive, and should tell Narvaez with friendly expressions and promises which we one and all made him, that we would do what his honour should command but that we begged him as a favour not to create a disturbance in the land, or to allow the Indians to see any division among us. This promise was made because we who formed the party of Cortés were only a few soldiers in comparison with those whom Narvaez had brought, and in order to gain his good will, and to see how he would act. So we offered ourselves as his servants, while at the same time, beneath all these good words, we did not neglect any chances to look for friends among the Captains of Narvaez, for the Padre Guevara and the Notary Vergara had told Cortés that Narvaez was not much liked by his captains, and advised us to send them some slabs and chains of gold, for "gifts break rocks." Cortés wrote to them that he and all his companions were rejoiced at their arrival at the port, and, as they were old friends, he begged Narvaez to do nothing towards the release of Montezuma who was a prisoner, or to cause a rising in the city, for it would involve the destruction of himself and his men as well as all our lives on account of the great power that Montezuma wielded; that he stated this because Montezuma was very much excited and all the city was in revolt on account of the messages that had been sent to him. That he (Cortés) thought and felt certain that things expressed in such a way and at such a time could never have come from the mouth of such a wise and valiant man as Narvaez, but were such things as Cervantes the jester and the soldiers he had with him might say. Beside other words that were written in this letter, he placed his person and his property at the disposal of Narvaez, and said that he would do whatever Narvaez might command.

Cortés also wrote to the Secretary, Andrés de Duero, and to the Oidor, Lucas Vásquez de Ayllon, and he secretly ordered the Oidor to be given ingots and chains of gold. Then he begged the Padre de la Merced to follow the letters to the camp of Narvaez without delay, and he gave him more golden chains and ingots and some very valuable jewels to give to his friends there. So the first letter which Cortés wrote and sent by the Indians arrived before the Padre Guevara, and Narvaez went about showing it to his Captains and jeering at it and even at us. It is said that one of the Captains whom Narvaez had brought with him, named Salvatierra, who had come as Veedor, raised a clamour when he heard it, reproving Narvaez for reading such a letter from a traitor like Cortés, and saying that he ought to proceed against us at once, and not leave one of us alive, and he swore that he would roast Cortés' ears and eat one of them, and other such ribaldry. So Narvaez would not answer the letter, nor consider us worth a snap of the fingers.

Just at that time the priest Guevara and his companions arrived in camp, and told Narvaez that Cortés was a very excellent gentleman and a faithful servant of the King, and he told him of the great power of Mexico and of the many cities he had seen on the way, and that they understood that Cortés wished to serve him, and do all that he ordered, and it would be a good thing, if, peaceably and without disturbance, an agreement should be come to between them: he added that Señor

Narvaez should consider that all New Spain lay before him and he could take the people he had brought with him wherever he chose, and leave the other provinces to Cortés, for there were territories and to spare where one might settle. When Narvaez heard this, they say that he was so angry with Padre Guevara and Amaya that he would not see or listen to them again. When the people in the camp saw the Padre Guevara and the Notary Vergara and the others so greatly enriched, and the followers of Narvaez heard from them secretly so much good of Cortés and of all of us, and how they had seen such quantities of gold staked at play in our camp, many of them wished that they were already there. Just about this time our Padre de la Merced arrived at Narvaez's camp, with the ingots of gold which Cortés had given him and the private letters, and he went to kiss hands to Narvaez, and to tell him how Cortés wished for peace and friendship and was ready to obey his orders. But Narvaez who was very obstinate, and felt very aggressive, would not listen to him, and chose to say before the Padre himself, that Cortés and all of us were traitors, and because the Friar replied that on the contrary we were very loyal subjects of the King, Narvaez used abusive language to him.

Then the Friar very secretly distributed the ingots and chains of gold to those whom Cortés had named, and he got together and won over the chief persons in Narvaez's camp.

† LXXVIII

It appears that the Oidor Lucas Vásquez de Ayllon came in order to favour the cause of Cortés, and all of us, according to his instruction from the Royal Audiencia of Santo Domingo, who were aware of the many good and loyal services which we had done to God, and to our Lord the King. Moreover, in addition to what the Royal Audiencia had ordered him to do in his official capacity, the Oidor had now seen the letters from Cortés, and with them the blocks of gold; and whereas he had said previously that the despatch of the fleet was contrary to all right and justice, from this time forward he spoke so much more clearly and openly, and said so much good of Cortés and of all of those who were with him, that in the camp of Narvaez nothing else was talked about.

In addition to this it was seen that in Narvaez there was nothing but the utmost stinginess, for he took for himself all the gold and cloths which Montezuma had sent them and did not give a scrap of it either to a captain or a soldier, on the contrary he said very loudly to his steward, with a haughty voice, "See to it that not a mantle be missing, for they have all been noted down."

As they knew him to be so mean, and heard what I have already said about Cortés, and how we who were with him were very generous, his entire camp was more than half mutinous. Narvaez thought that the Oidor was at the bottom of it, and was sowing discord. Beside this, when Montezuma sent them food which the caterer or steward of Narvaez distributed, he did it without paying the attention to the Oidor or his servants that he should have done, and there was some irritation and uproar about it in the camp. Then owing to the advice given him by Salvatierra, and others, and above all trusting in the great support that he had received from the Bishop of Burgos, Narvaez had the daring to seize the King's Oidor and some of his servants and his clerk, and put them on board ship and send them as prisoners to Spain, or to the Island of Cuba. Also, because a gentleman, named Oblanca, a learned man, said that Cortés was a very good servant of the King, and it seemed to him wrong to call us traitors, Narvaez ordered him to be imprisoned. As Gonzalo de Oblanca was a very high-bred nobleman, he fretted himself to death within four days. Narvaez also made prisoners of two other soldiers whom he had brought in his ship who knew and spoke well of Cortés.

The Oidor, whom they were carrying as a prisoner to Castile, spoke kindly to the Captain and pilot and master who had charge of him on board the ship, but at the same time he frightened them by saying that when they arrived in Spain, that instead of paying them for what they had done, His Majesty would order them to be hanged. When they heard these words they told him that if he would pay them for their trouble they would take him to Santo Domingo and so they changed their course from what Narvaez had ordered and arrived and disembarked at the Island of Santo Domingo. When the Royal Audiencia heard the story of the Licentiate Lucas Vásquez de Ayllon, and took into consideration the great disrespect and effrontery that had been shown they felt it deeply, and were so much annoyed that they at once wrote to Castile to His Majesty's Royal Council.

Then certain soldiers, friends and relations of the Oidor Lucas Vásquez de Ayllon, seeing that Narvaez had committed that great disrespect and irregularity against an Oidor of His Majesty, agreed to flee from the sand dunes to the town where Captain Sandoval was stationed. Sandoval treated them with much honour, and learnt from them all that I have here related.

As soon as Narvaez had sent away the Oidor as a prisoner, he at once proceeded with all his baggage and supplies and munitions of war to form a camp in the town of Cempoala which at that time had a large population, and the first thing that he did was to take by force from the fat Cacique all the mantles and cloths and gold which Cortés had given into his charge before we left for Tlaxcala, and he also took the Indian women whom the Caciques of that town had given us, who had been left in the houses of their parents because they were daughters of chieftains, and too delicate to go to the war. When he did this the fat Cacique said many times to Narvaez that he must not touch any of the things that Cortés had left in his charge for if Cortés knew that anything had been taken he would kill him for it. He also complained to Narvaez himself of the many evil deeds and robberies that his people committed in the town, and told him that when Malinche was there with his people, they had not taken a single thing from them, and that he was very good and just, and that Narvaez should at once give him back his Indian women, and gold and mantles, for if he did not, he would send and complain to Malinche. When they heard that, they made fun of what he said, and the Veedor, Salvatierra, who was the one who boasted most, said to his friends and to Narvaez himself: "Don't you hear what a fright all these Caciques are in of this nonentity of a Cortés."

Let us go on and say that Cortés promptly took counsel with our Captains and all of us whom he knew to be his faithful followers, and whom he was accustomed to call in council in such important affairs as this. And it was decided by us all, that at once, without waiting for any more letters or other information, we should fall upon Narvaez and that Pedro de Alvarado should remain in Mexico to take charge of Montezuma with all the soldiers who were not inclined to go on that expedition, so that all those persons whom we suspected of being friends of Diego Velásquez could be left behind.

Just about that time, Cortés had sent to Tlaxcala for a large supply of maize, for there had been a bad seed time in the Mexican territory from want of rain, and we were in want of maize, for as we had with us many of our Tlaxcalan friends, there was great need of it. So they brought the maize and fowls and other food and we left it with Pedro de Alvarado, and we even made some barricades and fortifications for him and mounted some bronze cannon, and we left with him all the powder we possessed and fourteen musketeers, eight crossbowmen and five horses, and we left with him in all eighty soldiers.

† LXXIX

When as usual Cortés and the great Montezuma were conversing, Montezuma said to Cortés: "Señor Malinche, I noticed that all your captains and soldiers are agitated, and I have also observed that you only come to see me now and then, and Orteguilla the page tells me that you intend to go against those, your brothers, who have come in the ships, and to leave Tonatio here to guard me; do me the favour to tell me if there is anything I can do to assist you, for I will do it with the greatest good will. Moreover, Señor Malinche, I do not wish any calamity to befall you, for you have very few Teules with you, and those who have now come are five times as numerous, and they say that they are Christians like yourselves, and vassals and subjects of your Emperor, and they possess images and set up crosses and say Mass and say and announce that you are persons who have fled from your King, and that they have come to capture and kill you. I do not understand it at all, so take care what you are doing."

Cortés answered with a pretence of lightheartedness, and said through Doña Marina, who was always with him during all these conversations, that she should inform him that if he had not come to tell him all about it, it was because he loved him very much and did not wish to grieve him by our departure, and this was why he had postponed telling him, for he felt certain that Montezuma was well disposed towards him. That regarding what he said as to all of us being vassals of our great Emperor, it was true, also that they were Christians as we were, but as to what they said about our fleeing from our Lord the King, that it was not so, for our King had sent us to see him and tell him all that had been said and done in his royal name. As for what he said about their bringing many soldiers and ninety horses and many cannon and powder, and our being few in number, and that they had come to kill us and take us prisoners, that Our Lord Jesus Christ in whom we believe, and Our Lady Santa Maria, his blessed Mother, would give more strength to us than to them, for they were bad people and had come with a bad purpose. As our Emperor ruled over many kingdoms and principalities, there were great differences of race among them, some very valiant, and others even much more so. We came from Castile itself, which is called Old Castile, and we called ourselves Castilians, and the Captain who was now at Cempoala and the people he had brought with him came from another province, named Biscaya and called themselves Biscayans, and spoke like the Otomis of this land of Mexico, and he would see how we would bring them as prisoners. He need have no anxiety about our departure, for we would soon return victorious, and what he now begged of him was to stay quietly with his brother Tonatio and eighty soldiers. And, so that there should be no disturbance after we left the city, he must not countenance his captains and priests in doing anything for which, as soon as we returned, the rebellious ones would have to pay with their lives, and he begged him to provide our people with anything they might need in the way of food. Then Cortés embraced Montezuma twice, and Montezuma also embraced Cortés, and Doña Marina, who was very sagacious, said to him artfully that he was pretending sadness at our departure. Then Montezuma offered to do all that Cortés had asked him, and even promised that he would send five thousand warriors to our assistance. Cortés thanked him for it, but he well knew that he would not send them, and said that he needed no more than first of all the help of God, and then that of his companions.

Then Cortés spoke to Alvarado and all the soldiers who were remaining with him, and he charged them to take the greatest care that the great Montezuma did not escape, and to obey Pedro de Alvarado, and he promised with the help of our

Lord God, to make them all rich men. The Priest, Juan Díaz, also remained behind with them, as did also other suspected persons. Then we embraced one another and without taking any Indian women or any servants with us, and marching in light order, we set out on our journey for Cholula.

While on the road Cortés sent to Tlaxcala to beg our friends Xicotenga and Mase Escasi, to send us at once five thousand warriors, and they sent to say in reply that if it were against Indians like themselves they would do so, and even much more, but against Teules like us, and against lombards, and crossbows, they had no wish to fight. However they sent us twenty loads of fowls. Cortés also wrote to Sandoval that he should join us with all his soldiers as quickly as possible and that we were going to some towns about twelve leagues from Cempoala named Tanpaniguita and Mitlanguita.

Then as our scouts were marching on the look out, they saw Alonzo de Mata approaching, who said that he was a Notary, and was coming to serve the papers or copies of the decrees, and four Spaniards who came with him as witnesses. Two of our horsemen at once came to give notice, while the other scouts entered into conversation with Alonzo de Mata and his four witnesses. We hurried up and quickened our steps, and when they came near to us, they made deep bows to Cortés and to all of us, and Cortés dismounted from his horse, and as he knew why they came and that Alonzo de Mata wished to serve the decrees that he had brought, Cortés asked him if he was a King's Notary, and he replied yes; then he ordered him at once to exhibit his title, and if he had brought it that he should read the messages, and he [Cortés] would do what he should consider would be to the service of God and of His Majesty. That if he had not brought his title he should not read those documents, also that he [Cortés] must see the originals of the documents signed by His Majesty. So Mata, who was somewhat confused and timid, for he was not a King's Notary, and those who had come with him, did not know what to say. Cortés ordered them to be given food, for we were making a halt there, and he told them that we were going to some town named Tanpaniguita near the camp of Señor Narvaez, and that there he would be able to proclaim what his Captain might direct. Cortés was so tolerant that he never said a hard word about Narvaez, and he spoke privately with them and took their hands and gave them some gold, and soon afterwards they went back to their Narvaez, speaking well of Cortés and of all of us. As many of our soldiers at that time, out of ostentation, had jewels of gold on their arms and golden chains and collars round their necks, and these men who came to serve the decrees saw them, they told wonderful stories of us in Cempoala, and there were many of the principal people in the camp of Narvaez who wanted to come and make peace, and negotiate with Cortés, because they saw that we were all rich. So we arrived at Tanpaniguita, and the next day Captain Sandoval came with his soldiers numbering about sixty, for he had left behind all the old men and the invalids in a town named Papalote belonging to our Indian allies, so that they could be provided with food. There also came with him the five soldiers who were friends and relations of the Licentiate, Lucas Vásquez de Ayllon, who had fled from the camp of Narvaez, and came to kiss hands to Cortés, by whom they were all very well and gladly received.

Sandoval told Cortés that he had sent two soldiers disguised as Indians with Indians' clothes, to the camp of Narvaez, and Sandoval said that as they were dark-complexioned men they did not look like Spaniards, but like real Indians, and each one carried a load of plums on his back, for this was the plum season (this happened when Narvaez was still at the sand dunes, and before they had moved to the town of Cempoala), and they went to the hut of the fierce Salvatierra, who gave them a string of yellow beads for the plums, and when they had sold the plums, Salvatierra, believing them to be Indians, sent them to bring grass for his horse from the banks of a stream that ran near by the ranches. So they went and brought several loads of grass, and, as it was about the hour of Ave Maria when they returned with the grass, they squatted down on their heels like Indians in the hut until night fell, and they kept their eyes and ears open to what some of the soldiers of Narvaez were saying who had come to pay their respects to and keep company with Salvatierra. They reported that Salvatierra said to them: "Ah! at what a lucky moment we have come, for this traitor Cortés has collected more than seven hundred thousand dollars of gold, so we shall all be rich, and his captains and soldiers whom he has with him can hardly be less rich for they possess much gold!"—and they went on with their conversation. When it was quite dark our two soldiers silently crept out of the hut to where Salvatierra kept his horse, and as the bridle and saddle were close by, they saddled and bridled the animal and jumped on its back and rode off towards the town, and on the way they came upon another horse hobbled near the stream, and they took that also.

Cortés asked Sandoval where these horses were, and he replied that he had left them at the town of Papalote where he had placed the invalids, for the road by which he and his companions had come was impassable by horses, for it was very rough and crossed high mountains, and he had come that way so as not to fall in with any of the soldiers of Narvaez. When Cortés heard of the capture of Salvatierra's horse he was perfectly delighted, and said, "Now he will brag all the more since he finds it missing."

When Salvatierra woke up to find that the two Indians who had brought the plums for sale were missing, and could not find his horse or his saddle or his bridle, he said things that raised a laugh at his expense, for he soon found out that they were some of Cortés' Spaniards who had carried off his horse; and from that time on they kept watch.

† LXXX

As we had now all got together in that town, we agreed that another letter should be written to Narvaez to be carried by the Padre de la Merced, which, after an expression of respect and the utmost politeness, was more or less to the following effect: That we had rejoiced at his arrival and had believed that with his magnanimous character we should do great service to our Lord God and to His Majesty, but that he had replied to us nothing whatever; on the other hand he had called us who were loyal servants of His Majesty, traitors! and had stirred up trouble throughout the land by the messages he had sent to Montezuma; that Cortés had sent to beg him to choose whatever province he might prefer wherein to settle with his people, or that he should advance, and we would go to other territory and would undertake what it was the duty of faithful servants of His Majesty to accomplish; we had also begged as a favour that if he had brought any decrees from His Majesty that he would send the originals to us, so that we might examine them to see whether they had the royal signature and what orders they contained, so that with our breasts bowing before them on the ground, we might at once obey them. However, he would do neither one thing nor the other, but merely used abusive language to us and stirred up the country against us; that we begged and entreated him to send within three days and proclaim through His Majesty's Notary the Decrees he had brought, and we would obey; that if he had not brought the Decrees and wished to return to Cuba, he had better return and not disturb the country any more with threats, for if he made any more trouble, we would come against him and arrest him, and send him a prisoner to our Lord the King, because without the royal permission he had come to make war on us and disturb all the cities, and all the evils and deaths and burnings and losses that might thereon happen would be on his responsibility and not on ours; that he [Cortés] wrote and sent this letter now by hand, for no King's Notary dared to go to Narvaez to proclaim it for fear of being treated with as great disrespect as that with which Narvaez had treated the Oidor of His Majesty; where was there ever seen such audacity as to send him away a prisoner? In addition to what he had already said, he [Cortés] felt bound in duty to the honour and justice of our King, to punish that great disrespect and crime, and as Captain General and Chief Justice of New Spain which offices he held, he summoned and cited him on this charge and accused him, as in justice bound, for the crime in which he was involved was that of "laesio Majestatis," and that he called God to witness what he now said. Cortés also sent to tell Narvaez that he must at once return to the fat Cacique the mantles and cloth and jewels of gold which he had taken from him by force, and also the daughters of the chieftains who had been given to us by their parents, and that he must order his soldiers not to rob the Indians of that town nor of any other. After the usual expressions of courtesy, Cortés placed his signature, as did our Captains and some of the soldiers and I added mine. There accompanied the Friar a soldier named Bartolomé de Usagre, because he was a brother of the artilleryman Usagre who had charge of the artillery of Narvaez.

I will not waste further words on repeating how the Fraile

de la Merced reached the Camp of Narvaez, for he did what
Cortés ordered, which was to call together certain gentlemen
followers of Narvaez, and the gunners Rodrigo Martin and
Usagre. So as to be sure of attracting Usagre, his brother carried
some gold ingots which he secretly gave to him. In the same
manner the Friar distributed the gold as Cortés had commanded him, and told Andrés de Duero to come to our camp
soon to meet Cortés. In addition to this the Friar went to see
Narvaez, and speak to him and pretend to be his most humble
servant. While this was going on the partisans of Narvaez were
very suspicious of what our Friar was about and advised Narvaez to seize him at once, and this he was willing to do. When
Andrés de Duero heard of it he went to Narvaez and said to
him that he had been told that he wished to arrest the Fraile
de la Merced who was the messenger and Ambassador from
Cortés, and although some suspicions might be entertained
that the Friar was saying things in favour of Cortés, it would
not be wise to arrest him, for it had been clearly shown what
great honours and gifts Cortés bestowed on all the adherents of
Narvaez who went to visit him; that the Friar had spoken to
him [Andrés de Duero] as soon as he had arrived and given
him to understand his desire that he himself and other gentlemen from Cortés' camp should come to give Narvaez a reception, and that they should all be friends. Moreover, that it
would be mean to arrest a cleric. It were better that Usagre the
gunner whose brother had come to visit him should invite the
Friar to dinner and find out from him what it was that all
the followers of Cortés desired. With those and other palatable
speeches Andrés de Duero calmed Narvaez, and when this had
come to pass he took leave of him and secretly told the priest
what had taken place.

Narvaez sent at once to summon the Friar, and when he
came he showed him great respect, and the Friar half laughing,
for he was very sly and sagacious, begged him to come aside
with him in privacy, and Narvaez went strolling with him in a
courtyard, and the Friar said to him: "I know well that your
Honour wished to have me arrested but I wish you to know,
Sir, that you have no better or more devoted servant in the
camp than I am, and you may feel sure that many gentlemen
and captains among the followers of Cortés would be glad to
see him already in your hands, and I think that we shall all see

him there; and so as more surely to bring about his undoing they have made him write a nonsensical letter which was signed by the soldiers and was given to me to present to your Honour. I have not wished to show it until now, when we can chat together, and I longed to throw it in a river on account of the foolishness that it contains, and the soldiers and Captains of Cortés have done this so as to ensure his undoing." Narvaez said that the letter should be given to him, and the Friar replied that he had left it at his lodging and that he would go for it, and so he took his leave and went for the letter. Meanwhile the blustering Salvatierra came to the quarters of Narvaez.

The Friar quickly called Duero to go at once to the house of Narvaez for the presentation of the letter, for Duero and others among the Captains who had shown themselves favourable to Cortés, knew all about it, as the Friar carried it about with him, but he desired that many persons from that camp should be assembled to hear it read.

When the Friar arrived with the letter he at once gave it to Narvaez himself and said: "Do not be astonished at it, Sir, for Cortés talks as though out of his mind, but I know for certain that if your Honour will speak to him with affection he will promptly yield himself up with all his followers."

The Captains and soldiers told Narvaez to read the letter. When they heard it, Narvaez and Salvatierra roared with anger, the others laughed as though making fun of it, and then Andrés de Duero said: "Now I do not see how this can be, and I do not understand it, for this Cleric has told me that Cortés and all the rest would yield to your Honour, and now he writes these ravings." Then one Augustin Bermúdez, who was Captain and chief constable of the Camp of Narvaez, ably helped Duero and said: "I certainly learnt from this Friar of the Order of Mercy, in strict privacy, that if we were to send good mediators that Cortés himself would come to visit your Honour in order to give himself up with his soldiers, and it will be a good thing to send to his camp, which is not far off, the Señor Veedor Salvatierra and the Señor Andrés de Duero, and I will go with them": this he said purposely to see what Salvatierra would say. Narvaez at once said that Andrés de Duero and Salvatierra should go, but Salvatierra answered that he was indisposed, and that he would not go to see a traitor. The Friar said to him: "Señor Veedor, it is good to have moderation, for it is certain that you will have him a prisoner before many days."

As soon as the departure of Andrés de Duero was agreed upon, it seems that, in strict secrecy, Narvaez planned with Duero himself and three other Captains, that he should arrange with Cortés for an interview at some farms and Indian houses, which stood between the camp of Narvaez and ours, and that there an arrangement would be come to as to where we should go with Cortés to settle, and where boundaries should be drawn, and that during the interviews he [Narvaez] would arrest Cortés, and to this effect Narvaez had already bespoken twenty soldiers who were his friends.

The Friar knew about this at once, and so did Andrés de Duero, and they informed Cortés of everything.

† LXXXI

Let us go back. As soon as Cortés heard news of the fleet that Narvaez was bringing he at once despatched a soldier to a province called the land of the Chinantecs, near to where our soldiers had stayed when they went to search for mines, for the people of that province were very hostile to the Mexicans and they had accepted our friendship a few days before. They used as arms very long lances, longer than ours from Castile, with two fathoms of flint and stone knives, so he sent to beg them to bring him promptly three hundred of them, and to remove the knives, and, as they possessed much copper, to make for each one two metal points. The soldier took with him the model which the points should resemble, and they fashioned the points far more perfectly than those we sent to order from them. He also commanded our soldier to demand of them two thousand warriors, and by the day of the feast of Espíritu Santo to come with them to the town of Tanpaniguita, and that the two thousand men should bring lances. The Caciques said that they would come with the warriors, and the soldier soon came with a matter of two hundred Indians who carried the lances, and another of our soldiers remained behind to accompany the other warriors.

The lances proved to be extremely good, and the soldier trained us and taught us how to handle them, and how we were to cope with the horsemen. When we had made our muster and the list and record of all the soldiers and captains of our army, we found that there were two hundred and sixty-six including the drummer and fifer, and not counting the Friar. There were five horsemen and two small cannon, a few crossbowmen and fewer musketeers; what we relied on for fighting with Narvaez was the lances, and they were very good as will be seen further on.

I have already stated that when we were in Santiago de Cuba, Cortés settled with Andrés de Duero and with Amador de Lares that they should use their influence with Diego Velásquez to have [him] Cortés appointed Captain General to go with that fleet and, that he would divide with them all the gold, silver and jewels that might fall to his lot. As Andrés de Duero saw that his partner Cortés was at this moment so rich and powerful, under pretext of making peace and acting in favour of Narvaez, he concealed his real intention, which was to claim his share in the partnership, for his other partner Amador de Lares was already dead. As Cortés was far-sighted and crafty he not only promised to give Andrés de Duero great wealth, but also to give him a command over the whole force neither more nor less than he himself held, provided that he would induce Augustin Bermudez, who was Chief Constable in the camp of Narvaez, and other gentlemen (whom I will not name here), to endeavour to lead Narvaez astray, so that he should not escape with his life or honour and should be defeated.

The better to lure and bind Duero to what had been said, Cortés loaded his two Cuban Indians with gold, and it seems that Duero gave a promise to him. Cortés also sent many ingots and jewels of gold to Bermudez and to a priest named Juan de Leon and the priest Guevara.

Andrés de Duero stayed in our camp from the day of his arrival until after dinner the following day which was the feast of Espíritu Santo. He dined with Cortés and conversed a while with him in private. When dinner was over, Duero took leave of all of us both Captains and soldiers and then, already on horseback, he once more approached Cortés and said: "What are your orders, your honour; I wish to depart." Cortés answered him: "God be with you, and look to it, Señor Andrés de Duero, that what we have been talking about be well arranged, if not, by my conscience (for it was thus Cortés swore), before three days are passed I shall be there in your camp, and, if I find anything contrary to what we have agreed upon, your honour will be the first to be pierced by my lance."

Duero laughed and said: "I shall fail in nothing which concerns my service to your honour," and he set off at once, and when he arrived at his camp it is said that he told Narvaez that Cortés and all of us who were with him were very willing to go over to Narvaez himself.

Let us stop talking about this Duero affair and I will relate how Cortés promptly sent to summon one of our Captains named Juan Velásquez de Leon. When he had come before Cortés and made his salute he said: "What are your orders, sir," and as Cortés at times spoke honeyed words with a smile on his lips, he said half laughingly: "What made me summon the Señor Juan Velásquez is what Andrés de Duero has reported, which is that Narvaez says, and such is the report throughout his camp, that if your honour should go there that I would be at once undone and defeated, for they believe that you would join with Narvaez, and for this reason I have resolved that, for the life of me, if you really love me, you shall go on your good gray mare, and take all your gold and the *fanfarrona* (which was a very heavy golden chain) and other trifles that I will give you, in order to give them in my name to whomsoever I may direct. Your heavy *fanfarrona* you shall carry over one shoulder, and another chain which weighs even more than it, you shall wear wound twice round, then you will see how Narvaez loves you. Try to come away again soon, for then the Señor Diego de Ordás may go there, whom they wish to see in Narvaez's camp as he has been a Mayor-domo of Diego Velásquez."

Juan Velásquez answered that he would do what His Excellency commanded him, but that he would not take his own gold and his chains with him, only such as might be given him with orders to hand over to certain persons, but, wherever he might be, he would be at all times ready to render His Excellency such service as no amount of gold or diamonds could procure. "That was my belief," said Cortés, "and with this confidence in you, sir, I send you, but unless you take all your gold and jewels as I command, I do not wish you to go." Juan Velásquez replied: "Whatever your honour commands shall be done," but he did not wish to take his jewels. Cortés spoke to him then in private and he at once set out and took with him one of Cortés' orderlies named Juan del Rio to attend on him. Within two hours of the departure of Juan Velásquez, Cortés ordered Canillas to beat the drum and Benito de Beger our fifer to sound his tambourine, and he ordered Gonzalo de Sandoval who was Captain and Chief Constable to summon all the soldiers, and we at once began our march in quick time along the road to Cempoala. While we were on the march two native swine were killed which have a scent gland on the back, and many of the soldiers said that it was a sign of victory, and we slept on a bank near a small stream, with our scouts on ahead and spies and patrols.

When dawn broke we went straight along and marched until midday when we had a rest by a river where the town of Villa Rica de Vera Cruz now stands.[1]

† LXXXII

Juan Velásquez made such speed on the road, that he reached Cempoala by dawn and dismounted at the house of the fat Cacique, and thence went afoot to the quarters of Narvaez. The Indians recognized Juan Velásquez and were delighted to see and speak to him and said aloud to some of the soldiers of Narvaez, who were quartered in the house of the fat Cacique, that this was Juan Velásquez de Leon, one of Malinche's Captains. As soon as the soldiers heard this they went running to Narvaez to demand rewards for bringing the good news that Juan Velásquez de Leon had come.

When Narvaez heard of his arrival, before Juan Velásquez could reach his quarters, he went out to receive him in the street accompanied by some soldiers. On meeting they made a great show of reverence to one another, and Narvaez embraced Juan Velásquez, and asked him why he did not dismount at his quarters, and he ordered his servants to go at once for the horse and baggage, if he had brought any. Juan Velásquez replied that he wished to return at once, and that he had only come to kiss his hands and those of all the gentlemen of his

[1] The third site of the city, on the Rio Antigua.

camp, and to see if His Excellency and Cortés could agree to keep peace and friendship. Then it is said that Narvaez promptly repelled Juan Velásquez, greatly annoyed that such words should be spoken to him. "What! to make friends and peace with a traitor who had rebelled with the fleet against his cousin Diego Velásquez?"—and Juan Velásquez replied that Cortés was no traitor but a faithful servant of His Majesty, and that to appeal to our Lord and King as he had done should not be imputed to him as treason, and he begged Narvaez to use no such word in his presence. Then Narvaez began to bribe Juan Velásquez with great promises so as to persuade him to remain with him and to arrange with the followers of Cortés to give Cortés up and to come at once and place themselves under his command, promising him with oaths that he should be the foremost captain in all the camp and be the second in command. Juan Velásquez answered that it would be a great treason to desert the Captain to whom he had sworn obedience during war, and to abandon him knowing as he did that all that he had done in New Spain was in the service of God our Lord and His Majesty, and that Cortés could not avoid appealing, in the way he had appealed, to our King and Master, and he begged Narvaez to say no more about it.

By that time all the most important Captains from the Camp of Narvaez had come to see Juan Velásquez and they embraced him with the greatest courtesy, for Juan Velásquez was much of a courtier, well made, robust, of good presence and features and with a becoming beard, and he wore a great golden chain thrown over his shoulder giving it two turns under his arm, and it suited him well in the part of the gallant and brave captain.

It seems that at that time certain Captains of Narvaez advised him to arrest Juan Velásquez at once, for it seemed to them that he was speaking very freely in favour of Cortés. When Narvaez had already secretly ordered his Captains and Constables to take him prisoner, Augustin Bermudez and Andrés de Duero and our Padre de la Merced and a priest named Juan de Leon, and other persons from among those who had professed themselves friends of Cortés, heard about it, and they said to Narvaez that they were astonished at his ordering Juan Velásquez de Leon to be arrested, for what could Cortés do against him [Narvaez] even if he had another hundred Juan

Velásquezes in his Company? that Cortés might easily have arrested Andrés de Duero and the priest Guevara and others who had gone to his camp, and he did not do so; on the contrary, as they have stated, he paid them great honour; and it would be better once again to speak to Juan Velásquez with much courtesy and to invite him to dinner. This seemed to Narvaez to be good advice, and he promptly spoke again to Juan Velásquez in very affectionate terms so that he should be the mediator through whom Cortés might give himself up with all of us; and he invited him to dinner. Juan Velásquez replied that in that case he would do what he could, although he held Cortés to be very obstinate and stubborn in the matter, and that it would be better to divide the provinces, and his honour [Narvaez] should choose the land that pleased him best. This Juan Velásquez said in order to pacify him.

While these conversations were going on the Padre de la Merced whispered to Narvaez as his confidant and adviser which he had already become, "Order them to muster all your artillery and cavalry and musketeers and crossbowmen and soldiers so that Juan Velásquez de Leon and the orderly Juan del Rio may see them, and so that Cortés may fear your force." So on the advice of our Friar Narvaez held a review before Juan Velásquez de Leon and Juan del Rio, and in the presence of our cleric. When it was finished Juan Velásquez said to Narvaez: "You have brought a great force with you, may God increase it." Then Narvaez replied: "Ah, you can see that had I wished to go against Cortés I should have taken him prisoner and all of you that are with him." Then Juan Velásquez answered and said: "Look on him as taken and us soldiers too, but we shall know well how to defend ourselves," and so the conversation ended.

The next day Juan Velásquez was invited to dinner, and there was dining with Narvaez a nephew of Diego Velásquez the Governor of Cuba, who was also one of his captains, and while they were eating at table he began to talk of how Cortés had failed to surrender to Narvaez, and of the letter and summons that he sent him. And from one speech to another, the nephew of Diego Velásquez (who was also called Diego Velásquez like his uncle) exceeded all bounds and said that Cortés and all of us who were with him were traitors, because they did not come to submit themselves to Narvaez. When

Juan Velásquez heard this he rose from the chair on which
he was seated and with great ceremony said: "Señor Captain
Narvaez, I have already told you that I cannot acquiesce in
such words being spoken against Cortés or against any of
those who are with him, as those that have been uttered,
for it is truly malicious to speak evil of us who have served His
Majesty so loyally."

Diego Velásquez replied that his words were well said and
that he [Juan Velásquez] was upholding a traitor, and that
traitors were as worthless as he was, and that he was not a
good Velásquez. Juan Velásquez grasped his sword and said
that he lied and that he was a better gentleman than he was,
and a good Velásquez, better than him or his uncle, and that
he would let him know it, if the Señor Captain Narvaez would
give him leave. As there were many captains present, they
placed themselves between them and they advised Narvaez
that he should promptly order Juan Velásquez to leave the
camp, both him and the Friar and Juan del Rio for they felt
sure that they were doing no good there. At once without further delay they were ordered to leave, and they, who could
hardly await the hour of getting back to our camp, complied.

It is said that Juan Velásquez mounted on his good mare in
his coat of mail, which he always wore, and helmet and great
golden chain, went to take leave of Narvaez, and Diego Velásquez, the youth who had quarrelled, was there with Narvaez, and Juan Velásquez said to Narvaez: "What are your
Honour's orders for our camp?" Narvaez replied in a great
rage that he should get him gone and that it would have been
better had he never come, and the youth Diego Velásquez uttered threats and offensive words to Juan Velásquez, who answered that he was very audacious and deserved chastisement
for the words he had spoken, and placing his hand on his beard
he cried by this my beard I swear that I will see before many
days whether your courage is as good as your words. So they
parted, and keeping on their way they met us at the river near
Vera Cruz.

When they arrived where we were, what delight and happiness we all experienced, and how many caresses and what
praise did Cortés bestow on Juan Velásquez and on our Friar,
and he had good cause, for they were his faithful servants.

Then Juan Velásquez related, step by step, all that I have

already stated had happened to them with Narvaez and how he sent secretly to give the chains and ingots and jewels of gold to the persons whom Cortés had indicated. Then you should have heard our Friar! Being of a merry disposition, he well knew how to mimic his own behaviour as Narvaez's faithful servant, and to tell how, in sheer mockery, he advised him to hold the review and call out his artillery, and with what astuteness and cunning he gave him the letter. Then he next related what happened to him with Salvatierra, and told us what fierce threats Salvatierra uttered as to what he would do and what would happen when he captured Cortés and all of us, and that he even complained to him about the soldiers who had stolen his horse and that of the other captain, and we were all as delighted at hearing about it as though we were going to a wedding or a merrymaking, [although] we knew that the next day we should be going into battle and must conquer or die in it, we being but two hundred and sixty-six soldiers and those of Narvaez being five times as numerous as we were. We all marched at once, and we went to sleep near a small stream about a league from Cempoala where there was a bridge.

It seems that when Juan Velásquez and the Friar and Juan del Rio went back, Narvaez was told by his captains that a belief had arisen in the camp that Cortés had sent many jewels of gold, and had gained friends to his side in the camp itself, and that it would be well to be much on the alert, and to warn the soldiers to have their arms and horses ready. In addition to this the fat Cacique was in great fear of Cortés because he had allowed Narvaez to take the cloths and gold and to seize the Indian women, moreover he always had spies out to see where we slept and by what road we were coming, for so Narvaez had compelled him to do by force. When he knew that we were already arriving near to Cempoala the fat Cacique said to Narvaez: "What are you about? you are behaving very carelessly; do you think that Malinche and the Teules that he brings with him are the same as you are? Well, I tell you that when you least expect it he will be here and will kill you." Although they made fun of those words that the fat Cacique said to them, they did not fail to get ready, and the first thing they did was to declare war against us with fire and sword and free loot. This we heard from a soldier called El Galleguillo, who came fleeing from the camp of Narvaez, and he informed

Cortés about the proclamation and about other things that it was as well to know.

Let us return to Narvaez, who ordered all the artillery, horsemen, musketeers and crossbowmen to be taken out to a plain about a quarter of a league from Cempoala to await us there, and not to let one of us escape either death or capture. As it rained hard that day the followers of Narvaez had already had enough of waiting for us in the wet, and as they were accustomed neither to rain nor hardships and did not think we were of any account, his captains gave him notice that they would return to their quarters, as it was an outrage to be kept there waiting for two or three men, as they said we were. They further advised Narvaez to place his artillery, which numbered eighteen large cannon, in front of their quarters and that forty horsemen should remain all night waiting on the road by which we had to come to Cempoala; furthermore that he should station his spies by the ford of the river which we would have to cross, selecting good riders and lithe runners to carry messages, and that twenty horsemen should patrol throughout the night in the courtyards of their quarters. This plan which they communicated to him was to induce him to return to his quarters. Moreover, his captains said to him: "What, Señor? do you take Cortés to be so valiant as to dare with the three cats which he commands to come to this camp merely because this fat Indian says so? Don't you believe it, your Honour, he had only made this fuss and pretence of coming so that your Honour may grant good terms." It was in this way, as I have said, that Narvaez returned to his camp, and after his return he publicly promised to give two thousand pesos to whoever should kill Cortés or Gonzalo de Sandoval. He at once placed spies at the river, and the cry and countersign that he gave when they should fight against us in the camp was "Santa Maria, Santa Maria!"

† LXXXIII

When we arrived at the stream about a league from Cempoala, where there were some good meadows, Captain Cortés sent to summon us, both Captains and soldiers, and when he saw us assembled, he said to us that he begged the favour of silence.

Then he began a speech in such charming style, with sentences so neatly turned, that I assuredly am unable to write the like, so delightful was it and so full of promises, in which he at once reminded us of all that had happened to us since we set out from the Island of Cuba until then, and he said to us: "You well know that Diego Velásquez, the Governor of Cuba, chose me as Captain General, not that there were not many gentlemen among you worthy of the post, and you knew and believed that we were coming to settle, for thus it was published and proclaimed; however, as you have seen, he was merely sending to trade. You are already aware of what happened about my wishing to return to the Island of Cuba to render an account to Diego Velásquez of the task that he entrusted to me, in accordance with his instructions; but Your Honours ordered and obliged me to form a settlement in this country in His Majesty's name, and thanks to our Lord the settlement has been made and it was a very wise decision. In addition to this you made me your Captain General and the Chief Justice of the settlement until His Majesty may be pleased to order otherwise. As I have already mentioned there was certain talk of returning to Cuba among some of you, but I do not wish to dwell further on that; it is, so to say, a bygone and our staying was a blessed and good thing, for it is clear that we have done great service to God and His Majesty. You already know that we told His Majesty that this land is, so far as we have seen and know, four times larger than Castile and has great cities and is very rich in gold and mines, and how we begged His Majesty not to give it away to be governed in any other manner by any one whosoever, for we believe that the Bishop of Burgos would ask it from His Majesty for Diego Velásquez, or for some relation or friend of the Bishop's own. This land is so good that it would be proper to bestow it on an *Infante* or great Prince, and we are determined not to give it up to any one until His Majesty shall have heard our Proctors and we behold his royal signature and, approval, so that in all humility we may do what he may be pleased to order. You also know that we sent with the letters and placed at His Majesty's service all the gold and silver and jewels and everything that we possessed or had acquired, moreover you will well remember, gentlemen, how often we have been at the point of death in the wars and battles we have passed through; let me also remind you how inured we are to hardship, rains, winds and sometimes hunger, always having to carry our arms on our backs and to sleep on the ground whether it is snowing or raining, and if we examine it closely our skin is already tanned from suffering. I do not wish to refer to over fifty of our comrades who have died in the wars, nor to all of you who are bandaged in rags, and maimed from wounds which are not even yet healed. I should like to remind you of the troubles we had at sea and in the battles of Tabasco, and, those who were present at them, of the affairs of Almería or Cingapacinga, and how often in the mountains and on the roads attempts were made to take our lives. In what straits they placed us in the battles of Tlaxcala and how they handled us; then in the affair of Cholula, they had even prepared the earthen pots in which to cook our bodies; at the ascent of the passes you will not have forgotten the forces that Montezuma had gathered to exterminate us and you saw all the roads blocked with felled trees. Then during the dangers of the entry into and stay in the great City of Mexico, how many times did we look death in the face? who is able to count them?

"Then look at those among you who have come here twice before I did, first with Francisco Hernández de Córdova, and the other time with Juan de Grijalva; consider the hardships you underwent in discovering these countries, the hunger and thirst of the wounded and loss by death of so many soldiers and all the property of your own that you expended in those two voyages. Let us add now, gentlemen, that as Pánfilo de Narvaez marches against us with great fury and desire to get us in his power, calling us traitors and malefactors even before he had landed, and sends messages to the great Montezuma not in the words of a wise Captain, but of a mischief-maker, and as in addition to this he had the audacity to arrest one of His Majesty's Judges, for this great crime alone he deserves condign punishment. You have already heard how in his camp he has proclaimed war against us, and outlawed us as though we were Moors." Soon after saying this Cortés began to extol our appearance and courage in the late wars and battles, saying that then we were fighting to save our lives, and that now we had to fight with all our strength both for life and honour, for they were coming to capture us and drive us from our houses and rob us of our property. "Moreover," he added, "we do not even know if he brings authority from our King and Lord or only support from our opponent the Bishop of Burgos, and if by ill luck we should fall into the hands of Narvaez, which God prevent, all the services that we have done both to God and His Majesty will turn to disservice, they will bring law suits against us, saying that we killed and robbed and destroyed the land, where in truth they are the ones to rob, brawl and disserve our Lord and King but they will claim that they have served him"; then he said that all that he had related we had seen with our own eyes, and that as true gentlemen we were bound to stand up for His Majesty's honour and our own homes and properties; he left Mexico on that understanding with confidence in God and in us, that first he trusted everything in the hands of God and next in our hands, and let us consider what we thought of it.

Then one and all we answered him, jointly with Juan Velásquez de Leon and Francisco de Lugo and other captains, that he might feel sure that, God helping us, we would conquer or die over it, and he should look to it that they did not persuade him to terms, for if he should do anything underhand that we would stab him.

Then when he saw our determination he rejoiced greatly. When this was over he turned to beg us as a favour to keep silence. As the first thing to be done was to seize their artillery, which numbered eighteen cannon, and was posted in front of the quarters of Narvaez, he appointed a relation of his own to go as Captain, whose name was Pizarro, and he assigned to him sixty young soldiers, and he named me among them, and ordered that after the artillery was taken, we should all run to the quarters of Narvaez which were on a very lofty Cue. For the capture of Narvaez he named as Captain Gonzalo de Sandoval with sixty companions, and as he was chief Constable he gave him an order which read thus:—Gonzalo de Sandoval Chief Constable of this New Spain, in His Majesty's name I command you to seize the person of Pánfilo Narvaez, and should he resist, to kill him, for the benefit of the service of God and the King, insomuch as he has committed many acts to the disservice of God and of His Majesty, and arrested an Oidor. Given in this camp and signed Hernando Cortés, countersigned by his Secretary Pedro Hernández.

After issuing the order, he promised to give three thousand

pesos to the soldier who first laid hand on Narvaez, and to the second two thousand, and one thousand to the third. Then he chose Juan Velásquez de Leon to arrest the youth Diego Velásquez with whom he had had the quarrel, and gave him another sixty soldiers, and he likewise named Diego de Ordás to arrest Salvatierra and gave him another sixty soldiers, and there was Cortés himself ready for an emergency with another twenty soldiers, to hasten to where he was most needed, and where he intended to be present was at the capture of Narvaez and Salvatierra.

As soon as the lists were given to the Captains, Cortés said: "I well know that the followers of Narvaez are in all four times as numerous as we are, but they are not used to arms, and as the greater part of them are hostile to their captain, and many of them are ill, and we shall take them by surprise, I have an idea that God will give us the victory, and that they will not persist much in their defence, for we shall procure them more wealth than their Narvaez can. So, gentlemen, our lives and honour depend, after God, on your courage and your strong arms, I have no other favour to ask of you or to remind you of but that this is the touchstone of our honour and our glory for ever and ever, and it is better to die worthily than to live dishonoured." And as at that time it was raining and was late he said no more. There is one thing I have thought about since, he never told us: "I have such and such an arrangement in the camp made with so and so, which is in our favour," nor anything of that kind, but merely that we were to fight like brave men; and this omitting to tell us that he had friends in the camp of Narvaez, was the action of a very astute Captain, so that we should not fail to fight as very valiant men, and should place no hope in them, but only, after God, in our own great courage.

Later on they secretly gave us the password that we were to use while fighting, which was "Espíritu Santo, Espíritu Santo!" The followers of Narvaez had as their password and battle cry "Santa Maria, Santa Maria!"

When all this was finished, as I was a great friend and servant of Captain Sandoval, he begged me as a favour to keep by him that night and follow him if I were still alive after capturing the artillery, and I promised him that I would do so, as will be seen later on.

† LXXXIV

Let me say now that we spent part of the night in preparations and in thinking about what we had before us, for we had nothing at all on which to sup. I myself and one other soldier were posted as sentinels, and before long a scout came to ask me if I had perceived anything, and I said "No." Then came an officer and said that the Galleguillo who came from the camp of Narvaez had disappeared and that he was a spy sent by Narvaez, and that Cortés ordered us to march at once on the road to Cempoala, and we heard our fifer and the beating of the drum and the Captains getting their soldiers ready, and we began to march. The Galleguillo was found asleep under some cloths, for as it was raining and the poor fellow was not accustomed to be in the wet and cold he went there to sleep. Then going along at a good pace and without any playing on the fife or drum, and with the scouts reconnoitring the road, we reached the river where the spies of Narvaez were posted, and they were so little on the look out that we had time to capture one and the other fled shouting to the camp of Narvaez, crying "To arms! to arms! Cortés is coming."

I remember that when we passed through that river, as it was raining, it had become rather deep and the stones were slippery and we were much encumbered with our pikes and our arms, and I also remember that when the spy was captured he said to Cortés in a loud voice: "Take care, Señor Cortés, don't you go on there, for I swear that Narvaez is waiting for you in camp with all his army."

The order "To arms, to arms" and Narvaez calling to his captains, and our charging with our pikes and engaging the artillery, happened simultaneously, and the gunners had time only to fire four shots, and some of the balls passed overhead but one of them killed three of our comrades.

At that moment all our Captains came up with the fife and drum beating the charge, and as many of the followers of Narvaez were mounted, they were delayed for a few moments by them, but they promptly unhorsed six or seven of them. Then we who had seized the guns did not dare to leave them, for Narvaez was shooting at us with arrows and muskets from his quarters and wounded seven of us. At that moment Captain Sandoval arrived and made a rush to scale the steps, and, in spite of the strong resistance which Narvaez made with muskets, partisans and lances and flights of arrows, Sandoval and his soldiers still gained ground. Then as soon as we soldiers saw that the guns were ours and no one was left to dispute possession of them, we gave them over to our gunners, and Captain Pizarro and many of us went to the assistance of Sandoval, for the soldiers of Narvaez had driven them back down two of the steps. On our arrival he turned to ascend the steps again and we stood for some time fighting with our pikes which were very long, and when I was least expecting it we heard shouts from Narvaez who cried: "Holy Mary protect me, they have killed me and destroyed my eye."

When we heard this we at once shouted: "Victory, Victory for those of the password of Espíritu Santo, for Narvaez is dead; Victory! Victory! for Cortés, for Narvaez has fallen!" —but for all this we were not able to force the entrance to the Cue where they were posted, until a certain Martin López who was very tall set fire to the thatch of the lofty Cue and all the companions of Narvaez came tumbling down the steps. Then we seized Narvaez, and the first to lay hands on him was Pedro Sánchez Farfan, a good soldier, and I gave him to Sandoval and the other Captains who were with him, and we were still shouting and crying: "Long live the King, long live the King, and in his Royal Name, Cortés, Cortés, Victory, Victory, for Narvaez is dead!"

Let us leave this struggle and return to Cortés and the other Captains who were each one of them still fighting against the Captains of Narvaez who had not yet yielded, notwithstanding the shots that our gunners fired at them, and our shouts and the death of Narvaez, for they were posted in very lofty temples. As Cortés was very sagacious he promptly ordered it to be proclaimed that all the followers of Narvaez should come at once and yield themselves up under the banner of His Majesty, and to Cortés in his Royal name, under pain of death. Yet with all this the followers of the youth Diego Velásquez and those of Salvatierra did not give in, for they were in very lofty temples and could not be reached until Gonzalo de Sandoval went with half of us who were with him, with the cannon and the proclamation, and forced his way in and seized Salvatierra and those in his company as well as the youth

Diego Velásquez. Then Sandoval came with all those who had gone to capture Narvaez to put him in a safer place. And, after Cortés and Juan Velásquez and Ordás had made prisoners of Salvatierra and the youth Diego Velásquez and Gamarra, and Juan Yuste and Juan Bono the Biscayan and other persons of importance, Cortés came, without being recognized, in company with our Captains to where we held Narvaez. As the heat was great, and as Cortés was burdened with his arms, and had been going from place to place shouting to our soldiers and giving out proclamations, he arrived sweating and tired and panting for breath, and he spoke to Sandoval twice, and did not succeed in saying what he wanted on account of the trouble he was in; and he said: "What about Narvaez, what about Narvaez?"—and Sandoval said: "He is here; he is here and well guarded." Then Cortés, still much out of breath, turned to say: "Take care, my son Sandoval, that you do not leave him, and that you and your comrades do not let him break away while I go and attend to other matters, and see to it that these other captains who are prisoners with him are guarded in every way." Then he promptly went off to issue other proclamations to the effect that under pain of death all the followers of Narvaez should at once come to that place to surrender themselves under the banner of His Majesty and in his royal name to Hernando Cortés his Captain General and Chief Justice, and that no one should carry arms, but that all should give them up and hand them over to our Constables.

All this was done in the night, for it was not yet dawn, and it still rained from time to time; then the moon came out, but when we had arrived there it was very dark and was raining. However, the darkness was a help, for as it was so dark there were many fire-flies which give light by night, and the soldiers of Narvaez believed that they were the match fires of muskets.

Let us leave this and go on to say that as Narvaez was very badly wounded and had lost an eye, he asked leave of Sandoval for his surgeon named Maestre Juan, whom he had brought in his fleet, to attend to his eye and to the other captains who were wounded, and permission was given. While they were being doctored, Cortés came near by, on the sly, so that they should not recognize him, to see Narvaez. Some one whispered to Narvaez that Cortés was there, hardly was this said

to him than Narvaez exclaimed: "Señor Captain Cortés, you
must consider this a great feat, this victory which you have
won over me and the capture of my person"; and Cortés answered him that he gave many thanks to God for giving the
victory to him and to the gallant gentlemen and comrades who
had a share in it, but that to capture and defeat him [Narvaez]
who had seen fit to dare to arrest one of His Majesty's Judges,
was one of the least important things he had done in New
Spain. As soon as he had said this he went away and said no
more, but ordered Sandoval to place a strong guard over
Narvaez and to stay with him himself and not leave him in
charge of others. We had already placed two pairs of fetters
on him, and we carried him to an apartment and stationed
soldiers to guard him, and Sandoval designated me as one of
them, and privately he ordered me not to allow any of the
followers of Narvaez to speak to him until it was daytime and
Cortés could place him in greater security.

Let us leave this, and relate how Narvaez had sent forty
horsemen to wait for us on the road, when we were on our
way to his camp, and we were aware that they were still
wandering in the country and were fearful lest they should
come and attack us, and rescue their captains and Narvaez
himself whom we held prisoner. So we kept much on the
alert, and Cortés determined to send and beg them as a favour
to come into camp, and made great offers and promises to
them all.

He despatched Cristóbal de Olid, who was our quartermaster, and Diego de Ordás, to bring them in, and they went on
horses that we had captured from the followers of Narvaez
(for our horsemen brought no horses with them, but left them
picketed in a small wood near Cempoala; we brought only
pikes, swords, shields and daggers) and they went out into
the country with one of the soldiers of Narvaez who showed
them the track by which they had gone, and they came upon
them, and gave expression to so many offers and promises on
behalf of Cortés that they won them over, but some gentlemen
among them bore Cortés ill will.

Before they reached our camp it was broad daylight, and the
drummers brought by Narvaez, without word from Cortés or
any of us, began to beat their kettledrums and play on their
fifes and tambourines and cry: "Viva, Viva the gala of the

Romans! who few as they are have conquered Narvaez and his soldiers"; and a negro named Guidela whom Narvaez had brought with him, who was a very witty jester cried out and said: "Behold! The Romans never accomplished such a feat"; and although we told them to keep quiet and not to beat their drums, they would not do so until Cortés sent to arrest the drummer, who was named Tápia and was half crazy. At this moment came Cristóbal de Olid and Diego de Ordás and brought in the horsemen whom I have mentioned, and among them came Andrés de Duero and Augustin Bermúdez and many of our Captains' friends, who as soon as they came went to kiss hands to Cortés who with us around him was seated on an armchair, wearing a long orange-coloured robe with his armour beneath it. Then to see the graciousness with which he addressed and embraced them, and the flattering words that he said to them were matters worthy of note, and how cheerful he was, and he had good cause in seeing himself at that moment such a lord and so powerful, and so after kissing his hands each one passed to his quarters.

Let us speak now of those who were killed and wounded on that night. The standard-bearer of Narvaez named Fuentes, a gentleman from Seville, died. Another of Narvaez' captains named Rojas, a native of Old Castile, also died, and two of the other followers of Narvaez died. There also died one of the three soldiers who had belonged to us and had gone over to Narvaez. Many of the followers of Narvaez were wounded, and four of our men died and more were wounded, and the fat Cacique also was wounded, for when he knew that we were nearing Cempoala he took refuge in the quarters of Narvaez and there he was wounded, and Cortés at once ordered him to be well attended to and placed him in his house so that he should not be molested. Then the mad Cervantes and Escalona, who were those who had been of our party and had gone over to Narvaez, fared badly, for Escalona was severely wounded and Cervantes well beaten.

Let us go to those in the quarters of Salvatierra the fierce, of whom his soldiers say that never in all their lives did they see a more worthless man, or one so much alarmed at death when he heard us beat to arms. It is reported that when we cried out "Victory, Victory for Narvaez is dead," he promptly said that he was very sick at the stomach and was no good for anything. This I have related because of his threats and bravado; some of the men of his company were wounded.

Our Captain Juan Velásquez de Leon captured Diego Velásquez, him with whom he had the strife when he dined with Narvaez, and he took him to his quarters, and ordered him to be cared for and treated with all honour.

† LXXXV

I have already said that Cortés had sent to advise the towns of Chinantla that two thousand of their Indians with their lances should come to aid us, and they came late in the afternoon of this very day, after Narvaez had been made prisoner, under the command of their own Caciques. They entered Cempoala in good array, two by two, so gallantly that it was an affair worthy of note. When the followers of Narvaez beheld them they were astonished, and it is reported that they said to one another, if those people had caught them in the rear or had come in with us, what could have stopped them? Cortés thanked the Indian Captains for coming, and he gave them beads from Castile and ordered them to return at once to their towns.

After Pánfilo de Narvaez had been defeated, and all his followers disarmed, Cortés directed Captain Francisco de Lugo to proceed to the port where the fleet of Narvaez, which numbered eighteen ships, was lying, and to order all the mates and masters of the ships to come up to Cempoala, and to remove the sails, rudders and compasses, so that they should not carry the news to Diego Velásquez in Cuba, and that if they refused to obey him, he was to make them prisoners.

The Masters and mates promptly came to kiss hands to Captain Cortés, and he made them take an oath that they would not leave his command, and would obey whatever orders he gave them.

Then he appointed as Admiral and Captain of the Sea one Pedro Caballero who had been master of one of the ships of Narvaez, a person whom Cortés thoroughly trusted.

Orders were given that Juan Velásquez de Leon should proceed to conquer and form a settlement in the region of Panuco, and for this Cortés allotted him one hundred and twenty sailors, one hundred were to be followers of Narvaez with twenty of our men mixed with them as they had more experience in war.

He also gave another command to Diego de Ordás of another hundred and twenty soldiers to go and settle in the region of Coatzacoalcos.

In order that those Captains and their soldiers could set out fully armed, Cortés had them equipped, and ordered all the prisoners who were captains under Narvaez to be set free, except Narvaez himself and Salvatierra who said that he was ill of the stomach. Now as to furnishing them with all their arms, as some of our soldiers had already taken some of their horses, swords and other things, Cortés ordered them all to be given back to them, and over our refusal to give them up there occurred certain angry discussions. Cortés still contended that we must give them up, and as he was Captain General we had to do what he ordered. I gave them a horse which I had hidden away saddled and bridled, and two swords and three poignards and a dagger. Many others of our soldiers also gave up horses and arms. Alonzo de Ávila was a captain and a person who dared to speak his mind to Cortés, and he and the Padre de la Merced together spoke privately to Cortés, and told him that all the golden jewels that the Indians had presented to him, and all the food, he had given to the Captains of Narvaez forgetting us as though he had never known us, and it was not well done, but a very great ingratitude after we had placed him in his present position.

To this Cortés replied that all that he possessed both his person and his property was ours, but for the present he could do no less than propitiate the followers of Narvaez with gifts, good words and promises, for they were many in number, and we were few, lest they should rise against him and us and kill him.

Let us return now to Narvaez and a black man whom he brought covered with smallpox, and a very black affair it was for New Spain, for it was owing to him that the whole country was stricken and filled with it, from which there was great mortality, for according to what the Indians said they had never had such a disease, and, as they did not understand it, they bathed very often, and on that account a great number of them died; so that dark as was the lot of Narvaez, still blacker was the death of so many persons who were not Christians.

Let me say how ill luck suddenly turns the wheel, and after great good fortune and pleasure follows sadness; it so happened that at this moment came the news that Mexico was in revolt, and that Pedro de Alvarado was besieged in his fortress and quarters, and that they had set fire to this same fortress in two places, and had killed seven of his soldiers and wounded many others, and he sent to demand assistance with great urgency and haste. This news was brought by two Tlaxcalans without any letter, but a letter soon arrived by two other Tlaxcalans sent by Pedro de Alvarado in which he told the same story. When we heard this bad news, God knows how greatly it depressed us.

By forced marches we began our journey to Mexico, Narvaez and Salvatierra remaining as prisoners in Villa Rica.

Just at this moment, as we were ready to start, there arrived four great chieftains sent to Cortés by the great Montezuma to complain to him of Pedro de Alvarado, and what they said, with tears streaming from their eyes, was that Pedro de Alvarado sallied out from his quarters with all the soldiers that Cortés had left with him, and, for no reason at all, fell on their chieftains and Caciques who were dancing and celebrating a feast in honour of their Idols Huichilobos and Tezcatepuca, Pedro de Alvarado having given them leave to do so. He killed and wounded many of them and in defending themselves they had killed six of his soldiers. Thus they made many complaints against Pedro de Alvarado, and Cortés, somewhat disgusted, replied to the messengers that he would go to Mexico and put it all to rights. So they went off with that reply to their great Montezuma, who it is said, resented it as a very bad one and was enraged at it.

Cortés also promptly despatched letters to Pedro de Alvarado in which he advised him to look out that Montezuma did not escape, and that we were coming by forced marches, and he informed him about the victory we had gained over Narvaez, which Montezuma knew about already, and I will leave off here and tell what happened later on.

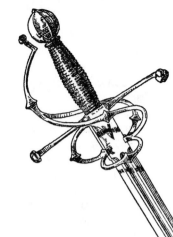

VII

The Flight from Mexico

† LXXXVI

When the news came which I have recorded that Pedro de
Alvarado was besieged and Mexico in revolt, the commands
that had been given to Juan Velásquez de Leon and Diego de
Ordás for the purpose of going to form settlements at Panuco
and Coatzacoalcos were rescinded and neither of them went,
for all joined with us. Cortés spoke to the followers of Narvaez,
for he felt that they would not accompany us willingly, and to
induce them to give that assistance, he begged them to leave
behind them their resentment over the affair of Narvaez, and
he promised to make them rich and give them office, and as
they came to seek a livelihood, and were in a country where
they could do service to God and His Majesty and enrich themselves, now was their chance; and so many speeches did he
make to them that one and all offered themselves to him to
go with us, and if they had known the power of Mexico, it
is certain that not one of them would have gone.

We were soon on our way by forced marches until we
reached Tlaxcala, where we learnt that up to the time that
Montezuma and his captains heard that we had defeated Narvaez they did not cease to attack, and had already killed seven
of Alvarado's soldiers and burnt his quarters, but as soon as
they heard of our victory they ceased attacking him; but they
added that Alvarado's company were much exhausted through
want of water and food, for Montezuma had failed to order
food to be given to them.

Some Tlaxcalan Indians brought this news at the very moment we arrived, and Cortés at once ordered a muster to be made of the men he had brought with him and found over thirteen hundred soldiers counting both our people and the followers of Narvaez, and over ninety-six horses and eighty crossbowmen, and as many musketeers, and with these it seemed to Cortés that he had force enough to enter Mexico in safety. In addition to this the Caciques of Tlaxcala gave us two thousand Indian warriors, and we at once set out by forced marches to Texcoco, and they paid no honour to us there and not a single chieftain made his appearance, for all were hidden away and ill disposed.

We arrived at Mexico on the day of Señor San Juan de Junio[1] 1520, and no Caciques or Captains or Indians whom we knew appeared in the streets, and all the houses were empty when we reached the quarters where we used to lodge. The great Montezuma came out to the courtyard to embrace and speak to Cortés and bid him welcome, and congratulate him on his victory over Narvaez, and as Cortés was arriving victorious he refused to listen to him, and Montezuma returned to his quarters very sad and depressed.

When each one of us was lodged in the quarters he had occupied before we set out from Mexico, and the following of Narvaez were lodged in other quarters, we then saw and talked with Pedro de Alvarado and the soldiers who had stayed with him; they gave us an account of the attacks made on them, and the straits in which the Mexicans had placed them, and we told them the story of our victory over Narvaez.

Cortés tried to find out what was the cause of the revolt in Mexico, for we clearly understood that it made Montezuma unhappy if we should think it had been his desire or had been done by his advice. Many of the soldiers who had remained with Pedro de Alvarado through that critical time said, that if Montezuma had had a hand in it, all of them would have been killed, but Montezuma calmed his people until they ceased to attack.

What Pedro de Alvarado told Cortés about the matter was that it was done by the Mexicans in order to liberate Montezuma, and because their Huichilobos ordered it, on account of our having placed the image of our Lady the Virgin Santa

[1] Midsummer day.

Maria and the Cross in his house. Moreover he said that many
Indians had come to remove the holy image from the altar
where we placed it, and were not able to move it, and that
the Indians looked upon it as a great miracle and had said so
to Montezuma, who had told them to leave it in the place
and altar in which it stood, and not to attempt to do otherwise,
and so it was left.

Pedro de Alvarado further stated that because Narvaez' message to Montezuma, that he was coming to release him from
prison and to capture us, had not turned out to be true, and
because Cortés had told Montezuma that as soon as we possessed ships we should go and embark and leave the country
entirely, and we were not going, and it was nothing but empty
words, and because it was evident that many more Teules were
arriving, it seemed well to the Mexicans to kill him (Pedro de
Alvarado) and his soldiers and release the great Montezuma
before the followers of Narvaez or our own men re-entered
Mexico, and afterwards not to leave one of us or of the followers of Narvaez alive.

Cortés turned and asked Pedro de Alvarado what was the
reason that he attacked them when they were dancing and
holding a festival. He replied that he knew for certain that as
soon as they had finished the festivals and dances and the
sacrifices that they were offering to their Huichilobos and
Tezcatepuca, they would at once come and make an attack
according to the agreement they had made between themselves,
and this and all the rest he learned from a priest and from
two chieftains and from other Mexicans.

Cortés said to him: "But they have told me that they asked
your permission to hold festivals and dances"; he replied that it
was true, and it was in order to take them unprepared and to
scare them, so that they should not come to attack him, that
he hastened to fall on them.

When Cortés heard this he said to him, very angrily, that
it was very ill done and a great mistake and that he wished
to God that Montezuma had escaped and not heard such an
account from his Idols. So he left him and spoke no more to
him about it.

Pedro de Alvarado himself also said that when he advanced
against them in that conflict, he ordered a cannon, that was
loaded with one ball and many small shot, to be fired, for as

many squadrons of Indians were approaching to set fire to his
quarters he sallied forth to fight them, and he ordered the
cannon to be fired, but it did not go off, and after he had
made a charge against the squadrons which were attacking
him, and many Indians were bearing down on him, while he
was retreating to the fortress and quarters, then, without fire
being applied to the cannon, the ball and the small shot was
discharged and killed many Indians; and had it not so happened the enemy would have killed them all, and they did on
that occasion carry off two of his soldiers alive.

Another thing Pedro de Alvarado stated, and this was the
only thing that was also reported by the other soldiers, for the
rest of the stories were told by Alvarado alone, and it is that
they had no water to drink, and they dug in the courtyard,
and made a well and took out fresh water, all around being
salt; in all it amounted to many gifts that our Lord God
bestowed on us.

† LXXXVII

When Cortés saw that they had given us no sort of a reception
in Texcoco, and had not even given us food, except bad food
and with bad grace, and that we found no chieftains with
whom to parley, and he saw that all were scared away and
ill disposed, and observed the same condition on coming to
Mexico, how no market was held and the whole place was
in revolt, and he heard from Pedro de Alvarado about the
disorderly manner in which he made his attack, and as it
appears that on the march Cortés had spoken to the Captains
of Narvaez glorifying himself on the great veneration and command that he enjoyed, and how on the road the Indians would
turn out to receive him and celebrate the occasion and give him
gold, and that in Mexico he ruled as absolutely over the great
Montezuma as over all his Captains, and that they would give
him presents of gold, as they were used to do, and when
everything turned out contrary to his expectations and they did
not even give us food to eat, he was greatly irritated, and
haughty towards the numerous Spaniards that he was bringing
with him, and very sad and fretful. At this moment the great
Montezuma sent two of his chieftains to beg our Cortés to go

and see him, for he wished to speak to him, and the answer that Cortés gave them was "Go to, for a dog, who will not even keep open a market, and does not order food to be given us." Then when our Captains, that is Juan Velásquez de Leon, Cristóbal de Olid, Alonzo de Ávila, and Francisco de Lugo, heard Cortés say this, they exclaimed: "Señor, moderate your anger and reflect how much good and honour this king of these countries has done us, who is so good that had it not been for him we should all of us already be dead, and they would have eaten us, and remember that he has even given you his daughters."

When Cortés heard this he was more angry than ever at the words they said to him, as they seemed to be a reproof, and he said: "Why should I be civil to a dog who was treating secretly with Narvaez, and now you can see that he does not even give us food to eat." Our Captains replied: "That is to our minds what he ought to do and it is good advice." As Cortés had so many Spaniards there with him in Mexico, both of our own party and of the followers of Narvaez he did not trouble himself a whit about anything, and he spoke angrily and rudely again, addressing the chieftains and telling them to say to their Lord Montezuma that he should at once order the markets and sales to be held, if not he would see what would happen.

The chieftains well understood the offensive remarks that Cortés made about their Lord and even the reproof that our Captains gave to Cortés about it, for they knew them well as having been those who used to be on guard over their Lord, and they knew that they were good friends of their Montezuma, and according to the way they understood the matter they repeated it to Montezuma. Either from anger at this treatment, or because it had already been agreed on that we were to be attacked, it was not a quarter of an hour later that a soldier arrived in great haste and badly wounded. He came from a town close by Mexico named Tacuba and was escorting some Indian women who belonged to Cortés, one of them a daughter of Montezuma, for it appears that Cortés had left them there in charge of the Lord of Tacuba, for they were relations of this same Lord, when we went off on the expedition against Narvaez. This soldier said that all the city and road by which he had come was full of warriors fully armed, and

that they had taken from him the Indian women he was bringing and had given him two wounds and that if he had not
let the women go, the Mexicans would have captured him, and
would have put him in a canoe and carried him off to be
sacrificed, and that they had broken down a bridge.

Let me go on and say that Cortés promptly ordered Diego
de Ordás to go with four hundred soldiers, and among them
most of the crossbowmen and musketeers and some horsemen,
and examine into what the soldier had reported, and that if
he found that he could calm the Indians without fighting and
disturbance that he should do so.

Diego de Ordás set out in the way that he was ordered
with his four hundred soldiers, but he had hardly reached the
middle of the street along which he was to march, when so
many squadrons of Mexican warriors fell on him and so many
more were on the roofs of the houses, and they made such
fierce attacks that on the first assault they killed eight soldiers
and wounded all the rest, and Diego de Ordás himself was
wounded in three places, and in this manner he could not
advance one step further but had to return little by little to
his quarters. During the retreat they killed another good soldier
named Lyscano who, with a broadsword, had done the work
of a very valiant man.

At that moment, while many squadrons came out against
Ordás, many more approached our quarters and shot off so
many javelins and stones from slings, and arrows, that they
wounded on that occasion alone over forty-six of our men,
and twelve of them died of their wounds; and such a number
of warriors fell upon us that Diego de Ordás, who was coming
in retreat, could not reach our quarters on account of the fierce
assaults they made on him, some from the rear and others in
front and others from the roofs.

Little availed our cannon, or our muskets, crossbows and
lances, or the thrusts we gave them, or our good fighting, for
although we killed and wounded many of them, yet they
managed to reach us by pushing forward over the points of
our swords and lances, and closing up their squadrons never
desisted from their brave attack, nor could we push them away
from us.

At last, what with cannon and muskets and the damage we
did them with our sword-thrusts, Ordás found an opportunity

to enter our quarters, and not until then, much as he desired it, could he force a passage with his badly wounded soldiers, fourteen fewer in number. Still many of the squadrons never ceased from attacking us, and telling us that we were like women, and they called us rogues and other abusive names. But the damage they had done us up to this time was as noth- ing to what they did afterwards, for such was their daring that, some attacking on one side and some on the other, they penetrated into our quarters and set fire to them, and we could not endure the smoke and the fire until it was remedied by flinging much earth over it, and cutting off other rooms whence the fire came. In truth, they believed that they would burn us alive in there. These conflicts lasted all day long, and even during the night so many squadrons of them fell on us, and hurled javelins, stones and arrows in masses, and random stones so that what with those that fell during the day and those that then fell in all the courts and on the ground, it looked like chaff on a threshing floor.

We passed the night in dressing wounds and in mending the breaches in the walls that the enemy had made, and in getting ready for the next day. Then, as soon as it was dawn, our Captain decided that all of us and Narvaez' men should sally out to fight with them and that we should take the cannon and muskets and crossbows and endeavour to defeat them, or at least to make them feel our strength and valour better than the day before. I may state that when we came to this decision, the Mexicans were arranging the very same thing. We fought very well, but they were so strong, and had so many squadrons which relieved each other from time to time, that even if ten thousand Trojan Hectors and as many more Roldans had been there, they would not have been able to break through them.

We noted their tenacity in fighting, but I declare that I do not know how to describe it, for neither cannon nor muskets nor crossbows availed, nor hand-to-hand fighting, nor killing thirty or forty of them every time we charged, for they still fought on in as close ranks and with more energy than in the begin- ning. Sometimes when we were gaining a little ground or a part of the street, they pretended to retreat, but it was merely to induce us to follow them and cut us off from our fortress and quarters, so as to fall on us in greater safety to themselves,

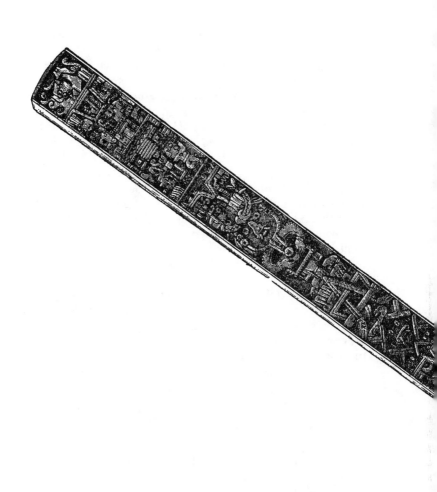

believing that we could not return to our quarters alive, for they did us much damage when we were retreating.

Then, as to going out to burn their houses, I have already said that between one house and another they have wooden drawbridges, and these they raised so that we could only pass through deep water. Then we could not endure the rocks and stones hurled from the roofs, in such a way that they damaged and wounded many of our men. I do not know why I write thus, so lukewarmly, for some three or four soldiers who were there with us and who had served in Italy, swore to God many times that they had never seen such fierce fights, not even when they had taken part in such between Christians and against the artillery of the King of France, or of the Great Turk, nor had they seen men like those Indians with such courage in closing up their ranks.

With great difficulty we withdrew to our quarters, many squadrons of warriors still pressing on us with loud yells and whistles, and trumpets and drums, calling us villains and cowards who did not dare to meet them all day in battle, but turned in flight.

On that day they killed ten or twelve more soldiers and we all returned badly wounded. What took place during the night was the arrangement that in two days' time all the soldiers in camp, as many as were able, should sally out with four engines like towers built of strong timber, in such a manner that five and twenty men could find shelter under each of them, and they were provided with apertures and loopholes through which to shoot, and musketeers and crossbowmen accompanied them, and close by them were to march the other soldiers, musketeers and crossbowmen and the guns, and all the rest, and the horsemen were to make charges.

When this plan was settled, as we spent all that day in carrying out the work and in strengthening many breaches that they had made in the walls, we did not go out to fight.

† LXXXVIII

I do not know how to tell of the great squadrons of warriors who came to attack us that day in our quarters, not only in ten or twelve places, but in more than twenty, for we were

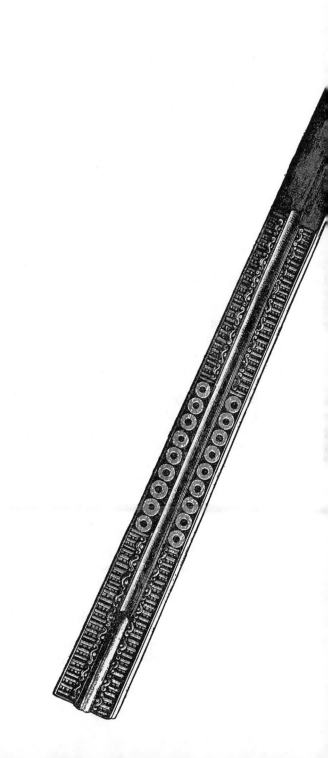

distributed over them all and in many other places, and while
we built up and fortified ourselves, as I have related, many
other squadrons openly endeavoured to penetrate into our quarters, and neither with guns, crossbows nor muskets, nor with
many charges and sword-thrusts could we force them back, for
they said that not one of us should remain alive that day and
they would sacrifice our hearts and blood to their gods, and
would have enough to glut their appetites and hold feasts on
our arms and legs, and would throw our bodies to the tigers,
lions, vipers and snakes, which they kept caged, so that they
might gorge on them, and for that reason they had ordered
them not to be given food for the past two days. As for the
gold we possessed, we would get little satisfaction from it or
from all the cloths; and as for the Tlaxcalans who were with
us, they said that they would place them in cages to fatten,
and little by little they would offer their bodies in sacrifice;
and, very tenderly, they said that we should give up to them
their great Lord Montezuma, and they said other things. Night
by night, in like manner, there were always many yells and
whistles and showers of darts, stones and arrows.

As soon as dawn came, after commending ourselves to God,
we sallied out from our quarters with our towers, with the
cannon, muskets, and crossbows in advance, and the horsemen
making charges, but, as I have stated, although we killed
many of them it availed nothing towards making them turn
their backs, indeed if they had fought bravely on the two previous days, they proved themselves far more vigorous and displayed much greater forces and squadrons on this day. Nevertheless, we determined, although it should cost the lives of all
of us, to push on with our towers and engines as far as the
great Cue of Huichilobos.

I will not relate at length the fights we had with them in
a fortified house, nor will I tell how they wounded the horses,
nor were the horses of any use to us, because although the
horsemen charged the squadrons to break through them, so
many arrows, darts and stones were hurled at them, that they,
well protected by armour though they were, could not prevail
against the enemy, and if they pursued and overtook them,
the Mexicans promptly dropped for safety into the canals and
lagoons where they had raised other walls against the horsemen, and many other Indians were stationed with very long

lances to finish killing them. Thus it benefited us nothing to turn aside to burn or demolish a house, it was quite useless, for, as I have said, they all stood in the water, and between house and house there was a movable bridge, and to cross by swimming was very dangerous, for on the roofs they had such store of rocks and stones and such defences, that it was certain destruction to risk it. In addition to this, where we did set fire to some houses, a single house took a whole day to burn, and the houses did not catch fire one from the other; thus it was useless toil to risk our persons in the attempt, so we went towards the great Cue of their Idols. Then, all of a sudden, more than four thousand Mexicans ascended it,[1] not counting other Companies that were posted on it with long lances and stones and darts, and placed themselves on the defensive, and resisted our ascent for a good while, and neither the towers nor the cannon or crossbows, nor the muskets were of any avail, nor the horsemen, for, although they wished to charge, the whole of the courtyard was paved with very large flagstones, so that the horses lost their foothold, and the stones were so slippery that the horses fell. While from the steps of the lofty Cue they forbade our advance, we had so many enemies both on one side and the other that although our cannon shots carried off ten or fifteen of them and we slew many others by sword-thrusts and charges, so many men attacked us that we were not able to ascend the lofty Cue. However with great unanimity we persisted in the attack, and without taking the towers (for they were already destroyed) we made our way to the summit.

Here Cortés showed himself very much of a man, as he always was. Oh! what a fight and what a fierce battle it was that took place; it was a memorable thing to see us all streaming with blood and covered with wounds and others slain. It pleased our Lord that we reached the place where we used to keep the image of Our Lady, and we did not find it, and it appears, as we came to know, that the great Montezuma paid devotion to Her, and ordered the image to be preserved in safety.

We set fire to their Idols and a good part of the chamber with the Idols Huichilobos and Tezcatepuc was burned. On that occasion the Tlaxcalans helped us very greatly. After this

[1] This was the Great Teocalli of Tenochtitlan, quite close to the Spanish Quarters. Cortés says that five hundred Mexicans ascended the Teocalli itself to defend it.

was accomplished, while some of us were fighting and others kindling the fire, as I have related, oh! to see the priests who were stationed on this great Cue, and the three or four thousand Indians, all men of importance. While we descended, oh! how they made us tumble down six or even ten steps at a time! And so much more there is to tell of the other squadrons posted on the battlements and recesses of the great Cue discharging so many darts and arrows that we could face neither one group of squadrons nor the other. We resolved to return, with much toil and risk to ourselves, to our quarters, our castles being destroyed, all of us wounded and sixteen slain, with the Indians constantly pressing on us and other squadrons on our flanks.

However clearly I may tell all this, I can never fully explain it to any one who did not see us. So far, I have not spoken of what the Mexican squadrons did who kept on attacking our quarters while we were marching outside, and the great obstinacy and tenacity they displayed in forcing their way in.

In this battle, we captured two of the chief priests, whom Cortés ordered us to convey with great care.

Many times I have seen among the Mexicans and Tlaxcalans, paintings of this battle, and the ascent that we made of the great Cue, as they look upon it as a very heroic deed. And although in the pictures that they have made of it, they depict all of us as badly wounded and streaming with blood and many of us dead they considered it a great feat, this setting fire to the Cue, when so many warriors were guarding it both on the battlements and recesses, and many more Indians were below on the ground and the Courts were full of them and there were many more on the sides; and with our towers destroyed, how was it possible to scale it?

Let us stop talking about it and I will relate how with great labour we returned to our quarters and if many men were then following us, as many more were in our quarters, for they had already demolished some walls so as to gain an entry, but on our arrival they desisted. Nevertheless, during all the rest of the day they never ceased to discharge darts, stones and arrows, and during the night yells and stones and darts.

That night was passed in dressing wounds and in burying the dead, in preparations for going out to fight the following day, in strengthening and adding parapets to the walls they had pulled down, and to other breaches they had made, and in

consulting how and in what way we could fight without suffering such great damage and death, and throughout the discussion we found no remedy at all.

Then I also wish to speak of the maledictions that the followers of Narvaez hurled at Cortés, and the words that they
used, cursing him and the country and even Diego Velásquez
who had sent them there when they were peacefully settled in
their homes in the Island of Cuba, and they were crazy and
out of their minds.

Let us go back to our story. It was decided to sue for peace
so that we could leave Mexico, and as soon as it was dawn
many more squadrons of Mexicans arrived and very effectually
surrounded our quarters on all sides, and if they had discharged
many stones and arrows before, they came much thicker and
with louder howls and whistles on this day, and other squadrons endeavoured to force an entrance in other parts, and cannon and muskets availed nothing, although we did them damage enough.

When Cortés saw all this, he decided that the great Montezuma should speak to them from the roof and tell them that
the war must cease, and that we wished to leave his city. When
they went to give this message from Cortés to the great Montezuma, it is reported that he said with great grief: "What more
does Malinche want from me? I neither wish to live nor to
listen to him, to such a pass has my fate brought me because
of him." And he did not wish to come, and it is even reported
that he said he neither wished to see nor hear him, nor listen
to his false words, promises or lies. Then the Padre de la
Merced and Cristóbal de Olid went and spoke to him with
much reverence and in very affectionate terms, and Montezuma said: "I believe that I shall not obtain any result towards
ending this war, for they have already raised up another Lord
and have made up their minds not to let you leave this place
alive, therefore I believe that all of you will have to die."

Montezuma was placed by a battlement of the roof with
many of us soldiers guarding him, and he began to speak to
his people, with very affectionate expressions telling them to
desist from the war, and that we would leave Mexico. Many of
the Mexican Chieftains and Captains knew him well and at
once ordered their people to be silent and not to discharge
darts, stones or arrows, and four of them reached a spot where

Montezuma could speak to them, and they to him, and with tears they said to him: "Oh! Señor, and our great Lord, how all your misfortune and injury and that of your children and relations afflicts us, we make known to you that we have already raised one of your kinsmen to be our Lord," and there he stated his name, that he was called Cuitlahuac, the Lord of Ixtapalapa, and moreover they said that the war must be carried through, and that they had vowed to their Idols not to relax it until we were all dead, and that they prayed every day to their Huichilobos and Texcatepuca to guard him free and safe from our power, and that should it end as they desired, they would not fail to hold him in higher regard as their Lord than they did before, and they begged him to forgive them. They had hardly finished this speech when suddenly such a shower of stones and darts were discharged that (our men who were shielding him having neglected for a moment their duty, because they saw how the attack ceased while he spoke to them) he was hit by three stones, one on the head, another on the arm and another on the leg, and although they begged him to have the wounds dressed and to take food, and spoke kind words to him about it, he would not. Indeed, when we least expected it, they came to say that he was dead. Cortés wept for him, and all of us Captains and soldiers, and there was no man among us who knew him and was intimate with him, who did not bemoan him as though he were our father, and it is not to be wondered at, considering how good he was. It was stated that he had reigned for seventeen years and that he was the best king there had ever been in Mexico, and that he had conquered in person, in three wars which he had carried on in the countries he had subjugated.

I have already told about the sorrow that we all of us felt about it when we saw that Montezuma was dead. We even thought badly of the Fraile de la Merced because he had not persuaded him to become a Christian, and he gave as an excuse that he did not think that he would die of those wounds, but that he ought to have ordered them to give him something to stupefy him. At the end of much discussion Cortés ordered a priest and a chief from among the prisoners to go and tell the Cacique whom they had chosen for Lord, who was named Cuitlahuac, and his Captains, that the great Montezuma was dead, and they had seen him die, and about the manner of his death and the wounds his own people had inflicted on him, and they should say how grieved we all were about it, and that they should bury him as the great king that he was, and they should raise the cousin of Montezuma who was with us, to be king, for the inheritance was his, or one of Montezuma's other sons, and that he whom they had raised to be king was not so by right, and they should negotiate a peace so that we could leave Mexico; and if they did not do so, now that Montezuma was dead, whom we held in respect and for that reason had not destroyed their city, we should sally out to make war on them and burn all their houses and do them much damage. So as to convince them that Montezuma was dead, he ordered six Mexicans who were high chieftains, and the priests whom we held as prisoners, to carry him out on their shoulders, and to hand the body over to the Mexican Captains, and to tell them what Montezuma had commanded at the time of his death, for those who carried him out on their backs were present at his death; and they told Cuitlahuac the whole truth, how his own people killed him with blows from three stones.

When they beheld him thus dead, we saw that they were in floods of tears and we clearly heard the shrieks and cries of distress that they gave for him, but for all this, the fierce assault they made on us never ceased, and then they came on us again with greater force and fury, and said to us: "Now for certain you will pay for the death of our King and Lord, and the dishonour to our Idols; and as for the peace you sent to beg for, come out here and we will settle how and in what way it is to be made," and they said that they had already chosen a good king, and he would not be so faint-hearted as to be deceived with false speeches like their good Montezuma, and as for the burial, we need not trouble about that, but about our own lives, for in two days there would not be one of us left—so much for the messages we had sent them. With these words they fell on us with loud yells and whistles and showers of stones, darts and arrows, while other squadrons were still attempting to set fire to our quarters in many places.

When Cortés and all of us observed this, we agreed that next day we would all of us sally out from our camp and attack in another direction, where there were many houses on dry land, and we would do all the damage we were able and go towards

the causeway, and that all the horsemen should break through
the squadrons and spear them with their lances or drive them
into the water, even though the enemy should kill the horses.
This was decided on in order to find out if by chance, with
the damage and slaughter that we should inflict on them, they
would abandon their attack and arrange some sort of peace,
so that we could go free without more deaths and damage. Although the next day we all bore ourselves very manfully and
killed many of the enemy and burned a matter of twenty
houses and almost reached dry land, it was all of no use, because of the great damage and deaths and wounds they inflicted
on us, and we could not hold a single bridge, for they were all
of them half broken down. Many Mexicans charged down on
us, and they had set up walls and barricades in places which
they thought could be reached by the horses, so that if we had
met with many difficulties up to this time, we found much
greater ones ahead of us.

† LXXXIX

Now we saw our forces diminishing every day and those of the
Mexicans increasing, and many of our men were dead and all
the rest wounded, and although we fought like brave men we
could not drive back nor even get free from the many squadrons which attacked us both by day and night, and the powder
was giving out, and the same was happening with the food and
water, and the great Montezuma being dead, they were unwilling to grant the peace and truce which we had sent to
demand of them. In fact we were staring death in the face, and
the bridges had been raised. It was therefore decided by Cortés
and all of us captains and soldiers that we should set out during
the night. That very afternoon we sent to tell them, through
one of their priests whom we held prisoner and who was a
man of great importance among them, that they should let us
go in peace within eight days and we would give up to them
all the gold; and this was done to put them off their guard
so that we might get out that night.

The order was given to make a bridge of very strong beams
and planks, so that we could carry it with us and place it
where the bridges were broken. Four hundred Tlaxcalan In-

dians and one hundred and fifty soldiers were told off to carry this bridge and place it in position and guard the passage until the army and all the baggage had crossed. Two hundred Tlaxcalan Indians and fifty soldiers were told off to carry the cannon, and Gonzalo de Sandoval, Diego de Ordás, Francisco de Sauzedo, Francisco de Lugo and a company of one hundred young and active soldiers were selected to go in the van to do the fighting. It was agreed that Cortés himself, Alonzo de Ávila, Cristóbal de Olid, and other Captains should go in the middle and support the party that most needed help in fighting. Pedro de Alvarado and Juan Velásquez de Leon were with the rearguard, and placed in the middle between them and the preceding section were two captains and the soldiers of Narvaez, and three hundred Tlaxcalans and thirty soldiers were told off to take charge of the prisoners and of Doña Marina and Doña Luisa; by the time this arrangement was made, it was already night.

In order to bring out the gold and divide it up and carry it, Cortés ordered his steward named Cristóbal de Guzman and other soldiers who were his servants to bring out all the gold and jewels and silver, and he gave them many Tlaxcalan Indians for the purpose, and they placed it in the Hall. Then Cortés told the King's officers named Alonzo Dávila and Gonzalo Mejía to take charge of the gold belonging to His Majesty, and he gave them seven wounded and lame horses and one mare, and many friendly Tlaxcalans, more than eighty in number, and they loaded them with parcels of it, as much as they could carry, for it was put up into very broad ingots, and much gold still remained in the Hall piled up in heaps. Then Cortés called his secretary and the others who were King's Notaries, and said: "Bear witness for me that I can do no more with this gold. We have here in this apartment and Hall over seven hundred thousand pesos in gold, and, as you have seen, it cannot be weighed nor placed in safety. I now give it up to any of the soldiers who care to take it, otherwise it will be lost among these dogs of Mexicans."

When they heard this many of the soldiers of Narvaez and some of our people loaded themselves with it. I declare that I had no other desire but the desire to save my life, but I did not fail to carry off from some small boxes that were there, four chalchihuites, which are stones very highly prized among the

Indians, and I quickly placed them in my bosom under my
armour, and, later on, the price of them served me well in
healing my wounds and getting me food.

After we had learnt the plans that Cortés had made about
the way in which we were to escape that night and get to
the bridges, as it was somewhat dark and cloudy and rainy, we
began before midnight to bring along the baggage, and the
horses and mare began their march, and the Tlaxcalans who
were laden with the gold. Then the bridge was quickly put in
place, and Cortés and the others whom he took with him in the
first detachment and many of the horsemen, crossed over it.
While this was happening, the voices, trumpets, cries and
whistles of the Mexicans began to sound and they called out in
their language to the people of Tlaltelolco, "Come out at once
with your canoes for the Teules are leaving; cut them off so that
not one of them may be left alive." When I least expected it, we
saw so many squadrons of warriors bearing down on us, and the
lake so crowded with canoes that we could not defend ourselves.
Many of our soldiers had already crossed the bridge, and while
we were in this position, a great multitude of Mexicans charged
down on us with the intention of removing the bridge and
wounding and killing our men who were unable to assist each
other; and as fortune is perverse at such times, one mischance
followed another, and as it was raining, two of the horses
slipped and fell into the lake. When I and others of Cortés'
Company saw that, we got safely to the other side of the bridge,
and so many warriors charged on us, that despite all our good
fighting, no further use could be made of the bridge, so that the
passage or water opening was soon filled up with dead horses,
Indian men and women, servants, baggage and boxes.

Fearing that they would not fail to kill us, we thrust ourselves ahead along the causeway, and we met many squadrons
armed with long lances waiting for us, and they used abusive
words to us, and among them they cried: "Oh! villains, are you
still alive?"—and with the cuts and thrusts we gave them, we
got through, although they then wounded six of those who
were going along with me. Then if there was some sort of
plan such as we had agreed upon it was an accursed one; for
Cortés and the captains and soldiers who passed first on horseback, so as to save themselves and reach dry land and make
sure of their lives, spurred on along the causeway, and they did

not fail to attain their object, and the horses with the gold and the Tlaxcalans also got out in safety. I assert that if we had waited (the horsemen and the soldiers one for the other) at the bridges, we should all have been put an end to, and not one of us would have been left alive; the reason was this, that as we went along the causeway, charging the Mexican squadrons, on one side of us was water and on the other azoteas,[1] and the lake was full of canoes so that we could do nothing. Moreover the muskets and crossbows were all left behind at the bridge, and as it was night time, what could we do beyond what we accomplished? which was to charge and give some sword-thrusts to those who tried to lay hands on us, and to march and get on ahead so as to get off the causeway.

Had it been in the day-time, it would have been far worse, and we who escaped did so only by the Grace of God. To one who saw the hosts of warriors who fell on us that night and the canoes full of them coming along to carry off our soldiers, it was terrifying. So we went ahead along the causeway in order to get to the town of Tacuba where Cortés was already stationed with all the Captains. Gonzalo de Sandoval, Cristóbal de Olid and others of those horsemen who had gone on ahead were crying out: "Señor Captain, let us halt, for they say that we are fleeing and leaving them to die at the bridges; let us go back and help them, if any of them survive"; but not one of them came out or escaped. Cortés' reply was that it was a miracle that any of us escaped. However, he promptly went back with the horsemen and the soldiers who were unwounded, but they did not march far, for Pedro de Alvarado soon met them, badly wounded, holding a spear in his hand, and on foot, for the enemy had already killed his sorrel mare, and he brought with him four soldiers as badly wounded as he was himself, and eight Tlaxcalans, all of them with blood flowing from many wounds.

While Cortés was on the causeway with the rest of the Captains, we repaired to the courtyard in Tacuba. Many squadrons had already arrived from Mexico, shouting out orders to Tacuba and to the other town named Atzcapotzalco, and they began to hurl darts, stones and arrows and attack with their long lances. We made some charges and both attacked them and defended ourselves.

[1] The flat roofs of the houses.

Let us go back to Pedro de Alvarado. When Cortés and the other Captains met him in that way, and saw that no more soldiers were coming along the causeway, tears sprang to his eyes. Pedro de Alvarado said that Juan Velásquez de Leon lay dead with many other gentlemen both of our own company and that of Narvaez, and that more than eighty of them were at the bridge; that he and the four soldiers whom he brought with him, after their horses had been killed, crossed the bridge in great peril, over the dead bodies, horses and boxes with which that passage at the bridge was choked. Moreover, he said that all the bridges and causeways were crowded with warriors. At the bridge of sorrow, which they afterwards called "Alvarado's leap," I assert that at the time not a single soldier stopped to see if he leaped much or little, for we could hardly save our own lives, as we were in great danger of death on account of the multitude of Mexicans charging down on us. I never heard of this leap of Alvarado until after Mexico was captured, and it was in some satirical verses made by a certain Gonzalo de Ocampo, which, as they were somewhat nasty, I will not fully quote here, except that he says: "Thou shouldst remember the leap that thou tookest from the bridge"; but I will not dwell on this subject.

Let us go on and I will relate how, when we were waiting in Tacuba, many Mexican warriors came together from all those towns and they killed three of our soldiers, so we agreed to get out of that town as quickly as we could, and five Tlaxcalan Indians, who found out a way towards Tlaxcala without following the main road, guided us with great precaution until we reached some small houses placed on a hill, and near to them a Cue or Oratory built like a fort, where we halted.

As we marched along we were followed by the Mexicans who hurled arrows and darts at us and stones from their slings, and the way in which they surrounded us and continually attacked us, was terrifying, as I have already said many times and am tired of repeating it.

We defended ourselves in that Cue and fortress, where we lodged and attended to the wounded and made many fires, but as for anything to eat, there was no thought of it. At that Cue or Oratory, after the great city of Mexico was captured, we built a church, which is called "Nuestra Señora de los

Remedios," and is very much visited, and many of the inhabitants and ladies from Mexico now go there on pilgrimages and to hold *novenas*.[1]

It was pitiable to see our wounds being dressed and bound up with cotton cloths, and as they were chilled and swollen they were very painful. However what was more to be wept over was the loss of the gentlemen and brave soldiers who were missing, namely, Juan Velásquez de Leon, Francisco de Sauzedo, Francisco de Morla, Lares the good horseman and many others of us followers of Cortés. I name these few only because it would be a long business to write the names of the great number of our companions who were missing. Of the followers of Narvaez, the greater number were left at the bridges weighed down with gold.

Let us go on to say how there were left dead at the bridges the sons and daughters of Montezuma as well as the prisoners we were bringing with us, also Cacamatzin the Lord of Texcoco and other kings of provinces. Let us stop relating all these hardships and say how we were thinking of what we had in front of us, for we were all wounded, and only twenty-three horses escaped; then of the cannon and artillery and powder, we saved nothing; the crossbows were few in number and we promptly mended their cords and made arrows but the worst of all was that we did not know what we should find the disposition of our friends the Tlaxcalans would be towards us. In addition to this, always surrounded by Mexicans who fell on us with yells, we determined to get out of that place at midnight with the Tlaxcalans in front as guides, taking every precaution. We marched with the wounded in the middle and the lame supported with staffs, and some, who were very bad and could not walk, on the croups of the horses that were lame and were not fit for fighting. Those horsemen who were not wounded went in front or were divided some on one side, some on the other, and marching in this manner all of us who were most free from wounds kept our faces towards the enemy. The wounded Tlaxcalans went in the body of our squadron and the rest of them who were sufficiently sound faced the enemy in company with us. The Mexicans were always harassing us with loud cries, yells and whistles, shouting out, "You are going where not one of you will be left alive," and we did not under-

---

[1] *Novenas*: religious exercises extending over nine days.

stand why they said so, but it will be seen later on. But I have
forgotten to write down how happy we were to see Doña
Marina still alive, and Doña Luisa the daughter of Xicotenga,
whose escape at the bridges was due to some Tlaxcalans, and
also a woman named Maria de Estrada, who was the only
Spanish woman in Mexico. Those who escaped and got away
first from the bridges were some sons of Xicotenga, the brothers
of Doña Luisa. Most of our servants who had been given to us
in Tlaxcala and in the city of Mexico itself were left behind
dead.[1]

[1] The distances traversed on the Noche Triste are approximately as follows:

		Yards.	Miles.
From the Spanish quarters to Tecpantzingo		1000	
"	Tecpantzingo to Tolteacalli	740	say 1¼
"	Tolteacalli to Toltecaacalopan	500	
"	Toltecaacalopan to the Ahuehuete Tree at Popotla on the margin of the lake		2¼
"	The Ahuehuete Tree to the Plaza of Tacuba		1
"	Tacuba to Los Remedios		4½
			9

† xc

That day we reached some farms and huts belonging to a large
town named Cuautitlan. Thence we went through some farms
and hamlets with the Mexicans always in pursuit of us, and
as many of them had got together, they endeavoured to kill us
and began to surround us, and hurled many stones with their
slings and javelins and arrows, and with their broadswords they
killed two of our soldiers in a bad pass, and they also killed a
horse and wounded many of our men, and we also with cut
and thrust killed some of them, and the horsemen did the same.
We slept in those houses and we ate the horse they had killed,
and the next day very early in the morning we began our
march, with the same and even greater precautions than we
observed before, half of the horsemen always going ahead. On
a plain a little more than a league further on (when we
began to think that we could march in safety) our scouts, who
were on the look out, returned to say that the fields were full
of Mexican warriors waiting for us. When we heard this we
were indeed alarmed but not so as to be faint-hearted or to fail

to meet them and fight to the death. There we halted for a short time and orders were given how the horsemen were to charge and return at a hand gallop, and were not to stop to spear the enemy but to keep their lances aimed at their faces until they broke up their squadrons; and that all the soldiers, in the thrusts they gave, should pass their swords through the bodies of their opponents, and that we should act in such a way as to avenge thoroughly the deaths and wounds of our companions, so that if God willed it we should escape with our lives.

After commending ourselves to God and the Holy Mary, full of courage, and calling on the name of Señor Santiago, as soon as we saw that the enemy began to surround us, and that the horsemen, keeping in parties of five, broke through their ranks, we all of us charged at the same time.

Oh! what a sight it was to see this fearful and destructive battle, how we moved all mixed up with them foot to foot, and the cuts and thrusts we gave them, and with what fury the dogs fought, and what wounds and deaths they inflicted on us with their lances and macanas. Then, as the ground was level, to see how the horsemen speared them as they chose, charging and returning, and although both they and their horses were wounded, they never stopped fighting like very brave men. As for all of us who had no horses, it seemed as if we all put on double strength, for although we were wounded and again received other wounds, we did not trouble to bind them up so as not to halt to do so, for there was not time, but with great spirit we closed with the enemy so as to give them sword thrusts. I wish to tell about Cortés and Cristóbal de Olid, Gonzalo de Sandoval, Gonzalo Domínguez and a Juan de Salamanca who although badly wounded rode on one side and the other, breaking through the squadrons; and about the words that Cortés said to those who were in the thick of the enemy, that the cuts and thrusts that we gave should be aimed at distinguished chieftains, for they all of them bore great golden plumes and rich arms and devices. Then to see how the valiant and spirited Sandoval encouraged us and cried: "Now, gentlemen, this is the day when we are bound to be victorious; have trust in God and we shall come out of this alive for some good purpose." They killed and wounded a great number of our soldiers, but it pleased God

that Cortés and the Captains whom I have already named
who went in his Company reached the place where the Captain General of the Mexicans was marching with his banner
displayed, and with rich golden armour and great gold and
silver plumes. When Cortés saw him with many other Mexican Chieftains all wearing great plumes, he said to our Captains: "Now, Señores, let us break through them and leave none
of them unwounded"; and commending themselves to God,
Cortés, Cristóbal de Olid, Sandoval, Alonzo de Ávila, and the
other horsemen charged, and Cortés struck his horse against
the Mexican Captain, which made him drop his banner, and
the rest of our Captains succeeded in breaking through the
squadron which consisted of many Indians following the Captain who carried the banner, who nevertheless had not fallen
at the shock that Cortés had given him, and it was Juan de
Salamanca, who rode with Cortés on a good piebald mare,
who gave him a lance thrust and took from him the rich plume
that he wore, and afterwards gave it to Cortés, saying that as
it was he who first met him and made him lower his banner
and deprived his followers of the courage to fight, that the
plume belonged to him (Cortés). However, three years afterwards, the King gave it to Salamanca as his coat of arms, and
his descendants bear it on their tabards.

Let us go back to the battle. It pleased Our Lord that when
that Captain who carried the Mexican banner was dead (and
many others were killed there) their attack slackened, and all
the horsemen followed them and we felt neither hunger nor
thirst, and it seemed as though we had neither suffered nor
passed through any evil or hardship, as we followed up our
victory killing and wounding. Then our friends the Tlaxcalans
were very lions, and with their swords and broadswords which
they there captured from the enemy behaved very well and
valiantly. When the horsemen returned from following up the
victory we all gave many thanks to God for having escaped
from such a great multitude of people, for there had never been
seen or found throughout the Indies such a great number of
warriors together in any battle that was fought, for there was
present there the flower of Mexico and Texcoco and all the
towns around the lake, and others in the neighbourhood, and
the people of Otumba and Tepetexcoco and Saltocan, who all
came in the belief that this time not a trace of us would be

left. Then what rich armour they wore, with so much gold and plumes and devices, and nearly all of them were captains and chieftains. Near the spot where this hard-fought and celebrated battle took place, and where one can say God spared our lives, there stands a town named Otumba.

Our escape from the City of Mexico was on the tenth of the month of July [1520], and this celebrated battle of Otumba was fought on the fourteenth of July.

I assert that within a matter of five days over eight hundred and sixty soldiers were killed and sacrificed, as well as seventy-two who were killed in a town named Tustepec, together with five Spanish women (those who were killed at Tustepec belonged to the company of Narvaez) and over a thousand Tlaxcalans were slain. At that time they also killed Juan de Alcántara the elder, with three other settlers from Villa Rica. If many more of the followers of Narvaez than those of Cortés died at the bridges, it was because they went forth laden with gold, and owing to its weight they could neither escape nor swim.

We went on to some other farms and a small town where there was a good Cue and strong house where we defended ourselves that night and dressed our wounds and got some rest. Although squadrons of Mexicans still followed us they did not dare to come up to us, and those who did come were as though they said "There you go out of our country."

From that small town where we slept, the hills over against Tlaxcala could be seen, and when we saw them we were as delighted as though they had been our own homes. But how could we know for certain that they were loyal to us or what their disposition was, or what had happened to those who were settled at Villa Rica, whether they were alive or dead? Cortés said to us that, although we were few in number, and there were only four hundred and forty of us left with twenty horses and twelve crossbowmen and seven musketeers, and we had no powder and were all wounded, lame, and maimed, we could see very clearly how our Lord Jesus Christ had been pleased to spare our lives, and for that we should always give Him great thanks and honour. Moreover, we had come again to be reduced to the number and strength of the soldiers who accompanied him the first time we entered Mexico, namely four hundred soldiers. He begged us not to give annoyance to the people in Tlaxcala, and not to take anything from them, and this he explained to the followers of Narvaez, for they were not used to obey their Captains in the wars as we were. Moreover, he said he trusted in God that we should find the Tlaxcalans true and very loyal, and that if it were otherwise, which God forfend, we must turn aside the blows of fate with stout hearts and strong arms, and for this we must be well prepared.

With our scouts ahead of us, we reached a spring on the hillside where there were some walls and defences made in past times, and our friends the Tlaxcalans said that this was the boundary between them and the Mexicans, and, in welcome tranquillity after the misery we had gone through, we halted to wash and to eat. Then we soon resumed our march and went to a Tlaxcalan town named Hueyotlipan where they received us and gave us to eat, but not much, unless we paid them with some small pieces of gold and chalchihuites which some of us carried with us; they gave us nothing without payment. There we remained one day resting and curing our wounds and we also attended to the horses. Then as soon as they heard the news at the Capital of Tlaxcala, Mase Escasi and Xicotenga the elder, and Chichimecatecle and many other Caciques and Chieftains and nearly all the inhabitants of Huexotzingo promptly came to us. When they reached the town where we were camped they came to embrace Cortés and all of us captains and soldiers, some of them weeping, especially Mase Escasi, Xicotenga, and Chichimecatecle, and Tapaneca, and they said to Cortés: "Oh! Malinche, Malinche! How grieved we are at your misfortunes and those of all your brothers, and at the number of our own people who have been killed with yours. We have told you so many times not to put trust in the Mexican people, for one day or the other they were sure to attack you, but you would not believe us. Now it has come to pass, and no more can be done at present than to tend you and give you to eat; rest yourselves for you are at home, and we will soon go to our town where we will find you quarters. Do not think, Malinche, that it is a small thing you have done to escape with your lives from that impregnable city and its bridges, and I tell you that if we formerly looked upon you as very brave, we now think you much more valiant; and although many Indian women in our towns will bewail the deaths of their sons, husbands, brothers and kinsmen, do not trouble yourself about that. Much do you owe to your Gods who have brought you here and delivered you from such a multitude of warriors who were awaiting you at Otumba. For four days I had known that they were waiting for you to slay you. I wanted to go in search of you with thirty thousand of our own warriors, but I could not start because they were not assembled and men were out collecting them."

Cortés and all our Captains and soldiers embraced them and told them that we thanked them, and Cortés gave to all the chieftains golden jewels and precious stones, and as every soldier had escaped with as much as he could carry some of us gave presents to our acquaintances from what we possessed. Then what rejoicing and happiness they showed when they saw that Doña Luisa and Doña Marina were saved, and what weeping and sorrow for the other Indians who did not come but were left behind dead. Especially did Mase Escasi weep for his daughter Doña Elvira and the death of Juan Velásquez de Leon to whom he had given her.

In this way we went to the Capital of Tlaxcala with all the Caciques, and Cortés lodged in the houses of Mase Escasi, and Xicotenga gave his quarters to Pedro de Alvarado, and there we tended our wounds and began to recover our strength, but, nevertheless, four soldiers died of their wounds and some other soldiers failed to recover.

† xci

We were also uneasy at not knowing about the people at Villa Rica, lest some disaster had happened to them, so Cortés at once wrote to them and sent the letter by three Tlaxcalans, and he asked them whether they had any powder or crossbows because he wished to return and scour the neighbourhood of Mexico. He also wrote to the officer named Caballero whom he had left there as Captain of the Sea, to keep watch that neither Narvaez nor any of the ships should leave for Cuba, and if he considered the two ships belonging to Narvaez which were in the harbour to be unfit for sea that he should destroy them and send their crews to him with all the arms they possessed.

Caballero wrote and said he would soon despatch the succour they were sending from Villa Rica, numbering seven in all, including four sailors. Their Captain was a soldier named Lencero, as they arrived at Tlaxcala thin and ill, we often for our own diversion and to make fun of them spoke of "Lencero's Help," for of the seven that came five had liver complaint and were covered with boils and the other two were swelled out with great bellies.

I will tell what happened to us there in Tlaxcala with Xicotenga the younger and his ill will. The truth is that when it became known in that City that we were fleeing from Mexico, and that the Mexicans had killed a great number of soldiers, and that we were coming for aid and shelter to Tlaxcala, Xicotenga the younger went about appealing to all his friends and relations and to others who he thought were on his side, and said to them that they should kill us and make friends with Cuitlahuac, the Lord of Mexico, and that in addition to this they should rob us of the cloaks and cloth which we had left in Tlaxcala to be taken care of, and the gold that we were now bringing from Mexico, and they would all become rich with the spoil.

This came to the ears of the elder Xicotenga, his father, who quarrelled with him and told him that no such thought should have entered his head, that it was disgraceful, but much as his father rebuked him he paid no heed nor did it stop him from talking about and working at his evil purpose. This reached the ears of Chichimecatecle, who was the mortal enemy of Xicotenga the younger, and he told it to Mase Escasi, and they called together Xicotenga the elder and the chiefs of Huexotzingo, and ordered Xicotenga the younger to be brought prisoner before them. Then Mase Escasi made a speech to them all and asked if they could remember or had heard it said that during the last hundred years there had ever been throughout Tlaxcala such prosperity and riches as there had been since the Teules had arrived in their country, or if in any of their provinces they had ever been so well provided for. For they possessed much cotton cloth and gold and they ate salt, and that wherever the Tlaxcalans went with the Teules, honour was paid to them out of respect to the Teules, and although many of them had now been killed in Mexico, they should bear in mind what their ancestors had said to them many years ago, that from where the sun rises there would come men who would rule over them. Why then was Xicotenga now going about with these treasons and infamies, scheming to make war on us and kill us? It was evilly done, and there was no excuse to be made for the knavery and mischief which he always had hidden in his breast, and now at the very moment when he saw us coming back defeated, when he ought to help us to recover ourselves, so as to turn again upon his enemies the towns of Mexico, he wished to carry out this treachery.

To these words Xicotenga the younger replied, that what he had said about making peace with the Mexicans was a very wise decision, and he said other things that they could not tolerate. Then Mase Escasi and Chichimecatecle and the old man, his father, blind as he was, arose and took Xicotenga the younger by the collar and by his mantle and tore it and roughly pushing him and with reproachful words they cast him down the steps with his mantle all torn, and had it not been for his father they would have slain him. The others who had been in his confidence were made prisoners. As we were all taking refuge there, and it was not the time to punish him, Cortés said nothing more about it.

I have called this to mind so that it may be seen how loyal and good were these people of Tlaxcala, and how much we are indebted to them, and especially to the good Xicotenga the elder, who is said to have ordered his son to be killed when he knew of his plots and treason.

Let us leave this, and I will relate how we remained twenty-two days in that town curing our wounds and recovering. Then Cortés determined that we should go to the province of Tepeaca which was near by. When Cortés told this to our Captains, and they were preparing the soldiers of Narvaez to go to the war, as these men were not accustomed to fighting, and having escaped from the defeat at Mexico and at the bridges, and from the battle of Otumba, they were most anxious to return to the Island of Cuba, to their Indians, and their gold mines, they cursed Cortés and his conquests. Especially was this the case with Andrés de Duero, the partner of Cortés. When they saw that words had no effect on Cortés, they drew up a formal requisition before a King's Notary demanding that he should go at once to Villa Rica and abandon the war, giving as a reason that we had neither horses nor muskets, crossbows nor powder, nor thread with which to make crossbow strings, nor stores, that we were all wounded, and out of all our company and the soldiers of Narvaez there only survived four hundred and forty, and that the Mexicans would hold the strongholds, sierras and passes against us, and that if we delayed any longer the ships would be eaten by worms and many other things were stated in this petition.

After Cortés had given his answer to the requisition, the men who were pressing their demands upon him saw that many of us, who stood firmly by Cortés, would put a stop to the importunity with which they expressed their demands merely by insisting that it would be neither to the service of God nor His Majesty to desert their captain during war time. At the end of much discussion they gave their obedience so far as to go with us on any expeditions that might be undertaken, but it was on condition that Cortés promised that when an opportunity should occur he would allow them to return to the Island of Cuba.

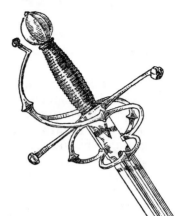

VIII

The Halt at Tepeaca

As Cortés had asked the Caciques of Tlaxcala for five thousand warriors, in order to overrun and chastise the towns where Spaniards had been killed, namely Tepeaca and Quecholac and Tecamachalco, distant from Tlaxcala six or seven leagues, they got ready four thousand Indians, with the greatest willingness.

Then as we were all ready, we began our march. On that expedition we took neither artillery nor muskets, for all had been lost at the bridges, and for the few that were saved, we had no powder. We had with us seventeen horses and six crossbows, and four hundred and twenty soldiers, most of them armed with sword and shield, and about two thousand friends of Tlaxcala.

The next day we had a fine battle with the Mexicans and Tepeacans, on a plain, and as the field of battle was among maize and maguey plantations, although the Mexicans fought fiercely, they were soon routed by those on horseback, and those who had no horses were not behindhand. Then to see with what spirit our Tlaxcalan allies attacked them and followed them up and overtook them! and many of the Mexicans and Tepeacans were slain, but of our Tlaxcalan allies only three were killed, and two horses were wounded, and one of them died, and two of our soldiers were wounded, but not in a manner to cause them any danger.

Then we went to the town of Tepeaca and founded a town

there, which was named La Villa de Segura de la Frontera, because it was on the road to Villa Rica, and it stood in a good neighbourhood of excellent towns subject to Mexico, and there was plenty of maize, and we had our allies the Tlaxcalans to guard the frontier. There, Alcaldes and Regidores were chosen, and orders were given that the neighbourhood subject to Mexico was to be raided, especially the towns where Spaniards had been killed. An iron was made with which to brand those whom we took for slaves, it was shaped thus ❡, which means *Guerra* [war]. From the Villa Segura de la Frontera we scoured the neighbourhood which included Quecholac and Tecamachalco, and the town of the Guayavas, and other towns of which I do not remember the names. It was in Quecholac that they had killed fifteen Spaniards in their quarters, and here we made many slaves, so that within forty days we had all these towns punished and thoroughly subdued.

At that time, in Mexico, they had raised up [to the throne] another Prince, because the Prince who had driven us out of Mexico had died of Smallpox. He whom they now made Lord over them was a nephew or very near relation of Montezuma, named Guatemoc, a young man of about twenty-five years, very much of a gentleman for an Indian, and very valiant, and he made himself so feared that all his people trembled before him, and he was married to a daughter of Montezuma, a very handsome woman for an Indian. When this Guatemoc, Prince of Mexico, learned that we had defeated the Mexican squadrons stationed in Tepeaca, and that the people of Tepeaca had given their fealty to His Majesty, and served us and gave us food, and that we had settled there, he feared that we should overrun Oaxaca and other provinces and bring them all into our alliance; so he sent messengers through all the towns and told them to be on the alert with all their arms, and he gave golden jewels to some Caciques, and to others he remitted their tribute, and above all he despatched great companies and garrisons of warriors to see that we did not enter his territory, and charged them to fight very fiercely against us, so that it should not happen again, as it did at Tepeaca and Quecholac.

Letters came to Cortés from Villa Rica to say that a ship had arrived in port, and that her Captain was a gentleman named Pedro Barba, a great friend of Cortés. He brought with him only thirteen soldiers, a horse and a mare, for the vessel that he came in was very small. He also brought letters for Pánfilo de Narvaez in the belief that New Spain was now his, and in these letters Velásquez sent to tell him that if he had not already killed Cortés that he should at once send him a prisoner to Cuba, so that he could be sent to Castile, for so it had been ordered by the Bishop of Burgos.

As soon as Pedro Barba arrived in port with his ship, and let go his anchor, Pedro Caballero went off to visit and welcome him in a boat well manned by sailors with their arms hidden.

They told Pedro Barba and his companions so many yarns that they induced them to go ashore in the boat, and when they had got them clear of their ship Pedro Caballero said to Pedro Barba, "Surrender, in the name of the Señor Capitan Hernando Cortés, my commander." Thus they were captured, and they were thunderstruck. Then they sent Pedro Barba and his companions to where we were stationed with Cortés in Tepeaca, and we were delighted to receive them for the help that it brought us in the very nick of time.

Cortés paid much honour to Pedro Barba, and made him Captain of the crossbowmen. Another small vessel arrived within eight days, and a gentleman named Rodrigo Morejon de Lobera came in her as Captain, and brought with him eight soldiers and six crossbows and much twine for making bowstrings, and one mare. In exactly the same way that they had taken Pedro Barba, so did they take this Rodrigo Morejon, and they were sent at once to Segura de la Frontera, and we rejoiced to see all of them, and Cortés paid them much honour and gave them employment.

† xciii

Guatemoc, the chieftain who had recently been raised to be King of Mexico, was sending garrisons to his frontiers, and in particular he sent one very powerful and numerous body of warriors to Guacachula and another to Izucar, distant two or three leagues from Guacachula. It seems that this host of warriors committed many robberies and acts of violence against the inhabitants of those towns where they were quartered; so much so, that four chieftains of Guacachula came very secretly to Cortés and asked him to send Teules and horses to put a stop to these robberies and injuries which the Mexicans were committing, and said that all the people of that town and others in the neighbourhood would aid us in slaying the Mexican squadrons.

When Cortés heard this he despatched Cristóbal de Olid as Captain with nearly all the horsemen and crossbowmen and a large force of Tlaxcalans. Cortés [also] told off certain captains from among those who had come with Narvaez, to accompany Captain Cristóbal de Olid, so he took with him over three hundred soldiers and all the best horses that we had.

About a league from Guacachula the Caciques of the town came out to tell them how and where the men of Culua were posted, and how they should be attacked, and in what way the Spaniards could be assisted, and they fell on the troops of Culua, and although the latter fought well for a good while and wounded some of our soldiers and killed two horses and wounded eight more at some barricades and ditches that were in the town, within an hour all the Mexicans were put to flight. Olid did not tarry long in that town but went on at once to Izucar, and with those who could follow him and with our allies from Guacachula he crossed the river and fell on the Mexican squadrons and quickly defeated them. There they killed two horses and gave Olid two wounds, one of them in the thigh, and his horse was badly wounded.

While we were stationed at Segura de la Frontera, letters reached Cortés to say that one of the ships which Francisco de Garay, the Governor of Jamaica, had sent to form a settlement at Panuco, had come into port, and that her Captain was named Camargo, and that she brought over sixty soldiers, all of them ill, and very yellow and with swollen bellies. They brought the news that the other Captain whom Garay had sent to settle at Panuco, whose name was Álvarez Pinedo, and all the soldiers and horses that had been sent to that province, had been killed by the Indians, and their ships burned. This Camargo, seeing how badly things had turned out, re-embarked his soldiers and came for help to the port, for they knew well that we had settled there. It was because they had to endure the constant attacks of the Indians of Panuco, that they had nothing to eat and arrived so thin and yellow and swollen. These soldiers and their captain came on very slowly (for they could not walk, owing to their weakness) to the town of Frontera. When Cortés saw them so swollen and yellow he knew that they were no good as fighting men and that we should hardly be able to cure them, and he treated them with much consideration. I fancy that Camargo died very soon, but I do not well remember what became of him, and many others of them died, and then for a joke we gave the others a nickname, and called them the "verdigris bellies" for they were the colour of death and their bellies were so swollen.

One Miguel Díaz de Auz arrived soon after, who had been sent as one of Francisco de Garay's captains to succour Captain Álvarez Pinedo, for he thought that Pinedo was at Panuco. When Miguel Díaz de Auz arrived at the port of Panuco and found no vestige, neither hide nor hair, of the Armada of Garay he understood at once from what he saw, that they were all dead. The Indians of that province attacked Miguel Díaz as soon as he arrived with his ship, and for that reason he came on to our port and disembarked his soldiers, who numbered more than fifty with seven horses, and he soon arrived where we were stationed with Cortés, and this help was most welcome just at the time when we needed it most.

A few days after Miguel Díaz de Auz had come to port, another ship arrived in port which Garay had also sent to help and succour his expedition, believing that they were all safe and well in the Rio de Panuco. The Captain who came in her was an old man named Ramírez. Thus, Francisco de Garay shot off one shaft after another to the assistance of his Armada, and each one went to assist the good fortune of Cortés and of us. It was of the greatest help to us, and all these men from Garay, as I have already said, came to Tepeaca where we were stationed. Because the soldiers brought by Miguel Díaz de Auz arrived very hearty and fat, we called them "the strong backs," and those who came with the elder Ramírez, who wore cotton armour so thick that no arrow could penetrate it, and it was very heavy, we called "the pack saddles." When the captains and soldiers whom I have mentioned, presented themselves before Cortés, he paid them much honour.

Cortés had now an abundance of soldiers and horses and crossbows. He had received news that in some towns named Zocotla and Xalatcinco and in others in the neighbourhood, many of the soldiers of Narvaez had been killed when on their way from Mexico, and also that it was in those towns that they had killed, and stolen the gold from Juan de Alcántara and the other two settlers from the town of Villa Rica.

Cortés sent Gonzalo de Sandoval, the chief Alguacil, as the captain of that expedition, a valiant man of good counsel, and he took with him two hundred soldiers, nearly all of them from us, the followers of Cortés, and twenty horsemen and twelve crossbowmen and a large force of Tlaxcalans.

Without relating anything more that happened on this expedition, I may say that the enemy were defeated and the Mexicans and the Caciques of those towns were put to flight.

They found in the Cues of that town clothes and armour and horses' bridles and two saddles, and other things belonging to horsemen, which had been offered to the Idols. Sandoval returned with a great spoil of women and boys who were branded as slaves, and Cortés was delighted when he saw him arrive strong and well, although eight soldiers had been badly wounded, and three horses killed, and Sandoval himself had one arrow wound.

I did not go on that expedition as I was very ill with fever and was vomiting blood, and thank God I got well for they bled me.

† XCIV

When Gonzalo de Sandoval arrived at the town of Segura de la Frontera after having made the expeditions I have spoken of, we had all the people of that province pacified. So Cortés decided, with the officials of the King, that all the slaves that had been taken should be branded so that his fifth might be set aside after the fifth had been taken for His Majesty, and to this effect he had a proclamation made in the town and camp, that all the soldiers should bring to a house chosen for the purpose all the women whom we were sheltering, to be branded, and the time allowed for doing this was the day of the proclamation and one more.

We all came with all the Indian women and girls and boys whom we had captured, but the grown-up men we did not trouble about as they were difficult to watch and we had no need of their services, as we had our friends the Tlaxcalans.

When they had all been brought together and had been marked with the iron which was like this 🐝, which stands for *guerra* [war], when we were not expecting it they set aside the Royal fifth, and then took another fifth for Cortés, and, in addition to this, the night before, after we had placed the women in that house as I have stated, they took away and hid the best looking Indian women, and there was not a good-looking one left, and when it came to dividing them, they allotted us the old and ugly women, and there was a great deal of grumbling about it against Cortés and those who ordered the good-looking Indian women to be stolen and hidden; so much so that some of the soldiers of Narvaez said to Cortés himself, that they took God to witness that such a thing had never happened as to have two Kings in the country belonging to our Lord the King, and to deduct two-fifths. One of the soldiers who said this to him was Juan Bono de Quejo, and moreover he said that they would not remain in such a country, and that he would inform His Majesty in Spain about it, and the Royal Council of the Indies. Another soldier told Cortés very clearly that it did not suffice to divide the gold which had been secured in Mexico in the way in which he had done it, for when he was dividing it he said that it was three hundred thousand pesos that had been collected, and when we were fleeing from Mexico, he had ordered witness to be taken that there remained more than seven hundred thousand; and that now the poor soldier who had done all the hard work and was covered with wounds could not even have a good-looking Indian woman; besides the soldiers had given the Indian women skirts and chemises, and all those women had been taken and hidden away. Moreover when the proclamation had been issued that they were to be brought and branded, it was thought that each soldier would have his women returned to him, and they would be appraised according to the value of each in pesos, and that when they had been valued a fifth would be paid to His Majesty and there would not be any fifth for Cortés; and other complaints were made worse than these.

When Cortés saw this, he said with smooth words that he swore on his conscience (for that was his usual oath) that from that time forward he would not act in that way, but that good or bad, all the Indian women should be put up to auction, and that the good-looking ones should be sold for so much, and

those that were not good looking for a lower price, so that
there should be no cause of quarrel with him. However, here
in Tepeaca no more slaves were made, but afterwards in Texcoco it was done nearly in this manner, as I will relate further
on.

I will stop talking about this and will refer to another matter almost worse than this of the slaves, which was that when
on that night of sorrow[1] we were fleeing from Mexico, Cortés
declared before a King's Notary that whoever should wish to
take gold from what was left there, might carry it off and welcome, for their own, as otherwise it would be lost. As in our
camp and town of Segura de la Frontera Cortés got to know
that there were many bars of gold, and that they were changing hands at play, and as the proverb has it: *"El oro y amores
eran malos de encubrir"* (gold and love affairs are difficult to
hide), he ordered a proclamation to be made, that under
heavy penalty they should bring and declare the gold that
they had taken, and that a third part of it should be returned
to them, and that if they did not bring it, all would be seized.
Many of the soldiers who possessed gold did not wish to give
it up, and some of it Cortés took as a loan, but more by force
than by consent, and as nearly all the Captains possessed gold
and even the officials of the King, the proclamation was all the
more ignored and no more spoken of; however, this order of
Cortés' seemed to be very wrong.

† xcv

When the Captains of Narvaez observed that now we had reinforcements both through those who had come from Cuba,
and those whom Francisco de Garay had sent to join his expedition from Jamaica, and they saw that the towns of the
province of Tepeaca were all at peace, after much discussion
with Cortés, and many promises and entreaties, they begged
him to give them leave to return to the Island of Cuba, as he
had promised. Cortés promptly granted their request, and even
promised them that if he regained New Spain and the city of
Mexico that he would give his partner Andrés de Duero much
more gold than he had given him before, and he made similar

[1] The *noche triste.*

promises to the other Captains, especially to Augustin Bermúdez, and he ordered them to be given supplies such as could be procured at that time, maize, and salted dogs, and a few fowls, and one of the best ships. Cortéz wrote to his wife, Doña Catalina Juarez, la Marcaida, and to Juan Juarez his brother-in-law, who at that time lived in the Island of Cuba, and sent them some bars and jewels of gold, and told them about all the disasters and hardships that had happened to us, and how we had been driven out of Mexico.

When Cortés gave the men leave to go, we asked him why he gave it, as we who remained behind were so few, and he replied that it was to avoid brawls and importunities, and that we could see for ourselves that some of those who were returning were not fit for warfare, and that it was better to remain alone than in useless company. Cortés sent Pedro de Alvarado to despatch them from the port, and told him that after they were embarked he was to return at once to the town.

I will now say that he also sent Diego de Ordás and Alonzo de Mendoza to Castile, with certain messages from himself, and I do not know if he sent any from us, for he did not tell us a thing about the business that he was negotiating with His Majesty.

Cortés also sent Alonzo de Ávila to the Island of Santo Domingo to give an account of all that had happened to the Royal Audiencia.

I well know that some inquiring readers will ask how without money could Diego de Ordás be sent on business to Castile, for it is clear that in Castile and elsewhere money is a necessity, and in the same way how could Alonzo de Ávila and Francisco Alvarez el Chico be sent on business to Santo Domingo, and to the Island of Jamaica for horses and mares? I may answer this, that when we were fleeing from Mexico by Cortés' orders more than eighty Tlaxcalan Indians were laden with gold, and they were amongst the first who got clear of the bridges, so that it is clear that many loads of it were saved, and it was not all lost on the causeway.

Let us leave this subject, and I will say that now as all the towns in the neighbourhood of Tepeaca were at peace, Cortés settled that one Francisco de Orozco should stay in our town of Segura de la Frontera as captain, with a batch of twenty soldiers who were wounded or ill, and that all the rest of the army should go to Tlaxcala. He also gave orders that timber should be cut for the building of thirteen launches so that we could return to Mexico again, for we knew for certain that we could never master the lake without launches, nor carry on war, nor enter that great city another time by the causeways, without great risk to our lives.

He who was the expert to cut the wood and make the model and the measurement, and give instructions how the launches were to be fast sailors and of light draught for their special purpose, and the one who built them, was Martin López, who certainly, besides being a good sailor in all the wars, served His Majesty very well in this matter of the launches and worked at them like a strong man.

When we arrived at Tlaxcala our great friend Mase Escasi had died of smallpox. We all grieved over his death very much and Cortés said he felt it as though it were the death of his own father, and he put on mourning of black cloth, and so did many of our Captains and soldiers. Cortés and all of us paid much honour to the children and relations of Mase Escasi. As there were disputes in Tlaxcala about the Cacique-ship and command, Cortés ordered and decreed that it should go to a legitimate son of Mase Escasi, for so his father had ordered before he died, and he had also said to his sons and relations, that they should take care always to obey the commands of Malinche and his brethren, for we were certainly those who were destined to govern the country, and he gave them other good advice.

Xicotenga the elder and Chichimecatecle and nearly all the other caciques of Tlaxcala offered their services to Cortés, both in the matter of cutting wood for the launches and anything else he might order for the war against Mexico. Cortés embraced them with much affection and thanked them for it, especially Xicotenga the elder and Chichimecatecle, and soon persuaded them to become Christians and the good old Xico-tenga with much willingness said that he wished to be a Christian, and he was baptized by the Padre de la Merced with the greatest ceremony that at that time it was possible to arrange in Tlaxcala, and was given the name of Don Lorenzo Vargas.

Let us go back to speak of the launches. Martin López made

such speed in cutting the wood with the great assistance rendered him by the Indians, that he had the whole of it cut within a few days, and each beam marked for the position for which it was intended to occupy, after the manner that the master carpenters and boat builders have of marking it. He was also assisted by another good soldier named Ándrez Nuñez, and an old carpenter who was lame from a wound, called Ramírez the elder.

Then Cortés sent to Villa Rica for much of the iron and the bolts of the ships which we had destroyed, and for anchors, sails and rigging and for cables and tow and all the other material for building ships, and he ordered all the blacksmiths to come, and one Hernando de Aguilar who was half a blacksmith and helped in the forging. Cortés sent a certain Santa Cruz as Captain to Villa Rica with orders to bring all the material I have mentioned. He brought everything, even to the cauldrons for melting the pitch, and all the things that they had taken out of the ships, and transported them with the help of more than a thousand Indians, for all the towns of those provinces were enemies of the Mexicans, and at once gave men to carry the loads. Then as we had no pitch with which to caulk the launches, and the Indians did not know how to extract it, Cortés ordered four sailors who understood the work to go and make pitch in some fine pine woods near Huexotzingo.

As soon as Cortés saw that the timber for the launches was cut, and the persons named by me had started for Cuba he settled that we should go with all our soldiers to the city of Texcoco. Over this there were many and great discussions, for some of the soldiers said that there was a better position, and better canals and ditches in which to build the sloops at Ayotzingo near Chalco than in the ditch and lake [at Texcoco], and others contended that Texcoco was the better, as it was nearer to many other towns, and that when we held that city in our power, we could make expeditions to the country in the vicinity of Mexico, and that once stationed in that city we could form a better opinion as to how things were going on.

News now reached us that a large ship had arrived from Spain and the Canary Islands, laden with a great variety of merchandise, muskets, powder, crossbows and crossbow cords, and three horses, and other arms. Cortés sent at once to buy all the arms and powder and everything else that she carried, and Juan de Burgos, the owner of the ship, and Amedel the sailing master, and all the passengers on board soon came to our camp, and we were very well satisfied at receiving such timely assistance.

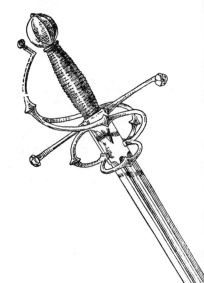

IX

The Return to the Valley

† XCVI

When Cortés saw that he possessed such a goodly store of muskets and powder and crossbows and realized the strong desire of all of us, both Captains and soldiers, again to attack the great City of Mexico, he decided to ask the Caciques of Tlaxcala to give him ten thousand Indian warriors to join us on an expedition to Texcoco; which after Mexico is one of the largest cities in the whole of New Spain. Xicotenga the elder promptly said that he would give him with the utmost willingness not only ten thousand men but many more if he chose to take them, and that another valiant Cacique, our great friend Chichimecatecle would go as their captain. On the day after the feast of the Nativity in the year 1520 we began our march, and slept at (Tesmelucan) a pueblo subject to Tlaxcala, and the people of the town gave us what we needed. From there onward it was Mexican territory, and we went more cautiously, for it was well known in Mexico and Texcoco that we were marching towards their city. That day we met no obstacles whatever and camped at the foot of the Sierra, a march of about three leagues. The night was very cold, but we got through it safely thanks to our patrols, and scouts. When the dawn came we began to ascend a small pass and in some difficult places like barrancas the hillside had been cut away so that we could not pass, and many pine trees and other timber had been placed across the track, but having so many friendly Tlaxcalans with us, a clearing was soon made, and

sending a company of musketeers and crossbowmen in advance
we marched on with the utmost caution, our allies cutting and
pushing aside trees to enable the horsemen to pass, until we
got to the top of the range. Then we descended a little and
caught sight of the lake of Mexico and its great cities standing
in the water, and when we saw it we gave great thanks to God
for allowing us to see it again.

We descended the mountain to where we saw great smoke
signals, and marching onward we came upon a large squadron
of Mexican and Texcocan warriors who were waiting for us at
a pass through a rocky thicket where there was an apparently
broken down wooden bridge, and a deep gulch and waterfall
below it. However, we soon defeated the squadron and passed
in perfect safety. To hear the shouts that they gave from the
farms and from the barrancas! However they did nothing else,
and shouted only from places where the horsemen could not
reach them. Our friends the Tlaxcalans carried off fowls and
whatever else they could steal, and they did not abstain from
this although Cortés had ordered them not to make war on the
people if they were not attacked. The Tlaxcalans answered
that if the people were well disposed and peaceable they
would not come out on the road and attack us as they did at
the passage of the barranca and bridge, where they tried to
stop our advance.

We went to sleep that night at (Coatepec) a deserted
pueblo subject to Texcoco, and took every precaution lest we
should be attacked during the darkness.

As soon as dawn came we began our march towards
Texcoco, which was about two leagues distant from where we
slept. However, we had not advanced half a league when we
saw our scouts returning at a breakneck pace and looking very
cheerful, and they told Cortés that ten Indians were approaching unarmed and carrying golden devices and banners, and
that yells and shouts no longer came from the huts and farms
they had passed on the road as had happened the day before.

Then Cortés ordered a halt until seven Indian Chieftains,
natives of Texcoco, came up to us. They carried a golden banner, and a long lance, and before reaching us they lowered the
banner and knelt down (which is a sign of peace), and when
they came before Cortés who had our interpreters standing by
him, they said: "Malinche, our Lord and Chieftain of Texcoco,

Coanacotzin sends to beg you to receive him into your friendship, and he is awaiting you peaceably in the City, and in proof thereof accept this banner of gold, and he begs as a favour that you will order your Tlaxcalans and your brethren not to do any harm to his land, and that you will come and lodge in the city where he will provide you with all that you need." Moreover they said that the troops which had been stationed in the ravines and bad passes did not belong to Texcoco, but were Mexicans sent by Guatemoc.

When the message had been considered Cortés at once sent for the Tlaxcalan Captains and ordered them, in the most friendly way, not to do any damage nor to take anything whatever in this country because peace had been made, and they did as he told them, but he did not forbid their taking food if it were only maize and beans, or even fowls and dogs, of which there was an abundance, all the houses being full of them.

Then Cortés took counsel with his Captains, and it seemed to them all that this begging for peace was a trick, for if it had been true it would not have been done so suddenly, and they would have brought food. Nevertheless, Cortés accepted the banner, which was worth about eighty pesos, and thanked the messengers and said to them, that he was not in the habit of doing evil or damage to any vassals of His Majesty, and if they kept the peace which they had announced he would protect them against the Mexicans; that as they might have seen, he had already ordered the Tlaxcalans not to do any damage in their country, and they would avoid doing so for the future, although they knew how in that city over forty Spaniards our brethren, and two hundred Tlaxcalans had been killed at the time when we were leaving Mexico, and many loads of gold and other spoil which belonged to them had been stolen, and that he must beg their chieftain Coanacotzin and the other chiefs and captains of Texcoco to restore to us the gold and the cloths, but as to the death of the Spaniards, there was no remedy for it, he would therefore not ask them for any.

The messengers replied that they would report to their Lord as he ordered them to do, but that he who had ordered the Spaniards to be killed and who took all the spoil was a chieftain named Cuitlahuac who had been chosen King of Mexico after Montezuma's death, and that they took to him in Mexico nearly all the Teules and they had been promptly sacrificed to Huichilobos.

When Cortés heard that reply, he made no answer, lest he should lose his temper or threaten them, but he bade them Godspeed. One of the ambassadors remained in our company, and we went on to a suburb of Texcoco called Coatlinchan, and there they gave us plenty to eat and all that we had need of, and we cast down some Idols that were in the houses where we lodged, and early the next day we went to the city of Texcoco. In none of the streets nor houses did we see any women, boys or children, only terrified looking men. We took up our quarters in some great rooms and halls, and Cortés at once summoned the captains and most of us soldiers and told us not to leave the precincts of the great courts, and to keep well on the alert until we could see how things were going, for it did not seem to him that the city was friendly. He ordered Pedro de Alvarado and Cristóbal de Olid and some other soldiers, and me among them, to ascend the great Cue which was very lofty, and to look from the lofty Cue over the City and the lake, and what we saw was that all the inhabitants were moving off with their goods and chattels, and women and children, some to the hills and others to the reed thickets in the lake, and that the lake was thronged with canoes great and small.

As soon as Cortés knew this he wanted to capture the Lord of Texcoco who had sent him the golden banner, and when certain priests whom Cortés sent as messengers went to summon him, he had already placed himself in safety, for he was the very first to flee to Mexico with many other chieftains. We passed that night with great precautions, and very early the next day Cortés ordered all the Indian chieftains who had remained in Texcoco to be summoned before him, for as it was a very large city there were many other chieftains of the parties opposing the Cacique who had fled, with whom there had been discussions and disputes about the command and Kingship of that city. When they came before Cortés he learned from them how and since when Coanacotzin had ruled over the city. They told him that Coanacotzin in his desire to seize the power had infamously killed his elder brother Cuicuitzcatzin with the assistance given him for that purpose by Cuitlahuac, the Prince of Mexico, the one that made war on

us when we were fleeing after the death of Montezuma. Furthermore, there were among them other Lords who had a
better right to the kingdom of Texcoco than he who now held
it, and that it should go to a youth who at that time became a
Christian with much religious pomp, and was named Don
Hernando Cortés, for our Captain was his Godfather. They
said that this youth was the legitimate son of Nezahualpilli, the
Lord and King of Texcoco, and presently without any further
delay, and with the greatest festive celebration and rejoicing
throughout Texcoco, they appointed him their natural Lord
and King, with all the ceremonies which they were accustomed
to render to their so-called Kings; and in perfect peace and
with the love of all his vassals, and of the neighbouring
towns, he governed absolutely and was obeyed. For his better
instruction in the matters of our faith and to improve his manners, and so that he should learn our language, Cortés ordered
that he should have as his tutors Antonio de Villa Real, and a
Bachelor of Arts named Escobar; Cortés then asked for a large
force of Indian labourers to broaden and deepen the canals
and ditches through which we were to draw the launches to
the lake when they were finished and ready to sail. He also
explained to Don Hernando himself and the other chieftains
what was the reason and purpose in having the launches built,
and how we were going to blockade Mexico. Don Hernando
offered all the assistance within his power, and of his own ac-
cord promised to send messengers to all the neighbouring
pueblos and tell them to become vassals of His Majesty, and
accept our friendship and authority against Mexico.

† xcvii

After spending twelve days in Texcoco the Tlaxcalans had exhausted their provisions, and they were so numerous that the
people of Texcoco were unable to furnish them with sufficient
food. As we were unwilling that they should become a burden
to the people of Texcoco and as the Tlaxcalans themselves
were most desirous of fighting the Mexicans and avenging the
death of the many Tlaxcalans who had been killed and offered
as sacrifices during their past defeats, Cortés determined that
we should set out on our march to Iztapalapa with himself as

Commander in Chief, and with Andrés de Tápia, Cristóbal de
Olid, and thirteen horsemen, twenty crossbowmen, six musketeers and two hundred and twenty soldiers, and our Tlaxcalan
allies, besides twenty chieftains from Texcoco given us by Don
Hernando. I have already said that more than half the houses
in Iztapalapa were built in the water and the other half on
dry land. We kept on our way in good order, and as the Mexicans always held watchmen and garrisons and warriors ready
to oppose us and to reinforce any of their towns, when they
knew that we were going to attack them, they warned the
people of Iztapalapa to be prepared, and sent over eight thousand Mexicans to help them. Like good warriors they awaited
our coming on dry land, and for a good while they fought
very bravely against us. Then the horsemen broke through
their ranks, followed by the crossbows and muskets, and all our
Tlaxcalan allies who charged on them like mad dogs, and the
enemy quickly abandoned the open ground and took refuge
in the town. However, they had arranged a stratagem, and
this was the way they did it; they fled and got into their
canoes which were in the water, and into the houses which
stood in the lake, others retired among the reeds, and as it was
a dark night, they gave us a chance to take up quarters in
the town, well contented with the spoil we had taken and still
more with the victory we had gained. While we were in this
situation, when we least expected it such a flood of water
rushed through the whole town, that if the chieftains whom
we had brought from Texcoco had not cried out, and warned
us to get out of the houses to dry land as quickly as we could,
we should all have been drowned, for the enemy had burst
open the canals of fresh and salt water and torn down a
causeway, so that the water rose up all of a sudden. As our
allies the Tlaxcalans were not accustomed to water and did
not know how to swim, two of them were drowned, and we, at
great risk to our lives, all thoroughly drenched and with our
powder spoilt, managed to get out without our belongings, and
in that condition, very cold, and without any supper, we
passed a bad night. Worst of all were the jeers and the shouts
and whistles which the people of Iztapalapa and the Mexicans
uttered from their houses and canoes. However, there was still
a worse thing to happen to us, for as they knew in Mexico
about the plan that had been made to drown us by breaking

down the causeway and canals, we found waiting for us on land and in the lake many battalions of warriors, and, as soon as day dawned, they made such an attack on us that we could hardly bear up against it; but they did not defeat us, although they killed two soldiers and one horse, and wounded many both of us and the Tlaxcalans. Little by little the attack slackened and we returned to Texcoco, half ashamed at the trick and stratagem to throw us into the water, and also because we gained very little credit in the battle they fought against us afterwards, as our powder was exhausted. Nevertheless, it frightened them, and they had enough to do in burying and burning their dead, and curing their wounds and rebuilding their houses.

When we had been two days in Texcoco after our return from the expedition to Iztapalapa, three pueblos came peaceably to Cortés to beg pardon for the past wars and the deaths of Spaniards whom they had killed.

As Cortés saw that there was nothing else to be done at the time, he pardoned them, but he gave them a severe reprimand, and they bound themselves by many promises always to be hostile to the Mexicans and to be the vassals of His Majesty, and to serve us, and so they did.

About the same time the inhabitants of the pueblo named Mixquic, which is also called Venezuela, which stands in the lake, came to beg for peace and friendship. These people had apparently never been on good terms with the Mexicans, and in their hearts they detested them. Cortés and all of us were greatly pleased at these people coming to seek our friendship, because their pueblo was in the lake, and through them we hoped to get at their neighbours who were likewise established on the water, so Cortés thanked them greatly and dismissed them with promises and gentle speeches. While this was taking place they came to tell Cortés that great squadrons of Mexicans were advancing on the four pueblos which had been the first to seek our friendship, one named Coatlinchan and others whose names I forget, and they told Cortés that they did not dare to stay in their houses and that they wished to flee to the mountains or to come to Texcoco where we were, and they said so many things to Cortés to induce him to help them, that he promptly got ready twenty horsemen and two hundred soldiers, thirteen crossbowmen, and ten musketeers and took with him Pedro de Alvarado and Cristóbal de Olid, and went to the pueblos, a distance from Texcoco of about two leagues. It appeared to be true that the Mexicans had sent to threaten them and warn them that they would be destroyed for accepting our friendship, but the point of dispute over which they uttered the worst threats concerned some large maize plantations lying near the lake which were ready for the harvest, whence the people of Texcoco were providing our camp. The Mexicans wanted to take the maize, for they said that it was theirs, for it had been the custom for those four pueblos to sow and harvest the maize plantations on that plain for the priests of the Mexican Idols. Over this question of the maize field many Indians had been killed. When Cortés understood about it, he promised the people that when the time came for them to go and gather maize, he would send a Captain and many horsemen and soldiers to protect those who went to fetch it. They were well pleased with what Cortés had said to them, and we returned to Texcoco. From that time forward, whenever we had need of maize in our camp, we mustered the Indian warriors from all those towns and with our Tlaxcalan allies and ten horsemen and a hundred soldiers, with some musketeers and crossbowmen, we went after the maize. I say this because I went twice for it myself and on one occasion we had a capital skirmish with some powerful Mexican Squadrons which had come in more than a thousand canoes, and awaited us in the maize fields, and as we had our allies with us, although the Mexicans fought like brave men, we made them take to their canoes, but they killed one of our soldiers and wounded twelve, and they also wounded some Tlaxcalans, but the enemy had not much to brag about for fifteen or twenty of them were lying dead, and we carried off five of them as prisoners.

The next day we heard the news that the people of Chalco and Tlamanalco and their dependencies wished to make peace, but on account of the Mexican garrisons stationed in their towns, they had no opportunity to do so, and that these Mexicans did much damage in their country and took their women, especially if they were handsome.

We had also heard that the timber for building the launches had been cut and prepared at Tlaxcala, and as the time was passing, and none of the timber had yet been brought to

Texcoco, most of the soldiers were a good deal worried about it. Then, in addition to this, the people came from the pueblo of Mixquic and from other friendly pueblos to tell Cortés that the Mexicans were coming to attack them because they had accepted our friendship. Moreover some of our friends the Tlaxcalans, who had already grabbed clothing and salt and gold and other spoil, wished to return home, but they did not dare to do so because the road was not safe.

† xcviii

When Cortés found that to succour some of those towns that clamoured for help and to give assistance to the people of Chalco as well would make it impossible to give security to either one or the other, he decided to put aside all other matters and first of all to go to Chalco and Tlamanalco. For that purpose he sent Gonzalo de Sandoval and Francisco de Lugo with fifteen horsemen and two hundred soldiers and musketeers and crossbowmen and our Tlaxcalan allies, with orders by all means to break up and disperse the Mexican garrisons and to drive them out of Chalco and Tlamanalco, and leave the road to Tlaxcala quite clear, so that one could come and go to Villa Rica without any molestation from the Mexican warriors. As soon as this was arranged he sent some Texcocan Indians very secretly to Chalco to advise the people about it, so that they might be fully prepared to fall on the Mexican garrison either by day or night. As they wished for nothing better, the people of Chalco kept thoroughly prepared.

When Gonzalo de Sandoval marched with his army he left a rearguard of five horsemen and as many crossbowmen to protect the large number of the Tlaxcalans, who were laden with the spoil that they had seized. The Mexicans knew that our people were marching on Chalco, and had got together many squadrons of warriors, who fell on the rearguard where the Tlaxcalans were marching with their spoil, and punished them severely, and our five horsemen and the crossbowmen could not hold out against them, for two of the crossbowmen were killed and the others were wounded, and although Gonzalo de Sandoval promptly turned round on the enemy and defeated them, and killed ten Mexicans, the lake was so near by that the enemy managed to take refuge in the canoes in which they had come.

When the enemy had been put to flight and Sandoval saw that the five horsemen, in the rearguard with the musketeers and crossbowmen, were wounded both they and their horses, and that two crossbowmen were dead and the others wounded, although, I repeat, he saw all this, he did not fail to say to them that they were not worth much for not having been able to resist the enemy and defend themselves and our allies, and that he was very angry with them; they were from among those who had lately come from Spain, and he told them that it was very clear that they did not know what fighting was like. Then he placed in safety all the Tlaxcalan Indians with their spoil, and he also despatched some letters which Cortés was sending to Villa Rica. In these Cortés told the Captain, who had remained in command there, that if there were any soldiers who were disposed to take part in the fighting, that he should send them to Tlaxcala, but that they should not go beyond that town until the roads were safer, for they would run great risk.

When the messengers had been despatched and the Tlaxcalans sent off to their homes, Sandoval turned towards Chalco. As he marched on he saw many squadrons of Mexicans coming against him, and on a level plain, where there were large plantations of maize and magueys, they attacked him fiercely with darts, arrows, and stones from slings, and long lances with which to kill the horses. When Sandoval saw such a host of warriors opposed to him, he cheered on his men and twice broke through the ranks of the enemy, and with the aid of the muskets and crossbows, and the few allies who had stayed with him, he defeated them, although they wounded five soldiers and six horses, and many of our allies. However, he had fallen on them so quickly and with such fury that he made them pay well for the damage they had first done. When the people of Chalco knew that Sandoval was near, they went out to receive him on the road with much honour and rejoicing. In that defeat eight Mexicans were taken prisoner, three of them chieftains of importance.

When all this had been done, Sandoval said that on the following day he wished to return to Texcoco, and the people of Chalco said they wanted to go with him to see and speak to

Malinche and take with them the two sons of the Lord of that province who had died of small-pox a few days before, and before dying had charged all his chieftains and elders to take his sons to see the Captain, so that by his hand they might be installed Lords of Chalco, and that all should endeavour to become subjects of the Great King of the Teules, for it was quite true that his ancestors had told him that men with beards who came from the direction of the sunrise would govern these lands, and from what he had seen, we were those men.

Sandoval soon returned with all his army to Texcoco and took in his company the sons of the Lord of Chalco and the other chieftains, and the eight Mexican prisoners and Cortés was overjoyed at his arrival. The Caciques presented themselves at once before Cortés, and, after having paid him every sign of respect, they told him of the willingness with which they would become vassals of His Majesty, as their father had commanded them to do, and begged that they might receive the chieftainship from his hands. When they had made their speeches, they presented Cortés with rich jewels worth about two hundred pesos de oro. When Cortés thoroughly understood what they had said, he showed them much kindness and embraced them, and under his hand gave the Lordship of Chalco to the elder brother with more than the half of the subject pueblos, and those of Tlamanalco and Chimal he gave to the younger brother together with Ayotzingo and other subject pueblos.

Cortés begged the chieftains to wait in Texcoco for two days, as he was about to send a Captain to Tlaxcala, for the timber and planking, who would take them in his company, and conduct them to their country, so that the Mexicans should not attack them on the road; for this they thanked him greatly and went away well contented.

Let us stop talking about this and say how Cortés decided to send to Mexico the eight prisoners, whom Sandoval had captured in the rout at Chalco, to tell the Prince named Guatemoc, whom the Mexicans had then chosen as king, how greatly he desired to avoid being the cause of his ruin and that of so great a city; he therefore begged them to sue for peace, and he would pardon them for the losses and deaths we had

suffered, and would ask nothing from them. He reminded
Guatemoc that it is easy to remedy a war in the beginning but
very difficult towards the middle and at the end, and that it
would end in their destruction and how could Guatemoc desire all his people to be slain and his city destroyed? He should
bear in mind the great power of our Lord God in whom we
believe and whom we worship, and who always helps us, and
he should always remember that all the pueblos in the neighbourhood were now on our side, that the Tlaxcalans had no
wish but for war, in order to avenge the deaths of their com-
patriots. Let the Mexicans lay down their arms and make
peace, and he [Cortés] would promise them that he would always treat them with great honour. Doña Marina and Aguilar
made use of many other sound arguments and gave them good
advice on the subject. Those eight Indians went before
Guatemoc, but he refused to send any answer whatever, and
went on making dykes and gathering stores, and sending to all
the provinces an order that if any of us could be captured
straying, we should be brought to Mexico to be sacrificed, and
that when he sent to summon them, they should come at once
with their arms, and he sent to remit and free them from
much of their tribute.

†   xcix

As we were always longing to get the launches finished, and to
begin the blockade of Mexico, our Captain Cortés, so as not to
waste time to no purpose, ordered Gonzalo de Sandoval to go
for the timber, and to take with him two hundred soldiers,
twenty musketeers and crossbowmen, fifteen horsemen and a
large company of Tlaxcalans as well as twenty chieftains from
Texcoco; also to take in his company the youths and the elders from Chalco and to place them in safety in their towns.

Before they set out Cortés established a friendship between
the Tlaxcalans and the people of Chalco.

Cortés also ordered Gonzalo de Sandoval to go to a pueblo
subject to Texcoco, where more than forty soldiers of the followers of Narvaez and some of our own men and many Tlaxcalans had been killed, and the people had also stolen three
loads of gold, when we were turned out of Mexico.

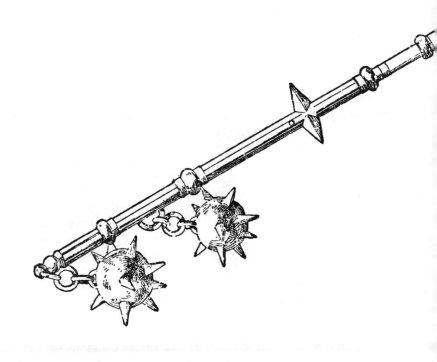

Before our soldiers arrived at this pueblo the people already knew through their spies that they were coming down on them and they abandoned the pueblo and fled to the hills, and Sandoval followed them and killed only three or four of them, for he felt pity for them, but they took some women and girls and captured four chieftains. Much blood of the Spaniards who had been killed was found on the walls of the Temple in that pueblo, for they had sprinkled their Idols with it, and Sandoval also found two faces which had been flayed, and the skin tanned like skin for gloves, the beards were left on, and they had been placed as offerings upon one of the altars. There were also found four tanned skins of horses very well prepared, with the hair on and the horse shoes, and they were hung up before the Idols in the great Cue. There were also found many garments of the Spaniards who had been killed hung up as offerings to these same Idols, and on the pillar of a house where they had been imprisoned there was found written with charcoal: "Here was imprisoned the unfortunate Juan Yuste and many others whom I brought in my company." This Juan Yuste was a gentleman, and was one of the persons of quality whom Narvaez had brought with him. Sandoval and all his soldiers were moved to pity by all this and it grieved them greatly, but, how could the matter now be remedied except by being merciful to the people of the pueblo, however they had fled and would not wait, and had taken their women and children with them. A few women who were captured wept for their husbands and fathers, and when Sandoval saw this, he liberated four chieftains whom he had captured and all the women and sent them to summon the inhabitants of the pueblo, who came and begged for pardon and gave their fealty to His Majesty, and promised always to oppose the Mexicans and to serve us well with all possible affection and good will. When they were asked about the gold they had stolen from the Tlaxcalans who passed that way, they replied that they had taken three loads of it from them, but the Mexicans and the lords of Texcoco had carried it off, for they said that the gold had belonged to Montezuma, who when he was a prisoner had taken it from their temples and given it to Malinche.

So Sandoval went on his way towards Tlaxcala, and when

near the capital where the Caciques reside, he met eight thousand men carrying on their backs all the timber and boards for the launches, and as many more men with their arms and plumes acting as a guard, and two thousand others who brought food and relieved the carriers. There came as commanders of the whole force of Tlaxcalans, Chichimecatecle, and all came in the charge of Martin López who was the Master carpenter who cut the timber and gave the model and dimensions for the boards. When Sandoval saw them approaching he was delighted that they had relieved him from his task, for he expected to be detained some days in Tlaxcala waiting for them to get off with all the timber and planking. In the same order in which they came up to us we accompanied them for two days until we entered Mexican territory. The Mexicans whistled and shouted from their farms and from the barrancas and from other places where we could do them no harm either with our horsemen or our muskets.

Then Martin López said that it would be as well to change the order in which they had hitherto marched for the Tlaxcalans had told him they feared that the powerful forces of Mexico might make a sudden attack in that part of the road, and might defeat them, as they were so heavily laden and hampered by the timber and food they were carrying. So Sandoval at once divided the horsemen and musketeers and crossbowmen, so that some should go in advance and others on the flanks, and he ordered Chichimecatecle to take charge of the Tlaxcalans who were to march behind as a rearguard with Gonzalo de Sandoval himself. The Cacique was offended at this, thinking that they did not consider him a brave man, but they said so much to him on that point, that he became reconciled, seeing that Sandoval himself was to remain with him, and that he was given to understand that the Mexicans always made their attacks on the baggage which was kept towards the rear. When he clearly understood this he embraced Sandoval and said that he felt honoured by what had been done.

Another two days' march brought them to Texcoco, and before entering the city they put on very fine cloaks and plumes, and marched in good order to the sound of drums and trumpets, and in an unbroken line they were half a day marching into the City, shouting, whistling and crying out "Viva, Viva for the Emperor our Lord and Castile! Castile and Tlaxcala! Tlaxcala!"

From that time forward the greatest despatch was used in building the thirteen launches. Martin López was the Master builder, aided by other Spaniards and two blacksmiths with their forges, and some Indian carpenters; and all worked with the greatest speed until the launches were put together, and they only needed to be caulked, and their masts, rigging and sails to be set up. I want to say how great were the precautions that we took in our camp while this was being done, in the matter of spies and scouts and guards for the launches, for they lay near the Lake, and three times the Mexicans tried to set them on fire, and we even captured fifteen of the Indians who had come to set fire to them, and from these men Cortés learned fully what was being done in Mexico and what Guatemoc was planning, and it was that they would never make peace but would either all die fighting, or kill every one of us.

I wish now to mention the summonses and messengers that the Mexicans sent to all their subject pueblos, and how they remitted their tribute, and the work that they carried on both by day and night, of digging ditches and deepening the passages beneath the bridges, and making strong entrenchments and preparing their darts and dart throwers and making very long lances with which to kill the horses, to which were attached the swords that they had captured from us on the night of our defeat.

Let us also speak of the canal and trench by which the launches were to go out into the great Lake, for it was already very broad and deep so that ships of considerable size were able to float in it, for, as I have already said, there were eight thousand Indians always employed on the work.

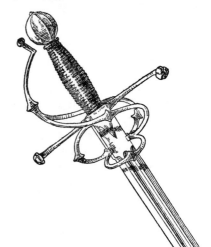

X

Preliminary Expeditions

† c

As over fifteen thousand Tlaxcalans had come to Texcoco with the timber for the launches, and had already been five days in the city without doing anything worth mentioning, and, as they had not brought supplies with them, food was getting scarce, and Chichimecatecle the Captain of the Tlaxcalans being a very valiant and proud man said to Cortés that he wished to go and render some service to our great Emperor by fighting against the Mexicans, both to show his strength and the good will he bore us, as well as to avenge the deaths of his brethren and his vassals, and he begged as a favour from Cortés that he would command and instruct him in what direction he should go and encounter our enemies. Cortés replied to him that he thought very highly of his good-will, and said that he wished to go himself, the next day, to a pueblo named Saltocan, five or six leagues distant from the City of Texcoco, where, although the houses were built in the waters of a lake, there was an entrance from the land. He had sent three times to summon the people of that pueblo to make peace and they refused to do so, but ill-treated the messengers and wounded two of them, and sent as an answer that if we came there we would find forces and a fortress as strong as Mexico, and come when we might, we would find them on the field of battle, for they had received word from their Idols that they would kill us there, and their Idols had advised them to send this reply.

Cortés got ready to go in person on this expedition, and ordered two hundred and fifty soldiers to go in his company with thirty horsemen, and he took with him, Pedro de Alvarado and Cristóbal de Olid and many musketeers and crossbowmen, and all the Tlaxcalans, and a company of warriors from Texcoco, nearly all of them chieftains. He left Gonzalo de Sandoval on guard at Texcoco, and told him to keep a good look out both on the Texcocoans, and the launches and the camp, and see that no attack was made on it by night for, as I have already said, we had always to keep on the alert, on the one hand to guard against the Mexicans themselves and on the other, because we were in such a great city, as was Texcoco, where all the inhabitants of the city were relations and friends of the Mexicans. He also ordered Sandoval and Martin López to have the vessels ready to be launched and to sail within fifteen days.

Then after hearing Mass, Cortés set out with his army; and not far from Saltocan he met great squadrons of Mexicans who were awaiting him in a place where they believed that they could get the better of our Spaniards and kill the horses. Cortés ordered the horsemen as soon as the muskets and crossbows had been discharged, to break in upon the enemy; however, they killed only a few of the Mexicans, who at once took refuge in the bush, and in places where the horsemen could not follow them, but our friends the Tlaxcalans captured and killed about thirty of them.

That night Cortés went to sleep at some huts, and kept a good look-out for they were in a thickly peopled country, and he knew that Guatemoc had sent many squadrons of warriors to Saltocan as reinforcements, and these troops had come in canoes along some deep creeks. Early the next morning the Mexicans and the people of Saltocan began to attack our troops and they shot many darts and arrows at them and slung stones from their slings, from the canals where they were posted, and they wounded ten of our soldiers and many of our Tlaxcalan allies, and our horsemen could do them no hurt, for they could not gallop nor cross the creeks. The causeway and road by which they were used to enter the town from the land had been destroyed and broken down by hand only a few days before. Owing to this, our soldiers found no way by which they could enter the town, or do any damage to its defenders, although they kept up a fire against those who went about in canoes, but the canoes were protected by bulwarks of wood, and besides they took good care not to expose themselves. Our soldiers seeing that they could gain no advantage whatever, and that they could not hit on the road and causeway which was there before, because it was all covered with water, cursed the town and our profitless expedition, and were half ashamed because the Mexicans and townspeople shouted at them and called them women, and said that Malinche was a woman too, and that his only bravery was in deceiving them with stories and lies. Just at this moment, two of the Indians, who had come there with our people, who belonged to the pueblo Tepetezcuco and were very hostile to the people of Saltocan, said to one of our soldiers that three days before they had seen the people of Saltocan breaking open the causeway and they made a ditch across it and turned the water of another canal into it, but that not very far ahead the road began again and led to the town. When our soldiers thoroughly understood this, the musketeers and crossbowmen were ranged in good order, and little by little and not altogether, sometimes skipping along and at other times wading waist deep, all our soldiers crossed over, with many of our allies following them. Cortés and the horsemen, turning their backs on our soldiers, kept guard on the land, for they feared that the Mexican squadrons might again fall on our rear. When our men had passed the canals, the enemy fell on them with fury, and wounded many of them, but as they had made up their minds to gain the causeway which was close by, they still forged ahead until they could attack the enemy on land, clear of the water, and then they got to the town. Without further waste of words they fell on the enemy so fiercely that they killed many of them and repaid them well for the trick they had played. Much cotton cloth and gold and other spoil was taken, but, as the town was built in the lake, the Mexicans and the inhabitants soon got into their canoes with all the property they were able to carry, and went off to Mexico.

When our people saw the town deserted, they burned some of the houses, and as they did not dare to sleep there because the town stood in the water, they returned to where Captain Cortés was awaiting them.

The next day they marched to the great pueblo named

Guautitlan, and as they went on their way, the Indians from the neighbouring villages, and many Mexicans who had joined them, yelled and whistled and shouted insults at our men, but they kept to the canals and the places where the horsemen could not gallop and no harm could be done to them. In this way, our troops arrived at the town, which had been abandoned that same day and all property carried off. That night they slept there, well guarded by sentinels and patrols, and the following day marched on to the great pueblo called Tenayuca. They found this pueblo deserted like the last, and all the Indian inhabitants had assembled together in another town further on called Tacuba. From Tenayuca they marched to Atzcapotzalco, about half a league distant one from the other, and this too was deserted. This town of Atzcapotzalco was where they used to work the gold and silver for the great Montezuma. From there they marched to Tacuba, a distance of half a league, and this is the place where we halted on that sad night when we came out from Mexico routed.

Before our army could reach the town it was met in the open by a large number of troops which were lying in wait, gathered from all the pueblos through which our army had passed, as well as those from Tacuba and Mexico, for Mexico was close by. All of them together began an attack on our people in such a manner that our Captain and the horsemen had all they could do to break through their ranks, so close did they keep together. However, our soldiers with good sword play forced them to retreat; then, as it was night-time, they went to sleep in the town after posting sentinels and watchmen.

If there had been many Mexicans gathered together that day, there were many more on the next morning, and in excellent order they advanced to attack our people with such energy that they killed and wounded some of our soldiers. Nevertheless, our men forced them to retreat to their houses and fortresses, so that they found time to enter Tacuba and burn and sack many of the houses. When this was known in Mexico, many more squadrons were ordered to go forth from the city to fight against Cortés, and it was arranged that when they fought with him, they should pretend to turn in flight towards Mexico, and little by little they should draw our army on to the causeway until they had them well on to it, and that they should behave as though they were retreating out of fear.

As it was arranged, so they carried it out, and Cortés, believing that he was gaining a victory, ordered the enemy to be followed as far as a bridge. When the Mexicans thought that they had already got Cortés in their trap, and the bridge had been crossed, a huge multitude of Indians turned on him, some in canoes and others by land, and others on the azoteas, and they placed him in such straits and matters looked so serious that he believed himself to be defeated, for at the bridge that he had reached, they fell on him with such force that he could effect little or nothing. A standard bearer, in resisting the charge of the enemy, was badly wounded and fell with his banner from the bridge into the water, and was in danger of being drowned, and the Mexicans had even seized him to drag him into a canoe, but he was so strong that he escaped with his banner. In that fight they killed four or five of our soldiers and wounded many of them, and Cortés, recognizing the great audacity and want of forethought that he had shown in going on to the causeway in the way I have related, and feeling that the Mexicans had caught him in a trap, ordered all his followers to retire in the best order possible without turning their backs, but with their faces towards the enemy and hand to hand as though resisting an onset. The horsemen made some charges, but they were very few, for the horses were soon wounded. In this way, Cortés escaped that time from the power of the Mexicans, and when he got on dry land he gave great thanks to God.

During the five days that Cortés stayed in Tacuba, he had encounters and battles with the Mexicans, and he then returned to Texcoco along the road by which he had come.

By long marches, Cortés arrived at a pueblo subject to Texcoco, named Aculman, about two leagues and a half distant from Texcoco, and as soon as we knew that he had arrived there we went out with Gonzalo de Sandoval to see him and receive him, accompanied by the Caciques of Texcoco. We were greatly delighted at the sight of Cortés, for we had known nothing of what had happened to him for fifteen days. After welcoming him we returned to Texcoco that afternoon, for we did not dare to leave the camp without a sufficient guard. The Tlaxcalans, as they were now rich and came laden with spoil, asked leave to return to their homes, and Cortés granted it, and they went by a road where the Mexicans could not spy on them and saved their property.

At the end of four days, during which our Captain was resting, and hurrying on the building of the launches, the people from some pueblos on the North Coast came to ask for peace and offer themselves as vassals to His Majesty. At this same time, there came messengers from other pueblos who had become our friends, saying that we must come and help them because great squadrons of Mexicans were coming against them and had entered their territory and were carrying off many of their Indians as prisoners, and had wounded others. There also came people from Chalco and Tlamanalco who said that if we did not come to their assistance they would all be lost, and told a most pitiful tale, and brought a piece of henequen cloth, painted with an exact representation of the squadrons of Mexicans which had come against them. Cortés did not know what to say, nor how to answer them or help them, for he had seen that many of our soldiers were wounded and ill, and eight had died of pains in the back, and from throwing up clotted blood mixed with mud from the mouth and nose, and it was from the fatigue of always wearing armour on our backs, and from the everlasting going on expeditions and from the dust that we swallowed. In addition to this, three or four horses had died of their wounds, yet we never stopped going on expeditions. So the answer he gave to the first pueblos was to flatter them, and to say that he would soon come to help them, but that while he was on the way they should get help from their neighbours. He said so much to them, through our interpreters, that he encouraged and put heart into them. As Cortés had ordered them, they awaited the Mexicans in the open and fought a battle with them, and with the help of our allies, their neighbours, they did not do badly.

Let us return to the people of Chalco; as our Cortés saw how important it was for us that this province and the road through it should be freed from Mexicans (for it was the way we had to come and go to Villa Rica de la Vera Cruz and to Tlaxcala, and we had to supply our camp from that province, for it was a land that produced much maize), he at once ordered Gonzalo de Sandoval to get ready to start the next morning for Chalco, and he ordered him to take twenty horsemen and two hundred soldiers, twelve crossbowmen and ten musketeers and the Tlaxcalans who were in camp, who were very few (for the greater number of them had gone to their homes laden with spoil) and Sandoval also took with him a company of Texcocoans, and Captain Luis Marin who was his intimate friend. Cortés and Pedro de Alvarado and Cristóbal de Olid remained behind to guard the city and the launches.

Introductory Note

During the expeditions described in the four following chapters, the Spaniards passed out of the Valley of Mexico through the gap between the Serrania of Ajusco and the slopes of Popocatapetl, and descended into the plains of Morelos and Cuernavaca. The towns of Yecapixtla, Oaxtepec, Yautepec, and Cuernavaca all stand at somewhat the same altitude, about 5,000 ft. above the level of the sea and a little more than 2,000 ft. below the level of the Valley of Mexico. The Serrania of Ajusco, with its innumerable extinct craters and somewhat recent lava fields, and the mass of Popocatapetl, form a lofty barrier to the north of these towns, which is edged near Tepostlan and towards the East by a fringe of broken and abrupt conglomerate rock, forming hills and cliffs, with spurs running southward into the plains of Morelos and Cuernavaca. Just to the south of this rampart, several isolated hills of a few hundred feet in height arise somewhat abruptly from the plain, and it was on one of these hills (probably Tlayacapan), which lies halfway between Yecapixtla and Tepostlan, that the Indians took refuge.

Neither Bernal Díaz nor Cortés appear to have visited Yecapixtla, and their descriptions of its position are somewhat misleading. The town is not situated on a lofty eminence, but, like Cuernavaca, although on slightly rising ground, it hardly stands out from the surrounding plain. These plains slope gradually to the south, and are deeply scored by the numerous small streams which, flowing from the mountains to the north, have cut their way deep down through soil and rock, forming ravines or barrancas, which, in chosen spots, render fortifications almost unnecessary. Both Yecapixtla and Cuernavaca are nearly surrounded by such ravines.

†   CI

After hearing Mass, Sandoval set out on the 12th March in the year 1521, and slept at some farms belonging to Chalco, and on the next morning arrived at Tlamanalco where the Caciques and Captains gave him a good reception and provided food, and advised him to go at once in the direction of a great pueblo called Oaxtepec, for he would find the whole of the Mexican forces either assembled at Oaxtepec or on the road thither; and they said that all the warriors from the province of Chalco would accompany him.

Sandoval set out at once, and went on to sleep at a pueblo subject to Chalco called Chimaluacan, for the spies, sent by the people of Chalco to watch the Culuas, came to report that the enemy's forces were lying in wait for them in some rocky defiles in the neighbourhood of that town. As the enemy was posted in broken ground and it was not known if they had dug pits or raised barricades, Sandoval wished to keep his soldiers well in hand so as to avoid any disaster.

As he continued his march he saw the Mexican squadrons approaching him in three divisions, shouting and whistling and sounding trumpets and drums, and they came on to the attack like fierce lions. Sandoval told the horsemen to charge them at once before they could reach our men. Cheering on his troops by shouting: "Santiago and at them!" Sandoval led the charge himself, and by that movement, he routed some of the Mexican squadrons, but not all of them, so that they soon turned and showed a firm front, for they were helped by the bad track and broken ground, and the horsemen owing to the rough ground were not able to gallop and could not get in rear of them. To finish my story, the Mexicans were forced into retreat but their flight was towards other bad passes. Sandoval and the horsemen went in pursuit, but overtook only three or four of the enemy. During that pursuit, owing to the badness of the road, the horse of a cavalryman, named Gonzalo Domínguez, fell with his rider beneath him, and the man died from his injuries within a few days. I call this to mind because Gonzalo Domínguez was one of the best horsemen and one of the most valiant men that Cortés had brought in his Company, and we held him in much esteem for his valour, so that we all felt the loss greatly.

To go back to Sandoval and his army; they followed the enemy to the neighbourhood of the pueblo of Oaxtepec, but before reaching the town, over fifteen thousand Mexicans emerged from it and began to surround our soldiers and wounded many of them and five horses, but as the ground was level in some places, our horsemen, making a united effort, broke up two of their squadrons, and the rest turned tail and fled towards the town in order to guard some barricades which they had raised, but our soldiers and the allies followed so close that they had no time to defend them, and the horsemen kept up the pursuit in other directions until they had shut the enemy up in a part of the town where they could not be reached. Thinking that the enemy would not again renew the attack on that day, Sandoval ordered his men to rest and tend their wounds, and they began to take their food. While they were eating, two horsemen and two soldiers who had been told off as scouts before the men began to eat, ran in crying: "To arms, to arms; the Mexicans are coming in great force." As they were always accustomed to have their arms in readiness, the horsemen were soon mounted and they came out into a great plaza. At that moment the enemy were upon them, and there they fought another good battle. After the enemy had been for some time showing us a good front from some barricades and wounding some of our men, Sandoval fell on them so suddenly with his horsemen that with the help of the muskets and crossbows and the sword-play of the soldiers, he drove them from the town into some neighbouring barrancas, and they did not come back again that day.

When Captain Sandoval found himself free from that struggle, he gave thanks to God and went to rest and sleep in an orchard within the town, which was so beautiful and contained such fine buildings that it was the best worth beholding of anything we had seen in New Spain. There were so many things in it to look at that it was really wonderful and was certainly the orchard of a great prince, and they could not go all through it then, for it was more than a quarter of a league in length.

Let us stop talking about the orchard and say that I did not go myself on this expedition, nor did I then walk about this orchard, but I went there about twenty days later when, in company with Cortés, we made the round of the great towns of the lakes, as I shall tell later on. The reason why I did not go this first time was because I had been badly wounded by a spear-thrust in the throat, and was in danger of dying from it, and I still bear the scar. The wound was given me during the Iztapalapa affair, when they tried to drown us.

On the following day Gonzalo de Sandoval sent messengers to treat for peace, but the Caciques did not dare to come in for fear of the Mexicans.

†   CII

The same day, Sandoval sent to another large pueblo called Yecapixtla, about two leagues distant from Oaxtepec, to tell the people to take warning from what had happened to the squadrons of Culuas stationed in the pueblo of Oaxtepec, and to make peace and expel the Mexican garrisons who were guarding their country, and that if they did not do so he would come and make war on them and chastise them. The answer returned was that the Spaniards might come when they liked, for they were looking forward to feast on their flesh and provide sacrifices for their Idols.

When this reply was given, the Caciques from Chalco, who were with Sandoval, knew that there must be a large force of Mexicans in garrison at Yecapixtla ready to make war on Chalco as soon as Sandoval should retire; and for this reason they begged him to go to Yecapixtla and drive the Mexicans out of the place. However, Sandoval was not willing to go, one reason being that many of his soldiers and horses were wounded, and the other that he had already fought three battles and he did not wish to exceed the instructions that Cortés had given him. Moreover, some of the gentlemen whom he had brought in his company, men from the army of Narvaez, advised him to return to Texcoco and not go to Yecapixtla, which was strongly fortified, lest some disaster should befall him. However, the Captain, Luis Marin, counselled him not to fail to go to that fortress and do what he could, for the Caciques from Chalco said that if he turned back without defeating the force which was assembled in that fortress, that as soon as they saw or heard that he had returned to Texcoco, the enemy would at once attack Chalco. Sandoval, therefore, decided to go to Yecapixtla.

As soon as he came in sight of the town, a host of warriors came out and began to shoot darts and arrows and cast stones from their slings, so that they fell like hail, and three horses and many soldiers were wounded without our men being able to do any harm to the enemy.

As Sandoval observed that the Caciques from Chalco and their Captains and many of the Indian warriors were manoeuvring round about without daring to attack the enemy, on purpose to try them and to see what they would answer, Sandoval said to them, "What are you doing: why don't you begin to fight and get into the town and fortress, for we are here and will defend you." They replied that they did not dare to do it, that the enemy were in a stronghold, and it was for this very purpose that Sandoval and his brother Teules had come with them and that the people of Chalco had come under his protection relying on his help to drive the enemy out.

So Sandoval and all his soldiers began the attack, and many were wounded as they clambered up [the sides of the ravines] and Sandoval himself was again wounded in the head, and many of our allies were wounded, for they too entered the town and did much damage to it, and it was the Indians from Chalco and our allies from Tlaxcala who did most damage to the enemy, for our soldiers after breaking up their ranks and putting them to flight, would not give a sword-thrust at the enemy, for it seemed to them mere cruelty, and they were chiefly occupied in looking out for pretty Indian women or seeking for plunder, and they frequently quarrelled with our allies on account of their cruelty, and took the Indian men and women away from them to prevent their being killed.

I must go on to say that when this was over, Sandoval and all his army returned to Texcoco with much spoil, especially of good-looking Indian women.

When the lord of Mexico, who was called Guatemoc, heard of the defeat of his armies it is said that he showed much resentment at it, and still more at the thought that the people of Chalco, who were his subjects and vassals, should dare to take up arms three times against his forces.

He was so angry that he resolved that as soon as Sandoval

should return to his camp at Texcoco he would send out a great force of warriors, which he at once assembled in the city of Mexico, and another force which was got together from the lake, equipped with every sort of arms, and would despatch this force, numbering over twenty thousand Mexicans, in two thousand large canoes to make a sudden descent on Chalco, to do all the damage that it was possible to do.

This was all accomplished with such skill and rapidity that Sandoval had hardly arrived at Texcoco and spoken to Cortés, when again messengers came in canoes across the lake begging help from Cortés, telling him that more than two thousand canoes carrying over twenty thousand Mexicans had come to Chalco, and they begged him to come at once to their assistance.

At the very moment that Cortés heard this news Sandoval came to speak to him and to give him an account of what he had done during the expedition from which he had just then returned, but Cortés was so angry with him he would not listen to him, believing that it was through some fault or carelessness on his part that our friends at Chalco were experiencing this trouble, and without any delay, and without listening to him, Cortés ordered Sandoval to leave all his wounded men in camp and to go back again in all haste with those who were sound.

Sandoval was much distressed at the words Cortés used to him, and at his refusal to listen to him, but he set out at once for Chalco where his men arrived tired out with the weight of their arms and their long march. It appears that the people of Chalco, learning through their spies that the Mexicans were coming so suddenly upon them, and that Guatemoc had determined that they should be attacked, before any help could reach them from us, had sent to summon aid from the people of the province of Huexotzingo which was near by, and the men from Huexotzingo arrived that same night, all equipped with their arms, and joined with those from Chalco, so that in all there were more than twenty thousand of them. As they had already lost their fear of the Mexicans they quietly awaited their arrival in camp and fought like brave men, and although the Mexicans killed many of them and took many prisoners, the people of Chalco killed many more of the Mexicans and took as prisoners fifteen captains and chieftains and many other warriors of lesser rank. The Mexicans looked upon this battle as a much greater disgrace, seeing that the people of Chalco had defeated them, than if they had been defeated by us.

When Sandoval arrived at Chalco and found that there was nothing for him to do, and nothing more to be feared as the Mexicans would not return again to Chalco, he marched back again to Texcoco and took the Mexican prisoners with him.

Whereat Cortés was delighted but Sandoval showed great resentment towards our captain for what had happened, and did not go to see or speak to him, until Cortés sent to tell him that he had misunderstood the affair, thinking that it was through some carelessness on his part that things had gone wrong, and that although he had set out with a large force of soldiers and horsemen he had returned without defeating the Mexicans.

I will cease speaking about this matter, for Cortés and Sandoval soon became fast friends again and there was nothing Cortés would not do to please Sandoval.

As Gonzalo de Sandoval had arrived in Texcoco with a great booty of slaves and there were many others which had been captured in the late expeditions, it was decided that they should at once be branded. When proclamation was made, most of us soldiers took those slaves that we possessed to be marked with the brand of His Majesty, in the way that we had already arranged with Cortés. We thought that our slaves would be returned to us after the Royal fifth had been paid, and that a price would be put on the women slaves in accordance with the value of each one of them. However it was not so done, and if the affair was badly managed at Tepeaca, it was managed much worse here at Texcoco. From this time on many of us soldiers when we captured good-looking Indian women hid them away and did not take them to be branded, but gave out that they had escaped; or if we were favourites of Cortés we took them secretly by night to be branded, and they were valued at their worth, the Royal fifth paid and they were marked with the iron. Many others remained in our lodgings and we said that they were free servants from the pueblos that had made peace, or from Tlaxcala.

About this time a ship arrived from Spain in which came Julian de Alderete, as His Majesty's Treasurer.

A great store of arms and powder was also brought in this ship, in fact as was to be expected in a ship coming from Spain it came well laden, and we rejoiced at its arrival and at the news from Spain that it brought.

Cortés now saw that the building of the launches was finished, and noted the eagerness of all of us soldiers to commence the siege of Mexico.

† CIII

As Cortés had told the people of Chalco that he was coming to help them so that the Mexicans should no longer come and attack them (for we had been going there and back every week to assist them) he ordered a force of soldiers to be prepared, and they were three hundred soldiers, thirty horsemen, twenty crossbowmen and fifteen musketeers, and the Treasurer Julian de Alderete, Pedro de Alvarado, Andrés de Tápia, Cristóbal de Olid, and the Friar Pedro Melgarejo went also, and Cortés ordered me to go with him, and there were many Tlaxcalans and allies from Texcoco in his company. He left Gonzalo de Sandoval behind with a good company of soldiers and horsemen to guard Texcoco and the launches.

On the morning of Friday the 5th April, 1521, after hearing Mass we set out for Tlamanalco, where we were well received, and we slept there. The next day we went to Chalco, for the one town is quite close to the other, and there Cortés ordered all the Caciques of the province to be called together, and he made them a speech, in which he gave them to understand that we were now going to try whether we could bring to peace some of the towns in the neighbourhood of the lake, and also to view the land and position before blockading Mexico, and that we were going to place thirteen launches on the lake, and he begged them to be ready to accompany us on the next day with all their warriors. When they understood this, all with one voice promised that they would willingly do what we asked.

The next day we went to sleep at Chimaluacan, and there we met more than twenty thousand allies from Chalco, Texcoco, and Huexotzingo and from Tlaxcala and other towns, and in all the expeditions in which I have been engaged in New

Spain, never have I known so many of our allied warriors to accompany us as joined us now.

About this time we received news, that in a plain near by, there were many companies and squadrons of Mexicans and all their allies from the country round about waiting to attack us. So Cortés held us in readiness and after hearing Mass we set out early in the morning from the pueblo of Chimaluacan, and marched among some high rocks between two hills where there were fortifications and barricades, where many Indians both men and women were safely sheltered, and from these strongholds they yelled and shouted at us, but we did not care to attack them, but kept quietly on our way, and arrived at a plain where there were some springs with very little water. On one side was a high rocky hill[1] with a fortress very difficult to subdue, as the attempt soon proved, and we saw that it was crowded with warriors, and from the summit they shouted at us and threw stones and shot darts and arrows, and wounded three of our soldiers. Then Cortés ordered us to halt there, and said: "It seems that all these Mexicans who shut themselves up in fortresses make mock of us as long as we do not attack them," and he ordered some horsemen and crossbowmen to go round to the other side of the hill and see if there was a more convenient opening whence to attack them. They returned to say that the best approach was where we then were, for there was no other place where it was possible to climb up, for it was all steep rock. Then Cortés ordered us to make an attack. The Standard Bearer Cristóbal del Corral led the way with other ensigns and all of us followed him while Cortés and the horsemen kept guard on the plain, so that no other troops of Mexicans should fall on the baggage or on us during our attack on the stronghold. As we began to climb up the hill, the Indians who were posted above rolled down so many huge stones and rocks that it was terrifying to see them hurtling and bounding down, and it was a miracle that we were not all of us killed. One soldier named Martínez fell dead at my feet; he had a helmet on his head but he gave no cry and never spoke another word. Still we kept on, but as the great *Galgas,* as we call these big rocks in this country, came rolling and tearing and bounding down and breaking in pieces, they soon killed two more good soldiers, Gaspar Sánchez,

[1] Probably Tlayacapan.

nephew of the Treasurer of Cuba, and a man named Bravo, but still we kept on. Then another valiant soldier named Alonzo Rodríguez was killed, and two others were wounded in the head, and nearly all the rest were wounded in the legs, and still we persevered and pushed on ahead.

As I was active in those days, I kept on following the Standard Bearer Corral, and we got beneath some hollows and cavities which there were in the hillside so as to avoid a chance rock hitting us and I clambered up from hollow to hollow to escape being killed. The Standard Bearer Cristóbal del Corral sheltered himself behind some thick trees covered with thorns which grow in these hollows, his face was streaming with blood and his banner was broken, and he called out: "Oh Señor Bernal Díaz del Castillo, it is impossible to go on any further, keep in the shelter of the hollow and take care that none of those galgas or boulders strike you, for one can hardly hold on with one's hands and feet, much less climb any higher." Just then I saw that Pedro Barba, a captain of the crossbowmen, and two other soldiers were coming up in the same way that Corral and I had done, climbing from hollow to hollow. I called out from above: "Señor Capitan, don't come up any further, for you can't hold on with hands and feet, but will roll down again." When I said this to him he replied as though he were very valiant, or some great lord and could make no other reply: "Go ahead." I took that reply as a personal insult, and answered him: "Let us see you come to where I am," and I went up still higher. At that very moment such a lot of great stones came rolling down on us from above where they had stored them for the purpose, that Pedro Barba was wounded and one soldier killed, and they could not climb a single step higher.

Then the Standard Bearer Corral cried out that they should pass the word to Cortés, from mouth to mouth, that we could not get any higher, and that to retreat was equally dangerous.

When Cortés heard this he understood what was happening, for there below where he stood on the level ground two or three soldiers had been killed and seven of them wounded by the great impetus of the boulders which were hurled down on them, and Cortés thought for certain that nearly all of us who had made the ascent must have been killed or badly wounded, for from where he stood he could not see the folds in the hill. So by signs and shouts and by the shots that they fired, we up above knew that they were meant as signals for us to retreat, and in good order we descended from hollow to hollow, our bodies bruised and streaming with blood, the banners rent, and eight men dead. When Cortés saw us he gave thanks to God and they related to him what had happened between Pedro Barba and me. Pedro Barba himself and the Standard Bearer Corral were telling him about the great strength of the hill and that it was a marvel that the boulders did not carry us away as they flew down, and the story was soon known throughout the camp.

Let us leave these empty tales and say how there were many companies of Mexicans lying in wait in places where we could neither see nor observe them, hoping to bring help and succour to those posted on the hill, for they well knew that we should not be able to force our way into the stronghold, and they had arranged while we were fighting to attack us in the rear. When Cortés knew that they were approaching, he ordered the horsemen and all of us to go and attack them, and this we did, for the ground was level in places as there were fields lying between the small hills, and we pursued the enemy until they reached another very strong hill.

We killed very few Indians during the pursuit for they took refuge in places where we could not reach them. So we returned to the stronghold which we had attempted to scale, and seeing that there was no water there, and that neither we nor the horses had had anything to drink that day, for the springs which I have spoken about as being there contained nothing but mud, because the many allies whom we had brought with us crowded into them and would not let them flow. For this reason orders were given to shift our camp, and we went down through some fields to another hill which was distant from the first about a league and a half, thinking that we should find water there, but we found very little of it. Near this hill were some native mulberry trees and there we camped, and there were some twelve or thirteen houses at the foot of the stronghold. As soon as we arrived the Indians began to shout and shoot darts and arrows and roll down boulders from above.

There were many more people in this fortress than there were in the first hill, and it was much stronger, as we afterwards found out.

Our musketeers and crossbowmen fired up at them but they
were so high up and protected by so many barricades that we
could not do them any harm, besides there was no possibility
of climbing up and forcing our way in. Although we made
two attempts, from the houses that stood there, over some steps
by which we could mount up for two stages, beyond that it
was worse than the first hill, so that we did not increase our
reputation at this stronghold any more than at the first, and the
victory lay with the Mexicans and their allies.

†   CIV

That night we slept in the mulberry grove and were half dead
with thirst. It was arranged that on the next day all the musketeers and crossbowmen should go to another hill which was
close by the large one, and should climb up it, for there was a
way up although it was not an easy one, to see if from that hill
their muskets and crossbows would carry as far as the stronghold on the other, so that they could attack it. Cortés ordered
Francisco Verdugo and the Treasurer Juan de Alderete, who
boasted that they were good crossbowmen, and Pedro Barba
who was a Captain, to go as leaders, and all the rest of the soldiers to attack from the steps and tracks above the houses
which I have already spoken of, and to climb up as best we
could. So we began the ascent, but they hurled down so many
stones both great and small that many of the soldiers were
wounded, and in addition to this it was quite useless to attempt
the ascent, for even using both our hands and feet we could
climb no further. While we were making these attempts the
musketeers and crossbowmen from the other hill of which I
have spoken, managed to reach the enemy with their muskets
and crossbows but they could only just do it, however they
killed some and wounded others. In this way we went on attacking them for about half an hour when it pleased our Lord
God that they agreed to make peace. The reason why they did
so was that they had not got a drop of water, and there was a
great number of people on the level ground on the hill top and
the people from all the neighbourhood round had taken refuge
there both men, women and children and slaves. So that we
down below should understand that they wished for peace, the

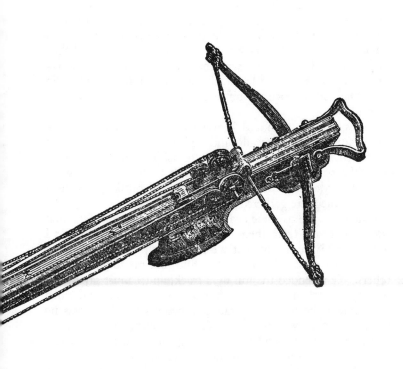

women on the hill waved their shawls and clapped the palms of their hands together as a sign that they would make bread or tortillas for us and the warriors ceased shooting arrows and darts and hurling down stones.

When Cortés observed this he ordered that no more harm should be done to them, and by signs he made them understand that five of their chiefs should come down to treat for peace. When they came down with much reverence they asked Cortés to pardon them for having protected and defended themselves by taking refuge in that stronghold. Cortés replied somewhat angrily that they deserved death for having begun the war, but as they had come to make peace, they must go at once to the other hill and summon the Caciques and chiefs who were stationed there and bring in the dead bodies, and that if they came in peace he would pardon what had happened, if not, that we should attack them and besiege them until they died of thirst, for we knew well that there too they had no water, for there is very little in all that part of the country. So they went off at once to summon the Caciques as they were told to do.

Cortés sent the Standard Bearer Corral, and two other captains namely Juan Jaramillo and Pedro de Ircio and me, who happened to be there with them, to ascend the hill and see what the stronghold was like, whether there were many Indians wounded or killed by the arrows and muskets and how many people were gathered there.

· When he gave us these orders he said, "Look to it, Sirs, that you do not take from them a single grain of maize," and as I understood it he meant that we should help ourselves, and it was for that reason that he sent us and told me to go with the others. We ascended the hill by a track, and I must say that it was stronger than the first hill for it was sheer rock, and when we reached the top the entrance into the stronghold was no wider than the two mouths of a silo or an oven. At the very top it was level ground and there was a great breadth of meadow land all crowded with people, both warriors and many women and children, and we found twenty dead men and many wounded, and they had not a drop of water to drink. All their clothes and other property was done up in bundles and there were many bales of cloaks which were the tribute they paid to Guatemoc, and when I saw so many loads of cloths and knew

that it was intended for tribute I began to load four Tlaxcalans, my free servants whom I had brought with me, and I
also put four other bales on the backs of four other Indians
who were guarding the tribute, one bale on each man's back.
When Pedro de Ircio saw this he said that the bales should not
be taken, and I contended that they should, but as he was Captain, I did as he ordered, for he threatened to tell Cortés about
it. Pedro de Ircio said to me that I had heard what Cortés had
said, that we should not take a single grain of maize, and I replied that was true, and that it was on account of those very
words I wished to carry off these robes. However, he would not
let me carry off anything at all, and we went down to tell
Cortés what we had seen. Then Pedro de Ircio said to Cortés:
"I took nothing from them although Bernal Díaz del Castillo
had already laden eight Indians with cloth and would have
brought them away loaded had I not stopped him." Then
Cortés replied, half angrily: "Why did he not bring them, you
ought to have stayed there with the cloth and the Indians,"
and he added: "See how they understand me, I send them to
help themselves, and from Bernal Díaz, who did understand
me, they took away the spoil which he was taking from those
dogs who will sit there laughing at us in the company of those
whom we have killed and wounded."

When Pedro de Ircio heard this he wished to go up to the
stronghold again, but he was told that there was no reason for
his going, and that on no account should he return there.

Let us leave this talk and say that the people from the other
hill came in, and, after much discussion about their being pardoned for their past deeds, all gave their fealty to His Majesty.
As there was no water in that place we went at once to a fine
pueblo already mentioned by me in the last chapter called
Oaxtepec, where is the garden which I have said is the best
that I have ever seen in all my life, and so said the Treasurer
Alderete and the monk Fray Pedro Melgarejo and our Cortés.
When they saw it and walked about in it they admired it
greatly and said that they had never seen a better garden in
Spain. I must add that we all found quarters in the garden that
night. The Caciques of the town came to speak and offer their
services to Cortés, for Gonzalo de Sandoval had already
brought them to peace when he entered the town. That night
we slept there and the next morning very early we left for

Yautepec and we met some squadrons of Mexicans who had
come out from that town and the horsemen pursued them
more than a league and a half until they took refuge in another
large pueblo called Tepostlan where the inhabitants were so
completely off their guard that we fell upon them before their
spies whom they had sent to watch us could reach them.

Here we found some very good-looking Indian women and
much spoil, but none of the Mexicans nor any of the inhabitants waited for us in the town, so Cortés sent three or four
times to summon the Caciques to come and make peace, and
said that if they did not come he would burn the town and go
in search of them. They replied that they did not mean to
come, therefore, so as to strike fear into the other pueblos,
Cortés ordered half the houses round about to be set on fire.
At that very moment the Caciques from the pueblo that we
had passed that day called Yautepec came and gave their fealty
to His Majesty. The next day we took the road for a much better and larger town named Coadlabaca (at the present time we
usually alter the spelling and call it Cuernavaca), and it was
garrisoned by many warriors both Mexican and Native, and
was very strong on account of the Barrancas more than eight
fathoms deep, with running water at the bottom, but the volume of water is small. However, they make the place into a
stronghold and there was no way of entering for horses except
by two bridges which had already been broken down. This
protection was sufficient to prevent our forcing an entrance so
we fought with them from across the stream and ravine, and
they shot many arrows and lances at us and hurled stones from
their slings, so that they fell thicker than hail. While this was
happening Cortés was informed that about half a league further on there was a place where horses could pass, and he at
once set off with all the horsemen while all of us remained
looking for some way to get across, and we saw that by means
of some trees which stood near the edge one could get over to
the other side of that deep ravine, and although three soldiers
fell from the trees into the water below, and one of them broke
his leg, nevertheless we did cross over although the danger was
great. As for me I will say truly that when I was crossing and
saw how bad and dangerous the passage was, I turned quite
giddy, still I got across, I and others of our soldiers and many
Tlaxcalans, and we fell on the rear of the Mexicans who were

shooting stones and darts and arrows at our people, and when they saw us they could not believe it and thought that we were more numerous than we were. At that moment Cristóbal de Olid and Andrés de Tápia and other horsemen who at great risk had crossed by a broken bridge, arrived on the scene and we fell on the enemy so that they turned their backs and fled into the thickets about the deep ravine where we could not reach them. Soon afterwards Cortés himself arrived with the rest of the horsemen.

In this town we took great spoil both of large bales of cloth as well as good-looking women. Cortés ordered us to remain there that day and we all found quarters in the beautiful garden of the chief of the town.

Although I feel bound to speak many times in the course of this story about the great precautions of sentinels, spies and scouts which were taken wherever we were, whether encamped or on the march, it would be tedious to repeat it too often, and for this reason I will go on and say that our scouts came to tell Cortés that twenty Indians were approaching, and that from their movements and appearance they seemed to be Caciques and chieftains who were bringing messages or coming to seek for peace. They proved to be the Caciques of the town, and when they arrived where Cortés was standing they paid him great respect and presented him with some gold jewels and asked him to pardon them for not meeting him peacefully, but they said the Lord of Mexico commanded them to stay in their stronghold and thence to make war on us, and had sent a large force of Mexicans to aid them, but from what they had now seen, there was no place, however strong it might be, that we would not attack and dominate, and they begged Cortés to have mercy and make peace with them. Cortés received them graciously, and they then gave their fealty to His Majesty.

†   cv

The next day we set out towards Xochimilco,[1] which is a great city where nearly all the houses are built in a fresh water lake,

[1] The march from Cuernavaca to Xochimilco must have been very arduous, as it was necessary to cross the desolate Serrania de Aljvisco by a pass of not less than 10,000 feet in altitude.

distant about two and a half leagues from Mexico. We marched
with great circumspection and in close order and we passed
through some pine forests, but there was no water whatever
along the road. As we carried our arms on our backs and it was
already late and the sun was very hot we suffered much from
thirst, but we did not know if there was any water ahead of us,
for we had marched two or three leagues, and we were still
uncertain how far off was the pool which we had been told
was on the road. When Cortés saw that the whole of the army
was tired out and our allies the Tlaxcalans were dispirited, and
one of them had died of thirst, and I believe one of our soldiers
who was old and ailing also died of thirst, he ordered a halt to
be made in the shade of some pine trees and sent six horsemen
ahead on the road to Xochimilco to see how far off the nearest
village, or farm, or pool of water might be, so that we might
know if it were near and might go and sleep there.

When the horsemen set out, I made up my mind to step
aside so that neither Cortés nor the horsemen should see me,
and with my three strong and active Tlaxcalan servants I followed behind the horsemen until they observed me coming
behind them, and stopped in order to turn me back for fear
that there should be some unexpected attack by Mexican warriors from which I could not defend myself. Nevertheless I
preferred to go on with them, and Cristóbal de Olid, as he was
a friend of mine, said that I might go but should keep my
hands ready to fight and my feet ready to place myself in safety
if there was any fear of warriors, however, my thirst was so
great that I would have risked my life to satisfy it. About half
a league ahead there were a number of farms and cottages on
the hillsides belonging to the people of Xochimilco. The horsemen left me and went to search for pools of water and they
found some and satisfied their thirst, and one of my Tlaxcalans
brought out of a house a large pitcher of very cold water (for
they have very large pitchers in that country) from which I
quenched my thirst, and so did they.

Then I determined to return to where Cortés was resting,
for the dwellers in the farms were already giving the call to
arms and shouting and whistling at us. With the help of the
Tlaxcalans I carried along the pitcher full of water and I
found Cortés who was beginning to march again with his
army. I told him that there was water at the farms near by and

that I had already had a drink and was bringing water in a pitcher which the Tlaxcalans were bringing very carefully hidden, so that it should not be taken from me, for thirst has no laws, and Cortés and some of the other gentlemen drank from it, and he was well satisfied and all were rejoiced and hastened on their march so that we arrived at the farms before the sun had set.

Water was found in the houses, but not very much of it, and owing to the hunger and thirst that they suffered some of the soldiers ate some plants like thistles which hurt their tongues and mouths.

Just then the horsemen returned and reported that the pool of water was a long way off, and that all the country was being called to arms, and that it would be advisable to sleep where we were. So sentinels and watchmen and scouts were at once posted and I was one of the watchmen, and I remember that it rained a little that night and there was a very high wind.

The next day very early in the morning we began our march again and about eight o'clock we arrived at Xochimilco. I cannot estimate the great number of the warriors who were waiting for us, some on the land and others in a passage by a broken bridge, and the great number of breast works and barricades which had been thrown up, and the lances which they carried made from the swords captured from us during the great slaughter on the causeways at Mexico. I say that all the mainland was covered with warriors, and at the passage of that bridge we were fighting them for more than half an hour and could not get through, neither muskets nor crossbows nor the many great charges that we made were of any avail, and the worst of all was that many other squadrons of them were already coming to attack us on our flanks. When we saw that, we dashed through the water and bridge, some half swimming and others jumping, and here some of our soldiers, much against their will, had perforce to drink so much of the water beneath the bridge that their bellies were swollen up from it.

To go back to the battle, at the passage of the bridge many of our soldiers were wounded, but we soon brought the enemy to the sword's point along some streets where there was solid ground ahead of us. Cortés and the horsemen turned in another direction on the mainland where they came on more than ten thousand Indians, all Mexicans, who had come as reinforcements to help the people in the city, and they fought in such a way with our troops that, with their lances in rest, they awaited the attack of the horsemen and wounded four of them. Cortés was in the middle of the press and the horse he was riding, which was a very good one, a dark chestnut called "el Romo" [the flat-nosed] either because he was too fat or was tired (for he was a pampered horse) broke down, and the Mexican warriors who were around in great numbers laid hold of Cortés and dragged him from the horse; others say that by sheer strength they threw the horse down. Whichever way it may have happened, Cortés and the horse fell to the ground, and at that very moment many more Mexican warriors pressed up to see if they could carry him off alive. When some Tlaxcalans and also a very valiant soldier named Cristóbal de Olea saw what had happened, they at once came up and with good cuts and thrusts they cleared a space so that Cortés could mount again although he was badly wounded in the head. Olea was also very badly wounded with three sword cuts. By that time all of us soldiers who were anywhere near came to their help. At that time, as every street in the City was crowded with squadrons of warriors and as we were obliged to follow their banners, we were not able all to keep together, but some of us to attack in some places and some of us in others as Cortés commanded us. However we all knew from the shouts and cries, yells and whistles that we heard, that where Cortés and the horsemen were engaged the fight was hottest, and, without further explanation, although there were swarms of warriors round us, we went at great risk to ourselves to join Cortés. Fifteen horsemen had already joined him and were fighting near some canals where the enemy had thrown up breastworks and barricades. When we came up we put the Mexicans to flight, but not all of them turned their backs on us, and because the soldier Olea who had helped our Cortés was very badly wounded with three sword cuts and was bleeding, and because the streets of the city were crowded with warriors, we advised Cortés to turn back to some barricades, so that he and Olea and the horse might be attended to.

So we turned back, but not without anxiety on account of the stones, arrows and javelins which they fired at us from the barricades, for the Mexicans thought that we were turning to retreat and they followed us with great fury. At this moment

Andrés de Tápia and Cristóbal de Olid came up, and all the
rest of the horsemen who had gone off with them in other directions. Blood was streaming down Olid's face, and from his
horse and from all the rest of them, for everyone was wounded,
and they said that they had been fighting against such a host of
Mexicans in the open fields that they could make no headway
against them, for when we had passed the bridge which I have
mentioned it seems that Cortés had divided the horsemen so
that half went in one direction and half in the other, one half
following one set of squadrons and the other half another set of
squadrons.

While we were treating the wounds by searing them with oil,
there was a great noise of yells, trumpets, shells and drums
from some of the streets on the mainland, and along them
came a host of Mexicans into the court where we were tending
the wounded, and they let fly such a number of javelins and
stones that they at once wounded many of our soldiers. However, the enemy did not come very well out of that incursion
for we charged on them and with good cuts and thrusts we left
most of them stretched out on the ground.

The horsemen too were not slow in riding out to the attack
and killed many of them, but two of the horses were wounded.
We drove them out of that court, and when Cortés saw that
there were no more of the enemy we went to rest in another
great court where stood the great oratories of the city.

Many of our soldiers ascended the highest temple where the
Idols were kept, and from thence looked over the Great City
of Mexico and the lakes, for one had a commanding view of it
all, and they could see approaching more than two thousand
canoes full of warriors who were coming straight towards us
from Mexico. Later on we learnt that Guatemoc had sent them
to attack us that night or next day, and at the same time he
sent another ten thousand warriors by land so that by attacking
us both on one side and the other, not one of us should go out
of that city alive. He had also got ready another ten thousand
men as a reinforcement when the attack was made. All this
we found out on the following day from five Mexican captains
who were captured during the battle.

However, our Lord ordained that it should be otherwise, for
when that great fleet of canoes was observed and it was known
that they were coming to attack us, we agreed to keep a very

good watch throughout the camp, especially at the landing places and canals where they had to disembark. The horsemen were waiting very much on the alert all night through, with the horses saddled and bridled on the causeway and on the mainland, and Cortés and all his captains were keeping watch and going the rounds all night long. I and two other soldiers were posted as sentinels on some masonry walls, and we had got together many stones where we were posted, and the soldiers of our company were provided with crossbows and muskets and long lances, so that if the enemy should reach the landing place on the canals we could resist them and make them turn back.

While my companions and I were watching we heard a sound of many canoes being paddled, although they approached with muffled paddles, to disembark at the landing place where we were posted, and with a good shower of stones and with the lances we opposed them so that they did not dare to disembark. We sent one of our companions to give warning to Cortés, and while this was happening there again approached many more canoes laden with warriors, and they began to shoot darts and stones and arrows at us, and as we again opposed them, two of our soldiers were wounded in the head, but as it was night time and very dark the canoes went to join the captains of the whole fleet of canoes and they all went off together to disembark at another landing place where the canals were deeper. Then as they were not used to fighting during the night, they all went to join the squadrons that Guatemoc had sent by land which already numbered more than fifteen thousand Indians.

I also wish to relate, but not for the purpose of boasting about it, that when our companions went to report to Cortés that many canoes full of warriors had reached the landing place where we were watching, Cortés himself accompanied by ten horsemen came at once to speak to us, and as he came close to us without speaking we cried out, I and Gonzalo Sánchez, a Portuguese from Algarve, and we shouted: "Who comes there, are not you able to speak, what do you want?" and we threw three or four stones at him. When Cortés recognized my voice and that of my companion he said to the Treasurer Julian de Alderete and to Fray Pedro Melgarejo and Cristóbal de Olid, who were accompanying him on his rounds:

"We need no further security here than the two men who are here stationed as watchmen, they are men who have been with me from the earliest times and we can fully trust them to keep a good look out even in a case of still greater danger," and then they spoke to us and explained the danger that was threatening us.

In the same way without saying more to us they went on to examine the other outposts and we heard how they flogged two soldiers who were lounging through their watch, these were some of Narvaez's men.

There is another matter which I call to mind, which is that our musketeers had no more powder, and the crossbowmen no arrows, for on the day before they had fired so quickly that all had been used up. That same night Cortés ordered the crossbowmen to get ready all the arrows they possessed and to feather them and fix on the arrow heads, for on these expeditions we always carried many loads of materials for arrows and over five loads of arrow heads made of copper, so that we could always make arrows when they were needed. So all that night every crossbowman was occupied feathering and putting heads on the arrows, and Pedro Barba, who was their Captain, never ceased from overseeing the work and from time to time Cortés assisted him.

† CVI

As soon as there was daylight we saw all the Mexican squadrons closing in on the court where we were encamped, and, as they never caught us napping, the horsemen in one direction where there was firm ground, and we and our Tlaxcalan allies in another, charged through them and killed and wounded three of their captains who died the next day, and our allies made a good capture and took as prisoners five chieftains, from whom we learnt what orders had been given by Guatemoc.

Many of our soldiers were wounded in that battle, but this encounter was not the end of the fighting, for our horsemen, following on the heels of the enemy, came on the ten thousand warriors whom Guatemoc had sent as reinforcements. The Mexican Captains who came with this force carried swords captured from us, and made many demonstrations of the valour with which they would use them saying that they would slay us with our own arms. When our horsemen who were few in number found themselves close to the enemy and saw the great number of squadrons, they feared to attack them, and they moved aside so as not to meet them until Cortés and all of us could come to their aid. When we heard of this, without a moment's delay, all the horsemen who were left mounted their horses although both men and horses were wounded, and all the soldiers and crossbowmen and our Tlaxcalan allies marched out and we charged in such a way that we broke the ranks of the enemy and got at them hand to hand and with good sword play made them abandon their unlucky enterprise and leave us the field of battle.

We captured some other chieftains there and heard from them that Guatemoc had ordered another great flotilla of canoes to be despatched and was sending many more warriors by land, and had said to his warriors that when we were weary from our recent encounters and had many dead and wounded, we would become careless, thinking that no more squadrons would be sent against us, and that with the large force he was then sending they would be able to defeat us. When this was known, if we had been on the alert before we were much more so now, and it was agreed that the next day we should leave the city and not wait for more attacks. That day we spent in attending to the wounded, and in cleaning our arms and making arrows.

It appears that in this city there were many rich men who had very large houses full of mantles and cloth and Indian cotton shirts, and they possessed gold and feather work and much other property. It so happened that while we were occupied as I have described, the Tlaxcalans and some of our soldiers chanced to find out in what part of the town these houses were situated, and some of the Xochimilco prisoners went with them to point them out. These houses stood in the fresh water lake and one could reach them by a causeway but there were two or three small bridges in the causeway where it crossed some deep canals, and as our soldiers went to the houses and found them full of cloth and no one was guarding them, they loaded themselves and many of the Tlaxcalans with the cloth and the gold ornaments and came with it to the camp. Some of the other soldiers when they saw this, also set out for the houses, but while they were inside taking the cloth out of some huge wooden boxes, at that very moment a great flotilla of canoes arrived full of Indians from Mexico who fell upon them and wounded many of the soldiers, and carried off four of them alive and took them to Mexico, but the rest escaped.

When these four soldiers were taken to Guatemoc he learnt how few of us we were who had come with Cortés and that many of us were wounded, and all that he wished to know about our journey. When he had thoroughly informed himself about all this, he ordered the arms, feet and heads of our unfortunate companions to be cut off and sent them to the towns of our allies, to those that had already made peace with us, and he sent to tell them that he did not think there would be one of us left alive to return to Texcoco. The hearts and blood were offered to the Idols.

Let us leave this and say how he at once sent many fleets of canoes full of warriors, and other companies by land, and told them to see to it that we did not leave Xochimilco alive. As I am tired of writing about the many battles and encounters which we fought against the Mexicans in those days, and yet cannot omit to mention them, I will say that as soon as dawn broke there came such a host of Mexicans by the waterways and others by the causeways and by the mainland, that we could hardly break them up. So we then went out from the city to a great Plaza which stood at a little distance from the town, where they were used to hold their markets, and halted there with all our baggage ready for the march. Cortés then began to make us a speech about the danger in which we were placed, for we knew for certain that in the bad passes on the roads, at the creeks and on the canals the whole power of Mexico and its allies would be lying in wait for us, and he told us that it would be a good thing, and it was his command, that we should march unencumbered and should leave the baggage and the cloths so that it should not impede us when it came to fighting. When we heard this with one voice we answered that, please God we were men enough to defend our property and persons and his also, and that it would show great cowardice to do such a thing. When Cortés knew our wishes and heard our reply he said that he prayed God to help us, and then, knowing the strength and power of the enemy, we arranged the order of march, the baggage and the wounded in the middle, the

horsemen divided so that half of them marched ahead and
half as a rearguard. The crossbowmen and our native allies we
also placed near the middle as a security, for the Mexicans were
accustomed to attack the baggage. Of the musketeers we did
not take much count for they had no powder left.

In this order we began our march, and when the squadrons
of Mexicans whom Guatemoc had sent out that day saw us retreating from Xochimilco they thought that it was from fear
and that we did not dare to meet them, which was true, and so
great a host of them started off at once and came directly
against us that they wounded eight soldiers of whom two died
within eight days, and they thought to defeat us and break
into the baggage, but as we marched in the order I have described they were not able to do it. However, all along the
road until we reached a large town called Coyoacan, about
two leagues distant from Xochimilco, the warriors never ceased
to make sudden attacks on us from positions where we could
not well get at them, but whence they could assail us with
javelins and stones and arrows, and then take refuge in the
neighbouring creeks and ditches.

When we arrived at Coyoacan about ten o'clock in the morning we found it deserted.

As this large town stands on level ground, we determined to
rest there that day and the next so as to attend to the wounded
and to make arrows, for we understood very· well that we
should have to fight more battles before returning to our camp
at Texcoco.

Next day but one early in the morning we began our march,
following the road to Tacuba, which stands about two leagues
from our starting place. At one place on the road many
squadrons of warriors divided into three parties came out to attack us, but we resisted all three attacks, and the horsemen
followed the enemy over the level ground until they took refuge in the creeks and canals.

As we kept on our way Cortés left us with ten horsemen
and four pages, intending to prepare an ambush for the Mexicans who came out from the creeks and made attacks on us.
The Mexicans pretended that they were running away and
Cortés with the horsemen and servants followed them. Then
Cortés saw that there was a large force of the enemy placed in
ambush who fell upon him and his horsemen and wounded

some horses, and if they had not retreated at once they would all have been killed or taken prisoner. As it was, the Mexicans carried off two alive out of the four soldiers who were pages to Cortés, and they carried them to Guatemoc who had them sacrificed.

We arrived at Tacuba with our banners flying and with all the army and the baggage. The rest of the horsemen had come in with Pedro de Alvarado and Cristóbal de Olid, but Cortés and the ten horsemen who were with him did not appear, and we had an uncomfortable suspicion that some disaster might have overtaken him. Then Pedro de Alvarado and Cristóbal de Olid and other horsemen went in search of him, in the direction of the creeks where we had seen him turn off. At that moment the other two pages who had gone with Cortés and who had escaped with their lives came into camp, and they told us all that I have already related, and said that they had escaped because they were fleet of foot, and that Cortés and the others were following slowly because their horses were wounded. While we were talking Cortés appeared, at which we all rejoiced, although he had arrived very sad and almost tearful.

When we reached Tacuba it rained heavily and we took shelter for nearly two hours in some large courts, and Cortés with some other captains and many of us soldiers ascended the lofty temple of that town whence one had a good view of the city of Mexico which is quite near, and of the lake and the other cities which are built in the water.

We continued our march, and passed by Atzcapotzalco, which we found to be deserted, and went on to Tenayuca. This town was also deserted. From thence we went to Guatitlan, and throughout the day it never ceased raining with heavy rainstorms, and as we marched with our arms shouldered and never took off our harness by day or night, what with the weight and the soaking we got, we were quite broken down. We arrived at that large town when night was falling but it also was deserted. It never ceased raining all night long and the mud was very deep. The natives of the place and some squadrons of Mexicans yelled at us all night from the canals and other places where we could do them no harm. As it was raining and very dark no sentinels could be posted or rounds made, and no order was kept, nor could we find those who were posted, and this I can myself assert for they stationed me as a watchman for the first watch, and neither officer nor patrol visited me, and so it was throughout the camp.

Let us leave this carelessness and say that the next day we continued our march to another large pueblo[1] of which I do not remember the name; the mud was very deep in it, and we found it deserted. The following day we passed by other deserted pueblos and the day after we reached a pueblo called Aculman, subject to Texcoco. When they knew in Texcoco that we were coming, they came out to receive Cortés, and there were many Spaniards who had lately come from Spain. Captain Gonzalo de Sandoval with many soldiers also came out to receive us and with him came the Lord of Texcoco.

Cortés had a good reception both from our own people and from those recently come from Spain, and a still more cordial reception from the natives of the neighbouring towns, who at once brought food.

That night Sandoval returned to Texcoco with all his soldiers to protect his camp, and the next morning Cortés and all of us continued our march to Texcoco. So we marched on weary and wounded, having left many of our soldier companions behind us dead, or in the power of the Mexicans to be sacrificed and instead of resting and curing our wounds we had to meet a conspiracy organized by certain persons of quality who were partisans of Narvaez for the purpose of killing Cortés and Gonzalo de Sandoval, Pedro de Alvarado and Andrés de Tápia.

† CVII

As I have already said we returned broken up and wounded from the expedition that I have recorded. It appears that a great friend of the Governor of Cuba named Antonio de Villafaña, a native of Zamora or Toro, planned with other soldiers of the party of Narvaez (I will not mention their names for their honour's sake), that when Cortés should thus return from that expedition they would kill him with dagger thrusts. As a Spanish ship had arrived at that time it was to happen in this way: when Cortés should be seated at table dining with his

[1] Citlaltepec.

Captains, one of the persons who had made the plot should bring him a letter firmly closed up and sealed as though it came from Castile, and should say that it came from his father Martin Cortés, and while he was reading it they should stab him with daggers, both Cortés and all the Captains and soldiers who should happen to be near him and would defend him.

When all that I have spoken about had already been talked over and prepared, it pleased Our Lord that those who had arranged it should give a share in the affair to two important persons (I wish also to avoid mentioning their names) who had gone on the expeditions with us, and in the plan that had been made they had named one of these persons to be captain general when they had killed Cortés, and other soldiers of the party of Narvaez they appointed chief alguacil and ensign, and alcaldes, magistrates, treasurer and inspector and other officers of that sort; and they had even divided among themselves our property and horses, and this plot was kept secret until two days after our arrival at Texcoco.

It pleased Our Lord God that such a thing should not come to pass, for New Spain would have been lost and all of us, for parties and follies would have sprung up at once.

It seems that a soldier divulged the plot to Cortés, who at once put a stop to it before more fuel could be added to the fire, for that good soldier asserted that many persons of quality were concerned in it. When Cortés knew of it, after making great promises and gifts, which he gave to the man who disclosed it to him, he at once secretly informed all our Captains, namely, Pedro de Alvarado, Francisco de Lugo, Cristóbal de Olid, Andrés de Tápia, Gonzalo de Sandoval and me, and the two alcaldes who were on duty that year, namely, Luis Marin and Pedro de Ircio and all of us who were adherents of Cortés.

As soon as we knew about it we got ready, and without further delay went with Cortés to the lodging of Antonio de Villafaña, and there were present with him many of those who were in the conspiracy, and with the aid of four alguaciles whom Cortés had brought with him we promptly laid hands on Villafaña, and the Captains and soldiers who were with him at once began to flee and Cortés ordered them to be seized and detained. As soon as we held Villafaña prisoner Cortés drew from his [Villafaña's] breast the memorandum which he possessed with the signatures of all who were in the conspiracy, and after he had read it and had seen that there were many persons of quality in it, so as not to dishonour them, he spread the report that Villafaña had swallowed the memorandum and that he [Cortés] had neither seen nor read it, and he at once brought him to trial. When Villafaña's statement was taken he spoke the truth and with the many witnesses of good faith and credibility whose evidence they took on the case, the regular Alcaldes jointly with Cortés and the Quartermaster Cristóbal de Olid gave sentence, and after Villafaña had confessed with the priest Juan Díaz, they hanged him from the window of a room where he had lodged.

Cortés did not wish that anyone else should be dishonoured in that affair, although at that time many were made prisoners in order to frighten them, and to make a show that he wished to punish others, but as the time was not suitable he overlooked it.

Cortés at once agreed to have a guard for his person, and the Captain of it was a gentleman named Antonio de Quiñones, a native of Zamora, with six soldiers, good and valiant men who guarded Cortés day and night. And he begged us, whom he knew belonged to his party, to look after his person. Although from that time forth he showed great kindness to those who were in the conspiracy, he distrusted them.

Let us leave this subject and say that he at once ordered it to be proclaimed that, within two days, all the Indian men and women that we had captured on those expeditions should be brought to be branded, and a house was designated for the purpose.

So as not to waste more words in this story about the way that they were sold at the auction (beyond what I have said at other times on the two other occasions when they were branded) if it were done badly before, it was done much worse this time, for, after taking out the royal fifth, Cortés took his fifth and further thefts for Captains, and if those we sent to be branded were handsome and good Indian women they stole them by night from the crowd, so that they should not reappear from then till doomsday and on this account many women were left out, who we afterwards kept as free servants.

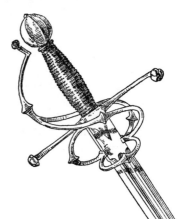

XI

The Siege and Fall of Mexico

After Antonio de Villafaña had been punished, and those who had joined with him in the conspiracy had quieted down, Cortés examined the sloops which were already built and had their rigging, sails and oars in place, and spare oars for each sloop. Moreover the canal by which the sloops were to pass out to the lake was already broad and deep. So Cortés sent to advise all the friendly pueblos near Texcoco to make eight thousand arrow heads of copper in each pueblo, and he also ordered them to make and trim for him in each pueblo eight thousand arrows of a very good kind of wood, and for these they also carried away a sample, and messengers and letters were then sent to our friend Xicotenga the elder, and to his son Xicotenga the younger and to his brothers, and to Chichimecatecle, informing them that when the day of Corpus Christi was passed, we were going to leave this city to proceed against Mexico and to invest it. He told them to send him twenty thousand warriors from their own people at Tlaxcala, and from those of Huexotzingo and Cholula, for all were now friends and brothers in arms, and they all knew the time of meeting and the plan, as he had informed them by their own Indians who were continually leaving our camp laden with the spoils from the expeditions we had made.

He also gave warning to the people of Chalco and Tlamanalco and their vassals, to be prepared when we should send to summon them, and he gave them to understand that we were about to invest Mexico, and the time when we should set out, and he said the same to Don Fernando the Lord of Texcoco and to his chieftains and to all his vassals, and to all the other towns friendly to us. One and all replied that they would do exactly what Cortés sent to order them, and that they would come.

After the orders were given, Cortés decided with our Captains and soldiers that on the second day of the feast of Espíritu Santo (this was the year one thousand five hundred and twenty-one) a review should be held. This review was held in the great Courts of Texcoco and there were present eighty-four horsemen, six-hundred-and-fifty soldiers with swords and shields and many with lances, and one-hundred-and-ninety-four crossbowmen and musketeers. From these there were chosen to man the thirteen launches those that I will now mention—For each launch, twelve crossbowmen and musketeers; in addition to them there were also set apart another twelve men, six on each side as rowers for each launch. And besides these there was a Captain for each launch and an artilleryman.

Cortés also divided among them all the boat guns and falconets we possessed and the powder he thought they would need. When this was done, he ordered the following rules, which we all had to observe, to be proclaimed.

First, no man should dare to blaspheme Our Lord Jesus Christ, nor Our Lady, His Blessed Mother, nor the Sainted Apostles, nor any other saints under heavy penalty.

Second, no soldier should illtreat our allies, since they went to help us, or should take anything away from them even if they should be spoils gained by war, whether Indian men or women or gold or silver or Chalchihuites.

Another was, no soldier should dare to depart either by day or night from our camp to go to any pueblo of our allies, or anywhere else, either to fetch food or for any other matter, under heavy penalties.

Another, all the soldiers should wear very good armour, well quilted, a neck guard, head piece, leggings and shield, for we knew about the great number of javelins and stones and arrows and lances, and for all of them it was necessary to wear the armour which the proclamation mentioned.

Another, no one should gamble for a horse or arms on any account, under heavy penalty.

Another, no soldier, horseman, crossbowman, or musketeer should go to sleep unless he were fully armed and shod with his sandals, unless it were under the stress of wounds or because he was suffering from illness, so that we might be fully prepared whatsoever time the Mexicans might come to attack us.

In addition to these, the laws were proclaimed which were ordered to be observed in soldiering; that is, that anyone who sleeps when on guard or leaves his post should be punished with death, and it was proclaimed that no soldier should go from one camp to another without leave from his Captain under pain of death.

Another, that any soldier deserting his Captain in war or battle, should suffer death.

After the review had taken place, Cortés saw that not enough men who knew how to row could be found for the launches, although those who had been brought in the ships which we destroyed when we came with Cortés were thoroughly experienced and the sailors from the ships of Narvaez and those from Jamaica also knew how to row, and all of them were placed on the list and had been warned. Yet counting all of them, there was not a full supply, as many of the men refused to row. So Cortés made enquiries to find out who were seamen, or had been seen to go out fishing, and if they came from Palos or Triana or from any other port or place where there were sailors, and he ordered them under pain of heavy penalties to go on board the launches. However high-born they might say they were, he made them go and row, and in this way he got together one hundred and fifty men as rowers, and they were much freer from hardships than we were who were stationed on the causeways fighting, and they became rich from plunder as I will relate further on.

After Cortés had decided who should go in the launches, he divided the crossbowmen and musketeers and the powder, cannon and arrows and everything else that was necessary among them and ordered them to place in each launch the royal banners and other banners with the name that was given to each launch, besides other things which were needed, and he named as Captains of the launches those whom I will now mention here:—Garcí Holguin, Pedro Barba, Juan de Linpias, Carvajal the deaf, Juan Jaramillo, Jerónimo Ruiz de la Mota, his companion Caravajal, and one Portillo who had just come from Castile, a good soldier who had a handsome wife and a Zamora who was a ship's mate, a Colmenero who was a seaman and a good soldier, a Lema, a Jínes Nórtes, one Briones a native of Salamanca, another Captain whose name I do not remember, and Miguel Díaz de Auz.

After he had named them, he gave instructions to each Captain what he was to do, and to what part of the causeways he was to go, and with which one of the Captains who were on land he was to co-operate.

When he had finished arranging all that I have mentioned, they came to tell Cortés that the Captains from Tlaxcala with a great number of warriors were approaching, and that Xicotenga, the younger, was coming as their commander in chief, and that he was bringing in his company his two brothers, sons of the good old man Don Lorenzo de Vargas. Xicotenga was also bringing a great force of Tlaxcalans under the command of Chichimecatecle and men from Huexotzingo, and another regiment of Cholulans, although they were few in number, because, from what I always observed after we had punished the people of Cholula, they never afterwards sided with Mexicans nor yet with us, but were keeping on the lookout [to see which side to take] and even when we were expelled from Mexico they were not found in opposition to us.

When Cortés knew that Xicotenga and his brothers and other Captains were approaching (and they were coming one day before the time he had told them to come) Cortés went out a quarter of a league from Texcoco to receive them with Pedro de Alvarado and others of our Captains, and as soon as he met Xicotenga and his brothers, Cortés paid them great respect and embraced them and all the other Captains. They approached in fine order, all very brilliant with great devices, each regiment by itself with its banners unfurled, and the white bird, like an eagle with its wings outstretched, which is their badge. The ensigns waved their banners and standards, and all carried bows and arrows, two handed swords, javelins and spear throwers; some carried macanas and great lances and others small lances. Adorned with their feather head-dresses, and moving in good order and uttering shouts, cries, and whistles, calling out: "Long live the Emperor our Master," and "Castile, Castile, Tlaxcala, Tlaxcala," they took more than three hours entering Texcoco.

Cortés ordered them to be lodged in good quarters, and to be supplied with everything we had in our camp. After many embraces and promises to enrich them, he took leave of them and told them that next day he would give them orders what they were to do, and that now they were tired and should rest.

† CIX

Cortés appointed Pedro de Alvarado Captain of one hundred and fifty sword and shield soldiers (and many of them carried lances) and thirty horsemen and eighteen musketeers and crossbowmen, and he named his brother Jorge de Alvarado, and Gutiérrez de Badajoz and Andrés de Monjaraz to go together with him, and these he appointed to be Captains of fifty soldiers and to divide among the three of them the musketeers and crossbowmen, as many in one Company as in the other. Pedro de Alvarado was to be Captain of the horsemen and General of the three companies, and he gave him eight thousand Tlaxcalans and their Captains, and he selected me and ordered me to go with him, and told us to go and take up our position in the City of Tacuba. He ordered that the armour we took with us should be very good headpieces, neck coverings, and leggings, for our defence was to go well armoured.

Let us go on to the next division. He gave to Cristóbal de Olid, who was quartermaster, other thirty horsemen and one hundred and seventy-five soldiers and twenty musketeers and crossbowmen all provided with armour in the same way as the soldiers he gave to Pedro de Alvarado, and he appointed three other Captains who were Andrés de Tápia, Francisco Verdugo, and Francisco de Lugo, and between all three Captains were divided all the soldiers and crossbowmen and musketeers. Cristóbal de Olid was Captain General of the three Captains and of the horsemen, and he gave him another eight thousand Tlaxcalans, and ordered him to go and establish his camp in the city of Coyoacan, which is two leagues from Tacuba.

Cortés made Gonzalo de Sandoval, the chief Alguacil, Captain of the other division of soldiers, and gave him twenty-four horsemen, fourteen musketeers and crossbowmen, one hundred and fifty sword, shield and lance soldiers, and more than eight thousand Indian warriors from the people of Chalco and Huexotzingo and of some other friendly pueblos through which Sandoval had to pass, and he gave him as companions and captains, Luis Marin and Pedro de Ircio who were Sandoval's friends, and ordered the soldiers, crossbowmen and musketeers to be divided between the two captains, and that Sandoval should have the horsemen under his command and be the General, and that he should place his camp near to Iztapalapa, and attack it and do it all the damage he could, until Cortés should send him other orders. Sandoval did not leave Texcoco until Cortés, who was Commander in chief of the regiments and of the launches, was quite ready to set out for the lake with the thirteen launches.

So as to avoid confusion on the road, we sent on ahead all the regiments of Tlaxcalans, until they should reach Mexican Territory.

As the Tlaxcalans with their Captain, Chichimecatecle and other Captains with their men, marched carelessly, they did not notice whether Xicotenga, the younger, who was their Captain General, accompanied them and when Chichimecatecle asked and enquired what had become of him, and where he had stopped, they found out that he had that night returned secretly to Tlaxcala, and was going to seize forcibly the caciqueship and vassals and lands of Chichimecatecle himself. The Tlaxcalans said that the reasons for his so doing were that when Xicotenga, the younger, saw the Captains of Tlaxcala, especially Chichimecatecle, going to the war, [he knew that] there would be nobody to oppose him, for he did not fear his father Xicotenga, the blind, who, being his father would aid him, and our friend Mase Escasi was already dead, and the only man he feared was Chichimecatecle. They also said that they always knew that Xicotenga had no wish to go to the war against Mexico, for they heard him say many times that all of us and of them would be killed. As soon as the Cacique Chichimecatecle heard and understood this, he turned back from the march more than swiftly, and came to inform Cortés about it.

Cortés at once ordered five Texcocan chieftains and two

from Tlaxcala, friends of Xicotenga, to go and force him to return, and to tell him that Cortés begged him to come back at once and go against his enemies the Mexicans, and to reflect that if his father Don Lorenzo de Vargas were not so old and blind he would come against Mexico himself and as all Tlaxcalans were and are very loyal servants of His Majesty, that it did not become him to dishonour them as he was now doing. And he sent to make him many offers and promises that he would give him gold and cloths if he would return. The reply Xicotenga sent was that if the old man his father, and Mase Escasi would have believed him, that Cortés would not have so lorded it over them and made them do all that he wished, and not to waste more words, he said that he did not intend to return. When Cortés heard that answer he at once gave an order for an Alguacil and four horsemen and five Indian chieftains from Texcoco to go in all haste and wherever they should overtake him to hang him, and he said: "There is never any improvement in this Cacique, but he must be traitor and ill-disposed towards us and of bad counsel," and that there was no time to put up with him any longer, or to ignore what had passed. When Pedro de Alvarado knew of it he petitioned strongly on Xicotenga's behalf, and Cortés gave him a favourable answer, but secretly he ordered the Alguacil and the horsemen not to leave Xicotenga alive. And so it was done and in a town subject to Texcoco they hanged him, and thus his treason was put an end to. There were some Tlaxcalans who said that Don Lorenzo de Vargas, the father of Xicotenga, sent to tell Cortés that this son of his was a bad man and he would not vouch for him, and that he begged Cortés to kill him.

Let us leave this story as it is, and say that for this reason we remained that day without setting out from Texcoco, and the next day we set out, both divisions, together, for Cristóbal de Olid and Pedro de Alvarado had both to take the same road. We went to sleep at a pueblo subject to Texcoco named Aculman, and it happened that Cristóbal de Olid sent on ahead to that pueblo to secure quarters, and had green branches placed above the roof of each house as a sign. When we arrived with Pedro de Alvarado we found no place where we could lodge, and over this [matter] the men of our Company had already put hands to their weapons against those of Cristóbal de Olid and even the Captains were defying one another, but there were not wanting on both sides gentlemen who got between us and somewhat appeased the clamour, yet not so much but that we still all remained dissatisfied, and from that place they sent to inform Cortés, and he at once despatched Fray Pedro de Melgarejo, and the Captain Luis Marin in all haste, and wrote to the Captains and all of us reproving us, and when they arrived we made friends, but from that time on, the Captains, Pedro de Alvarado and Cristóbal de Olid were not on good terms.

† cx

The next day [Thursday, 23rd May] the two Divisions continued their March together and we went to sleep at a large town [Zitlaltepec] which was deserted, for we were already in Mexican territory. The day following we went to sleep at Cuautitlan, and it also was without inhabitants, and the next day we passed through Tenayuca and Atzcapotzalco, which were also deserted, and at the hour of vespers we arrived at Tacuba and at once took up our quarters in some large houses and rooms, for this town also was deserted, and there, too, all our friends the Tlaxcalans found quarters, and that very afternoon we went through the farms belonging to those towns and brought in food to eat. We slept there that night after stationing good watchmen, sentinels and scouts, for as I have already said, Mexico was close by Tacuba, and when night fell we heard great shouts which the Mexicans raised at us from the lake, crying out much abuse, that we were not men enough to come out and fight them. They had many of their canoes full of warriors and the causeways also were crowded with fighting men, and these words were said with the idea of provoking us to come out that night and fight; but as we had gained experience from the affair of the causeways and bridges we would not go out until the next day, which was Sunday [26th May].

After hearing Mass, which was said by Father Juan Díaz, and commending ourselves to God, we agreed that with the two Divisions together, we should go out and cut off the water of Chapultepec by which the city was supplied which was about half a league distant from Tacuba.

As we were marching to break the pipes, we came on many warriors who were waiting for us on the road, for they fully understood that would be the first thing by which we could do them damage, and so when they met us near some bad ground, they began to shoot arrows at us and hurl javelins and stones from slings, and they wounded three of our soldiers, but we quickly made them turn their backs and our friends the Tlaxcalans followed them so that they killed twenty and we captured eighteen of them.

As soon as these squadrons had been put to flight we broke the conduits through which the water flowed to the city, and from that time onwards it never flowed into Mexico so long as the war lasted. When we had accomplished this, our Captains agreed that we should go at once to reconnoitre and advance along the causeway from Tacuba, and do what was possible towards gaining possession of a bridge. When we had reached the causeway, there were so many canoes on the lake full of warriors, and the causeways also were so crowded with them, that we were astounded at it; and they shot so many arrows and javelins and stones from slings that at the first encounter they wounded over thirty soldiers. Still we went on marching along the causeway towards the bridge, and from what I understand they gave way for us to reach it, so as to get us on the other side of the bridge. When they had got us there, I declare that such a host of warriors charged down on us, that we could not hold out against them; for on the causeway, which was eight paces wide, what could we do against such a great force as was stationed on one side and the other of the causeway, and struck at us as at a mark, for although our musketeers and crossbowmen never ceased loading and firing at the canoes, they did them but very little damage for they brought the canoes very well protected with bulwarks of wood. Then when we attacked the squadrons that fought on the causeway itself, they promptly threw themselves into the water, and there were so many of them that we could not prevail against them. Those on horseback did not make any progress whatever, for the Indians wounded their horses from one side and from the other, and as soon as they charged after

the squadrons the Indians threw themselves in the water. The
enemy had raised breastworks where other warriors were stationed in waiting, with long lances which they had made like
scythes from the weapons which had been captured from us
when they drove us fleeing out of Mexico.

In this manner we stood fighting with them about an hour,
and so many stones were showered on us that we could not
bear up against them, and we even saw that there was approaching us in another direction a great fleet of canoes to cut
off our passage, so as to turn our flanks, and knowing this,
and because we saw that our friends the Tlaxcalans whom we
had brought with us were greatly obstructing the causeway,
and, if they went off of it, it was clear enough that they could
not fight in the water, our Captains and all of us soldiers agreed
to retreat in good order and not to go further ahead.

When the Mexicans saw us retreating and the Tlaxcalans
escaping beyond the causeway what shouts and howls and
whistles they gave us, and how they came on to join us foot
to foot. I declare that I do not know how to describe it, for
all the causeway was heaped up with javelins, arrows, and
stones that had been hurled at us, and many more of them
must have fallen in the water. When we found ourselves on
dry land we gave thanks to God for having freed us from
that battle, for by that time eight of our soldiers had fallen
dead, and more than fifty were wounded. Through all this,
they yelled out at us and shouted abuse from the canoes, and
our friends the Tlaxcalans told them to come on land and
even if they were double the number they would fight them.
These were the first things that we did to cut off the water
and reconnoitre the lake, although we gained no honour by
them. That night we stayed in our camp while the wounded
were attended to, and one horse died, and we posted a good
force of sentinels and scouts.

The next morning Captain Cristóbal de Olid said that he
wished to go to his station at Coyoacan, a league and a half
away, and notwithstanding that Pedro de Alvarado and other
gentlemen begged him not to separate the two divisions, but
to keep them together, he would not do so; for as Cristóbal
de Olid was very courageous, and in the reconnaissance which
we made of the lake, the day before, we had not done well,
he said that it was Pedro de Alvarado's fault that we had

advanced so rashly, so that he would not stay and went off
to Coyoacan where Cortés had sent him. We remained in our
camp, for it was not right to separate one division from the
other at that time, and if the Mexicans had known how few
soldiers we were during the four or five days that we were
there apart before the launches could come, and had fallen on
us and on the division of Cristóbal de Olid separately, we
should have incurred great hardship and they would have done
us great damage. So we stayed in Tacuba and Cristóbal de
Olid in his camp, without daring to reconnoitre any further
nor to advance along the causeways, and every day we had
skirmishes with many squadrons of Mexicans who came on
land to fight with us, and even challenged us so as to place
us in situations where they could master us and we could do
them no damage.

I will leave them there and I will tell how Gonzalo de
Sandoval set out from Texcoco four days after the feast of
Corpus Christi[1] and came to Iztapalapa; almost all the march
was among friends, subjects of Texcoco, and when he reached
the town of Iztapalapa he at once began to make war and to
burn many of the houses that stood on dry land, for all the
rest of the houses stood in the lake. However, not many hours
passed before great squadrons of Mexicans came promptly to
the aid of that city and Sandoval had a good battle with them
and great encounters when they fought on land; and when
they had taken refuge in their canoes they shot many javelins,
arrows and stones at him and wounded his soldiers. While they
were thus fighting they saw that on a small hill[2] that was
close to Iztapalapa on dry land, great smoke signals were being
made, and they were answered by other smoke signals from
other towns standing in the lake, and it was a sign to assemble
all the canoes from Mexico and all the towns around the lake,
for they saw that Cortés had already set out from Texcoco with
the thirteen launches.

[1] Friday, 31st May.
[2] Cerro de la Estrella.

[The following description of Cortés's movements is taken from his third letter to the Emperor Charles V.]

31st May: As soon as I had despatched Sandoval I embarked in the launches and set out using both sails and oars, and while Sandoval was fighting and setting fire to the city of Iztapalapa we came in sight of a lofty hill standing in the water, which was strongly fortified[1] where many people had got together both from the neighbouring pueblos round the lake as well as from Tenochtitlan, for they knew I should make my first attack on Iztapalapa, and they were stationed there in its defence as well as to attack us if they could do so. When they saw our fleet approach they began to cry out and make great smoke signals to warn the cities on the lake so that they might be on the alert. Although it was my intention to attack that part of the City of Iztapalapa which stood in the water I turned aside to that hill and landed on it with one hundred and fifty men, and although it was very steep and high with much difficulty we began the ascent and captured the barricades which they had raised on the summit for their defence, and fell on them in such a way that none but the women and children escaped.

In this combat twenty-five Spaniards were wounded, but it was a very beautiful victory.

As the people of Iztapalapa had made smoke signals from some Idol towers on a high hill[2] near the city, the people of Tenochtitlan and of the other cities which stand in the water were aware that I had already entered the lake with the launches, and they at once got together a great fleet of canoes, and as far as we could judge there were about five hundred of them, to come and attack us and to find out what the launches were like. When I saw that they were coming straight towards us, I and the men who had landed on that hill re-embarked in haste.

I ordered the captains of the launches to make no movement whatever, so that those in the canoes, in the belief that we were afraid to move against them, might be led to attack us. Thus they began to drive their fleet against us headlong, but at

[1] Tepepolco, the Peñon del Marqués.
[2] Cerro de la Estrella.

the distance of two crossbow shots they stopped short and remained still.

As I was very anxious that our first encounter should be a victorious one and should be made in such a way that they should be deeply impressed with fear of the launches, for the launches were the key of the whole war, and it was on the water that a decision would be come to, it pleased God that as we halted gazing at one another a favourable breeze should spring up from the land to enable us to join battle with them, and I promptly ordered the captains to fall upon the fleet of canoes and follow them until they were shut up in the city of Tenochtitlan. As the breeze was very strong, although they fled as fast as they were able we dashed into the midst of them and broke up numberless canoes and killed and drowned many of our enemies. It was the most wonderful sight in the world to behold! We pursued them fully three leagues and shut them in among the houses of the city. There it pleased our Lord to grant us even a greater and better victory than we had hoped and prayed for.

When the garrison at Coyoacan saw us pursuing the canoes most of the horsemen and foot soldiers who were stationed there set out on the march for Tenochtitlan and fought fiercely with the Indians on the causeway, and captured the barricades they had made; and with the help of the launches which came close to the causeway they captured and passed across many of the places where the bridges had been removed, both the foot soldiers and the horsemen. Our friends the Indians from Tlax-cala as well as the Spaniards followed up the enemy and slew them and forced them into the water on the other side of the causeway where the launches could not go. They followed up their victory for more than a league of the causeway until they reached the place where I had halted with the launches, as I will go on to tell.

We chased the canoes with our launches for a good three leagues; those that escaped us took refuge among the houses in the city, and as it was already past Vespers I ordered the launches to be recalled and we approached the causeway with them, where I decided to land with thirty men to capture two small Idol towers which were surrounded by a low masonry wall (Acachinango). As we jumped ashore they fought fiercely to defend them from us, but we captured them with great effort, and risk to ourselves, and I promptly landed three large cannon I had brought with me.

The distance along the causeway between this place and the city was about half a league, and it was crowded with the enemy and the water on either side of the causeway was covered with canoes full of warriors, so I had one of the cannon aimed and fired along the causeway, which did much damage to the enemy. Through the carelessness of the gunner, at the moment of firing he set fire to the gunpowder we had with us. However, it was only a small quantity. That same night I despatched a launch to Iztapalapa where Sandoval was stationed, a distance of about two leagues, to bring back all the gunpowder he possessed.

Although it was originally my intention when I set out with the launches to go to Coyoacan, yet when I landed on the causeway and captured those two towers I decided to make my headquarters (Acachinango) there and to keep the launches there near the towers, and that half the force from Coyoacan and fifty of Sandoval's men should join me there the following day.

Having arranged for this, that night we kept on the alert, for we were in great danger, and at midnight a great host of men came in canoes and along the causeway to attack our camp, and truly they caused us great surprise and alarm, because they came by night and up to that time they had never done such a thing, nor have they ever been known to fight by night unless sure of victory.

However, as we were keenly on the look-out we began to fight with them as did those on the launches, for each one carried a small field piece and they began to fire them, and the crossbowmen and musketeers did likewise.

So the enemy did not dare to advance any further, nor did they approach close enough to do us any damage. So they left us for the rest of the night without troubling us any further.

1st June: The next day at dawn fifteen crossbowmen and musketeers, and fifty men armed with swords and shields and seven or eight horsemen from the Coyoacan garrison arrived at my encampment on the causeway. When they reached us we were already being attacked by the enemy in such numbers that both on land and water we could see nothing but men and they raised such cries and yells that it seemed as though the world were sinking.

We began to fight with them along the causeway and captured an opening where they had removed the bridge, and a barricade which had been raised at the approach to it. However with our cannon and horsemen we did them so great damage that we almost shut them in among the first houses of the city.

Because many canoes gathered on the other side of the causeway and did us great harm with darts and arrows which they shot at us on the causeway, and as our launches were not able to pass through I had a portion of the causeway broken through near our camp and sent four launches through to the other side, and they drove all the canoes back among the houses of the city, and they followed in after them which up to that time they had not dared to do, for there were many shallows and stakes to impede them. When they found canals where they could enter safely they fought with the canoes and captured some of them and set fire to many of the houses in the suburbs. Thus we passed all that day fighting.

2nd June: The next day Sandoval with the men he had with him in Iztapalapa, both Spaniards and allies, left for Coyoacan. From Iztapalapa to the mainland there is a causeway about a league and a half in length, and as Sandoval began his march of about a quarter of a league along it he reached a small city which also stands in the water, but through a good part of it one can ride on horseback, and the natives of the town began to attack him. He defeated and killed many of them and destroyed and burnt the town. As I knew that the Indians had broken down many parts of the causeway and our men would not be able to pass along it I sent two launches to aid them in the passage and they used them as bridges and they went to lodge at Coyoacan. Sandoval himself with the horsemen took the road along the causeway on which we were camped, and when he reached us found us fighting, and he and those with him dismounted and began to fight with those on the causeway whom we were driving back. As Sandoval began to fight the enemy pierced his foot with a dart, and although they wounded him and others that day, what with the cannon, crossbows and muskets we did so much execution that neither those in the canoes nor those on the causeway dared to approach us and they showed more fear and less pride than was usual.

During the following six days we went on fighting in this way and the launches went about burning all the houses they could in the neighbourhood of the city, and they discovered a canal by which they could enter the suburbs and even reach the main part of the city, which was very fortunate as it put a stop to the coming of the canoes so that not one of them dared to show themselves within a quarter of a league of our camp.

One day Alvarado who was in command of the garrison at Tacuba sent to tell me that on the other side of the city the people of Mexico came and went as they pleased along a causeway which led to some towns on the mainland and by another small causeway near to it, and in order that the city should be completely invested I sent Sandoval (though he was wounded) to fix his camp at a small pueblo [Tepeyac, now Guadelupe] at the end of the causeway, so he set out with twenty-three horsemen, one hundred and ten foot soldiers and eighteen crossbowmen and musketeers and set up his camp where I told him. As I had at my camp on the causeway two hundred Spanish foot soldiers including twenty-five crossbowmen and musketeers, and more than two hundred and fifty men in the launches and many friendly Indian warriors, I decided to push along the causeway into the city as far as I was able with the launches protecting our flanks, and I ordered some of the troops from Coyoacan to join me at my camp and ten horsemen to remain at the entrance of the causeway and the remainder of the garrison of Coyoacan and ten thousand Indian allies to protect our rear, for some of the pueblos in the lake were still hostile. I also ordered Sandoval and Alvarado to attack in force on the same day.

I set out from the camp along the causeway in the morning and soon came upon the enemy at one of the breaches they had made in the causeway, a lance in length and two lance lengths in depth, and a barricade they had raised to defend it. Both sides fought stoutly but in the end we prevailed and followed along the causeway until we reached the entrance to the city where stood one of their Idol towers[1] and at the foot of it a

---

[1] Xoluco.

great bridge[1] which spanned a broad canal. The bridge had been raised and the place defended by a very strong barricade. They began to attack us as we approached, but with the launches on both sides of us we captured it without loss, which would have been impossible but for the help of the launches. As soon as they began to abandon the barricade the men from the launches jumped ashore and we crossed the canal with more than eight thousand of our allies from Tlaxcala, Huexotzingo, Chalco and Texcoco.

While we filled in the place of the bridge with stones and adobes the Spaniards captured another barricade in the street which is the broadest and most important street in the city; as there was no canal at this barricade it was easier to carry it. They pursued the enemy along the street until they reached another canal [2] where the bridge had been removed excepting one broad beam across which the enemy passed in safety and then promptly removed it. On the other side of the canal they had raised a great barricade of earth and adobes. When we reached it we could not advance unless we threw ourselves in the water, and this would have been very dangerous as the enemy were fighting very valiantly and a countless number of them were attacking us fiercely from the azoteas on either side of the street. However, when the musketeers and crossbowmen came up and we fired with two cannon up the street we did the enemy great damage, and observing this some of the Spaniards threw themselves in the water and got to the other side, but it took us more than two hours to overcome the defence.

When the enemy saw us crossing over they abandoned the barricade and the azoteas and took to flight along the street. Then all our men got across and I made them fill in the site of the bridge and destroy the barricade. Meanwhile the Spaniards and our Indian allies went ahead along the street a distance of two crossbow shots to another bridge[3] which was close to the Plaza and principal buildings of the city. This bridge had not been removed nor had any barricade been raised, for they never thought that we should gain as much as we had done that day, nor did we think we should get half so far.

[1] Puente de San Antonio Abad.
[2] Huitzlau (Hospital de Jesus Nazarino).
[3] Puente de Palacio.

At the entrance to the Plaza we placed a cannon and with it did great execution, for the enemy were so numerous that the Plaza would not hold them all. The Spaniards seeing that there was no water there (which was our greatest danger) determined to enter the Plaza, and when the enemy saw this carried into effect and observed the multitude of our allies (although they had no fear of them unless they were in our company) they fled with our allies after them until they were shut up in the court of the Temple, which was enclosed with a masonry wall.

This enclosure would be large enough to hold a town of four hundred houses. However, a breach was made and the Spaniards and allies captured it and remained there and on the Towers for a good while. When the people of the city saw that there were no horsemen with us they turned again on the Spaniards and drove them from the towers and courts, and as our men were in great danger, for it was worse than a retreat, they took refuge in the porticoes of the courts; however, the enemy had chastened them so severely that they abandoned these and retreated to the Plaza whence they were driven out into the street and were obliged to abandon the cannon which had been placed there.

The Spaniards, unable to withstand the onset of the enemy, retreated in great danger and would have suffered great loss had it not pleased God that at that moment three horsemen should arrive who entered the Plaza, and when the enemy beheld them they thought that there were more of them and began to flee and the horsemen killed some of them and we regained the courts and enclosure. On the most important and highest tower which has over a hundred steps to reach the summit, ten or twelve Indian chieftains had sheltered themselves, and four or five of the Spaniards clambered up, and, although the Indians fought bravely, they gained the summit and slew them all.

Five or six more horsemen had now arrived, and they and the others arranged an ambuscade by which they killed over thirty of the enemy.

As it was already late I got the men together and ordered a retreat, and as we retired such a host of the enemy fell upon us that had it not been for the horsemen the Spaniards must have suffered great loss. However, as I had had all the bad

places in the street and causeways thoroughly filled in and repaired by the time we retired, the horsemen were able to come
and go over them, and as the enemy attacked our rearguard so
the horsemen charged back on them and speared and killed
many of them, and as the street is a long one they did this
four or five times.

Although the enemy knew how much they were suffering
they came like mad dogs, and nothing could check them or
prevent them pursuing us. In this way we returned along the
causeway to our camp without losing any Spaniards, although
some were wounded. We set fire to most of the houses bordering that street, so that when we should return again they
could do no harm from the azoteas.

[*At this time Cortés was joined by a great number of Indians
from Texcoco and Xochimilco who threw in their lot with the
Spaniards.*]

As the launches had burnt many of the houses in the suburbs of the city and no canoe dared to venture out, it seemed
as though six launches would suffice for the protection of our
camp, so I decided to send three launches each to the camps
of Sandoval and Alvarado. This proved a most successful plan,
for they performed some wonderful exploits, capturing many
of the enemy's men and canoes.

When this was arranged and the reinforcements had arrived
I gave out that in two days' time I was going to enter and
attack the city.

Sunday, 16th June: When the day came, after hearing Mass
and giving instructions to my captains I left our camp with
fifteen or twenty horsemen, three hundred Spaniards and a
huge host of our allies, and soon came on a yelling crowd of
our enemies. As we had not attacked them for three days they
had removed all our fillings from the breaches in the causeway
and made the openings much more dangerous and difficult for
us to capture. As the launches on either side of the causeway
could get close up to the enemy they did great execution with
their cannon, muskets and crossbows. Moreover, the men leapt
ashore and carried the barricade and breach and we all got
across in pursuit of the enemy. Again and again the Indians
made stands behind breaches and barricades, but we carried

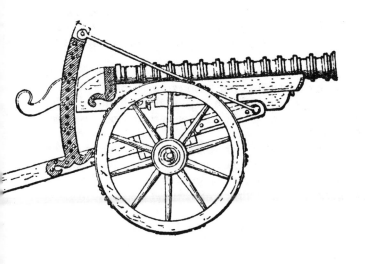

them all and drove the enemy from the street and from the Plaza where stand the principal houses of the city. I ordered the Spaniards to advance no further, as I was busy with the help of ten thousand allies in filling in the water openings and breaches in the street and causeway.

This occupied us until Vespers, meanwhile the Spaniards were skirmishing with the people of the city and killing many of them. I rode through the city for a short time with the horsemen, charging along the streets which were free from water, and the enemy no longer dared approach us on dry land. All I had seen forced me to two conclusions, the one that we should regain little of the treasure the Mexicans had taken from us; the other that they would force us to destroy and kill them all, and this last weighed on my soul. I began to wonder how I could terrify them and bring them to a sense of their error. It could only be done by burning and destroying their houses and the towers of the Idols, and so as to impress it on them this day I set fire to the great houses round the Plaza where before we were driven from the city the Spaniards and I had been lodged, and they were so extensive that a prince and six hundred of his household and followers might have been lodged in them.

Near these there were others, which although smaller were newer and more elegant, and Montezuma kept all kinds of birds in them and although I suffered in doing it, in order that they should suffer more I decided to burn them, and this scared both them and their allies.

As it was already late I ordered the troops to return to camp, and as we retired a numberless host of the enemy fell on the rearguard, but as the street was now in good condition for charging, the horsemen turned on them and speared many of them.

17th June: The next day I returned to the city in the same way so that the enemy should not have time to open the breaches and raise barricades, but early as we set out, two of the canals which cross the street had been opened just as they were the day before, and it was very difficult to pass them so that the fighting lasted until an hour after noon, and we had used up almost all our arrows and ammunition. It may seem that after being exposed to so great danger in crossing these canals and capturing the barricades that we were negligent in

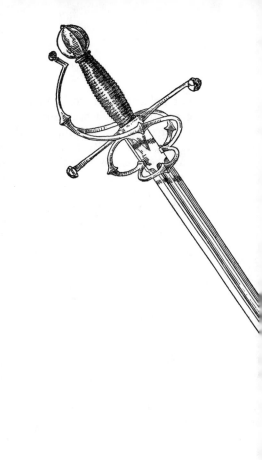

not holding them so as to avoid having to repeat the work every day, but it was not possible, for we should have had either to move the camp into the Plaza or to have left guards at the bridges. By placing our camp in the city we should have been exposed to attacks from all sides both by day and night, and as we were few in number and they were many the strain would have been unbearable.

As to guarding the bridges by night, the Spaniards were so exhausted by day that they could not have endured night guards in addition, so we were forced to do the work over again each time we entered the city.

As it was late we did not do much more this day than capture and fill in the site of the two bridges and set fire to many fine houses on the main road which goes from the city to Tacuba. Although the enemy well knew the loss they suffered when following us as we retired, yet they never omitted to follow and attack us until they saw us clear of the city.

The natives of Iztapalapa, Churubusco, Mexicaltzingo, Culuacan, Mixquic and Cuitlahuac, all towns on the fresh water lake, seeing that we were victorious over the people of Tenochtitlan and on account of the injury they were receiving from our allies, came to beg for peace and freedom from attack from our friends at Chalco. I received them favourably and told them that my only enmity was against the people Tenochtitlan and said that they could show the sincerity of their friendship by aiding me with their canoes, and as it was the rainy season and we were lodged in wretched huts, by building houses for us on the causeway.

This they did so well that on either side of the two towers on the causeway they built so many that they extended for the distance of three or four crossbow shots. The causeway was so wide here that there was space between the houses for a road where footsoldiers and horsemen could freely pass.

For several days in succession we entered the city and were always victorious over our enemies. I then arranged to enter the city in three or four divisions and summoned all the people from the towns on the lake to come in their canoes.

23rd June: That morning there were more than a hundred thousand allies at our camp and I ordered four launches with half the canoes (which must have numbered fifteen hundred) to go in one direction and the other three launches and half the canoes to go in another direction and scour the city and burn and destroy all they could.

I myself entered by the principal street and found everything clear as far as the Plaza and none of the breaches re-opened. I went on to the street which goes to Tacuba in which there were other six or seven bridges. There I arranged that one captain should advance along another street with sixty or seventy Spaniards and six horsemen to guard the rear, and with them went ten or twelve thousand of our allies, and I ordered another captain to do the same along another street while I advanced along the Tacuba street, where I captured three bridges and filled them in. The other three bridges we left for another day as it was already late.

I was very anxious to clear that street so as to communicate with the camp of Pedro de Alvarado and pass from one camp to the other. However, it was a day of great victory on land and water both for us and the companies under Sandoval and Alvarado.

[*We must now return to Bernal Díaz who was with Pedro de Alvarado at Tacuba, and go back to the 31st May, when Cortés fought his first battle on the lake.*]

† CXI

I will now relate what we did in our camp at Tacuba, for, as we knew that Cortés was going about the lake, we advanced along our causeway with great caution, and not like the first time, and we reached the first bridge, the crossbowmen and musketeers acting in concert some firing while others loaded. Pedro de Alvarado ordered the horsemen not to advance with us but to remain on dry land to guard our rear, fearing lest the pueblos I have mentioned through which we had passed, should attack us on the causeway. In this way we stood sometimes attacking, at others on the defensive so as to prevent the Mexicans reaching land from the causeway, for every day we had encounters and in them they killed three soldiers, and we were also engaged in filling up the bad places.

When we saw ourselves reinforced with the four launches sent by Cortés, Pedro de Alvarado ordered two of them to go on one side of the causeway and two on the other side, and we began to fight very successfully, for the launches vanquished the canoes which were wont to attack us from the water, and so we had an opportunity to capture several bridges and barricades, and while we were fighting, so numerous were the stones from the slings and the javelins and arrows that they shot at us that although all the soldiers were well protected by armour they were injured and wounded, and not until night parted us did we cease contending and fighting.

From time to time the Mexicans changed about and relieved their squadrons as we could tell by the devices and distinguishing marks on their armour. Whenever we left a bridge or barricade unguarded after having captured it with much labour, the enemy would retake and deepen it that same night, and construct stronger defences and even make hidden pits in the waters, so that the next day when we were fighting, and it was time for us to retire, we should get entangled among the defences. To prevent the launches from coming to our assistance, they had fixed many stakes hidden in the water so that they should get impaled on them.

When we drew off in the night we treated our wounds by searing them with oil, and a soldier named Juan Catalan blessed them for us and made charms, and truly we found that our Lord Jesus Christ was pleased to give us strength in addition to the many mercies he vouchsafed us every day, for the wounds healed rapidly.

Wounded and tied up in rags as we were we had to fight from morning until night, for if the wounded had remained in camp without coming out to fight, there would not have been twenty men in each company well enough to go out.

Then I wish to speak of our captains and ensigns and our standard bearers, who were covered with wounds and their banners ragged, and I declare that we had need of a fresh standard bearer every day for we all came out in such a condition that they were not able to advance fighting and carry the banners a second time.

Then with all this did we perchance have enough to eat? I do not speak of want of maize cakes, for we had enough of them, but of some refreshing food for the wounded. The cursed stuff that kept life in us was some herbs that the Indians eat,

and the cherries of the country while they lasted, and afterwards tunas,[1] which came into season at that time.

Tlatelolco and the towns on the Lake had been warned by
Guatemoc that on seeing a signal on the great Cue of Tlatelolco
they should hasten to assist some in canoes and others by land;
and the Mexican captains had been fully prepared and advised
how and when and to what points they were to bring assistance.

When we saw that however many water openings we captured by day the Mexicans returned and closed them up again,
we agreed that we should all go and station ourselves on the
causeway[2] in a small plaza where there were some Idol towers
which we had already taken, and where there was space to
erect our "ranchos," although they were very poor ones and
when it rained we all got wet, and they were fit for nothing
but to cover us from the dew.

We left the Indian women who made bread for us in Tacuba,
and all the horsemen and our friends the Tlaxcalans were left
to guard them, and to watch and guard the passes so that the
enemy should not come from the neighbouring pueblos and
attack our rearguard on the causeway while we were fighting.

So when once we had set up our ranchos where I have
stated, thenceforward we endeavoured quickly to destroy the
houses and blocks of buildings and to fill up the water openings
that we captured. We levelled the houses to the ground, for if
we set fire to them they took too long to burn, and one house
would not catch fire from another, for each house stood in the
water, and one could not pass from one to the other without
crossing bridges or going in canoes. If we wanted to cross the
water by swimming they did us much damage from the azoteas, so that we were more secure when the houses were
demolished. As soon as we had captured some barrier or bridge
or bad pass where they offered much resistance, we endeavoured to guard it by day and by night. This was the way in
which all our companies kept guard together during the night.
The first company, which numbered more than forty soldiers,
kept watch from nightfall until midnight, and from midnight

[1] Fruit of the *Nopal cactus*, prickly pears.
[2] About Thursday, 20th June. Alvarado must have turned off from the Tacuba
Causeway to the left on entering the outskirts of the city, and followed a causeway
leading direct to Tlatelolco, making his camp about half-way between the Tacuba
Causeway and the great Teocalli of Tlatelolco.

until two hours before dawn another company, also of forty men, kept watch, and the first company did not leave their post but we slept there on the ground; this second watch is called the *modorra*,[1] and soon another forty soldiers came and kept the *alba* [dawn] watch, which is the two hours until daylight, but those who watched the modorra could not leave, but had to stay there, so that when dawn came there were over one hundred and twenty soldiers all on watch together. Moreover on some nights, when we judged that there was special danger we kept watch together, from nightfall until dawn, awaiting a great sally of the Mexicans in fear lest they should break through.

On several nights great squadrons came to attack us and break through at midnight, and others during the modorra and others during the dawn watch, and they came sometimes without commotion and at others with loud yells and whistles, and when they arrived where we were keeping night watch, what javelins and stones and arrows they let fly, and there were many others with lances, and although they wounded some of us, yet we resisted them, and sent back many of them wounded. Then, notwithstanding all the precautions we took, they would turn on us and open some bridge or causeway which we had captured, and we could not defend it from them in the night so as to prevent them doing it, and the next day it was our turn again to capture it and stop it up, and then they would come again to open it and strengthen it with walls, until the Mexicans changed their method of fighting which I will tell about in its proper time.

The Mexicans still brought in much food and water from the nine towns built on the lake, so to prevent these supplies being brought to them, it was arranged between all the three camps that two launches should cruise in the lake by night and should capture all the canoes they were able, and destroy or bring them to our camps. But even with all this, many laden canoes did not fail to get in, and as the Mexicans went about in their canoes carrying supplies, yet there was never a day when the launches did not bring in a prize of canoes and many Indians hanging from the yards.

The Mexicans then armed thirty *piraguas,* which are very large canoes, with specially good rowers and warriors, and by

---

[1] *Modorra* = the drowsy time, before dawn.

night they posted all thirty amongst some reed beds in a place where the launches could not see them; then they sent out before nightfall, with good rowers, two or three canoes covered over with branches as though they were carrying provisions or bringing in water. In the track which, in the opinion of the Mexicans, the launches would follow them when they were fighting with them, they had driven numerous strong timbers made pointed like stakes so that they should get impaled on them. Then as the canoes were going over the lake showing signs of being afraid and drew near to the reed beds, two of our launches set out after them, and the two canoes made as though they were retreating to the land, to the place where the thirty piraguas were posted in ambush, and the launches followed them and as soon as they reached the ambush all the piraguas together sallied out and made for the launches and quickly wounded all the soldiers, rowers, and captains, and the launches could go neither in one direction or another on account of the stakes that had been fixed. In this way the Mexicans killed a captain named de Portilla, an excellent soldier who had been in Italy, and they wounded Pedro Barba who was another very good captain, and they captured his launch, and within three days he died of his wounds. These two launches belonged to the camp of Cortés, and he was greatly distressed about it.

Let us leave this and say that when the Mexicans saw that we were levelling all the houses to the ground and were filling up the bridges and openings they decided on another way of fighting, and that was, to open a bridge and a very wide and deep channel which we had to pass wading through the water, and it was sometimes out of our depth, and they had dug many pits which we could not see under the water and had made walls and barricades both on the one side and the other of the opening, and had driven in many pointed stakes of heavy timber in places where our launches would run on to them if they should come to our assistance when we were fighting to capture this fort, for they well knew that the first thing we must do was to destroy the barricade and pass through that open space of water so as to reach the City. At the same time they had prepared in hidden places many canoes well manned with warriors and good rowers. One Sunday morning [23rd June] great squadrons of warriors began to approach from three directions and attacked us in such a way that it was all we could do to hold our own and prevent them from defeating us.

At that time Pedro de Alvarado had ordered half the horsemen who used to stay in Tacuba to sleep on the causeway, for there was not so much risk as at the beginning, as there were no longer any azoteas, for nearly all the houses had been demolished. To go back to my story, three squadrons of the enemy came on very fearlessly, the one from the direction of the great open space of water, the other by way of some houses that we had pulled down, and the other squadron had taken us in the rear from the direction of Tacuba, and we were surrounded. The horsemen with our Tlaxcalan friends broke through the squadron that had taken us in the rear and we all of us fought very valiantly with the other two squadrons until we forced them to retreat. However, that seeming flight that they made was a pretence, but we captured the first barricade where they made a stand, and we, thinking that we were victorious, crossed that water at a run, for where we passed there were no pits and we followed up our advance among some great houses and temple towers. The enemy acted as though they were still retreating, but they did not cease to shoot javelins and stones from slings and many arrows and when we were least expecting it a great multitude of warriors who were hidden in a place we were not able to see, and many others from the azoteas and houses joined the combat, and those who at first acted as though they were retreating, turned round on us all at once and dealt us such treatment that we could not withstand them. We then decided to retreat with great caution, but at the water opening which we had captured, that is to say at the place where we had crossed the first time, where there were no pits, they had stationed such a fleet of canoes that we were not able to cross at that ford, and they forced us to go across in another direction, where the water was very deep, and they had dug many pits. As such a multitude of warriors were coming against us, and we were in retreat, we crossed the water by swimming and wading, and nearly all the soldiers fell in the pits; then the canoes came down upon us and there the Mexicans carried off five of our companions, and took them alive to Guatemoc, and they wounded nearly all of us. Moreover, the launches which were guarding us could not come to our assistance because they were impaled on the stakes which had been fixed there, and from the canoes and azoteas the Mexicans attacked them so fiercely with javelins and arrows that they killed three soldiers and rowers and wounded many of us. To go back to the pits and the opening, I declare it was a wonder that we were not all killed in them. Concerning myself, I may say that many Indians had already laid hold of me, but I managed to get my arm free, and our Lord Jesus Christ gave me strength so that by some good sword thrusts that I gave them I saved myself, but I was badly wounded in one arm, and when I found myself out of that water in safety, I became insensible and without power to stand on my feet and altogether breathless, and this was caused by the great strain that I exerted in getting away from that rabble and from the quantity of blood I had lost. I declare that when they had me in their clutches, that in my thoughts I was commending myself to our Lord God and to our Lady His Blessed Mother and He gave me the strength I have spoken of by which I saved myself; thank God for the mercy that He vouchsafed me.

There is another thing I wish to mention, that Pedro de Alvarado and the horsemen, when they had thoroughly routed the squadrons that came on our rear from Tacuba, did not any of them pass that water or the barricades, with the exception of one horseman who had come only a short time before from Spain, and there they killed him, both him and his horse. The horsemen were already advancing to our assistance when they saw us coming back in retreat, and if they had crossed there, and should have then had to retreat, there would not have been one of them, nor of the horses, nor of us left alive. Flushed with the victory they had gained, the Mexicans continued during that whole day, which as I have said was a Sunday, to send so vast a host of warriors against our camp, that we could not prevail against them, and they expected for certain to rout us, but we held our own against them by the help of some bronze cannon and hard fighting, and by all the companies together keeping guard every night.

Let us leave this and say when Cortés heard of it he was very angry. Then when we saw that it was our fault that great disaster had happened, we began then and there to fill in that opening, and although it meant great labour and many wounds which the enemy inflicted while we were at work, and the death of six soldiers, in four days we had it filled in,[1] and at night we kept watch on the place itself, all three companies in the order I have already mentioned.

Let me now say that the towns situated in the lake when they saw how day by day we were victorious both on water and on land, and that the people of Chalco, Tlaxcala, and other pueblos had made friends with us, decided to sue Cortés for peace and with great humility they asked pardon if in any way they had offended us, and said that they had been under orders and could not do otherwise.[2] The towns that came in were Iztapalapa, Churubusco, Culuacan, and Mixquic and all those of the fresh water lake, and Cortés told them that we should not move the camp until the Mexicans sued for peace or he had destroyed them by war. He ordered them to aid us with all the canoes that they possessed to fight against Mexico, and to come and build ranchos for Cortés and to bring him food, and they replied that they would do so, and they built the ranchos but brought very little food. However, our ranchos where we were stationed were never rebuilt so we remained in the rain, for those who have been in this country know that through the months of June, July and August it rains every day in these parts.

We made attacks on the Mexicans every day and succeeded in capturing many idol towers, houses, canals, and other openings and bridges which they had constructed from house to house, and we filled them all up with adobes and the timbers from the houses that we pulled down and destroyed and we kept guard over them, but notwithstanding all this trouble that we took, the enemy came back and deepened them and widened the openings and erected more barricades. And because

[1] By Friday, 28th June.
[2] From Cortés' account the submission of these towns appears to have taken place about 18th June.

our three companies considered it a dishonour that some should be fighting and facing the Mexican squadrons and others should be filling up passes and openings and bridges, Pedro de Alvarado, so as to avoid quarrels as to who should be fighting or filling up openings, ordered that one company should have charge of the filling in and look after that work one day, while the other two companies should fight and face the enemy, and that this should be done in rotation one day one company, and another day another company, until each company should have had its turn, and owing to this arrangement there was nothing captured that was not razed to the ground, and our friends the Tlaxcalans helped us. So we went on penetrating into the City, but at the hour for retiring all three companies had to fight in union, for that was the time when we ran the greatest risk. First of all we sent all the Tlaxcalans off the causeway, for it was clear that they were considerable embarrassment when we were fighting.

Guatemoc now ordered us to be attacked at all three camps at the same time by all his troops and with all the energy that was possible both on land and by water, and he ordered them to go by night during the modorra watch, so that the launches should not be able to assist us on account of the stakes. They came on with so furious an impetus that had it not been for those who were on the watch, who were over one hundred and twenty soldiers well used to fighting, they would have penetrated into our camp, and we ran a great risk as it was, but by fighting in good order we withstood them; however, they wounded fifteen of our men and two of them died of their wounds within eight days.

Also in the camp of Cortés they placed our troops in the greatest straits and difficulties and many were killed and wounded, and in the camp of Sandoval the same thing happened, and in this way they came on two successive nights and many Mexicans also were killed in these encounters and many more wounded. When Guatemoc and his captains and priests saw that the attack that they made on those two nights profited them nothing, they decided to come with all their combined forces at the dawn watch and attack our camp, and they came on so fearlessly that they surrounded us on two sides, and had even half defeated us and cut us off, when it pleased our Lord Jesus Christ to give us strength to turn and

close our ranks, and we sheltered ourselves to a certain degree
with the launches, and with good cut and thrust, and advancing shoulder to shoulder, we drove them off. In that battle
they killed eight and wounded many of our soldiers and they
even injured Pedro de Alvarado. If the Tlaxcalans had slept
on the causeway that night we should have run great risk
from the embarrassment they would have caused us on account
of their numbers, but the experience of what had happened
before made us get them off the causeway promptly and send
them to Tacuba, and we remained free from care. To go back
to our battle, we killed many Mexicans and took prisoner four
persons of importance. I well understand that interested readers will be surfeited with seeing so many fights every day but
one cannot do less, for during the ninety and three days that
we besieged this strong and great City we had war and combats
every day and every night as well. However, when it seemed
to us that we were victorious, great disasters were really coming upon us, and we were in the greatest danger of perishing
in all three camps, as will be seen later on.

[*To return to Cortés' account of his doings.*]

24*th June*: When on my return to camp in the evening
(of the 24th June) I heard about Pedro de Alvarado's reverse,
I decided to go to his camp on the following morning and
reprimand him for what had happened and to see how far he
had advanced and where he had placed his camp. When I arrived there I was astonished to see how far he had penetrated
into the city and the formidable passes and bridges which he
had captured, and having seen them I could not impute much
blame to him, and after talking over what was to be done I
returned to my own camp.

I made several advances into the city during the next few
days and was everywhere victorious. However, we had now
been continuously fighting for more than twenty days, and
every attack exposed us to great risk for the enemy were united
and powerful and ready to fight to the death. The Spaniards,
irritated at the delay, importuned me to advance and capture
the market place [of Tlatelolco] for having gained that the
enemy would have little space in which to defend themselves,
and if they would not give in, would die of hunger and thirst

for they had nothing to drink but the salt water of the lake.

When I demurred to this plan, your Majesty's Treasurer (Julian de Alderete) told me that the whole camp was set on it and I ought to do it, and in the end they pressed me so greatly that after consultation with others I gave way. The next day (29th June) I called together the most important persons in the camp and we agreed to give notice to Sandoval and Pedro de Alvarado that on the following day we should advance into the city and endeavour to reach the market place of Tlatelolco and I also sent them written instructions and asked them to send me seventy or eighty foot soldiers.

The following day (30th June) after hearing Mass there set out from our camp seven launches, more than three thousand canoes of our allies, and I followed with twenty-five horsemen and all my foot soldiers and those who had come from Tacuba, and when we reached the city I divided my force as follows: —From the position we had already gained there are three streets leading to the market place, or Tianginz as the Indians call it, of Tlatelolco. Along the principal street I sent your Majesty's treasurer and accountant (Julian de Alderete) with seventy men and fifteen or twenty thousand of our allies and seven or eight horsemen as a rearguard, and as they carried the barricades they were to fill in the bridge openings, and for this purpose a dozen men carried mattocks, and our allies were very useful at this work. The other two streets lead from the Tacuba street to the market place, and they are narrower and there are causeways with bridges and canals. By the broadest of these two I ordered two captains to advance with eighty men and more than ten thousand Indian allies. At the entrance to the Tacuba street I posted two large cannon with eight horsemen to guard them. I myself with eight horsemen and one hundred foot soldiers including twenty-five crossbowmen and musketeers and a great host of our allies went on so as to advance along the narrowest street as far as possible.

At the entrance of the street I halted the horsemen and ordered them to stay there and not to follow me unless I sent for them. Then I dismounted and we reached a barricade at the end of a bridge and with the help of a small field piece and the musketeers and crossbowmen we carried it and went along the causeway, which had been broken down in two or three places. In addition to the three lines of attack which we were following, our allies were so numerous that they swarmed over the azoteas in all directions and it seemed as if nothing could harm us. As the Spaniards carried those bridges and barricades our allies followed us along the causeway without making good, and I halted with about twenty Spaniards where there was an island, for I saw that some of our allies were surrounded by the enemy who sometimes drove them back and thrust them into the water, but with our help they rallied. In addition to this we had to take care that the people of the city did not emerge from the cross streets and attack in the rear the Spaniards who had advanced along the street, and who at this time sent to tell me that they had made great gains and were not far from the market place, and that in any case they should press forward, for they already heard the noise of battle which Sandoval and Pedro de Alvarado were waging from their side. I sent to tell them on no account to go ahead without first thoroughly filling in the bridge openings so that in case of retreat the water should not trouble or impede them, for they knew that there lay the greatest danger. They sent back to say that every place they had captured had been made good, and I could go there and verify it for myself.

Having some misgiving lest they might err and be wanting in caution about filling in the bridge openings I went there and found that they had advanced across one breach in the street which was ten or twelve paces in width and the depth of the water that filled it was twice a man's height. In order to cross it they had thrown in timber and bundles of reeds and as they crossed with care, a few at a time, the timber and reeds had not given way with them, and they in the joy of victory were so dull witted as to think that they had left it quite firm.

At the moment that I reached that wretched bridge I saw that the Spaniards and many of our allies were retreating in full flight with the enemy setting on them like dogs and, when I saw that great disaster I began to shout: "Hold on!" and when I got to the water I found it full of Spaniards and Indians as though not a straw had been thrown into it, and the enemy in order to kill the Spaniards charged into the water after them, and canoes manned by the enemy came along the canals and carried off the Spaniards alive. The whole affair was so sudden that seeing how the people were being killed I determined to stay there and die fighting.

All that I and those with me could do was to give a hand to some unfortunate Spaniards who were drowning and drag them out; some got out wounded and others half drowned, and others without arms, and we sent them to the rear. Then such numbers of the enemy charged on me and the dozen or fifteen Spaniards in my company that they completely surrounded us. As I was busy helping those who were drowning I did not see or think of the danger we were in and some of the Indians seized me and would have carried me off but for a captain of fifty (Cristóbal de Olea) who always attended me, and a youth (named Serma) of his company, who, after God, saved my life. Like the valiant man he was, Olea in saving my life lost his own.

Meanwhile the defeated Spaniards got along the causeway, and as it was small and narrow and on a level with the water, for the dogs had been careful to make it so, and many of our routed allies were pouring along it, it became so crowded that movement was slow and the enemy had time to reach it by water on either side and capture and kill at their will. A captain who was with me named Antonio Quiñones said to me: "Let us get away from here and save yourself, for you know that without you none of us will escape," but he could not prevail on me to go, and seeing this he seized me by the arms to urge me to flight, and although I was better pleased with death than with life, at the urgency of that captain and other companions who were present we began to retreat fighting with our swords and shields against the enemy who came rushing against us.

Then one of my servants arrived on horseback and cleared a small space, but at that moment from a roof he received a spear thrust in the throat which made him turn back, and while we were battling fiercely, waiting for the people to pass along that narrow causeway and gain safety and keeping back the enemy, another servant of mine brought a horse for me to mount, but such was the mud on the causeway from those who fell in and scrambled out of the water, that no one could keep his feet, all the more from the jostling of one against another in the efforts to save themselves.

I mounted, but not with the intention of fighting on the causeway for that was impossible on horseback, and if it could have been done the eight horsemen whom I had left on the island at the entrance of the causeway would have done so, but they could do no more than retreat along it, and even this was dangerous enough and two mares ridden by two of my servants fell from the causeway into the water, one being killed by the Indians and the other rescued by some foot soldiers. Another of my servants named Cristóbal de Guzman mounted a horse on the island to bring it to me so that I could escape, but before reaching me the Indians killed both him and the horse. His death caused grief throughout the camp and grief is still intense among those who knew him.

Notwithstanding all these dangers it pleased God that we who survived should reach the Calle de Tacuba which is very broad, and collect the troops while I and nine horsemen formed a rearguard. The enemy came on so greatly elated by victory and pride it seemed as though no one would be left alive, and retiring as best I could I sent to tell the treasurer and accountant to retreat to the Plaza with great caution, and I sent to say the same to the other two captains who had advanced by the street leading to the market place. Both one and the other had fought valiantly and captured many barricades and bridges which they had carefully filled in which was the reason of their suffering no loss in their retreat.

Before the treasurer and accountant retired the people of the city threw from the barricade where they were fighting the heads of two or three Spaniards which they had cut off, and the Treasurer could not tell at the time if they came from our troops or from those of Pedro de Alvarado.

We all got together in the Plaza when such hosts of the enemy charged on us from all directions that it was all we could do to keep them off, and this in a place where before our defeat they did not dare to await the approach of three horsemen or ten foot soldiers. Then they promptly burned incense of perfumes and resins of the country on the summit of a lofty tower near the Plaza as an offering to their Idols and as a sign of victory, and however much we might wish to prevent it, nothing could be done, for already our people were hastening towards our camp.

In this defeat the enemy killed thirty-five or forty Spaniards, and more than a thousand of our Indian allies, and I was wounded in the leg, and we lost a small field piece, and many crossbows, muskets and other arms.

[*We must now turn to Bernal Díaz's account of the happenings on the 30th June.*]

† CXIII

As Cortés saw that it was impossible to fill in all the openings, bridges, and canals of water that we captured day by day, which the Mexicans reopened during the night and made stronger than they had been before with barricades, and that it was very hard work fighting and filling in bridges and keeping watch all of us together (all the more as we were most of us wounded and twenty had died), he decided to consult his captains and soldiers who were in his camp, that is Cristóbal de Olid, Francisco Verdugo, Andrés de Tápia, the ensign Corral and Francisco de Lugo, and he also wrote to us in the camp of Pedro de Alvarado and to the camp of Sandoval to take the opinion of all us captains and soldiers. The question he asked was, whether it seemed good to us to make an advance into the City with a rush, so as to reach Tlatelolco, which is the great market of Mexico, and is much broader and larger than that of Salamanca, and that if we could reach it, whether it would be well to station all our three camps there, as from thence we should be able to fight through the streets of Mexico without having such difficulty in retreating and should not have so much to fill in, or have to guard the bridges. As was likely to happen in such discussions and consultations, some of us said that it was not good advice or a good idea to intrude ourselves so entirely into the heart of the City, but that we should remain as we were, fighting and pulling down and levelling the houses. We who held the latter opinion gave as the most obvious reason for it that if we stationed ourselves in Tlatelolco and left the causeways and bridges unguarded and deserted, the Mexicans—having so many warriors and canoes —would reopen the bridges and causeways and we would no longer be masters of these. They would attack us with their powerful forces by night and day, and as they always had many impediments made with stakes ready prepared, our launches would not be able to help us, thus by the plan that Cortés was proposing we would be the besieged and the enemy would have possession of the land, the country and the lake, and we wrote to him about his proposal so that "it should not happen to us as it had happened before" (as the saying of the Mazegatos runs), when we went fleeing out of Mexico.

After Cortés had heard our opinions and the good reasons we gave for them the only result of all the discussion was that on the following day we were to advance with all the energy we could from all three camps, horsemen as well as crossbowmen, musketeers and soldiers and to push forward until we reached the great market place at Tlatelolco. When all was ready in all the three camps and our friends the Tlaxcalans had been warned as well as the people of Texcoco and those from the towns of the lake who had again given their fealty to His Majesty, who were to come with their canoes to help the launches, one Sunday morning (30th June) after having heard mass, we set out from our camp with Pedro de Alvarado, and Cortés set out for his camp, and Sandoval with his companies, and in full force each company advanced capturing bridges and barricades, and the enemy fought like brave warriors and Cortés on his side gained many victories, so too did Gonzalo de Sandoval on his side. Then we on our side had already captured another barricade and a bridge, which was done with much difficulty because Guatemoc had great forces guarding them, and we came out of the fight with many of our soldiers wounded, and one soon died of his wounds, and more than a thousand of our Tlaxcalan friends alone came out of it injured; however, we still followed up our victory very cheerfully.

[*Bernal Díaz here gives an account of the disaster which overtook the division under Cortés which has already been given in Cortés' own words.*]

Let us cease speaking about Cortés and his defeat and return to our army, that of Pedro de Alvarado, and say how we advanced victoriously, and, when we least expected it, we saw

advancing against us with loud yells very many squadrons of
Mexicans with very handsome ensigns and plumes, and they
cast in front of us five heads streaming with blood which they
had just cut off the men whom they had captured from Cortés,
and they cried:—"Thus will we kill you as we have killed
Malinche and Sandoval, and all whom they had brought with
them, and these are their heads and by them you may know
them well," and saying these words they closed in on us until
they laid hands on us and neither cut nor thrust nor crossbows
nor muskets availed to stop them, all they did was to rush at
us as at a mark. Even so we lost nothing of our order in retreating, for we at once commanded our friends the Tlaxcalans
to clear off quickly from the causeways and bad passages, and
this time they did it with a will, for when they saw the five
heads of our companions dripping with blood and heard the
Mexicans say that they had killed Malinche and Sandoval and
all the Teules whom they had brought with them, and that so
they would do to us also and to the Tlaxcalans, they were
thoroughly frightened, thinking it was true, and for this reason,
I say, they cleared off the causeway very completely.

As we were retreating we heard the sound of trumpets from
the great Cue, which from its height dominates the whole City,
and also a drum a most dismal sound indeed it was, like an
instrument of demons, as it resounded so that one could hear it
two leagues off, and with it many small tambourines and shell
trumpets, horns and whistles. At that moment, as we afterwards learnt, they were offering the hearts of ten of our comrades and much blood to the idols.

Simultaneously there came against us many squadrons which
Guatemoc had newly sent out, and he ordered his horn to be
sounded. When this horn was sounded it was a signal that his
captains and warriors must fight so as to capture their enemies
or die in the attempt, and the sound that it made echoed in
their ears, and when his captains and squadrons heard it, the
fury and courage with which they threw themselves on us, in
order to lay hold of us, was terrifying, and I do not know how
to describe it here; even now when I stop to remember, it is as
though I could see it all at this minute, and were present again
in that fight and battle. But I reassert that our Lord Jesus Christ
saved us, for if he had not given us strength, seeing that we
were all wounded, we should never otherwise have been able

to reach our ranchos, and I give thanks and praise to God for it, that I escaped that time with many others from the power of the Mexicans.

To go back to our story, the horsemen made charges, and with two heavy cannon that we placed near our ranchos with some loading while others fired we held our own, for the causeway was crowded to the utmost with the enemy and they came after us up to the houses, as though we were already conquered, and shot javelins and stones at us, and as I have said, with those cannon we killed many of them. The man who was most helpful that day was a gentleman named Pedro Moreno Medrano, for he acted as gunner because the artillerymen we used to have with us were some of them dead and the others wounded, and Pedro Moreno besides always being a brave soldier was on that day a great help to us. Being as we were in that condition, thoroughly miserable and wounded, we knew nothing of either Cortés or Sandoval nor of their armies, whether they had been killed or routed, as the Mexicans told us they were when they cast before us the five heads which they brought tied together by the hair and the beards, saying that Malinche and all the Teules were already dead, and that thus they were going to kill all of us that very day. We were not able to get news from them because we were fighting half a league apart one from the other, and for this very reason we were much distressed, but by all of us both wounded and sound keeping together in a body we held out against the shock of the fury of the Mexicans who came against us, and who did not believe that there would be a trace of us left after the attack that they made upon us.

Then they had already captured one of our launches and killed three soldiers and wounded the captain and most of the soldiers who were in it, and it was rescued by another launch of which Juan Jaramillo was captain. Yet another launch was impaled in a place from which it could not move, and its captain was Juan de Linpias Caravajal, who went deaf at that time. He himself fought most valiantly and so encouraged his soldiers, who were rowing the launch that day, that they broke the stakes on which they were impaled and got away, all badly wounded, and saved their launch. This Linpias was the first to break the stakes and it was a great thing for all of us.

Cortés sent Andrés de Tápia with three horsemen post-haste

by land,[1] at the risk of their lives, to our camp, to find out if we were alive. The Captain Andrés de Tápia made great haste, although he and two of those who came with him were wounded. When they reached our camp and found us fighting with the Mexican force which was still close to us, they rejoiced in their hearts and related to us what had happened about the defeat of Cortés. However, they did not care to state that so many were dead, and said that about twenty-five had been killed and that all the rest were well.

† CXIV

Let us stop talking of this and turn to Sandoval and his captains and soldiers, who marched on victoriously in the part and streets they had captured, and when the Mexicans had defeated Cortés they turned on Sandoval and his army and captains so effectively that he could make no headway, and they killed six soldiers and wounded all whom he had brought with him, and gave Sandoval himself three wounds one in the thigh, another in the head and another in the left arm. While Sandoval was battling with the enemy they placed before him six heads of Cortés' men whom they had killed, and said they were the heads of Malinche and of Tonatio and other Captains, and that they meant so to do with Sandoval and those who were with him, and they attacked him fiercely. When Sandoval saw this he ordered all his captains and soldiers to show a brave spirit and not be dismayed, and to take care that in retreating there should not be any confusion on the causeway which was narrow, and first of all he ordered his allies, who were numerous, to clear off the causeway so as not to embarrass him, and with the help of his two launches and of his musketeers and crossbowmen, with great difficulty he retired to his quarters, with all his men badly wounded and even discouraged and six of them dead. When he found himself clear of the causeway, although he was surrounded by Mexicans, he encouraged his people and their captains and charged them all to be sure to keep together in a body by day and by night so as to guard the camp and avoid defeat. Then when he learned from the cap-

[1] Round by Coyoacan.

tain Luis Marin, that they were well able to do it, wounded and bound up in rags as he was, he took two other horsemen with him and rode post-haste to the camp of Cortés. When Sandoval saw Cortés he said: "Oh Sir Captain, what is this? Are these the counsels and stratagems of warfare that you have always impressed on us, how has this disaster happened?" Cortés replied, with tears springing to his eyes: "Oh my son Sandoval, for my sins this has been permitted; however, I do not deserve as much blame in the matter as all my captains and soldiers impute, but the Treasurer Julian de Alderete to whom I gave the order to fill in that passage where they defeated us, and he did not do it."

The Treasurer in turn blamed Cortés for not ordering the many allies that he had with him to clear off the causeway in good time, and there were many other discussions and replies from Cortés to the Treasurer which as they were spoken in anger, will be left untold. At that moment there arrived two launches which Cortés kept in the lake and by the causeway, and they had not come in nor had anything been known about them since the defeat. It seems that they had been detained and impaled on some stakes, and, according to what the captains reported, they had been kept there surrounded by canoes which attacked them, and they all came in wounded, and said that God in the first place aided them with a wind, and thanks to the great energy with which they rowed they broke the stakes; at this Cortés was well pleased, for up to that time, although he did not publish it so as not to dishearten the soldiers, he knew nothing about the launches and had held them as lost.

Cortés strongly advised Sandoval to proceed at once post-haste to our camp of Pedro de Alvarado, and see whether we were routed, or how we stood, and if we were alive to help us to keep up the defence so that they should not break into our camp, and he told Francisco de Lugo, who accompanied Sandoval (for he well knew that there were Mexican squadrons on the road), that he had already sent Andrés de Tápia with three horsemen to get news of us, and he feared that they had been killed on the road. After saying this to him and taking leave of him he went to embrace Sandoval, and said: "Look here, my son, as I am not able to go everywhere, for you can see that I am wounded, I commit this work to your care so that you may inspire confidence in all three camps. I know well that Pedro de Alvarado and all his captains and brothers and soldiers have fought valiantly and acted like gentlemen, but I fear the great forces of these dogs may have defeated him, and as for me and my army, you observe in what condition I am."

Sandoval and Francisco de Lugo came post-haste[1] to where we were and when he arrived it was a little after dusk and it seems that the defeat of Cortés took place before noon. When Sandoval arrived he found us fighting with the Mexicans who wanted to get into our camp by way of some houses which we had pulled down, and others by the causeway, and many canoes by the lake, and they had already got one launch stranded on the land, and of the soldiers who were in it two were dead and most of them wounded. Sandoval saw me and six other soldiers standing more than waist high in the water helping the launch to get off into deep water, and many Indians attacking us with swords which they had captured from us (and they gave me an arrow wound and a sword cut in the leg) so as to prevent us helping the launch, which, judging from the energy they were displaying, they intended to carry off with their canoes. They had attached many ropes to it with which to tow it off and place it inside the City. When Sandoval saw us in that position he said to us: "Oh! Brothers put your strength into it and prevent them carrying off the launch," and we exerted so much strength that we soon hauled it out in safety, although as I have said, all of the sailors came out wounded and two dead.

At that time many companies of Mexicans came to the causeway and wounded the horsemen as well as all of us, and they gave Sandoval a good blow with a stone in the face. Then Pedro de Alvarado and other horsemen went to his assistance. As so many squadrons approached I and twenty other soldiers faced them, and Sandoval ordered us to retreat little by little so that they should not kill the horses, and because we did not retreat as quickly as he wished he said to us with fury: "Do you wish that through your selfishness they should kill me and all these horsemen? For the love of me, dear brothers, do fall back"—at that moment the enemy again wounded him and his horse. Just then we cleared our allies off the causeway, and we retreated little by little keeping our faces to the enemy and not turning our backs, as though to form a dam. Notwithstanding

[1] By way of Coyoacan and Tacuba to the camp on the causeway.

the number of Mexicans that the balls were sweeping away, we could not fend them off, on the contrary they kept on following us thinking that this very night they would carry us off to be sacrificed.

When we had retreated near to our quarters and had already crossed a great opening where there was much water the arrows, javelins and stones could no longer reach us. Sandoval, Francisco de Lugo and Andrés de Tápia were standing with Pedro de Alvarado each one relating what had happened to him and what Cortés had ordered, when again there was sounded the dismal drum of Huichilobos and many other shells and horns and things like trumpets and the sound of them all was terrifying, and we all looked towards the lofty Cue where they were being sounded, and saw that our comrades whom they had captured when they defeated Cortés were being carried by force up the steps, and they were taking them to be sacrificed. When they got them up to a small square in front of the oratory, where their accursed idols are kept, we saw them place plumes on the heads of many of them and with things like fans in their hands they forced them to dance before Huichilobos, and after they had danced they immediately placed them on their backs on some rather narrow stones which had been prepared as places for sacrifice, and with stone knives they sawed open their chests and drew out their palpitating hearts and offered them to the idols that were there, and they kicked the bodies down the steps, and Indian butchers who were waiting below cut off the arms and feet and flayed the skin off the faces, and prepared it afterwards like glove leather with the beards on, and kept those for the festivals when they celebrated drunken orgies, and the flesh they ate in *chilmole*. In the same way they sacrificed all the others and ate the legs and arms and offered the hearts and blood to their idols, as I have said, and the bodies, that is their entrails and feet, they threw to the tigers and lions which they kept in the house of the carnivores which I have spoken about in an earlier chapter.

When we saw those cruelties all of us in our camp said the one to the other: "Thank God that they are not carrying me off to-day to be sacrificed."

It should also be noted that we were not far away from

them,[1] yet we could render them no help, and could only pray God to guard us from such a death.

Then, at the moment that they were making the sacrifices, great squadrons of Mexicans fell on us suddenly and gave us plenty to do on all sides and neither in one way or the other could we prevail against them.

And they cried: "Look, that is the way in which you will all have to die, for our gods have promised it to us many times." Then the words and threats which they said to our friends the Tlaxcalans were so injurious and evil that they disheartened them, and they threw them roasted legs of Indians and the arms of our soldiers and cried to them: "Eat of the flesh of these Teules and of your brothers, for we are already glutted with it, and you can stuff yourselves with this which is over, and observe that as for the houses which you have destroyed we shall have to bring you to rebuild them much better with white stone and well worked masonry, so go on helping the Teules, for you will see them all sacrificed."

There was another thing that Guatemoc ordered to be done when he won that victory, he sent to all the towns of our allies and friends and to their relations, the hands and feet of our soldiers and the flayed faces with the beards, and the heads of the horses that they had killed, and he sent word that more than half of us were dead and he would soon finish us off, and he told them to give up their friendship with us and come to Mexico and if they did not give it up promptly, he would come and destroy them, and he sent to tell them many other things to induce them to leave our camp and desert us, and then we should be killed by his hands.

As they still went on attacking us both by day and by night, all of us in our camp kept watch together, Gonzalo de Sandoval and Pedro de Alvarado and the other captains keeping us company during our watch, and although during the night great companies of warriors came against us we withstood them. Both by day and night half the horsemen remained in Tacuba and the other half were on the causeway.

There was another greater evil that they did us; no matter how carefully we had filled in the water spaces since we ad-

[1] They must have been at their camp on the causeway—they could not have seen this from Tacuba.

vanced along the causeway, they returned and opened them all
and constructed barricades stronger than before. Then our
friends of the cities of the lake who had again accepted our
friendship and had come to aid us with their canoes believed
that they "came to gather wool and went back shorn," for
many of them lost their lives and many more returned
wounded, and they lost more than half of the canoes they had
brought with them, but, even with all this, thenceforth they
did not help the Mexicans for they were hostile to them, but
they carefully watched events as they happened.

Let us cease talking about misfortunes and once again tell
about the caution, and the manner of it, that from now on we
exercised, and how Gonzalo de Sandoval and Francisco de
Lugo and Andrés de Tápia and the other soldiers who had
come to our camp thought it would be well to return to their
posts and to give a report to Cortés as to how and in what position we stood. So they went post-haste and told Cortés that
Pedro de Alvarado and all his soldiers were using great caution
both in fighting as well as in keeping watch, and moreover
Sandoval, as he considered me a friend, said to Cortés that he
had found me and the soldiers fighting more than waist high
in water defending a stranded launch, and that if it had not
been for us the enemy would surely have killed the captain and
soldiers who were on board, and because he said other things in
my praise about when he ordered me to retreat, I am not going to repeat them here, for other persons told of it, and it was
known throughout the camp of Cortés and in our own, but I
do not wish to recite it here. When Cortés clearly understood
the great caution that we observed in our camp it greatly eased
his heart, and from that time onwards he ordered all three
camps not to fight with the Mexicans either too much or too
little, meaning that we were not to trouble about capturing
any bridge or barricade, and, except in defence of our camps,
we were not to go out to fight with the enemy.

Nevertheless the day had hardly dawned when they were attacking our camp, discharging many stones from slings, and
javelins and arrows and shouting out hideous abuse, and as we
had near the camp a very broad and deep opening of water we
remained for four days in succession without crossing it. Cortés
remained as long in his camp and Sandoval in his. This determination not to go out and fight and endeavour to capture the

barricades which the Mexicans had returned to open and fortify, was because we were all badly wounded and worn out with hardships, both from keeping watch and bearing arms without anything sustaining to eat; and because we had lost the day before over sixty and odd soldiers from all the camps, and eight horses and so that we might obtain some rest, and take mature counsel as to what should be done. From that time onwards, Cortés ordered us to remain quiet, as I have said, so I will leave off here and tell how and in what way we fought and everything else that happened in our camp.

† cxv

The Mexicans continued with their attacks every day, and our friends, the people of Tlaxcala and Cholula and Huexotzingo, and even those of Texcoco and Chalco and Tlamanalco, decided to return to their own Countries, and nearly all of them went off without Cortés or Pedro de Alvarado or Sandoval knowing about it. There only remained in Cortés' camp Ixlilxochitl, who was afterwards baptized and named Don Carlos (he was the brother of Don Fernando the Lord of Texcoco and was a very valiant man) and about forty of his relations and friends. In Sandoval's camp there remained another cacique from Huexotzingo with about fifty men, and in our camp there remained two sons of Lorenzo de Vargas and the brave Chichimecatecle with about eighty Tlaxcalans, his relations and vassals. When we found ourselves with so few allies we were distressed, and Cortés and Sandoval each of them asked the allies that remained in his camp, why the others had gone off in that way, and they replied that they had observed Mexicans speaking with their Idols during the night who promised them that they should kill us, and they believed it to be true; so it was through fear that they left, and what made it more credible was seeing us all wounded and many of us dead, and of their own people more than twelve hundred were missing, and they feared that we should all be killed. In conversations which Cortés had with Ixlilxochitl, he said to him: "Señor Malinche, do not be distressed because you cannot fight every day with the Mexicans, get your foot well, and take my advice, and that is to stay some days in your camp, and tell

Tonatio to do the same and stay in his camp and Sandoval in Tepeaquilla, and keep the launches on the move night and day to prevent supplies of provisions or water from getting to the enemy for there are within this great City so many thousand *xiquipeles*[1] of warriors that they must of necessity eat up the food that they possess, and the water they are now drinking is from some springs they have made, and it is half salt, and as it rains every day and sometimes at night they catch the water and live on that, but what can they do if you stop their food and water? They will suffer more from hunger and thirst than from war." When Cortés understood this advice, he threw his arms round him and thanked him for it and made him promises that he would give him pueblos. This advice many of us soldiers had already discussed, but, such is our nature, that we did not wish to wait so long a time, but to advance into the city. When Cortés had well considered what the cacique had said, he ordered two launches to go to our camp and to that of Sandoval to tell us that he ordered us to remain another three days without advancing into the city. As at that time the Mexicans were victorious he did not dare to send out one launch alone. There was one thing that helped us much, which was that our launches now ventured to break the stakes that the Mexicans had placed in the lake to impale them, and they did it in this way, they rowed with all their strength, and so that the rowing should carry greater impetus they set about it from some distance back and got wind into their sails and rowed their best, so they became masters of the lake and even of a good many houses that stood apart from the city, and when the Mexicans saw this they lost some of their courage.

As now we had no allies, we ourselves began to fill in and stop up the great opening that, I have said before, was near our camp, and the first company on the rota worked hard at carrying adobes and timber to fill it in, while the other two companies did the fighting, and in the four days that all of us worked at it we had it filled in and levelled. Cortés did the same in his camp where the same arrangement prevailed, and even he himself was at work carrying adobes and timber, until the bridges and causeways and openings were secure so that a retreat could be effected in safety; and Sandoval did neither more nor less in his camp. With our launches close by us, and

[1] A division numbering 8,000 men.

free from any fear of stakes we advanced in this manner little by little.

Let me say now what the Mexicans did during the night on their great and lofty Cues and that was to sound the cursed drum, which I again declare had the most accursed sound and the most dismal that it was possible to invent, and the sound carried far over the country, and they sounded other worse instruments and diabolical things, and they made great fires and uttered the loudest yells and whistles, for at that moment they were sacrificing our comrades whom they had captured from Cortés and we knew that it took them ten days in succession to complete the sacrificing of all our soldiers, and they left to the last Cristóbal de Guzman whom they kept alive for twelve or thirteen days, according to the report of the three Mexican captains whom we captured. Whenever they sacrificed them then their Huichilobos spoke to them and promised them victory, and that we should die by their hands within eight days, and told them to make vigorous attacks on us although many should die in them and in this way he kept them deluded.

Once more as soon as another day dawned all the greatest forces that Guatemoc could collect were already down upon us, and as we had filled up the opening and causeway and bridge they could pass it dryshod. My faith! They had the daring to come up to our ranchos and hurl javelins and stones and arrows, but with the cannon we could always make them draw off, for Pedro Moreno, who had charge of the cannon, did much damage to the enemy. I wish to say that they shot our own arrows at us from crossbows, for while they held five crossbowmen alive, and Cristóbal de Guzman with them, they made them load the crossbows and show them how they were to be discharged, and either they or the Mexicans discharged those shots deliberately, but they did no harm with them.

Every day we had very hard fights, but we did not cease to advance, capturing barricades, bridges and water openings, and as our launches dared to go wherever they chose in the lake, and did not fear the stakes, they helped us very much. Let me say that as usual the launches that Cortés had at his camp cruised about giving chase to the canoes that were bringing in supplies and water and collecting in the lake a sort of ooze which when it was dried had the flavour of cheese, and these launches brought in many Indian prisoners. Twelve or thirteen days had gone by since the defeat of Cortés, and as soon as Ixlilxochitl observed that we had thoroughly recovered ourselves, and what the Mexicans said that they were sure to kill us within ten days was not true (which was what their Huichilobos and Tezcatepuca had promised them), he sent to advise his brother Don Fernando to send to Cortés, at once, the whole force of warriors that he could muster in Texcoco, and within two days of the time of his sending to tell him, more than two thousand warriors arrived.

When Cortés saw such a good reinforcement he was greatly delighted and said flattering words to them. At that time many Tlaxcalans with their captains also returned and a cacique from Topeyanco named Tecapaneca came as their general. Many Indians also came from Huexotzingo and a very few from Cholula. When Cortés knew that they had returned he ordered that all of them, as they arrived, should come to his camp so that he could speak to them. Before they arrived he ordered guards of our soldiers to be placed on the roads to protect them, in case the Mexicans should come out to attack them. When they came before Cortés he made them a speech through Doña Marina and Jerónimo de Aguilar and told them that they had fully understood and knew for certain about the good will with which he had always regarded them and still bore them, both because they had served His Majesty, as well as for the good offices that we had received at their hands, and if he had, after reaching this city, commanded them to join us in destroying the Mexicans, he intended them to profit by it, and return to their land rich men, and to revenge themselves on their enemies, and not that we should capture that great City solely for his benefit, and although he had always found them useful and they had helped us in everything, they must have seen clearly that we ordered them off the causeways every day, because we were less hampered when we fought without them, and that he who gave us victory and aided us in everything was Our Lord Jesus Christ, in whom we believe and whom we worship as he had already often told them and warned them at other times. Because they went away at the most critical time of the war they were deserving of death, for deserting their captains when they were fighting and for forsaking them, but as they did not understand our laws and ordinances he pardoned them, and in order to understand the situation better they should observe that without their help we still continued destroying houses and capturing barricades. From that time forward he ordered them not to kill any Mexicans, for he wished to conquer them by kindness. When he had made this speech to them he embraced Chichimecatecle and the two youthful Xicotengas, and Ixlilxochitl, and promised to give them territory and vassals in addition to what they now held. After the conversation with them he ordered them to depart, and each one went to his camp.

From all three camps we were now advancing into the City, Cortés on his side, Sandoval on his and Pedro de Alvarado on our side, and we reached the spot where the spring was, that I have already spoken about, where the Mexicans drank the brackish water, and we broke it up and destroyed it so that they might not make use of it. Some Mexicans were guarding it and we had a good skirmish with them. We could already move freely through all parts of the streets we had captured, for they were already levelled and free from water and openings and the horses could move very easily.

Thus the ten Companies of Pedro de Alvarado advanced fighting and reached Tlatelolco, and there were so many Mexicans guarding their Idols and lofty cues, and they had raised so many barricades that we were fully two hours before we were able to capture them and get inside. Now that the horses had space to gallop, although most of them were wounded, they helped us very much, and the horsemen speared many Mexicans. As the enemy were so numerous the ten[1] companies were divided into three parts to fight against them, and Pedro de Alvarado ordered the company commanded by a captain named Gutierre de Badajoz to ascend the lofty Cue of Huichilobos, which has one hundred and fourteen steps, and he fought very well against the enemy and against the many priests who were in the houses of the oratories, but the enemy attacked Gutierre de Badajoz and his company in such a way that they sent him rolling down ten or twelve steps, and we promptly went to his assistance.

As we advanced the squadrons with which we were fighting followed us, and we ran great risk of our lives, but nevertheless we ascended the steps which as I have said before were one hundred and fourteen in number. It is as well to mention here

[1] In the text "dos capitanias," evidently a mistake for "diez capitanias" as above.

the great danger we were in, both one [company] and the other, in capturing those fortresses which were very lofty, and in those battles they once more wounded us all very badly, nevertheless we set the oratories on fire and burned the idols, and we planted our banners and were fighting on the level after we had set fire to the oratories until night time, but we could do nothing against so many warriors.

[*Extract from the third letter of Cortés to the Emperor Charles V.*]

About 15*th July*: By now the Spaniards who had been wounded at the time of our defeat had recovered. Moreover, a vessel belonging to Ponce de Leon arrived at Vera Cruz, and the people of the town sent me some powder and crossbows, of which we had great need.

The people in the surrounding country had, thank God, now declared in our favour, and I, seeing how those of the city were still hostile and showing as clearly as any people could do a determination to die in its defence, was at a loss to know how to free ourselves from the dangers and hardships we were enduring without totally destroying their city, for it is the most beautiful city in the world. It was useless to tell them that we would not raise the siege, and that the launches would not cease to fight them on the water, nor that we had already destroyed the people of Matalcingo and Malinalco, and that there was no one left in the land to bring them succour, and that there was nowhere whence they could procure maize, meat, fruit, water, or other necessaries, for the more we repeated this to them the less faintheartedness they showed. On the contrary, both in fighting and in stratagems we found them more undaunted than ever.

This being so, and seeing that the siege had lasted already more than forty-five days, I decided to take other means for our security and for the reduction of the enemy. The plan was to demolish every house on each side of the street as we penetrated into the city and not to advance a step until all was levelled to the ground, and what had been water was dry land, no matter what delay this would entail.

For this purpose I called together all the chieftains and leading men among our allies and explained my plan to them, and told them to summon all their labourers and order them to bring their *coas* which are like Spanish hoes. They replied that they would do so very willingly and were delighted at the plan, for it seemed to them the best way of destroying the city, which they desired above all things in the world.

Three or four days were occupied making arrangements, then one morning after hearing mass, we set out for the city, and on reaching the water opening and barricade near the great houses of the Plaza with the intention to attack it, the people of the city asked to desist, as they wished to make peace, and that a chieftain from the city was coming to speak to me. In this way they detained me for more than an hour, but in truth they had no desire for peace for while we were standing at ease they began to shoot arrows and darts and stones at us. When I saw this we attacked and carried the barricade. On entering the Plaza we found it all strewn with great stones and that the horsemen could not gallop, and we found one street barricaded with a dry stone wall and another street also full of stones. In this day we filled in the canal which goes out of the Plaza in such a way that the Indians were never able to open it again, and from this point onwards we began little by little to demolish the houses and to fill in the canals, and as on that day we had one hundred and fifty thousand warriors with us, we accomplished a good deal . . .

In this way we penetrated into the city during the following five or six days, and always on retiring we sent off our allies first while some of the Spaniards stayed in ambush among the houses, and the horsemen who were in the rear pretended to retreat hastily so as to draw the enemy out into the Plaza, and by this means and with the foot soldiers in ambush we managed to spear some of the enemy every afternoon.

†

We knew already that the Indians in the city were much discouraged, and we heard from two wretched Indians who had left the city by night and come to our camp that the people were dying of hunger and that they came out by night to search among the houses and in those parts of the city we had already captured, seeking for firewood and herbs and roots for food. As we had already filled in many of the canals and made good many of the bad places I decided to enter the city before dawn and do all the damage we were able, so the launches set out before daybreak, and I with twelve or fifteen horsemen and some foot soldiers and allies entered with a rush, but first of all while we were in hiding we stationed some spies who as soon as day dawned gave us the signal to advance, and we fell on a great multitude of people, but as they were the poor wretches who had come out hunting for food they were most of them unarmed and were women and children, and we did so much damage to them whenever we could get about the city that prisoners and dead between them numbered over eight hundred.

The launches also captured many canoes with Indians who were out fishing. When the captains and chieftains of the enemy saw us advancing through the city at this unusual hour they were dismayed, and did not dare to come out and fight us, so we returned to our camp with booty and food for our allies.

The next day we again entered the city and as our allies observed the orderly method with which we were carrying out its destruction they accompanied us every day in untold numbers. That day we succeeded in gaining the whole of the Tacuba street and filling in the bad places in such a way that we could communicate with the camp of Pedro de Alvarado through the city, and we also captured two bridges on the principal street leading to the market place, and solidly filled in the canals. We also set fire to the houses of the Lord of the City, a youth of eighteen years named Guatemoc, who was the second Lord after the death of Montezuma. These houses were large and well fortified and were surrounded by water. We also gained two bridges near this on the other streets leading to the market place, so that three quarters of the city were already in our hands and the Indians were forced to retire to their stronghold, which was among the houses more completely surrounded by water.

25th July: The next day, which was the festival of the apostle Santiago (St. James), we entered the city in the same order and followed the great street which leads to the market place, and captured a very large water-opening which the enemy thought they held securely. It was a very dangerous operation and caused much delay as the opening was so wide, and we were not able that day to fill it in solidly so that the horsemen could pass. Observing this, the Indian reinforcements, splendid in appearance, attacked us, but as we continued to face them and had with us many crossbowmen we drove them back to their barricades.

26th July: When we returned very early next morning we found the water-opening we had been filling up in the same state as we had left it, and advancing two bowshots ahead we captured two great water-openings which the enemy had broken through the road-bed, and we reached a small idol tower, where we found the heads of some of the Christians whom the enemy had killed, which caused us great grief. This street which we had been following leads directly to the cause-way to Sandoval's camp, and a street to the left leads to the market place. In this latter street there was no water except one water-opening which the enemy were defending against us and on that day, when we were getting ready to enter the city at nine in the morning, we observed from our camp that smoke was ascending from the two lofty towers which stand in Tlatel-olco, the market place of the city, and could not think what it could be, for it was more copious than the smoke of incense which the Indians offer to the Idols, and we concluded that Pedro de Alvarado's men must have got there, which turned out to be the fact, though we could hardly believe it.

That day we did not attempt to capture the bridge and canal which separated us from the market place, but contented our-selves by filling in and levelling all the bad places. On retir-ing the enemy attacked us fiercely although at great cost to themselves. The next morning we had only to capture the canal across the road and its barricade which was near the Idol tower to reach the market place. When we began the attack a standard bearer and two or three other Spaniards threw them-selves into the water and the enemy gave way before them, and we began to fill in the opening so that the horsemen could cross; and while this was being done, Pedro de Alvarado with four horsemen came along the street, and this gave the greatest delight to all of us, for it meant the speedy end of the war.

Pedro de Alvarado placed guards to defend our flanks, and as the opening was soon filled I ordered my troops not to ad-

vance any further, and went forward myself with a few horsemen to see the market place. We rode for a short time about the
Plaza, observing the arcades where the enemy were clustered
in great numbers on the roofs, but as they saw us riding freely
about the great Plaza they did not dare to approach us.

Then I ascended the great tower which is near the market
place, and on it and on others we found the heads of the Christians they had killed and offered to their Idols, as well as the
heads of our Tlaxcalan allies. From the great tower I could see
that we had captured seven-eighths of the city, and knew that
the enemy were so numerous that they could not exist in that
narrow space, especially as the houses left to them were small
and each one stood by itself in the water. And above all, knowing of the great hunger they were suffering, for we had found
in the streets gnawed roots and bark of trees, we determined to
cease fighting for a day, and derive some means to save such a
multitude from destruction. However they said they would
never make peace, and that if only one was left he would die
fighting. . . .

Several days passed without fighting, and then one day when
we returned to the City we found the streets full of women
and children and other miserable people, thin and afflicted,
who were dying of hunger, the most pitiable thing in the world
to see and I ordered our allies to do them no hurt, but not a
single warrior appeared where he could be got at although we
saw them on the roofs, covered with their cloaks and unarmed.

Again I tried this day to bring them to peace but their replies
were evasive. After passing most of the day in these efforts I
sent to tell them I should attack them and that they must call in
all their people, otherwise I should allow our allies to kill them.
They still said they wanted peace, so I replied that I did not see
there the Lord with whom I could treat for peace and that if
he would come I would give him all the security he might ask
for and that we would discuss peace.

However, when we saw that it was all a mock and that they
were all getting ready to attack us, after having warned them
many times so as to constrain them to the utmost necessity, I
ordered Pedro de Alvarado and all his men to enter the large
quarter which the enemy still held, which consisted of more
than a thousand houses, while I entered with all my men from

the other side on foot, as the horsemen were useless there. The battle was waged fiercely until we captured the whole of the quarter and the slaughter effected by our allies was so great that dead and prisoners numbered more than twelve thousand souls, and the cruelty of our allies was so great that on no account would they spare a life in spite of our reproofs and example.

[*To return to Bernal Díaz.*]

† CXVI

As we were all of us now in Tlatelolco, Cortés ordered all the companies to take up their quarters, and keep watch there, because from our camp we had to come more than half a league to where we were now fighting. So we stayed there three days without doing anything worth mentioning, because Cortés ordered us not to advance any further into the City nor to destroy more houses, for he wished to stop and demand peace. During those days that we were waiting in Tlatelolco Cortés sent to Guatemoc begging him to surrender, and not to have any fear, and with many promises he undertook that his (Guatemoc's) person should be much respected and honoured by him, and that he should govern Mexico and all his territory and cities as he was used to do, and he sent him food and presents such as tortillas, poultry, tunas and cacao, for he had nothing else to send. Guatemoc took counsel with his captains and what they advised him to reply was that he desired peace but that he would wait three days before giving an answer, and that at the end of three days Guatemoc and Cortés should meet and make arrangements about the peace, and that during those three days they would have time to know more fully the wishes and reply of their Huichilobos, and he might have added to mend bridges and to make openings in the causeway and prepare arrows, javelins, and stones and make barricades.

Guatemoc sent four Mexican chieftains with that reply, and we believed that the promise of peace was true, and Cortés ordered the messengers to be given plenty to eat and drink and then sent them back to Guatemoc, and with them he sent more refreshments the same as before. Then Guatemoc sent other messengers, and by them two rich mantles, and they said that Guatemoc would come when everything was ready. Not to waste more words about the matter he never intended to come (for they had counselled him not to believe Cortés and had reminded him of the end of his uncle the great Montezuma, and of his relations and the destruction of all the noble families of Mexico; and had advised him to say that he was ill) but intended that all should sally out to fight and that it would please their Gods to give them the victory they had so often promised them. As we were waiting for Guatemoc and he did not come, we understood their deceit and at that very moment so many battalions of Mexicans with their distinguishing marks sallied out and made an attack on Cortés that he could not withstand it, and as many more went in the direction of our camp and in that of Sandoval's. They came on in such a way that it seemed as though they had just then begun the fighting all over again, and as we were posted rather carelessly, believing that they had already made peace, they wounded many of our soldiers, three of them very severely, and two horses, but they did not get off with much to brag of, for we paid them out well. When Cortés saw this he ordered us again to make war on them and to advance into the City in the part where they had taken refuge. When they saw that we were advancing and capturing the whole City, Guatemoc sent two chiefs to tell Cortés that he desired to speak with him across a canal, Cortés to stand on one bank and Guatemoc on the other and they fixed the time for the morning of the following day. Cortés went, but Guatemoc would not keep the appointment but sent chieftains who said that their Lord did not dare to come out for fear lest, while they were talking, guns and crossbows should be discharged at him and should kill him. Then Cortés promised him on his oath that he should not be molested in any way that he did not approve of, but it was no use, they did not believe him and said "lest what happened to Montezuma should happen to him." At that time two of the chieftains who were talking to Cortés drew out from a bag which they carried some tortillas and the leg of a fowl and cherries, and seated themselves in a very leisurely manner and began to eat so that Cortés might observe it and believe that they were not hungry. When Cortés observed it he sent to tell them that as they did not wish to make peace, he would soon enter into all their houses to see if they had any maize and how much more poultry.

We went on in this way for another four or five days without attacking them, and about this time many poor Indians who had nothing to eat, would come out every night, and they came to our camp worn out by hunger. As soon as Cortés saw this he ordered us not to attack them for perhaps they would change their minds about making peace, but they would not make peace although we sent to entreat them.

In Cortés' camp there was a soldier who said that he had been in Italy in the Company of the Great Captain[1] and was in the skirmish of Garallano and in other great battles, and he talked much about engines of war and that he could make a catapult in Tlatelolco by which, if they only bombarded the houses and part of the city where Guatemoc had sought refuge, for two days, they would make them surrender peacefully. So many things did he say to Cortés about this, for he was a very faithful soldier, that Cortés promptly set to work to make the catapult and they brought lime and stone in the way the soldier required, and carpenters and nails and all that was necessary for making the catapult, and they made two slings of strong bags and cords, and brought him great stones, larger than an arroba jar. When the catapult was made and set up in the way that the soldier ordered, and he said it was ready to be discharged, they placed a suitable stone in the sling which had been made and all this stone did was to rise no higher than the catapult and fall back upon it where it had been set up. When Cortés saw this he was angry with the soldier who gave the order for making it, and with himself for believing him, and he said that he knew well that in war one ought not to speak much about a thing that vexes one, and that the man had only been talking for talking's sake, as had been found out in the way that I have said. Cortés at once ordered the catapult to be taken to pieces. Let us leave this and say that, when he saw that the catapult was a thing to be laughed at, he decided that Gonzalo de Sandoval should go in command of all the twelve launches and invade that part of the City whither Guatemoc had retreated, which was in a part where we could not reach the houses and palaces by land, but only by water. Sandoval at

[1] Gonzalvo de Córdova.

once summoned all the captains of the launches and invaded
that part of the City where Guatemoc had taken refuge with
all the flower of his Captains and the most distinguished persons that were in Mexico. Cortés ordered Sandoval not to kill
or wound any Indians unless they should attack him, and even
if they did attack him, he was only to defend himself and not
do them any other harm, but he should destroy their houses
and the many defences they had erected in the lake. Cortés
himself ascended the great Cue of Tlatelolco to see how Sandoval advanced with the launches.

Sandoval advanced with great ardour upon the place where
the Houses of Guatemoc stood, and when Guatemoc saw himself surrounded, he was afraid that they would capture him or
kill him, and he had got ready fifty great piraguas with good
rowers so that when he saw himself hard pressed he could
save himself by going to hide in some reed beds and get from
thence to land and hide himself in another town, and those
were the instructions he had given his captains and the persons
of most importance who were with him in that fortified part
of the city, so that they should do the same.

When they saw that the launches were getting among the
houses they embarked in the fifty canoes, and they had already
placed on board the property and gold and jewels of Guatemoc
and all his family and women, and he had embarked himself
and shot out into the lake ahead, accompanied by many Captains. As many other canoes set out at the same time, the lake
was full of them, and Sandoval quickly received the news that
Guatemoc was fleeing, and ordered all the launches to stop destroying the houses and fortifications and follow the flight of
the canoes. As a certain García Holguin a friend of Sandoval,
was captain of a launch which was very fast and a good sailor
and was manned by good rowers Sandoval ordered him to follow in the direction in which they told him that Guatemoc was
fleeing with his great piraguas, and instructed him not to do
Guatemoc any injury whatever beyond capturing him in case
he should overtake him, and Sandoval went in another direction with other launches which kept him company. It pleased
our Lord God that García Holguin should overtake the canoes
and piraguas in which Guatemoc was travelling, and from the
style and the awnings and the seat he was using he knew that
it was Guatemoc the great Lord of Mexico, and he made sig-

nals for them to stop, but they would not stop, so he made as though he were going to discharge muskets and crossbows. When Guatemoc saw that, he was afraid, and said: "Do not shoot—I am the king of this City and they call me Guatemoc, and what I ask of you is not to disturb my things that I am taking with me nor my wife nor my relations, but carry me at once to Malinche." When Holguin heard him he was greatly delighted, and with much respect he embraced him and placed him in the launch, him and his wife and about thirty chieftains, and seated him in the poop on some mats and cloths, and gave him to eat of the food that he had brought with him, and he touched nothing whatever in the canoes that carried Guatemoc's property, but brought it along with the launch. By this time Gonzalo de Sandoval knew that Holguin had captured Guatemoc and was carrying him to Cortés, and he overtook Holguin and claimed the prisoner, and Holguin would not give him up and said that he had captured him and not Sandoval. When Cortés knew of this dispute he at once despatched Captain Luis Marin and Francisco de Verdugo to summon Sandoval and Holguin to come as they were in their launches without further discussion, and to bring Guatemoc and his wife and family with all signs of respect and that he would settle whose prisoner he was and to whom was due the honour of the capture.

While they were bringing him, Cortés ordered a guest chamber to be prepared as well as could be done at the time, with mats and cloths and seats, and a good supply of the food which Cortés had reserved for himself. Sandoval and Holguin soon arrived with Guatemoc, and the two captains between them led him up to Cortés, and when he came in front of him he paid him great respect, and Cortés embraced Guatemoc with delight, and was very affectionate to him and his captains. Then Guatemoc said to Cortés: "Señor Malinche, I have surely done my duty in defence of my City, and I can do no more and I come by force and a prisoner into your presence and into your power, take that dagger that you have in your belt and kill me at once with it," and when he said this he wept tears and sobbed and other great Lords whom he had brought with him also wept. Cortés answered him through Doña Marina and Aguilar very affectionately, that he esteemed him all the more for having been so brave as to defend the City, and he was deserving of no blame, on the contrary it was more in his favour than otherwise.

What he wished was that Guatemoc had made peace of his own free will before the city had been so far destroyed, and so many of his Mexicans had died, but now that both had happened there was no help for it and it could not be mended, let his spirit and the spirit of his Captains take rest, and he should rule in Mexico and over his provinces as he did before. Then Guatemoc and his Captains said that they accepted his favour, and Cortés asked after his wife and other great ladies, the wives of other Captains who, he had been told, had come with Guatemoc. Guatemoc himself answered and said that he had begged Gonzalo de Sandoval and García Holguin that they might remain in the canoes while he came to see what orders Malinche gave them. Cortés at once sent for them and ordered them all to be given of the best that at that time there was in the camp to eat, and as it was late and was beginning to rain, Cortés arranged for them to go to Coyoacan, and took Guatemoc and all his family and household and many chieftains with him and he ordered Pedro de Alvarado, Gonzalo de Sandoval and the other captains each to go to his own quarters and camp, and we went to Tacuba, Sandoval to Tepeaquilla and Cortés to Coyoacan. Guatemoc and his captains were captured on the thirteenth day of August at the time of vespers on the day of Señor San Hipólito in the year one thousand five hundred and twenty-one, thanks to our Lord Jesus Christ and our Lady the Virgin Santa Maria, His Blessed Mother. Amen.

APPENDIX

Commentary by the Translator

From the English Edition of 1908

Four eye-witnesses of the discovery and conquest of Mexico have left written records:

Hernando Cortés, who wrote five letters known as the *Cartas de Relacion* to the Emperor Charles V.

The First of these letters despatched from Vera Cruz, has never been found, but its place is supplied by a letter written to the Emperor at the same time by the Municipality of Vera Cruz, dated 10th July, 1519.

The Second letter, from Segura de la Frontera (Tepeaca), is dated 30th October, 1520.

The Third letter was written from Coyoacan, and dated 15th May, 1522.

The Fourth letter was written from the city of Temixtitan (Mexico), and dated 15th October, 1524.

The Fifth letter, written from Temixtitan (Mexico), dated 3rd September, 1526, deals with the march to Honduras.

The Anonymous Conqueror whose identity has never been ascertained.

The original of this document is lost, and its contents are preserved to us in an Italian translation. It deals only with the customs, arms, food, religion, buildings, etc., of the inhabitants of the city of Mexico, and adds nothing to our knowledge of events during the Conquest.

Andrés de Tápia, whose short but interesting account of the

expedition under Cortés ends with the defeat of Narvaez.
This document was only brought to light during the last
century.

Bernal Díaz del Castillo, whose stirring and picturesque
narrative is given in these pages.

To these may be added the *Itinerario de Grijalva,* an account
written by the chaplain who accompanied Grijalva on his
expedition when the coast of Mexico was first discovered; but
this account ends with the return of the expedition to Cuba,
and does not deal with the conquest of the country.

The original of this document has been lost, and it comes
down to us in an Italian translation. If the title is correct, it
must have been written by the priest Juan Díaz who accompanied the expedition. It seems to be written in a hostile spirit,
and its statements should be received with caution.

Many writers followed during the next forty years who had
conversed with actors in the events, and some of whom had
heard the story from the mouths of the conquered Indians,
and much additional information was thus added to the record;
but for a vivid impression of this daring plunge into the unknown, and the triumphant struggle of an isolated handful of
Spaniards against a powerful and warlike race, we must rely
on the accounts given by those two great soldiers and adventurers, leader and follower, Hernando Cortés and Bernal Díaz
del Castillo.

The scene of the principal part of Bernal Díaz's narrative
lies within the southern half of the present republic of Mexico,
Western Central America and the peninsula of Yucatan, a land
wholly within the tropics, which, however, owing to its physi-
cal conformation, furnishes almost every variety of climate.

A great range of volcanic mountains runs almost continuously through Mexico and the greater part of Central America,
near the Pacific Coast and parallel to it. A second range of
mountains not so continuous and distinct, runs almost parallel
to the Atlantic coast. The whole of the interior of the country
between these two ranges may be said to be mountainous but
intersected by many high-lying plains from 4,000 to 8,000 feet
above sea level, which form one of the most characteristic features of the country. These plains are sometimes seamed with
narrow *barrancas*[1] hundreds of feet in depth, often with pre-

[1] *Canyons,* ravines.

cipitous sides, caused by the washing away of the thick covering of light volcanic ash down to the bed rock. In common
speech the land is divided into the *tierra caliente,* the *tierra
templada,* and the *tierra fria,* the hot, temperate and cold lands.
As the slope of the mountains is rather more gradual towards
the Atlantic than towards the Pacific, the *tierra caliente* is more
extensive in the former direction. Three volcanic peaks, Orizaba, Popocatépetl and Ixtacíhuatl, almost in the middle of
Southern Mexico, rise above the line of perpetual snow and
reach a height of about 17,000 feet, and several of the somewhat lower peaks are snow-capped during some months of
the year. None of the rivers of Mexico west of the Isthmus
of Tehuantépec are navigable in the sense of being highways
of commercial importance. Passing to the east of the Isthmus of
Tehuantépec the country of Chiapas and Guatemala does not
differ materially in its general characteristics from that already
described, with the exception that the rivers flowing into the
Atlantic are relatively of greater importance, and the waters of
the Usumacinta and Grijalva form innumerable lagoons and
swamps before entering the Gulf of Mexico.

North and west of the Usumacinta and its tributaries, the
land, with the exception of the Cockscomb range in British
Honduras, is all low, and the peninsula of Yucatan appears to
be little more than a coral reef slightly raised above sea level.
There are no rivers, for the rain sinks easily through the
porous limestone rock, and the natives have often to seek their
drinking water 100 feet or more below the surface in the
great *cenotes* (*tznótes*) or limestone caverns.

The sea round the north and west coast of the peninsula
is very shallow, the 100 fathom line being in some parts as
much as ninety miles distant from the shore.

The wet season in Mexico and Central America may (subject to local variations) be said to extend from June to October,
but it lasts somewhat longer on the Atlantic than on the
Pacific slope. During these months the rainfall is often very
heavy, the States of Tabasco and Vera Cruz probably receiving
the larger amount.

During the winter months occasional strong cold gales sweep
the Gulf of Mexico from the North, the dreaded *Norte* so
often mentioned in Bernal Díaz's narrative. This wind causes
some discomfort even on the high plateau of the *tierra tem-*

plada, which, notwithstanding this drawback, may safely be said to possess one of the most perfect climates in the world.

The first question always asked regarding the Conquest is: "Who were the Mexicans, and how did they get to Mexico?" and to these questions no certain answer can be given. All that can be said is that the whole American race, although it may have originated from more than one stock, reached America in a very early stage of human development, and that the Nahua tribes to which Mexicans belong came from the northwest coast, which is generally assumed to have been the earliest home of the American race. Whether the people came from Asia at a time when the Northern continents were continuous is a question not easily settled, but if such were the case, the migration must have taken place before the cultivation of cereal crops or the smelting of iron ore was known to the Northern Asiatics, for no iron implements were found in America, and no cereal was found there that was known in the East, the only cereal cultivated in America being the Indian corn or maize, and this is clearly of indigenous origin.

It is, therefore, not necessary to consider further such a very distant connection, if such existed, between the extreme east and west.

There is, of course, the possibility of isolated drifts from Asia to America; several instances of Polynesians having drifted in their canoes almost incredible distances in the Pacific are on record, and derelict junks have been known to reach the coast of America; but the survivors of such drifts, although they may have introduced a new game or some slight modification of an existing art, are not likely to have affected very materially the development of American culture.

The waves of migration from north to south, due probably to pressure of population or search for supplies of food, must necessarily have been intermittent and irregular, and must have been broken up by numerous cross currents due to natural obstacles. It seems natural to speak of a wave of migration, and to treat it as though it followed the laws governing a flow of water; but to make the simile more complete we must imagine not a flow of water, but of a fluid liable to marked chemical change due to its surroundings, which here may slowly crystallize into a stable form, and there may boil over with noticeable energy, redissolving adjacent crystals and mixing again with a neighbouring stream. There is no reason to suppose that this process had not been going on in America as long as it had in other parts of the world, but there we are often helped to understand the process by written or carved records, which go back for hundreds and even thousands of years, whereas in America written records are almost non-existent, and carved records are confined to a small area, and both are almost undecipherable.

In Mexico and Central America accepted tradition appears to begin with the arrival of the Toltecs, a branch of the Nahua race, and history with that of the later Nahua tribes, but as to who the people were whom the Toltecs found in possession of the country, tradition is silent.

The commonly accepted story is that the Toltecs, whose capital was at Tula, were a people of considerable civilization, who, after imparting something of their culture to ruder Nahua hordes that followed them from the North, themselves migrated to Guatemala and Yucatan, where they built the great temples and carved the monuments which have been so often described by modern travellers. I am not, however, myself able to accept this explanation of the facts known to us. The monuments and architectural remains of Guatemala and Yucatan are undoubtedly the work of the Mayas, who, although nearly related to the Nahuas, are admitted to be a distinct race, speaking a different language; and I am inclined to believe that the Maya race formerly inhabited a considerable portion of Central and Southern Mexico, and it is to it that we must give credit for Tula, Cholula, and, possibly, Teotehuacan, all lying within Central Mexico, as well as for the highest culture ever attained by natives on the continent of North America.

Driven from their Mexican homes by the pressure of Nahua immigrants, they doubtless took refuge in the high lands of Chiapas and Guatemala, and along the banks of the Rivers Usumacinta and Motagua, and pressed on as far as the present frontier of Guatemala and Honduras; but it must be admitted that, so far, no account of this migration and settlement is known to us.

Once settled in Central America, the Mayas would have held a strong defensive position against Nahua invaders, for they were protected on the Gulf side by the intricate swamps and waterways which Cortés found so much difficulty in crossing on his march to Honduras, and on the land side by the mountain ranges which rise abruptly to the east of the Isthmus of Tehuantépec. The passes through the great volcanic barrier which runs parallel to the Pacific Coast could have been easily defended, while a road was left open along the lowlands between the mountains and the sea, of which the Nahua hordes apparently availed themselves, for Nahua names and dialects are found as far east as Nicaragua.

Judging from the architectural remains and the sculptured stones, it may be safely assumed that it was in Central America that the Mayas reached the highest point of their culture, and that they there developed their peculiar script. No Maya hieroglyphic inscriptions have yet been found in Central Mexico, and it is only within the last few years that attention has been called to what appears to be a somewhat crude form of Maya script unearthed as far west as Monte Alban in the State of Oaxaca.

I am further inclined to believe, that after some centuries of peaceful development had elapsed, the Maya defence failed, and that the people were again driven from their homes by invaders from the north-west, and leaving Chiapas and Guatemala, took refuge in Yucatan, where they founded Chichén-Itzá, Uxmal and the numerous towns whose ruins may still be seen throughout the northern part of the peninsula. It is worthy of note that weapons of war are almost entirely absent from the Central American sculptures, and at Copan one of the most important sculptured figures is that of a woman, whereas in Yucatan every man is depictured as a warrior with arms in his hands, and the only representation of a woman known to me is in a mural painting at Chichén-Itzá, where the women stand among the houses of a beleaguered town, apparently bewailing their fate, while the battle rages outside.

At the time of the Spanish conquest the highlands of Guatemala were held by tribes of the Maya Quiché race, who were probably descendants of the Mayas and their Nahua conquerors, and were of an entirely lower standard of culture than the pure Mayas.

Yucatan was still Maya, but the influence of its powerful Nahua neighbours was strongly felt, and civil wars had caused the destruction and abandonment of most of the old towns.

There is yet one Maya area which has so far not been mentioned, the land of the Huastecs around the mouth of the Rio Panuco (the river dividing the modern States of Vera Cruz and Tamaulipas). It seems probable that the Huastecs, and possibly also their neighbours the Totonacs, were the remnant of the Maya race left behind when the main body was driven to the south-east. If they were a Maya colony from the south, as has sometimes been asserted, they would certainly have brought with them the Maya script, but no Maya hieroglyphs have, so far as I know, ever been found in the Huastec country. If, however, they were a remnant left behind when the Mayas migrated to the south-east, we should not expect to find the Maya script in their country, for if my assumption is correct, at the time of the migration that script had not yet been developed. It should be noted that Tula, the reputed capital of the Toltecs, stands on the head waters of the Rio Panuco, and it may be that if such people existed, on occupying Tula they acquired something of the Maya culture, and thus gained their reputation of great builders and the teachers of the later Nahua immigrants.

The exact reason for the disappearance of the earlier races who inhabited Mexico, and of the abandonment of the Central American cities, may never be known, but religious differences cannot be left out of the question, and one way of regarding the change is as the triumph of the ruthless and sanguinary War God Huitzilopochtli over the mild and civilizing cult of Quetzalcoatl or Kukulcan. Were I asked to give definitely all my reasons in support of the foregoing statements, which differ very considerably from those made by such a recent authority as Mr. Payne in his history of the American people, I must own that I should be at a loss how to do so. However, I think it will be admitted by all students of the subject that we are a very long way indeed from having collected and sifted all the evidence procurable, and until the architecture, sculpture and other remains of the very numerous ruined towns which may be found throughout the country are more carefully studied and classified, and until the inscriptions have been deciphered, we must put up with such working hypotheses as may best enable us to group such information as has already been obtained.

In my own case, a somewhat intimate acquaintance with the sculptures and ruined buildings both in Central America and

Mexico has left impressions on my mind as to their relation to one another which it is not always easy to express in definite terms. In another place[1] I have given my reasons for believing that the ruined towns of Central America, and probably the majority of those of Yucatan, had been abandoned by their inhabitants long before the Spanish conquest, and consequently the Spaniards are not responsible for the amount of damage that is sometimes attributed to them.

In the story of Bernal Díaz we shall meet with the Mayas in the early pages describing the discovery of Yucatan and the passage of the three expeditions along the coast of the peninsula, and then again we shall come in touch with them after the conquest of Mexico on Cortés' journey across the base of the peninsula to Honduras.

No attempt was made to subdue the Mayas until 1527, six years after the fall of Mexico, and such redoubtable warriors did they prove themselves to be that, although Francisco de Montejo landed his forces and marched right across the northern part of the peninsula, he was eventually obliged to retreat, and by 1535 every Spaniard was driven out of the country. It was not until 1547 that the Spaniards brought the Mayas into subjection.

To turn now to the time of the Spanish conquest we find Mexico peopled by a number of different tribes more or less nearly alike in habits and customs, and not differing greatly from each other in race, but speaking different languages and dialects. Some of these people or tribes, such as the Zapotecs and Mixtecs of Oaxaca and the Tarascos of Michoacan, extended over a considerable extent of country; they were not, however, homogeneous nations acting under the direction of one chief or of a governing council. The township or *pueblo* appears to have been the unit of society, and the *pueblos* of the same race and speech acted together when compelled by necessity to do so, as it will be seen that the Tlaxcalans acted together owing to the continued hostility of the Mexicans. The main factor in the situation at the time when the Spaniards landed was the dominance of the *Pueblo* of Tenochtitlan or Mexico.

The Mexicans or Aztecs were a people of Nahua race who, after many years of wandering on their way from the North,

[1] *A Glimpse at Guatemala* (London, 1899).

finally settled in the high plain or valley, which still retains their name. For some years they appear to have been almost enslaved by other tribes of the Nahua race, who had already settled in the valley, and it was not until the fourteenth century that they established their home on the two small muddy islands of Tlatelulco and Tenochtitlan in the Great Lake.

By their own warlike prowess and diplomatic alliances with neighbouring towns they gradually increased in power until they gained the hegemony of the tribes and peoples of the valley, and then carried their warlike enterprises into distant parts of the country, even as far as Tabasco and Guatemala. In fact, they became the head of a military and predatory empire, dependent for their food, as well as their wealth, on tribute drawn from subject tribes and races. They were not a civilizing power, and as long as the tribute was paid, they did not appear to concern themselves with the improvement of the local government of their dependencies. The education of the sons and daughters of the upper classes was carefully attended to under the direction of the priesthood, but, as was only natural in a society so constituted, soldierly qualities were those most valued in the men, and the highest reward went to those who showed the greatest personal bravery in battle.

As the field of tribute extended, and wealth accumulated, the office of the principal *Cacique*[1] of Mexico, who was also the natural leader of their armies, rose in importance and dignity; and we learn from the narrative that Montezuma, who was the ninth in succession to the great *Caciques* of Mexico, was treated by his people with more than royal ceremonial.

The arms and armour of all the Indian tribes appear to have been nearly alike, and they are often described by the conquerors, and are shown in the native picture writings that have come down to us. They are the

Macana or *Maquahuitl,* called by the Spaniards a sword, a flat blade of wood three to four feet long, and three inches broad, with a groove along either edge, into which sharp-edged pieces of flint or obsidian were inserted, and firmly fixed with some adhesive compound.

Bows and stone-tipped *arrows.*

Slings.

---

[1] *Cacique* is the term usually employed by the Spaniards as equivalent to chief or king. It is not a Mexican but a Cuban word.

Long Spears with heads of stone or copper.

Javelins made of wood with points hardened in the fire (*varas tostadas*). These javelins, which were much dreaded by the Spaniards, were hurled from an *Atlatl* or throwing stick (*tiradera*).

It is worth noting that no bows or arrows are shown on any of the Maya sculptures, but in the stone carvings in Yucatan (on which weapons are always prominent) all the men are represented as armed with short spears or javelins and an *Atlatl*.

It may be that bows and arrows were unknown to the Mayas, until they were introduced by the Nahua races.[1]

The defensive armour consisted of padded and quilted cotton worn on the arms or body—a protection which the Spaniards themselves hastened to adopt—and shields, usually round shields made of wicker and covered with hide or other material, and often beautifully decorated. Sometimes they were oblong in shape, and large enough to cover the whole body; these latter could be folded up when not in use. Head-dresses or helmets, usually in the form of grotesque animals' heads, were used by the Chieftains and feathers were freely used in decoration, both in the form of beautiful feather patterns worked into cotton fabrics or as *penachos,* lofty head-dresses of feathers supported on a light wood or reed framework.

A Mexican army in battle array must have been both a beautiful and imposing spectacle, a blaze of colour and barbaric splendour.

This is not the place to discuss fully the moral aspects of the conquest, but in considering the conduct of the *Conquistadores* and their leader we must always keep in mind the traditions that influenced them and the laxity of the moral code of the time in which they lived. Some of the Spaniards had served in Italy under Gonsalvo de Córdova, *el gran Capitan,* and may have seen Cæsar Borgia himself—what can we expect from such associations? All of them were adventurers seeking for wealth; some, no doubt, were free-booting vagabonds who would have been a pest in any community. The wonder of it all is that Cortés with no authority from the Crown and

---

[1] I cannot call to mind any Mexican or Central American sculpture showing bows and arrows. Such representations appear to be confined to the *lienzos* (painted cloths) and picture writings, but I am not now able to verify this statement.

only a few ardent partisans to support him, could have kept the control of such a company for so long. He dared to cheat these men out of part of their hard-earned spoil that he might have gold with which to bribe the leaders of the force which he must always have known would be sent in pursuit of him. When the city fell he allowed Guatémoc to be tortured to force him to disclose the supposed secret of where his treasure was hidden—could even his authority have prevented it? It would have been a splendid act of heroism had he made the attempt; but we must think of the disappointed men around him, with the terrible strain of the siege suddenly relaxed, and all their hopes of riches dissipated. Then there is the greatest blot of all on Cortés' career, the execution of Guatémoc during the march to Honduras; no one can help feeling that it was wrong, but there is nothing to show that the reason advanced by Cortés was not a good one. It was only too probable that Mexicans longing to return to their homes, were plotting against the Spaniards to effect it. Had such a plot been successful the Spaniards were inevitably lost. That Cortés was not in a state of mind propitious to the careful weighing of evidence may at once be admitted; a long, dangerous and toilsome march through a tropical forest is not conducive to unruffled temper. However, the execution of Guatémoc, if it was an error, may have been more distinctly an error than a crime.

†

Neither in the sixteenth nor the twentieth century would troops that have seen their companions-in-arms captured and led to execution to grace the festival of a heathen god, and afford material for a cannibal feast, be likely to treat their enemies with much consideration, but the fate of the vanquished Mexicans were human to what it would have been had the victors been Tlaxcalans or other tribes of their own race and religion.

These concluding remarks are not made with the intention of whitewashing the character of the *Conquistadores,* their faults are sufficiently evident, but to impress on the reader the necessity of taking all the factors of the case into consideration when forming a judgment.

The bravery of the Indians was magnificent, and their courage and endurance during the last days of the siege of Mexico is unrivalled, but Bernal Díaz's narrative is written from the Spanish point of view, and it is on the conduct of the Spaniards alone that I feel the need of making any comment.

The character of Bernal Díaz himself shows clearly enough in his story; it is that of a lovable old soldier such as novelists have delighted to portray in Napoleon's "Old Guard", simple, enduring, splendidly courageous and unaffectedly vain.

Censure without stint has been heaped on Cortés and his followers for their treatment of the Indians, but no one has ever ventured to question the spirit and resource of that great leader nor the daring courage and endurance shown both by him and his followers.

I gladly take this opportunity of thanking Don Genaro García for permission to make the Translation from his Edition of the *True History* and for his unfailing courtesy and encouragement during the progress of the work, and of thanking Don José Romero of the Mexican Foreign Office for the loan of books of reference from his valuable collection and for other acts of kindness.

A.P.M.

APPENDIX II

Note on Spelling, etc.

Great difficulty has arisen over the spelling of the Indian names of persons and places. In the original text a native name has often several variants, and each one of these may differ from the more generally-accepted form.

In the Translation a purely arbitrary course has been adopted, but it is one which will probably prove more acceptable to the general reader. Such words as Montezuma (Motecuhzoma) and Huichilobos (Huitzilopochtli) are spelt as Bernal Díaz usually spells them; others, such as Guaçacalco, which occurs in the text in at least three different forms, has in the Translation always been given in the more generally-accepted form of Coatzacoalcos.

Spanish names are always printed in the Translation in the generally-accepted forms: thus Xpval de Oli of the text is printed as Cristóbal de Olid. The names of certain Spanish offices, such as Alguacil, Regidor, are retained in the Translation, as well as the "Fraile (or Padre) de la Merced" for the "Friar of the Order of Mercy", but all foreign words used in the Translation are printed in italics when they first occur, and are referred to in foot-notes.

Square brackets [ ] enclose words inserted by the Translator.

Notes to the Mexican Edition of 1904, edited by Sᵣ Don Genaro García, are marked "G. G."

The Sections have been divided into Chapters and Books with titles for convenience of reference. No such division or titles exist in the original Manuscript or in Sᵣ García's Mexican edition.

Itinerary

The dates given by Bernal Díaz, which are few in number, are placed on the left.

Orozco y Berra (*Hist. Antigua,* vol. iv) has compiled an account of the voyage, with dates, from many sources, including "The Itinerario", Oviedo, Las Casas, Herrera, Gomara, etc. These dates will be found on the right-hand column.

Places not mentioned by Bernal Díaz as stopping places of the expedition are printed in italics.

† THE EXPEDITION UNDER DE CORDÓVA

	Santiago de Cuba
8 Feb., 1517	Axaruco (Jaruco)
	Gran Cairo, Yucatan (near Cape Catoche)
Sunday, day of San Lázaro	Campeche (San Lázaro)
	Champotón (or Potonchan)
(Return Voyage)	Estero de los Lagartos
	Florida
	Los Martires—The Shoals of the Martyrs
	Puerto de Carenas (the modern Havana)

† THE EXPEDITION UNDER GRIJALVA

	Santiago de Cuba	
8 April, 1518	Matanzas	18 April, 1518
	Puerto de Carenas (Havana)	22 April, 1518
	Cape San Anton	1 May
The day of Santa Cruz, 3 May	Cozumel (Santa Cruz)	3–11 May
	Bahia de la Ascencion	13–16 May
	Champotón	25–28 May
	Boca de Términos (Puerto Deseado or P. Real)	31 May to 5 June
	Dio de Grijalva (Tabasco)	7–11 June
	Sighted Ayagualulco (La Rambla)	
	Sighted Rio de Tonalá (San Anton)	
	Sighted Rio de Coatzacoalcos	
	Sighted Sierra de San Martin	
	Rio de Papaloapan (Rio de Alvarado) and Tlacotlalpan	
	Rio de Banderas (Rio Jamapa)	
	Sighted Isla Blanca and Isla Verde	
	Isla de Sacrificios	17 June
St John's day, 24 June	San Juan de Ulua	18–24 June
	Sighted the Sierra de Tuxpan	
	Rio de Canoas (R. Tanguijo) (Cape Rojo)	28 June
Return Voyage	Sighted Rio de Coatzacoalcos	9 July
	Rio de Tonalá (San Anton)	12–20 July
	Puerto de Términos	17–22 August
	Puerto Deseado	1 September
	Small island near Champotón	3 September
	Campeche	5–8 September
	Bajos de Sisal (?)	11–12 September
	Rio de Lagartos	14–15 September
	Conil near Cape Catoche	21 September
	Sighted Cuba	29 September
	Puerto de Carenas (Havana)	30 September

| | Jaruco | 4 October |
| | Santiago de Cuba | 15 November[1] |

† EXPEDITION UNDER CORTÉS

	Santiago de Cuba	18th Nov., 1518
	Sailed from Trinidad	January, 1519
10 Feb., 1519	Sailed from (San Cristóbal ?) de Havana on the South Coast near Batabano	10th Feb., 1519
	Sailed from Cape San Anton	11th Feb., 1519
	Sailed from Cozumel	5th March
	Sailed from Punta de las Mujeres	6th March
	Returned to Cozumel	
4 March	Sailed from Cozumel	13th March
	Boca de Términos	
12 March[2]	Arrived at Rio de Grijalva or Tabasco	22nd March
25 March, Lady Day	Battle of Cintla	25th March
Palm Sunday	Sailed from Santa Maria de la Victoria	18th April
Holy Thursday	Arrived at San Juan de Ulua	21st April, Holy Thursday

[1] See Padre Augustin Rivera, *Anales Mexicanos,* vol. i, p. 47.
[2] This is clearly an error.

INDEX

Index